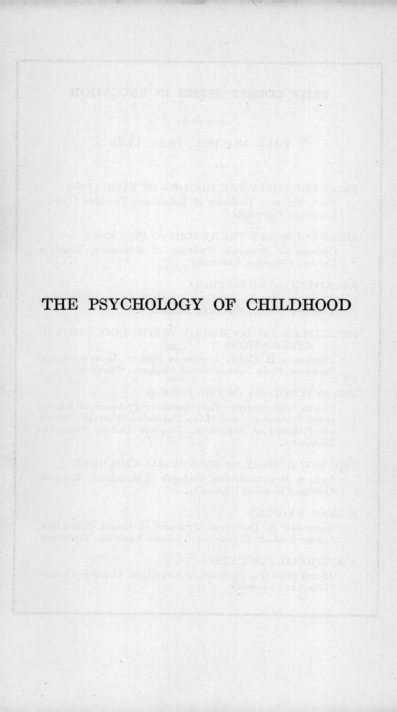

THE PSYCHOLOGY OF CHILDHOOD

BRIEF COURSE SERIES IN EDUCATION

EDITED BY

PAUL MONROE, Ph.D., LL.D.

BRIEF COURSE IN THE HISTORY OF EDUCATION
PAUL MONROE, Professor of Education, Teachers College, Columbia University.

BRIEF COURSE IN THE TEACHING PROCESS
GEORGE D. STRAYER, Professor of Education, Teachers College, Columbia University.

FOUNDATIONS OF METHOD
WILLIAM HEARD KILPATRICK, Professor of Education, Teachers College, Columbia University.

PRINCIPLES OF SOCIOLOGY WITH EDUCATIONAL APPLICATIONS
FREDERICK R. CLOW, Teacher of History, Economics, and Sociology, State Normal School, Oshkosh, Wisconsin.

THE PSYCHOLOGY OF CHILDHOOD
NAOMI NORSWORTHY, Late Associate Professor of Educational Psychology, and MARY THEODORA WHITLEY, Associate Professor of Education, Teachers College, Columbia University.

THE PSYCHOLOGY OF SUBNORMAL CHILDREN
LETA S. HOLLINGWORTH, Professor of Education, Teachers College, Columbia University.

SCHOOL HYGIENE
FLETCHER B. DRESSLAR, Professor of Health Education, George Peabody College for Teachers, Nashville, Tennessee.

VOCATIONAL EDUCATION
DAVID SNEDDEN, Professor of Education, Teachers College, Columbia University.

THE PSYCHOLOGY OF CHILDHOOD

BY

NAOMI NORSWORTHY, Ph.D.

LATE ASSOCIATE PROFESSOR OF EDUCATIONAL PSYCHOLOGY
TEACHERS COLLEGE, COLUMBIA UNIVERSITY

AND

MARY THEODORA WHITLEY, Ph.D.

ASSOCIATE PROFESSOR OF EDUCATION
TEACHERS COLLEGE, COLUMBIA UNIVERSITY

R. L. Gratto

Revised Edition

New York
THE MACMILLAN COMPANY
1933

Published August, 1918. Reprinted May, October, December, 1919; June, December, 1920; October, 1921; January, May, 1922; January, June, November, 1923; August, 1924; March, 1925; June, 1926; May, 1927; June, 1928; July, 1929; April, 1930; June, 1931; January, 1932.

Revised edition, March, 1933.

SET UP AND ELECTROTYPED BY T. MOREY & SON
· PRINTED IN THE UNITED STATES OF AMERICA ·

PREFATORY NOTE

The first rough draft of part of this book was prepared by Professor Norsworthy in 1913, when it was suddenly put aside on account of illness and never thereafter touched. Some of it was later incorporated into the text *How to Teach*, by Strayer and Norsworthy. When in 1916 it was urged that the preparation be resumed, since there seemed to be a felt need for a book of this type for use in normal schools, Miss Norsworthy's own physical condition precluded the attempt. Less than a fortnight before her death, when she was unable to talk over any details, she requested me to complete the work as arranged for in the plan of chapter titles. The task has involved a revision, partial rewriting, and the addition of several chapters. This may explain discrepancies in point of view and in style for which I can but apologize. Miss Norsworthy's many friends, to whom this book is affectionately dedicated, will, I am sure, understand that any adverse criticisms should be directed towards the reviser.

I am indebted for valuable help to Professor E. L. Thorndike, not only in retaining the many quotations from his works, and in the organization of the early part of the book, but also for much friendly criticism. My thanks are due also to Professors Strayer and Monroe, to Dr. Hollingworth for suggestions in Chapter XVI,[1] and to my cousin for assistance in proof reading.

MARY THEODORA WHITLEY

[1] Now Chapter XVII.

PREFACE TO THE SECOND EDITION

There has been so great a development of interest in the psychology of childhood, so much research work has appeared since 1918, that it seemed desirable to prepare a revision of this early, general text book, however great the present author's reluctance to approach the task.

A survey of the field shows a devitalizing of some problems, the emergence of others, changes in emphasis, and many additions to our knowledge about child development, since the first edition appeared. These changes are reflected in the present edition which omits or compresses treatment of some topics, greatly enlarges that of others, and adds four chapters, in consequence.

As before, it is intended for a textbook, not for reference reading. The needs of students in teacher training colleges and of teachers-in-training have been kept in mind, rather than the home situation of parents. The "practical exercises" appearing at the ends of the chapters consist of directions for observations, field work, simple investigations which can be carried on in the schools to which students have access for demonstration, and in the communities in which they are interested. It is recommended also that students select one child for intensive, comprehensive study during the months in which the course in psychology of childhood is given. No student should be expected to do all the exercises suggested; group discussion of the results of varied assignments proves very stimulating.

The references following each chapter are in no way supposed to be adequate indexes of source material; they do suggest diversified reading that may reasonably be required of a group of students working with a good sized library at command. The bibliography at the end will serve the needs of all but the specialist.

A course in general psychology is presupposed, since no space is devoted to the explanation of ordinary psychological terms, though a glossary is added for easy reference. A brief treatment of the various schools of thought among psychologists may help students orient their thinking. The main emphasis is not, however, on theoretical discussions of development but on principles of guidance for the children with whom the teacher must deal.

MARY THEODORA WHITLEY

NEW YORK CITY
February, 1933

TABLE OF CONTENTS

ix

THE
PSYCHOLOGY OF CHILDHOOD

CHAPTER I

PURPOSES AND METHODS OF CHILD STUDY

The aim in the study of childhood here presented is to describe the characteristics of little children, boys and girls and adolescents, and to trace the progressive development of their various abilities.

REASONS FOR FORMAL STUDY

Understanding and control. — Today the teaching profession realizes that the training its members receive cannot be concerned exclusively with the subject matter to be taught. It must include also the children who are to be educated — a far more important object of study. To understand the nature of any living, growing thing, plant, animal or human, is a prerequisite to intelligent treatment for its development. This involves a study of the original nature with which we have to deal in its characteristic ways of behaving to controlled elements in the environment, its needs at different stages of growth for perfection of development.

Human beings are worth it. — In the case of lower forms of life which we raise for our use, our enjoyment, our amusement, we have arrived at a very fair understanding; with the nature of grapes, roses, pigs, and elephants we are pretty well acquainted. But in the thousands of years we have been producing and rearing human young there has been less attentive,

1

purposeful study of their laws of growth, less careful provision for their nutrition and training.

Now that we are more scientifically minded we challenge the older philosophies that took certain beliefs about child nature for granted. We deprecate the hit or miss fashion in which knowledge of children was acquired by each teacher — largely at the expense of the children. We endeavor to utilize the best, vindicated methods of scientific approach to the fascinating problems of human development, and to pass on to each succeeding generation of parents, teachers, nurses, social workers, etc., such facts as are evidently of importance to know in order to provide the best education for every individual.

To avoid bias. — A complete study would include the observation of children at play, at work, learning, eating, sleeping, falling in love, getting into danger, worshiping, talking with their friends, daydreaming, and in many other phases of their active existence. For teachers, who deal with many children for relatively a few hours a week for fifteen to fifty weeks of their lives, it is particularly necessary to realize that, without care, their professional view may be just as partial and one sided as is that of the anxious parent whose one child is followed — perhaps too persistently — through every vicissitude for many years.

Nor is it enough for teachers to rely on recollections of their own childhood. Inevitably, we are all biased by the particular circumstances of our own upbringing. Apart from the limitations of reminiscence, we could have had intimate knowledge of only one type of home, probably. As adults we find our friends largely among those with a somewhat similar outlook to our own. We may be quite unable to appreciate others' ways of enjoying themselves, their social standards, their cultural level of conversation, their breadth or narrowness of view, the motives, even, that impel them. How, then, can we deal in unprejudiced fashion with children from homes so different from our own without the sympathy and understanding imagination stimulated by knowledge of facts that are factors in molding these children?

CHILD PSYCHOLOGY AS A SCIENCE

Nature of laws. — Since psychology is one example of a biological science we should expect to find laws not so absolutely prophetic of the reaction of individuals as are the laws of physics and chemistry, but laws similar to those in botany or zoölogy such as we apply in raising grapes or pigs for the market, or in training elephants for the circus. Some factors, not yet accounted for, provide variations in animals' reactions. They develop individuality in spite of the common treatment they receive. Even so with children. To whatever extent we standardize our procedures we shall not anticipate unvarying, uniform, 100 per cent responses. We may, however, measure the responses common to a group, or know that there is a 75 per cent chance of getting certain results in behavior if we control conditions in accordance with the principles already formulated from the outcome of experimental work. We can also realize that treatment and conditions suitable for the two-year-old would be highly unsuitable for the ten- or fifteen-year-old, and vice versa.

Content. — Since Child Psychology is but one branch of general psychology we should expect to find in it elements, both of facts and methods, which are common to the other branches of the science; and so we do.

So far as content goes, we get from *general* psychology our points of departure in investigations as to the differences between adults and children, our phraseology and classifications in describing the kinds and amounts of differences found. From *social* psychology we get facts about man's development among his fellows and his reactions to them that help us understand much of the behavior of children. From *animal* psychology we get knowledge about reactions in mammals and primates that helps us realize truths not only about instincts but also about the learning processes of children. From *abnormal* and *pathological* psychology we get, in addition, information which assists in the diagnosis of backward and feeble-minded children, which indicates the line of treatment for the mentally deranged adolescent or those in any way atypical, and which helps establish norms for the ordinary child at different stages. The allied sciences of anthropology, sociology, and physiology also add to our knowledge of the development and growth of children socially, industrially, spiritually, and physically, giving a key, through the study of heredity, to much of the general behavior and special aptitudes or deficiences in any given child. Child psychology in its turn makes its special contribution to *educational* psychology: since to direct the kind of changes desired in educating children, or the rate and method of making such changes, it is necessary to understand the nature of the beings in whom we endeavor to bring about these changes.

METHODS USED

Kinds of observation. — Since all scientific study involves observation in some form, we may note at once different classifications of the observational method before proceeding to describe and comment on each. According as it depends on introspection, reminiscence, the giving of opinions, describing feelings, and so on rather than noting muscular reactions in one's self or others, it is termed *subjective* or *objective*. According as to whether the observation is of many children or of one child, we speak of it as *extensive, collective* on the one hand, or *intensive, individual* on the other. Questionnaires belong to the former type, case histories, biographies, and so on to the latter. Experiments would generally be collective, and tests might be either, according to the immediate purpose. A check list answered by 6000 children would obviously be of the extensive type, so would standardized interviews with fifty selected children; so would a so-called group survey, or the recording of the physical measurements of all the children in a school.

If the observer sets himself no definite problem in advance except to be on the alert, and, as court recorder, to note everything so far as possible, it is termed *purposive* observation. When there is a problem formulated beforehand, and the observer's attention is narrowly directed, it is termed *purposeful*. In either case the children's activity may be perfectly free and spontaneous, or directed by questions, apparatus of various sorts. Tests, experiments, measurements belong obviously to the purposeful type. Finally, all these could be graded on a scale from the most casual, incidental sort of procedure up to the most highly systematized observation with very elaborate technique. The results can be treated statistically, even if the data are descriptive and qualitative.

In pioneer work chonologically, the methods of introspection, questionnaire, purposeful unsystematic observation were used, refined gradually into systematic observation, tests, experiments. Beginning students, whether in college or as parents in the community, are apt to be attracted to incidental intensive observation, case histories, questionnaires, utilizing experts to make measurements, give tests, and direct controlled experiments.

Introspection. — Quite obviously this is an impracticable method to use directly with very young children; indeed, even at ten years old it is difficult to make many understand and describe what is wanted. As a derived method, we find adults recounting childhood experiences in so graphic a manner that the readers may feel instantly the ring of truth in the interpretation, or detect the exaggerated strain for effect, or revolt at the namby-pamby didactic incorporated. But however interesting and true to life these reminiscent accounts seem there is the undeniable inaccuracy of memory both in the making of statements and in the joyful acceptance of them. We know how testimony is increasingly falsified by factors such as lapse of time, the presence of a desired coloring of events, the mere repetition of a narrative; and the subjective feel of the early life of even expert writers must likewise be distorted by these same facts. Nevertheless, some authors who combine sympathetic observation with vivid memories of events and emotions may produce tales which have great value in opening the eyes and understanding of many adults who are puzzled by children's conduct and who have largely forgotten "how things feel when you are small." Such books as *Emmy Lou, Anne of Green Gables, Paul and Fiametta, The Treasure-Seekers, Little Citizens, Penrod, The Madness of Philip, Phœbe and Ernest, The Golden Age, Jeremy,* not to mention hosts of others, may awaken not only a responsive thrill, but a more tender appreciation of the inner working of the child mind. They will always have their place in the reference library recommended for parents and others interested in the study of children.

Besides this literary form we have definite autobiographies such as those of Goethe, De Quincey, Tolstoi, George Sand, Marie Bashkirtseff, John Stuart Mill, Mary Antin, and many others. Here again, both the accuracy of the facts and the validity of the interpretation are open to the same criticisms as are expressed above. Moreover, we feel that people as exceptional in adult life as these may well have been exceptional as children, and therefore representative of only certain types of childhood. We need further introspective reports from still other nationalities — studies that could be more of a guide to missionaries and teachers in foreign countries, reconstructionists after the war, social workers among the foreign population of our cosmopolitan cities. Boys such as Tom Sawyer, David Copperfield (Charles Dickens largely), and Rabindranath Tagore seem very far apart by nature as well as by nurture.

Questionnaire. — Another form of the introspective method is sometimes seen when the questionnaire method is employed.

Formerly it aimed at securing data about child experience from parents' incidental observations, or from young adolescents' retrospections. Many sources of error were thus introduced, since these questionnaires were frequently sent to young people in special groups, in colleges and training schools for instance which are conveniently handy but do not represent the general population by any means. These young people, untrained as they are in the method necessary, are more prone to errors in accuracy than are thoughtful, observant adults, and are specially likely to be misled when reporting on whole sets of experiences in rather general terms. Moreover from this selected group, only those interested and therefore probably biased, may reply unless there is compulsion in the matter, when the very reluctance for the task may bring about a casual, careless, even mischievous response that still further reduces the reliability of the answers. Examples of this method of studying children are to be found in great plenty in the earlier numbers of the *Pedagogical Seminary,* and include such topics as the collecting instinct, adolescent ambitions, gangs, conversion experiences, doll-play, motor ability, ownership, the teacher's influence, interests in reading, exceptional children, imagination, moral influences, ideals, etc., etc.

Other disadvantages besides those of selected samples of people and reliance on faulty memory are that the questions may be so phrased as to be a strong suggestive force.

To offset these disadvantages investigators have usually had recourse to the supposed safety of numbers; but, as Thorndike suggests, there is a fallacy in concluding that ignorance, even if multiplied, is anything more than just ignorance. Moreover, the investigator, in the absence of any means of verification, is left to his probable misinterpretation of the replies; and, unless specifically trained as a statistician, may mislead the reader by his published averages, graphs, and other generalizations. It is perhaps the method that first occurs to persons who are in quest of information; for it seems so simple to interrogate people directly, so praiseworthy to ask large numbers of them, so valuable to employ printed forms. If the answers required can be of the simple *yes, no* type, or consist in checking one of several suggested answers a certain objectivity is gained, and certainly a simplification of procedure in tabulating the returns. However, when dealing with opinions, beliefs, ratings, and other subjective material this attempt to simplify the form may fail to secure the very facts wanted. For instance "Did you have a happy childhood? Yes. No." would be difficult for many to answer. Similarly, in asking children merely to check, in a list supplied, which games they played yesterday, we do not reach the important fact that one game lasted five minutes only and was played as a concession to a much younger child, while another was indulged in for over an hour and has been a favorite for nearly a year. Ambiguity in the questions is hardly to be avoided except by unusual care in framing them, and by testing them out before extensive use. "Are you afraid of water?" illustrates this difficulty. Its function, if carefully used so as to minimize the causes of error as stated above, is to give us a rough trip over the ground, so to speak, with impressionistic reports by the guide, which may suggest the aims and methods of the later, more careful, measured survey.

A better use is found for the questionnaire when the facts it attempts to secure are objective, as verifiable as physical measurements, and are already probably recorded in written form, as in the files of school reports, district nursing offices, and so forth.

Case histories, biographies. — These are alike in being intensive studies. The former is fairly common as physician, psychologist, visiting teacher, psychiatrist, case worker, and others pool their efforts to discover important facts about a given child. They delve into his past, study his heredity, his social environment, his school progress, home relationships. They take measurements, give tests, use many standard forms of questionnaire to ascertain the needed facts, do everything, in fact, that might be helpful in understanding the personality of the child. If the purpose is to redirect some undesirable tendency this is often called the clinical method. A biography is more rare. It is a longitudinal record, kept in quasi-diary form, of the development of a child as it occurs. Early examples of this are Preyer's [1] and Shinn's [2] studies of infants. More recent are Stern's [3] studies of his own children and that made by the Scupins [4] on their little son under Stern's direction. These may vary from strings of incidental observations through most exact

[1] Preyer, W., *Development of the Intellect.* Also *Senses and Will.*
[2] Shinn, M., *Biography of a Baby.*
[3] Stern, W., and C., *Monographen über die seelische Entwicklung des Kindes.*
[4] Scupin, E., and G., *Bubi's erste Kindheit.*

statements of spontaneous behavior up to experimental work with controlled conditions. Thus, Valentine,[1] in addition to recording general reactions of his children arranged to test certain assumptions of his about innate fears which were in contradiction to John Watson's theory. Such biographies can be kept only by well-trained experts in close contact with the child. Otherwise they become meaningless as they include biased interpretations rather than accurate noting of all the elements in the situation and the precise type of response made.

Systematic observation. — The term systematic applies rather to the observer's devices for recording and his preconceived purpose than to the fact of free or directed response. It may also be purposive, but is more likely to be purposeful. It is valuable to watch the spontaneous behavior of children in what, to them, are perfectly ordinary circumstances; but the unreliability of the incidental observations previously made in diary records and case studies has led to a great refinement of method. For instance, in studying behavior of children of nursery school age in the usual playroom a chart of the room is made. One observer, armed with chart and stop watch, traces the space traversed by a given child during a two-, or five-, or ten-minute period, noting places where he stopped and for how long, and his occupation every ten seconds. Another observer simultaneously records every word he says, preferably in shorthand. Another may record the type of social behavior indulged in, according to categories decided on beforehand using various symbols to indicate aggressive, passive, co-operative actions, and timing everything as before. A series of such timed samples of a child's behavior is recorded for successive intervals, perhaps on different days, perhaps by relays of observers for twenty-four-hour periods. Thomas,[2] and others under her guidance, has worked out detailed techniques for intensive studies of this

[1] Valentine, C. W., "The innate bases of fear," *Jo. Gen. Psy.*, v. 37, 1930.
[2] Thomas, Dorothy S., "Some new techniques for studying social behavior," *Ch. Dev. Mon. *1.*

sort. So has Goodenough,[1] in Minnesota, and Charlotte Bühler [2] in Vienna, and several others.

Gesell [3] uses moving-picture cameras from different angles trained upon infants in a special observation enclosure. In the playroom situation he uses a partition of a "one way screen" which looks opaque from the child's side but permits vision from the observer's side. This device eliminates any distraction in a test situation, or any self-consciousness on the part of the subjects observed.

Small groups, if not moving about, can be systematically observed provided the problem is a narrow one, *e.g.*, how many in the course of an hour exhibit a specific nervous habit, and how often.

Tests and measures. — In the physical field we think at once of finding a child's height, measuring his lung capacity, testing his speed of running, his strength of grip, etc. The standards are unambiguous; we know just what we mean when we speak of inches tall, feet per second, and so on, so that no question need arise as to the validity of the test. In school achievement, too, we have definiteness with regard to measures of spelling, speed of addition, knowledge of geographical facts, and the like. By the use of scaling devices we can assign objective values to children's handwriting, drawing, composition, and so on. When it comes to emotional stability, to intelligence, to personality traits, the complexity of that which is to be measured is so great that our approach can be only indirect. By the consistency of behavior in several tests supposedly measuring the same abilities and traits we infer that we have measured the factor in common, label it as we may. Statistical procedures further assure us that this consistency is not a chance occurrence. We conclude, therefore, that our tests are valid, *i.e.*, that they measure what they purport to measure.

[1] Goodenough, F. L., "Measuring behavior traits by means of repeated short samples," *Jo. Juv. Res.*, v. 12, 1928.
[2] Bühler, Ch., et al., *Soziologische und psychologische Studien über das erste Lebensjahr*.
[3] Gesell, A., *Infancy and Human Growth*, chs. 2, 3.

In the hands of well-trained persons tests that have been validated become tools of great value in diagnosing a particular child and ranking him with respect to age standards, grade standards, or other scales which may have nothing to do with age or grade. School achievement tests are in such form that any teacher can easily acquire the knowledge and skill necessary to employ them. By their use we can discover the kind and amount of improvement brought about in a group after a given period of teaching, and thus be in a position to judge whether or not our methods of instruction need overhauling. We can also rate children by a fixed standard rather than by one peculiar to the teacher, the school, the neighborhood, or the part of the country. Comparisons of racial differences will be more objective along these lines, also.

The best known intelligence test is the Stanford revision of the Binet "mental age" test, used as a criterion by which to judge the validity of many others. The Pintner-Paterson Performance Scale is especially adapted for use with foreign-speaking, or with deaf children. Several have been worked out for infants and little children. A great many group tests of intelligence are available.

Only those persons who have been trained to administer these should undertake to test children for any ulterior purpose. At one time a number of enthusiasts were at large in the country "doing Binets." If this were for their own experience that might not be so bad; but since physicians, immigration authorities, judges, and others have occasion to utilize the results of this form of work and on the basis of the diagnosis render decisions that may affect the whole future of the individual tested, it presented a grave social danger. It is sheer charlatanism for a college or normal school graduate who has read a book on the tests and seen a subject tested, to set up as an expert in this line. No one would dream of sending children to a quack dentist whose sole training had consisted of reading a little about dentistry and in watching a few processes of the profession; why then should children be sent to a quack psychologist whose preparation is equally scanty? Again, just as in other professions, say medicine, a person is expected to take first a general course, two years of college work at least, then to train for professional work, lastly to specialize in some particular branch of that, say throat and ear work; so one who aspires to be a clinical psychologist should take first a general higher education, then a thorough course in the general field of psychology, descriptive, pathological, experimental, educational; and only then specialize as a worker in the clinic. Even so, such an expert needs to work in close touch with a psychiatrist, since the level of mental ability is not an efficient index to many forms of mental trouble. Similarly, to use the elaborate statistical method which is necessary to deal adequately with the facts collected in experimental pedagogy means not only the devotion of more time to it than the teacher engaged in routine duties can afford, but also a very thorough, intensive preparation.

Ratings and rankings. — There are many qualitative statements we commonly make about children which we should find difficult to restate in quantitative fashion because we have no absolute units of measurement. Thus we form an opinion that Alice is very timid, John is rather conceited, Walter has great promise of leadership — from observations of occurrences which, if recorded simply in terms of muscular response to a specific situation would be less significant, besides being very numerous. Even such qualitative judgments can be handled by means of rating a child on a scale, or ranking individuals by comparing them with each other. A rating may be made more objective by having as standard brief descriptions of a trait in, say, a fivefold scale. Thus, there might be five numbered descriptions of "courteous," ranging from aggressively rude to thoughtfully polite. The child is then scored from 1 to 5 according as he, in the rater's opinion, is most like one of these standard, scaled descriptions. A graphic representation may be made by marking on a five-inch line whereabouts the child stands. With a dozen or so trait items in each of which a child is thus rated the graph becomes a *profile*, showing where in the rater's judgment, a child is strong or weak. If several people who know the child well use such a rating sheet a very fair picture can be obtained of how his characteristics strike others. Self-rating has proved valuable for children of twelve and over, particularly when compared with the consensus of opinion about them from those with whom they are most in contact. It often is a salutary check upon undesirable tendencies, it may be a stimulus to effort for improvement; it is frequently a revelation to the one concerned of the unanimity of opinion about him which is the reverse of his own. Ratings are frequently used to measure school achievement. In this case the child's performance is scaled relative to the norm for his age or grade, a profile drawn, and instant comparison is possible with a definite standard.

Ranking is a method useful for small groups whose members may be compared directly with each other. Thus, in the trait "courtesy," a dozen to twenty individuals might be ranked, the name of the most courteous at the top, the rudest at the bottom, the others in relative position in between. For large groups this is not feasible except as it picks the extreme cases.

Experiments. — Better than systematic observation from the standpoint of scientific method is the method of experimentation. By this we mean a technique by which we seek to solve a problem that has presented itself in the course of preliminary observations. We control all known factors in advance, vary one of them at a time and observe the difference in the resulting responses.

For example, Gesell and Thompson [1] experimented with identical twins from the age of forty-six weeks to determine the relative influence of training and maturation on the ability to climb stairs. While one received training the other not only received none but was not allowed to attempt any climbing or to witness any. After six weeks of practice the abilities of both were measured, then the procedure was reversed for two weeks and measures taken again. In this way checks were applied

[1] Gesell and Thompson, "Learning and growth in identical twins," *Gen. Psych. Mon.*, 1929.

apparatus, nor continue an experiment till its close unless heavily bribed with chocolate bars, might have no significance in the eyes of the investigator belonging to one school of thought, but be the most important result of all for another. Systematic observation, highly refined, of children under normal circumstances seems the most profitable method for those with a practical interest in children. The laboratory set-up may be more valuable for the specialist whose purpose is abstract theory.

Conclusion. — Such are the methods of child psychology, which serve its purpose of amassing information about children's natures as distinct from adults'. Its scope may be widened to include studies of child life on the physical side in connection with eugenics, infant mortality, tuberculosis, and the like; on the social side in connection with housing conditions, delinquency, dependency, child labor. Its main contribution is to the applied psychology of child-training and methods of instruction; in short, to the science and art of education.

EXERCISES AND OBSERVATIONS

1. Take ten individuals, children in one grade preferably, known to all in your study group. Arrange them in rank order for each of the qualities suggested below, and any others you choose. Score the one who shows most of the quality 1, the next 2, the next 3. Score the opposite end 10, 9, 8 respectively. Score the middle four simply M. Arrange as indicated in the sample. Compare your judgment with that of others in the group on the same children.

CHARACTERISTICS	ALICE	JOHN	AMY	BILLY	ETC.
Attentive, not careless	1	M	2	9	
Even tempered, not unstable	3	1	2	8	
Cautious, not heedless	2	M	M	10	
Generous, not stingy	M	2	8	M	
Courageous, not timid	8	3	M	2	
etc.					
etc.					

2. Fix in your mind a scale of five degrees for each of the qualities below. A rating of 5 will mean an extreme absence of a trait or the presence of its opposite. A rating of 1 will mean conspicuousness of the quality.

A rating of 3 will indicate an average amount. Select one child, consider him carefully from the point of view of each of these, and rate him graphically as in the sample shown. If desirable, get similar profiles from others who know the same child, and compare the composite judgments.

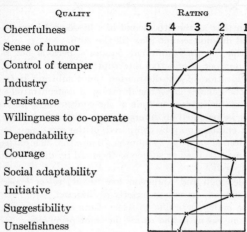

QUALITY	RATING
	5 4 3 2 1
Cheerfulness	
Sense of humor	
Control of temper	
Industry	
Persistance	
Willingness to co-operate	
Dependability	
Courage	
Social adaptability	
Initiative	
Suggestibility	
Unselfishness	

3. Observe a four- or five-year-old child in a playroom while he is engaged in some quiet, self-chosen occupation, such as painting, building with blocks, etc. Sit near, but do not attract his attention. Have a watch marking time in seconds, and 3 record sheets prepared thus, with 10 lines, 3 inches long, representing 30 seconds' worth of time each. Graph paper is desirable.

	0	5	10	15	20	25	30	Name
1st								Age
2nd								Date
3rd								Time
								Occupation
								Place

Observe the child for 5 minutes, tracing each line lightly marking with an x whenever he looks up or is otherwise distracted, and continuing with a heavy line till he resumes his occupation, which is to be marked with another cross. One line record, looking like this

would mean that at the 4th second of a 30-second interval he was distracted, and did not resume play till the 20th.

Repeat this for three different 5-minute periods not in succession. Count the number of effective interruptions in the total of 15 minutes. Total the duration of the distraction time; subtract it from the total playtime: the balance gives the duration of concentrated play. What percentage is the distraction time of the concentrated playtime?

This may be repeated on different days, with different play materials. Different children may be compared, of the same age.

Ten children at each age 24 months, 30 months, 36 months, 48 months, 60 months may be used as subjects, observed by different students; and results compared.

4. From Goodenough and Anderson (see below) select experiment 31 on pages 260–262, and carry out exactly as directed.
5. It would be highly desirable to select some one child, and, during the length of time spent in the course in child psychology, follow him up and study him from the angles suggested in the successive chapters of this book. This would involve a visit to his home, a conference with his parents besides various sorts of observations at appropriate times and places. Records from the physician's office and the school files will be important sources of information. Letters, stories he writes, drawings he makes, should be secured. Selected tests may be used to measure him, under the direction of the instructor.

FOR DISCUSSION

1. Of which type of observation would be the following:
   (a) Watching children on the street at play, counting how many were participating, how many looking on.
   (b) Asking ten observers to do this at different seasons, in different sections of the city, for standard lengths of time.
   (c) Getting help from a clinic to know how to deal with an eleven-year-old boy who steals.
   (d) Comparing eight-year-olds from bilingual homes and from unilingual homes in total vocabulary, language usage, reading comprehension, to decide which kind of home is more advantageous for language development.

(*e*) Asking fifty fourteen-year-olds to describe the content of their daydreams.

2. Which method of studying children would be suitable to discover:
   (*a*) Whether or not a given child is color-blind.
   (*b*) The total vocabulary of a child at two years old.
   (*c*) Whether stuttering is more common among left-handed children who have been taught to write with the right hand than it is in other children naturally right-handed.
   (*d*) The favorite reading material at different ages.
   (*e*) What is the normal level of difficulty in reasoning problems which ten-year-olds can solve.
   (*f*) The development of bladder control from ten to eighteen months of age.
   (*g*) Whether four-year-old children can keep time in walking to a 2–4 rhythm better than to a 3–4 rhythm.

3. Propose problems for which the following would be suitable methods to use:
   (*a*) A group ranking.
   (*b*) Observation of free activity.
   (*c*) Observation of directed response.
   (*d*) A check list form of questionnaire.

4. What are some disadvantages of the experimental method?

5. Besides the teacher and the judge, for whom else would you recommend child study?

6. Where besides school and home is a good place to study children?

7. What would be the difference in aim and methods between a mothers' club and a parent-teacher association?

8. In what form of child study would parents most likely be interested? Why?

9. How can the faults of the questionnaire method be to some extent avoided?

10. Describe the attitude desirable in a person who undertakes to observe children.

SELECTED REFERENCES

ANDERSON, J. E. "The methods of child psychology." In *Handbook of Child Psychology*. Clark University Press, 1931.

BARKER, MARGARET. "A technique for studying social activities of young children." *Child Development Monograph *3*. Teachers College Bureau of Publications, 1930.

BOTT, HELEN. "Observation of play activities in a nursery school." *Genetic Psych. Monograph *4*, v. 4 *1, 1928.

Dixon, C. M. *Children Are Like That.* John Day, 1930.

Gesell, Arnold. *The Mental Growth of the Pre-School Child.* Ch. 35. Macmillan, 1925.

Gesell, Arnold. *Infancy and Human Growth.* Pages 136–154. Macmillan, 1928.

Goodenough and Anderson. *Experimental Child Study.* Ch. 3 or part III. Century Co., 1931.

Hall, G. Stanley. "The contents of children's minds on entering school." In *Aspects of Child Life and Education.* Ginn & Co., 1907.

Major, D. R. *First Steps in Mental Growth.* Macmillan, 1906.

Van Alstyne, D. *Play Behavior and Choice of Play Materials of Pre-School Children.* University of Chicago Press, 1932.

CHAPTER II

ORIGINAL NATURE AND ITS MODIFICATION

It is not within the province of this study to go into the matter of the biological mechanisms of heredity. Our concern is rather to select such facts about human heredity as it is important for teachers dealing with children to know. For discussion and description of the way germ plasm acts the student should refer to any standard text on biology.[1]

LAWS OF HEREDITY

It will, however, be useful to review briefly the laws of heredity as they have been formulated by biologists.

Resemblance. — By heredity is meant an expected resemblance between offspring and parents. From the moment of conception certain constituents in the germ plasm called genes, by the method of dividing and combining of the chromosomes, determine what peculiarities shall be passed on and what shall be thrown out, so to speak, of the developing egg that will some day be born as a human infant. It is a fact so generally accepted that children resemble their parents that to utter it, much less dwell upon it, seems at first hardly necessary. "A chip of the old block," "his father's own child" are maxims of the race. The resemblances in families are among some of the most striking facts of common observation. In the realm of the physical we find resemblance in all of the features, eye and hair color, stature, cephalic index, shape of hands or face, so much so that a child is often said to be the "exact image" of father or grandmother because of this closeness of likeness. Just as good eyesight and longevity are family characteristics, so also color-blindness, left-handedness, some slight peculiarity of structure

[1] Thompson, J. A., *Heredity*, ch. 6. Conklin, Edwin G., *Heredity and Environment in the Development of Men.*

21

such as an extra finger or toe, or the Hapsburg lip, sense defects such as some forms of deafness or blindness, tendencies to certain diseases, especially those of the nervous system, — all these run in families. It is probable that certain mental traits likewise are handed down from parents to child, such as musical sensitivity, abilities in mathematics or the languages, artistic talent. In these ways and many others children resemble their parents.

Variability. — Two offspring of the same parents do not have identical heredity. In the pairing and dividing of the 24 pairs of chromosomes, derived half from the father, half from the mother, there are 16,777,216 different possibilities of arrangement, as any one who takes the trouble to work out the permutations of 48 taken 24 at a time can verify. This great variety possible explains why two children of very different, almost opposing natures, may be found in the same family, and this fact instead of a contradiction is really a proof of the closeness of family inheritance, as it is also a proof of the complexity and variability of the germs which produce human nature. Because of this variability, stupid parents may have gifted sons, quick-tempered parents stolid sons, short parents tall sons, inartistic parents artistic sons.

Two lines of ancestry. — The original nature in terms of family inheritance is not determined merely by the natures of the parents: there are two *lines* of ancestors concerned in the production of every child. Galton,[1] reached the conclusion that one half of a child's original equipment was due to the influence of his parents, one fourth to his grandparents, one eighth to his great-grandparents and so on back in geometric ratio. Thus it sometimes happens that though a child appears to be a change-ling, like no near relative, yet an investigation into the ancestral lines will usually explain the nature that seems a riddle when considering only the parent. Obviously, according to this an eminent great-grandfather contributes one eighth of one eighth, or one sixty-fourth of a given person's make-up, which should miti-

[1] Galton, F., *Hereditary Genius.*

gate undue pride in descent just as it may lessen the apprehension felt on discovering a scoundrel ancestor. However, this law is only one of several, and does not hold absolutely for one individual child. In mass studies, especially where large families are frequent, its working can be traced rather easily. Thus, if a characteristic was demonstrable in one grandparent, Woods [1] found it in one sixteenth of the grandchildren.

Inbreeding. — In raising stock, certain individuals are used over and over again, bred repeatedly within the closest family relationship. The result is a doubled, quadrupled chance of passing on some characteristics and of failing to find certain others. In human heredity where there is much intermarriage of near of kin, the same greater certainty of transmission of characteristics is seen. Where cousins marry, so that their offspring has only six great-grandparents instead of eight, whatever is in the common ancestry has twice as great a chance of being transmitted, be it strength or weakness.

Regression. — It is the exception to find the child of a great genius possessing ability equal to his father's, no matter in what the genius may be displayed. The ratings of children do not cluster immediately about the station occupied by their exceptional parents, but about a point somewhere between the extreme position occupied by their parents and the average. For example, the records of height of the children of a man three inches taller than the average will not cluster about that point, but about a point one or two inches above the average. Thus nature in the working of the laws of heredity is always pulling towards the average and so providing for solidarity and balance; at the same time, because of the principle of variation, new possibilities, genius, and talent are continually being produced.

Non-transmission of acquired traits. — The question as to whether the original nature of a child is directly influenced by the acquisition of the parents has been hotly discussed. Practically stated, the question is, can a man pass on to his offspring only the nature that he inherits, or also any acquisition or skill

[1] Woods, F. A., *Mental and Moral Heredity in Royalty.*

that has come as a result of education or training? For example, would the son of a man born at the height of his father's success as a writer be more likely to inherit literary ability than one born at the beginning of his career? Of course the obvious way to solve this question is by experiment, by allowing generation after generation — all the members of each — to acquire a certain habit, and then testing to see whether the acquisitions come more rapidly as generation succeeds generation. Following Lamarck, a school of psychologists and biologists declare their belief in the possibility and the fact of the transmission of acquired traits. Weismann and those who follow him take the opposite side of the question and declare that such transmission is impossible. Such facts as these: a parent is an expert baseball pitcher, and his son excels in the same line also; a parent is expert in the use of her needle, and her daughter shows the same trait; a parent is an expert linguist, and the children have the same talent, — all, according to Weismann, would be explained by the same reason, namely: because the characteristic was a part of the original equipment of each generation, a result, in other words, of heredity. The human race has changed from primitive times, language and culture have grown up, such facts as walking in an upright position and using the hands dexterously have attained their perfection, the traits of intellect and character have outgrown those of brute strength and sagacity, not as a matter of transmission directly from generation to generation, but as a result of gradually changing social conditions, and the working of the law of selection. Not the inheritance of acquisitions, but the selection of those who could acquire.

Mutation. — Changes take place in the genes, possibly of a simple chemical nature, which result, not simply in a fresh combination producing differentiated personal traits, but in a new trait which is itself heritable. The individual is called a "sport" if this new characteristic breeds true.

Reversion. — Sometimes, in the endless shifting of gene patterns, a characteristic that has not shown for generations will make its appearance. The offspring is referred to as a throwback. Since few people know much about all their ancestors more than two generations back, what is supposed to be a case of sport may often be a case of reversion, or atavism, as it is also called.

Sex linkage. — Some factors in heritability seem bound up with sex. To illustrate — a lack of coagulating power of the blood, called hæmophilia, producing a liability to copious, dangerous bleeding, is sex linked. Males are afflicted by it, though it may be transmitted through the female. This is true also of color-blindness which is more than four times as frequent among males as it is among females.

Mendel's law.[1] — This explains very clearly how characteristics may occur in children, making them surprisingly unlike either parent in this one particular, but entirely like some ancestor of three or four generations ago. It is very difficult to discern which method is followed by mental and temperamental traits, and at present little definite is known, because of the complexity of the thing called a trait or a characteristic. Certain features and traits of plants and animals have been analyzed into their unit characters, and the determiners of these have been controlled by those interested in the breeding of a certain stock, but with the human animal and with the more complex traits of the lower animals, hardly more than a beginning has been made. We are fairly sure that blue eyedness, the Hapsburg lip, follow Mendelian inheritance, as also many other physical characteristics. It is probable that feeble-mindedness and epilepsy are Mendelian recessives.

---

[1] When two varieties of a species, having different characteristics, are crossed in breeding, the resulting hybrid generation resembles one parent, the "dominant"; the "recessive" characteristic of the other is apparently suppressed, but is really latent, for it will appear in later generations. When the hybrids are inbred, 25 per cent of their offspring have the "recessive" characteristic of one grandparent, 25 per cent have the "dominant" characteristic of the other. The other 50 per cent may either resemble the hybrid parents, or be indistinguishable from the 25 per cent "dominants" till they in turn produce another generation. Thus, black (dominant) Andalusian fowls mated with white (recessive) produce nothing but slaty blue. The blue hybrids, if mated, produce in a brood of twelve, three white, three black, and six blue.

See Punnet, *Mendelism*, pp. 17–78, for a full account.

Possible modes of inheritance. — Some characteristics seem to be a *blend* — an equal mixture of paternal and maternal strain. This is true of skin color when negro and white mate. Some are *exclusive*, that is, the child is exactly like one side of the family or the other, though his own children may show the opposite characteristic. This is often seen in eye color. Some may be *particulate*. Piebald coated animals, having patches of hair like one parent and contiguous patches like the other, are not uncommon. In human beings we sometimes see one eye blue, one brown.

DIFFICULTIES IN STUDYING HUMAN HEREDITY

Inaccessibility of pedigrees. — The further back in any one's heredity we go the more ancestors he has, sixty-two by the fifth generation, for instance. Except in rare cases people do not know much about any of them except the nearest six, the parents and grandparents; and what they do not know, even about these near relatives, may be of considerable importance in determining heritability. Further, to make a complete study, not only the progenitors but the collaterals should be investigated. As families separate, even cousins often do not know reliable facts about each other, far less do second and third cousins. Still more infrequently do people retain interest in great-uncles and aunts. The case worker is hampered, then, by scanty information, some of that procurable only from the faulty memories of very old people.

Few offspring. — If the research worker's interests are at stake rather than those of the teacher or social worker, two other difficulties obstruct investigation. One is, that in order to prove Mendelian inheritance of two blends of a characteristic at least sixteen children would have to be born to each couple, and sixty-four if a third unit trait were in question. The fact that only two or three children are so frequently born, or at any rate survive infancy, limits the studies in the workings of the laws of heredity.

No experimentation. — Though we may observe results and control the breeding and training of animals we cannot do likewise with human stock but must use another approach. Conclusions drawn from studying animals' characteristics may not be wholly applicable to the interpretation of human inheriting.

Indefiniteness of terms. — Unfortunately, though physical characteristics are objective, indisputable evidence of inheritance, what is meant by a personal trait is open to question. Psychologists have not been able to agree on a definition of a trait, a tendency, a temperamental or mental characteristic, so that investigation is hampered by a vagueness in knowledge of what is to be sought for and, if possible, measured.

Methods available. — In spite of these difficulties, considerable progress has been made in studying pedigrees, taking case histories of nearly-related living people, measuring every one concerned who is willing to subject himself to the various testing devices we have so far perfected. Special statistical techniques are applied to discover the degree of likeness or unlikeness in some unit of personality.

RACE, NATIONALITY, AND SEX AS INFLUENCING ORIGINAL NATURE

Belief in racial differences. — One source of original nature is race. It has been customary to laud the white, and in particular the Anglo-Saxon race as that in which the intellect has most developed, the race that excels all others in its genius, its power to invent and to reason. In contrast to it the darker races have been held up to scorn. The keen sense power of the American Indian and the African Kaffir has been commented upon and the law of compensation has been called upon to explain why they have not progressed further. A critical reader will at once note that the evidence upon which these deductions are based is almost entirely anecdotal rather than scientific, depending upon untrained travelers' tales instead of upon objective tests. Hence no allowance has been made for training, for customs, or for surroundings.

One of the first serious investigations into race differences was made by R. S. Woodworth at the St. Louis Exposition in 1904. Summarizing his results and those of other investigators as to keenness of senses he says: "On the whole, the keenness of the senses seems to be about on a par in the various races of mankind." In tests of reaction time and power and of making simple judgments he found that the "results tend to show that simple sorts of judgments, being subject to the same disturbances, proceed in the same manner among various peoples: so that the similarity of the races in mental processes extends at least a step beyond sensation." When it comes to testing general intelligence, however, the matter becomes much more complicated. In reporting on a very simple test of intelligence he says: "If their results could be taken at their face value, they would indicate differences in intelligence between races, giving such groups as the Pygmy and Negrito a low station compared with most of mankind." [1] The doubt as to whether they can be taken at face value arises from the fact that the tests administered may not have been equally fair, equally novel to all the races. However, Woodworth's conclusion as to the low rank of the negroid races is borne out by such investigations as have been made into the relative standings of the white and negro children in the public schools even though these may be subjected to the same criticism noted, namely, the conditions may not have been identical.

Studies of negroes and Indians. — More recently there appeared a number of studies by Mayo, Pyle, Rowe, Perring, and others dealing with differences between negro and white, or Indian and white children in the schools of this country. Whether the Binet-Simon tests or the ordinary school grades were used as a measure the results appear in favor of the whites. Perring,[2] in the schools of Philadelphia, found twice as much retardation among negro as among white children, also that the amount of retardation was greater, being two years on the average for the negro, one and a half for the white. Pyle,[3] as a result of psychological tests given to over four hundred children

[1] Woodworth, R. S., *Racial Differences in Mental Traits*, pp. 176, 181.
[2] Perring, "A study of the retardation of negro and white pupils in a Philadelphia public school," *Psy. Cl.*, v. 8, 1915.
[3] Pyle, *Psy. Bull.*, 1915, 1916.

of each race in various towns in Missouri, shows that the girls in both races were better than the boys, that there was less difference between negro and white girls than there was between negro and white boys; that the racial difference was greater in the more difficult tests than in the easier ones. Taking all tests together, only one fifth of the negro children did as well or better than the average of the white children. In a later series of tests where there was a more direct measurement of learning capacity as the effects of environment were better eliminated, Pyle says that the negro children showed from three quarters to four fifths the ability of the white children. He notes also that the success of the negro increases with a greater proportion of white ancestry.

Later investigations. — With the development of group tests for intelligence many extensive comparisons were undertaken. The results of the Army Alpha and Beta tests administered to over a million and a half adults of the draft showed superior average performance by those of German, English, Jewish, Scotch, and American descent over those of Italian, Portuguese, Irish, negro, ancestry. Corresponding results appear when measuring children in our schools by group tests of intelligence. Taking 100 as an index to represent the average mentality of all white children, we find Chinese and Japanese — in this country, in our schools — averaging 99, northern negroes 85, Mexicans 78, southern negroes 75, full blood American Indians 70.

Averages, of course, tell us nothing about an individual's possibilities. In every race we find superior scores made by some children, inferior ones too; the total range of overlap in groups is very great. Garth,[1] in a survey of all types of research work into racial differences up to 1930, concludes that there is no indisputable evidence for differences in mentality for which modification and selection could not be responsible. All traits so far measured are distributed widely among all races. Individual differences within one race are greater than the differences between the averages, or between the extreme upper limits found of races.

[1] Garth, *Race Psychology.*

Popularly, we tend to believe in temperamental and other personality differences not only between races but between nationalities and the two sexes. At present we have very few means of testing and measuring such traits, so that we cannot say such differences are proved to exist however probable they may be.

Sex differences. — Thompson finds that "Motor ability in most of its forms is better developed in men than in women. In strength, rapidity of movement, and rate of fatigue, they have a very decided advantage, and in precision of movement a slight advantage. . . . The thresholds are on the whole lower in women, discriminative sensibility is on the whole better in men. . . . All these differences, however, are slight. As for the intellectual faculties, women are decidedly superior to men in memory, and possibly more rapid in associative thinking. Men are probably superior in ingenuity. . . . The data on the life of feeling indicate that there is little, if any, sexual difference in the degree of domination by emotion, and that social consciousness is more prominent in men and religious consciousness in women." [1] Thorndike finds the chief differences to be that the female varies less from the average standard, is more observant of small visual details, less often color-blind, less interested in things and their mechanisms, more interested in people and their feelings, less given to pursuing, capturing, and maltreating living things, and more given to nursing, comforting, and relieving them than is the male.

Burt,[2] measuring over 5000 children in school subjects such as language, arithmetic, and handwork found girls slightly superior in the average in speed of reading, speed of writing, spelling, quality of composition. Boys were slightly superior in subtraction and division computation, in speed and quality of handwork. Hunt,[3] under test conditions, found no marked difference in ability to remember names and faces or to interpret

---

[1] Thompson, *Mental Traits of Sex*, pp. 169, 170, 171.
[2] Burt, Cyril, *Mental and Scholastic Tests.*
[3] Hunt, Thelma, "The measurement of social intelligence," *Jo. Abn. Psy.*, v. 12, 1928.

emotions, though everyday experience would incline us to the belief that women surpass men in social and psychological "sense," just as men excel women in mechanical ability. Women's judgment in social situations requiring tact is superior.

The question of interest to the teacher is, what in nature is peculiar to the male sex and what to the female? What traits will be true of a boy, merely because he is a boy, and vice versa? This has been an extremely difficult question to answer, because of the difficulty encountered in trying to eliminate the influence of environment and training. Boys are what they are because of their original nature plus their surroundings. Some would claim that could we give boys and girls the same surroundings, the same social requirements, the same treatment from babyhood, there would be no difference in the resulting natures. Training undoubtedly accentuates inborn sex differences and it is true that a reversal of training does lessen this difference; however, the weight of opinion at present is that differences in intellect and character do exist because of differences of sex, but that these have been unduly magnified.

All the authors emphasize the smallness of the differences; and after all the striking thing is not the differences between the sexes but the great difference within the same sex in respect to every mental trait tested. The difference of man from man, and woman from woman, in any trait is almost as great as the differences between the sexes in that trait. Sex can be the cause then of only a fraction of the differences between the original nature of individuals.

NATURE AND NURTURE

An oft-debated question is — What is the relative importance of heredity and environment in determining the personality of a child? Answers to this vary all the way from a flat denial of any hereditary influence whatever — founded on a belief in the mechanistic method of learning — to the fatalistic statement that heredity predetermines a child's traits, no matter what the environment. The facts in the case are, of course, impossible to disentangle experimentally, since neither factor can be isolated.

Galton's studies. — The first comprehensive study of this question is the work done by Sir Francis Galton in his book entitled *Hereditary Genius*. He examined the careers of the relatives of 977 men of genius, each of whom would be ranked as one in four thousand for intellectual attainment, and then compared with these the careers of the relatives of 977 men of average ability of the same social rank. If nurture is the stronger factor, the proportion of eminent men in the two groups should be approximately the same, for the nurture was that of families of the same social standing in England. His results were as follows: In the first group he found 89 fathers, 114 brothers, 129 sons, — a total of 332 men of eminence; 52 grandfathers, 37 grandsons, 53 uncles, 61 nephews, — a total of 203 men of eminence. The 977 eminent men had 535 eminent relatives. In the second group he found one father, brother, or son; three grandfathers, grandsons, uncles, and nephews together. The 977 average men of the same social standing had but four eminent relatives.

Nature, not nurture, seems to be the determining factor.

Studies in royalty. — Woods in his study of *Mental and Moral Heredity in Royalty* reaches the same conclusion. He chose 671 persons in the royal families of Europe in general from as far back as the sixteenth, in some cases from the eleventh, century. This was excellent source material since pedigrees were very full and well kept, the families were usually large, the environmental conditions were as good as the times could make them, yet varied in different countries and through the centuries. He gave each a rating determined as objectively as possible on the scale of from 1 to 10 in intellect, also another rating in morality; then he studied the distribution of the ratings. The degree to which certain ratings cluster in families shows the influence of heredity, for were that not the influential factor, the various grades would be scattered at random. Imagining a complete chart to be constructed, large enough to contain all these 671 people arranged as in the familiar genealogical "tree," he says, "if such a great chart were constructed, we should see the geniuses, or (9) and (10) grades, not scattered at random over its entire surface, but isolated little groups of (9) and (10) characters (the individuals within each group contiguous to each other) would be found here and there. Those in the lowest grades for intellect would also be found close to others of the lowest type. . . . There would be certain regions composed almost entirely of grades from (4) to (7). . . . The upshot of it all is that as regards intellectual life, environment is a totally inadequate explanation. . . . Therefore it would seem that we are forced to the conclusion that all these rough differences in intellectual activity which are susceptible of grading on a scale of ten are due to predetermined differences in the primary germ cells." [1] He found that if there were strong contrasts in the ancestry there were also strong contrasts among the offspring. If a quality appeared in all the ancestry it surely appeared in the children; if it appeared in one parental line only it appeared in half the children, if in one parent only then in one fourth of the children — very pretty illustrations both of Galton's and Mendel's laws.

Studies of twins. — Twins are of two kinds, identical and fraternal. Identical twins are developed from the same ovum, are enclosed within the same placenta, are always of the same sex; they may be considered as having the same heredity. Fraternal twins develop from two separately fertilized ova, and are simply two children born at the same time. They do not have the same heredity, and need be no more alike than other offspring born at separate times. It is instructive, therefore, to measure the resemblance between twins of both kinds as compared with the resemblance between siblings and unrelated pairs of children taken at random.

Thorndike's study. — Following Galton's pioneer studies on twins, Thorndike studied fifty pairs of twins [2] taken from the

[1] Woods, *Mental and Moral Heredity in Royalty*, pp. 265, 266, 286.
[2] Thorndike, E. L., "Measurements of twins," *Columbia Contr. Phil. Psy.*, v. 13, *3.

New York public schools to see whether there was a greater degree of resemblance between them than between other brothers and sisters. A greater similarity between them would mean that nature was stronger than nurture, for it is in a greater identity of nature that twins differ from ordinary siblings. The results obtained showed an average resemblance in the mental abilities measured of .78.[1]

For the ordinary siblings but a few years apart in age in the tests that have been made the resemblance is less than half as great. Thorndike gives two additional reasons for believing that this close similarity could not have been caused by environmental conditions. In the first place, were environment the cause, the longer it had to act the greater should grow the resemblance, and twins of thirteen and fourteen years old should be more alike than those of nine and ten. This is not found to be the case. In the second place, if training is the cause the traits that are much open to the influences of training should show a greater similarity than those little subject to training; they do not show any greater similarity, however. Thorndike's evidence is then in accord with Galton's conclusion: namely, that nature is the prepotent influence in determining intellectual ability.

Other studies. — Many other studies have since been made on twin resemblance, also on family resemblance. Holzinger,[2] comparing 50 pairs of identical twins with 52 pairs of fraternal twins found high correlations, averaging nearly .90 for the identical twins in school achievement and intelligence tests, averaging around .60 for the fraternal twins. For ordinary siblings the resemblance is about .50, for cousins about .25. Between children and parents it is .40. Studies of siblings brought up in different homes show a resemblance of .25. Unrelated children brought up in the same foster home show a

[1] Resemblance is expressed statistically by an index, R, called the coefficient of correlation. Perfect resemblance would be indicated by +1.00; completely inverse relationship by −1.00; lack of any resemblance by 0.

[2] Holzinger, Karl J., "The relative effect of nature and nurture influences on twin differences," *Jo. Ed. Psych.*, v. 20, 1929.

resemblance in intelligence of .25 or more. These figures show, not only that heredity is the stronger factor in producing mental ability, but also that environment does have some influence. In general, the total contribution of the factor of heredity to mental ability is 75 to 80 per cent.

Foster children. — Children have been tested for intelligence before placement in foster homes, and again from one to five years later, with the result that no appreciable change was discovered from the better environment. In any retest of intelligence a variation of five points would be considered normal. Burks,[1] from a careful study of adopted children concluded that, on the average, less than 10 points of the intelligence quotient is due to environment. While in rare cases, about one in a thousand, the home environment may raise or depress the quotient as much as 20 points, heredity can do it 100 points. The extremes also, the geniuses and the low-grade feeble-minded, are accounted for by heredity alone.

Conclusions. — A child is what he is primarily because he is a member of a certain family, sex, and race. Those factors give him his inheritance, his capital, his stock in trade, and these birthday gifts bound his ultimate achievement. True, environment, training, education, play their part in the production of man as we idealize him, but that part is conditioned and limited by the nature which is being influenced. In other words, though Burbank may produce a prickless thistle by careful selection, and though we may improve a variety of figs immensely by careful regulation of the environment, yet we need never expect to gather figs from thistles, their natures being originally so differently determined. Nor is this limitation of human possibilities of growth a pessimistic doctrine. The sure realization of what has always been true is not pessimism, nor is it itself any curtailment of actual attainment. When the differences between the actual life of a savage in Central Africa and that of a civilized man are considered, the tremendous effect of environment

[1] Burks, Barbara S., "The relative influence of nature and nurture upon mental development," 27th *Yearbook*, N.S.S.E.

as a stimulating and selective force on races is overwhelming. The educator has still a task of infinite magnitude amid unknown potentialities, and to make due allowance for the sources and limitations of original nature will but make his work more effective and less wasteful. The recognition of the respective parts played by nature and nurture make it imperative for him to know the child mind in terms of its equipment, and to know the laws by means of which it may be changed.

Even if we could disentangle absolutely the factors operating to produce a given child what difference would it make? Teachers have to take children as they find them, complex results of heredity, home training, other environmental forces. Heredity is a condition of life which has to be dealt with, just as truly as is environment. Because a trait — granted that we could agree on what we mean by a trait — has been inherited, need not involve a fatalistic attitude. Traits can be modified, and that is the business of those, greatly in the majority so far as numbers are concerned, who are in a child's environment.

CHARACTERISTICS OF ORIGINAL NATURE

Functions depend on structure. — The inheritance of an individual, whether it be that of family, sex, or race, is in terms of physiological structure, not in terms of mental states. A baby is not heir to any ideas, his emotions or ideals are not ready-made, he does not inherit consciousness as such; he does inherit a complicated system of neurones acting upon muscles and glands as well as upon each other. He does inherit a chemical regulation of his body, so to speak, which has a profound effect on what we call his temperament. Physically, he is more or less subject to certain diseases, both of brain and body, than a baby in some other family. His whole system is bound by definite laws of growth. Psychologically and socially his development depends on the action of his nervous system.

The possibility of conduct or intelligence depends upon the connections at the synapses, — upon the possibility of the current affecting neurones in a certain definite way. The possession of an "original nature," then, means the possession, as a matter of inheritance, of certain connections between neurones, the possession of certain synapses which are in functional contact and across which a current may pass merely as a matter of structure.

Types of original responses. — Among these unlearned tendencies which make up the original nature of the human race we may note automatic or physiological actions and reflexes, instincts and capacities. Automatic actions are such as those controlling the heart-beats, digestive and intestinal movements; the contraction of the pupil of the eye from light, sneezing, swallowing, etc., are reflexes; to cringe when afraid, to slash out and fight when angry are called instincts, while the term capacities refers to those more subtle traits by means of which an individual becomes a good linguist, or is tactful, or gains skill in handling tools. However, there is no sharp line of division between these various unlearned tendencies. It seems better to consider them as of the same general character but differing from each other in simplicity, definiteness, uniformity of response, variableness among individuals, and modifiability. They range from movements such as the action of the blood vessels to those concerned in hunting and collecting; from the simple, definite, uniform knee-jerk, which is very similar in all people and open to very little modification, to the capacity for scholarship, which is extremely complex, vague as to definition, variable both as to manifestation in one individual and amounts amongst people in general, and is open to almost endless modification. This fund of unlearned tendencies is the capital with which each child starts, the capital which makes education and progress possible, as well as the capital which limits the extent to which progress and development in any line may proceed.

Law of sequence of maturation. — One characteristic true of the majority of these original tendencies is that they are delayed, that is, they are not present at birth. Of course, the physiological operations necessary for the life of the infant are active, but practically all of the capacities appear later. Their appearance is dependent on the growth and ripening of the connections between neurones.

No tendency appears till the organism is sufficiently mature. Birth is, after all, only one incident in the whole sequence of development; and maturation continues in as orderly a fashion as before birth. Just as we recognize the five months, seven months fetus as markedly less matured than the full term nine months infant, so that infant, at birth, is unable to perform many things he finds easy at six months old simply because he has matured further.

This law is perfectly well understood with regard to the vegetable world. We expect blossoms before fruit, for instance. But the rate of development is set as well as the sequence by the fact that currant bushes, cherry trees, oaks, are different in original nature. So too with human development. Children cut some teeth before they walk or talk, they can imitate vertical strokes with a crayon before a horizontal stroke, can draw a square before they can draw a diamond, can name objects in a picture before they can describe them, and so on; but the tempo of that development is set by each child's original nature.

In discussing this point of the delay in the appearance of original tendencies, it has been customary to talk of them as if they appeared suddenly, certain ages being the time above all others for certain instincts and capacities to mature. It seems very improbable that any ability is absent this week — or year even — and present the next. From all the studies that have been made — whether of the simple and definite instincts, or the more complex and vague capacities — the law seems to be one of gradual rather than of sudden maturing. We know now that the sex instinct is of long and slow development all through childhood rather than bursting into being during adolescence. Children tested from year to year show no time at which there is so sudden an increase in power that any certain age could be chosen as the one at which the instinct "appears." Of course, the interference of training and environment as a factor is undeniable; but the conclusion that though it is true that original tendencies are delayed they are also very gradual in their maturing, is not invalidated.

Crudity. — Children are often called "little savages," and so far as their inherited make-up is concerned, that is what they are. "Man's original equipment dates far back and adapts him, directly, only for such a life as might be led by a family group of wild men among the brute forces of land, water, storm and sun, fruit and berries, animals and other family groups of wild men." [1] The original traits and interests of man are not such as fit him to live in a civilized community in the twentieth century, and therefore the fact that these tendencies are modifiable is of tremendous importance. On this fact alone rests all the civilization of the world, all the culture of the ages, all the promise of the future. Here is the field and the function of education: to seize upon this capital and use it; to modify and direct the original capacities and instincts of children so that they are fitted to live in the best which adult society has to offer, to appreciate and to add to it.

METHODS OF MODIFYING ORIGINAL NATURE

The work of education is largely a matter of modification; few if any original tendencies are absolutely useless, few are so acceptable that they can be retained just as they are. The vast majority of them need to be modified, higher pleasures substituted for lower, certain elements eliminated by withholding the situation that calls them out when they will perish from disuse, or by following their manifestation with pain and discomfort of some kind, fixing the desirable traits or phases or elements by rewards or satisfaction.

By disuse or stimulation. — One method of controlling an instinct is to deal with the situation which evokes the response. The stimulus may be withheld to prevent the response recurring — illustrated in keeping dangerous but attractive objects out of a baby's reach, or it may be provided in superabundance so as

[1] Thorndike, *Education*, pp. 91–92.

to increase the likelihood of a response — illustrated by surrounding the kindergarten child with all sorts of suggestive implements. The former method, known as disuse, is obviously not a constructive way of training normal children, since no guarantee is given that the whole environment will be permanently emptied of such stimuli, nor is any provision made for teaching children how to respond when the inevitable situation is felt. In an emergency, or with very young, sick, or abnormal subjects the method of disuse may be necessary. For a rich, full life, the method of stimulation is always indicated.

By unpleasant or pleasant results. — A second method of control is to attach such consequences to the response that on a recurrence of the situation the response is either more or less likely to be made. Thus, love of being a cause, and manipulation are developed by the reward of seeing the object made or changed, and indiscriminate grabbing is checked by the pain of the burn or the slap that follows. In either case, the reward, satisfaction, pleasure feeling, or the punishment, dissatisfaction, pain feeling, needs to be closely associated in the child's own consciousness with the situation-response series rather than with accidental extraneous circumstances, or with the person who intensifies the affective tone of the results; also, the younger the child the more closely in time must the consequences be felt.

By substitution or sublimation. — A third method of control, known as substitution, attempts to reconstruct the situation-response series by forming a habit of responding in another than the primitive way whenever the situation occurs. Thus, when hungry and within sight, smell, and reach of food, children must learn to wait and help themselves in mannerly fashion rather than to grab, to eat rather than stuff and bolt their food, eventually to dine rather than to eat. A special form of this substitution method is known as sublimation. Here the emotional tone accompanying an original situation-response series is transferred to another complex and utilized in other, higher ways. Thus, the feelings of anger that might assist in striking out when pushed or interfered with bodily may be directed into energetic fighting for a cause, through newspaper publicity, speeches in the legislature, or similar means. And the feeling of derision or repugnance that by original nature is present when looking at anybody physically grotesque, awkward, or deformed, may be transferred to the mental contemplation of anything morally ugly; while by substitution, the response of sympathy may be felt in the first situation and helpful action follow.

This stimulation or disuse, reward or punishment, substitution and sublimation as methods of awakening, strengthening, or redirecting original nature does not wait until the child reaches school age, but begins in earliest babyhood; however, the pull and power of original nature is still strong during the child's school years, and it is the business of the teacher to make use of the energy, the tendencies which are there. To ignore them is wasteful, and may be definitely harmful. They are there to be used, neither to be ignored, nor just accepted. That education which knows what an individual will do apart from training, which makes use of natural interests and motives instead of forcing artificial ones, which works with rather than against original nature, that education will succeed in satisfying the deepest, most lasting, biggest human wants.

PRACTICAL EXERCISES

1. For the special child you have selected for intensive study, secure the "family tree" as far back as the grandparents. Include the related uncles, aunts, and cousins on both sides. Ask for any unusual facts about any of these that your informant can provide, such as physical characteristics, special aptitudes, vocational distinction.
2. Consult the school records for a given grade room to see what facts about racial or national heredity you can discover. If there are marked differences in scholastic aptitude in that room search further for any possible reasons suggested in the heredity involved.

FOR DISCUSSION

1. What difference would it make in education if inherited traits were unmodifiable?
2. What facts should any one offering vocational guidance find out about the heredity of the young people?
3. In what school subjects would you expect girls and boys respectively to excel? Why?

SELECTED REFERENCES

EAST, E. M. *Heredity and Human Affairs.*

EAST AND JONES. *Inbreeding and Outbreeding.*

GOODENOUGH, F. L. "Racial differences in the intelligence of school children." *Jo. Exp. Psych.*, v. 9, 1926.

GUYER, M. F. *Being Well Born.*

NEWMAN, H. H. "Mental and physical traits of identical twins." *Jo. Heredity*, v. 23, 1932.

POPENOE, P. B. *Child's Heredity.*

CHAPTER III

AFFECTIVE STATES AND EMOTIONS

SATISFIERS AND ANNOYERS

Physiological basis for satisfyingness. — Man is continually "wanting" something. All people are unremittingly doing the same thing, striving to satisfy their wants and desires, to obtain food, friends, reputation, public approval, to outdo others, to show kindliness, to collect, to gain results mental and manual, to rest, — or, on the other hand, to avoid deprivation of any of these things, to avoid scorn or rebuff, pain or failure. We spend our lives striving after certain situations, certain responses, and dodging other situations, other responses. Why should man spend his life for certain things, and pay no attention to others, or avoid them? There must be something in the original equipment of man to account for these differences in attitude, some situations must, because of structure, be satisfying to human nature, and others annoying.

To describe what is meant by "satisfying" and "annoying" is difficult. Pleasure and pain with their usual connotations are not synonymous terms. Thorndike says, "when any original behavior-series is started and operates successfully, its activities are satisfying, and the situations which they produce are satisfying," and vice versa, "when any original behavior-series is started, any failure of it to operate successfully is annoying." [1] Besides these "behavior" satisfiers and annoyers, there are some constant independent annoyers and satisfiers that need to be considered. Physical pain, bitter tastes, bad smells, slimy things, depression, solitude, disapproval, and intense sensory stimuli are almost always annoying, no matter what behavior-series is involved. "Sweet, meaty, fruity and nutty tastes,

[1] *Original Nature of Man*, pp. 123, 124.

43

glitter, color and motion in objects seen, being rocked, swung and carried (in childhood), rhythm in percepts and movements, elation, the presence of other human beings, their manifestation of satisfaction and their instinctive approving behavior" [1] are independent satisfiers.

Just what is the neurone condition which permits of this feeling of satisfaction or annoyance? If we think of reactions as depending on a chain of neurones with synapses in functional contact, then when such a series-with-synapses-ready-to-act is actually called upon to conduct, the mental accompaniment of the readiness is satisfaction; further, when such a series-ready-to-act is prevented from conducting, the mental accompaniment of the hindrance or checking is annoyance; or, when a series-unready-to-act is forced to conduct, the result is likewise annoyance. Compare by analogy the lack of friction when a line of people is prepared to pass water-buckets at a fire and is started doing so, and the friction occurring when either, being prepared, no buckets come their way, or when unprepared, buckets are started down the line. Now some neurone connections are always ready, others always unready; therefore we have independent, invariable, perennial annoyers and satisfiers. It must be borne in mind, that "readiness" depends on inner growth and maturity, as well as upon conditions of nutrition, disease, fatigue, and familiarity.

It is true, then, that merely as a matter of structure, certain situations are intrinsically satisfying to the human race, and others annoying. To have food, to hoard, to beat some one else in certain activities, to fight, to show kindliness, to tease, to display one's powers, to win approval, to be physically and mentally active, — these responses are to be desired and sought, they are in themselves satisfying emotionally. The reverse of them, *e.g.*, having to sit when the tendency to physical activity is ready, being told not to ask questions, being given no opportunity for mental activity, these situations are annoying. To fight when physically tired, or to collect when that occupation

[1] *Ibid.*, p. 130.

has continued all day, may be annoying owing to the depletion of the nerve centers. Each tendency as it works itself out produces in the animal a feeling of satisfaction. In these feelings is found the original basis for all interests, motives, desires, and wants, — those things which control the life, activities, and education of the human race. In order to attain and preserve satisfying states and to avoid annoying states, man is stimulated to learn. Herein is the continual incentive for the learning process. As the tendencies vary in strength, are delayed or transitory, so are the interests, and so must motives of appeal change. The satisfyingness of mere physical activity to the six-year-old is very great, and the annoyance at being deprived of it is proportionately great; the strength of the hunting or gang spirit in boys of ten or eleven makes the operation of these tendencies satisfying; later, when these tendencies have lost some of their original strength or have become merged in others, the interest in the corresponding situation is much less.

Utilization of affective states in education. — All this is of great importance in education, for it is by use of these original interests that the learning process is started, and it is by grafting the higher, more ideal interests into these crude ones that man's wants are made better. Gradually to draw a child's interest from personal approval to an interest in gaining approval for his group, and later to the approval of his own conscience; to develop a child's moral sense, so that instead of being merely interested in doing what brings immediate satisfaction he will be satisfied by doing what is right; so to train him that the social interests outweigh the non-social, — this work is the responsibility of the educator, for thus does man pass from the animal level into his human inheritance. The danger in educational practice here is the same as that pointed out before; the tendency is to ignore or suppress the fund of energy provided by these original interests, and instead of using these motives to bring out responses, to substitute for them artificial or adult motives. To ask a kindergarten child to do his work because he will need it some day, to appeal to him to be clean and neat because society demands it, to encourage him to tell the truth because it is right, in each case is to make an appeal that means nothing, because of lack of development. But to ask him to do his work so that he can use the desired toy, to appeal to him to be clean because then he can eat his lunch, to encourage him to tell the truth because it will pay in terms of pleasure right then, — these motives are those that he is working with every day, that have a basis in interests active at the time. No matter what the words used in appeal are, the work will be done, the child will be clean, and truth will be told, because, and only because of active interests; others cannot be operative because of the child's limitations in development, in experience, in knowledge. Why deceive both ourselves and the child by using more ideal motives? These are in place later, and if kept till the time when the interest is alive in the child they will have force to bring results. Used too early, they are likely to remain empty of true content. The individual is self-deceived, acting in response to motives worded in ideal terms, whereas the true motive is a selfish one. The danger in such appeals is not in calling on low and crude ones, but in constantly working on the same level and so failing to provide for the demands of progress and development. Meet the child fearlessly on the level where he is no matter where that may be, and then raise him to higher and higher levels by substitution and pleasurable results.

ÆSTHETIC EMOTIONS

Pleasure in perceptual experience. — The original tendencies which are built up into the æsthetic emotions are found in some situations in themselves satisfying. These roots are probably the satisfyingness of glitter and color, or rhythm in percepts and movements. From these crude beginnings comes the enjoyment of nature, of art, of poetry, of dancing, and of music. The fact that the mere presence of certain sensory stimuli causes in the organism feeling-responses of satisfaction makes possible, later, the yielding of one's self to the "perfect moment," when the whole being feels absorbed by, and identified with, beauty. The very nature and meagerness of the original equipment leave emotions in the field of the æsthetic extremely plastic. The kind of situation embodying the qualities that call out the satisfaction which is the æsthetic emotion will depend chiefly upon the individual's training and environment.

Just what any individual considers beauty or music or art is a matter of education; and there seems to be nothing else save the qualities mentioned necessary for æsthetic enjoyment, save possibly those which insure unity and ease of attention. The satisfaction aroused in a little child by a chromo or by strongly rhythmic music is just as truly an æsthetic emotion as that aroused in an educated adult by a Murillo Madonna, or a Beethoven symphony. From the enjoyment of the crude and elemental, the child must be raised to enjoyment of the artistic and complex. Here, as elsewhere, the beginning must be made on the level where original equipment places the child, not at some level far beyond; for the result of the latter method is to kill true æsthetic enjoyment. Strong, though good, color should be characteristic of the pictures given to children and those that hang on the walls of primary schoolrooms. It should be borne in mind that pictures are used for other purposes than that of æsthetic enjoyment, and therefore this need not hold true of those used for the sake of the story or the information. Gradually, from the appreciation of these pictures, the children may be brought to enjoy more delicate harmonies of color, black and white, the qualities of fine perspective. The music, the songs, and the poetry should have decided, simple rhythm at first, other qualities are of secondary importance; later, emphasis may be placed on harmony, on form and assonance. The development must be gradual, however, if true æsthetic appreciation of what is considered the best is to be cultivated.

Joy in construction is not identical with æsthetic pleasure. The satisfaction aroused by construction or creation is not necessarily an æsthetic emotion. It may be nothing more than pleasure in activity, or a feeling of achievement. Pleasure in the contemplation of beauty is more of a passive thing. Nothing but manipulative, "function," pleasure is seen in babies' first constructions. The tower of blocks is piled for the fun of piling. Not till about eighteen months of age is there a momentary pause to look at the finished product before demolishing it. When the connection is made between effortful activity and the looks of the result a new attitude is born towards materials; something beyond pure function pleasure is possible.

Not that constructive activity always thereafter arouses æsthetic pleasure — far from it — the two sources of pleasure are independent though sometimes connected. That one may be the condition of the arousal of the other, there can be no question. The production by an individual of a beautiful object is often followed by a contemplation of the beauty which is æsthetic; and the satisfaction in terms of æsthetic appreciation of something beautiful may stimulate the constructive interest. However, the two attitudes are different, and the training and development of one need not involve the training or development of the other. One may readily enjoy sensory appeals and be trained to appreciation of the beautiful in sound, color, line, or proportion without developing any ability to create in these lines, perhaps with only partial success in imitating others' work without offending good taste. Most people can have this passive enjoyment educated, fewer can reproduce acceptably without rigid training in technique, and fewest of all among us so create that the rest can contemplate our productions with real æsthetic pleasure.

Training æsthetic appreciation. — The methods of training appreciation are not well developed; comparatively little is done in the schools to direct the æsthetic emotion in the face of the fact that few, very few, of the thousands of children who leave every year can be producers to any extent, whereas all can enjoy, if the power has been developed. The great works of art, literature, music, and nature are ever present, offering the greatest of all opportunities for æsthetic appreciation. However, certain developments in the schools are evidence of the recognition of the power and the value of the æsthetic emotions. The separation of literature from the structural study of English in the high school; the introduction of the victrola, broadcasting, or other planning for the children to hear good instrumental and vocal music and compositions; visits to art museums, not for criticism, but enjoyment; the excursions into the woods or down to the river, not for nature study, but to develop emotional response; allowing children to read for the sheer pleasure of it rather than for the purpose of reproducing the story, telling the plot, or discussing the style; placing copies of famous statues and pictures in our school corridors and rooms; — all these are endeavors to develop that form of satisfaction which we call æsthetic, whose roots are in the original nature of man.

FUNDAMENTAL EMOTIONS

Original nature and emotions. — Closely allied to the other type of satisfiers, that is, the action of any behavior-series which is ready, are the primitive emotions. These emotions are also part of the life of feeling, part of the original equipment of man. John B. Watson, [1] observing the behavior of newborn infants, concludes there are three distinctly different types of emotional responses present even then. Fear is stimulated by either a loud sound or by loss of support, such as twitching the blanket on which the infant is lying, or letting him drop one inch. Rage is stimulated by simple bodily restraint, such as holding the ankles together, or the arms close to the sides. Satisfaction or "love" is stimulated by stroking or patting. Pillsbury accepts the statement that "emotion is the conscious side of instinct." McDougall says, "Each of the principal instincts conditions, then, some one kind of emotional excitement whose quality is specific or peculiar to it." [2] Thus each of the primary instincts on its affective side is linked to one definite emotion, *e.g.*, the instinct of flight to the emotion of fear, the instinct of pugnacity to the emotion of anger, the parental instinct to the tender emotion. That instinct and the coarser

[1] Watson, J., and R., "Studies in infant psychology," *Sci. Mo.*, v. 13, 1912.
[2] McDougall, *Social Psychology*, p. 47.

emotions are closely connected, both having their roots in original nature, there can be no doubt; but that there is a one-to-one correspondence between instinct and emotion seems very unlikely. According to this theory, fighting should always be accompanied by anger, and this is surely not true. A small boy may be fighting another, and during the process, experience several emotions, anger, fear, exhilaration, joy of victory, and self-conscious display. In Gesell's study of jealousy [1] almost as many situations are given as the original causes of that emotion. Other students believe it to be a much simpler state of affairs. In the various theories and studies of laughter the same complexity and lack of agreement are found. When the opposite end of the behavior-series is studied, and the question is asked, "Just what are the responses that are originally connected with an anger-provoking or a laughter-provoking situation?" the answer is just as indefinite. The same thing is true when one inquires into the kind of mental state that is aroused. The very fact that the emotions in themselves are so complex means that they elude analysis and description. Every one knows what an emotion is, since because of general nature every one experiences them; but the cause, the bodily response, and even the states themselves await further study.

Conditioning, or substitution of stimuli. — Responses not originally called out by certain situations may be attached to them by the process called conditioning, from the work of Pavlov with the conditioned reflex. He showed how the reflex of salivation in the dog, occurring originally to the sight and smell of food, could be produced merely by the sound of a bell provided the bell and the food were presented simultaneously a certain number of times. Watson [2] has shown how a child might be made afraid of furry animals which he did not originally fear, by striking a metal bar loudly just as he reached for the animal. The negative, fear reaction of crying and shrinking originally attached to the loud sound, was prepotent even in the

---

[1] Gesell, A., "Jealousy," *A. J. P.*, v. 17, pp. 437–496.
[2] *Op. cit.*, also *Psychology from the Standpoint of a Behaviorist.*

complex situation. Very soon it was made to the sight of the animal alone, that is, to the other element in the complex situation. It had been transferred, we can say, or, a substitute stimulus was now effective. Similarly, apparently any stimulus may be substituted for another in the S — R pattern so long as, at some time or other, the new stimulus is presented simultaneously with the old, potent stimulus.

Since this is true, the attempt to discover what is the original S — R pattern is less useful than the realization, in clinic cases particularly, that whole chains of substitutions have been forged, and that retraining must take place along the lines of effecting new substitutions, new transferences that will bring desirable responses.

Bodily changes. — Cannon's [1] work with animals has revealed to us the profound changes that go on in the body when intense emotions are experienced. For instance, the neurone action of the sympathetic section of the autonomic system checks action of the stomach and intestines, changes the rate of the heart-beat, contracts the blood vessels supplying the inner organs, enlarges those supplying the limbs, and stimulates various glands, for example the sweat glands, tear glands, adrenal glands into action. The adrenalin secretion, carried by the blood to all parts of the body reinforces chemically the action started by the sympathetic system. The liver secretes more sugar which acts as fuel or energy for the muscles. The blood itself, if exposed to the air, will clot more rapidly than usual. The value to the animal in times of danger of greater available energy is so obvious that Cannon formulated what is known as the Emergency theory of the emotions. The sensations aroused in the cortex caused by these organic changes are what we commonly speak of as the emotions.

The wear and tear on the body is considerable. The heart and lungs are overworked, digestion is upset, so much blood sugar is produced that, if elimination is not provided for, it may act as a toxic substance. The immediate physical after effects may be

[1] Cannon, W. B., *Bodily Changes in Pain, Hunger, Fear and Rage.*

very bad. Vomiting or diarrhœa may occur if a child is forced to eat after a screaming fit. Many adolescents confess great difficulty in controlling temper. Even if they inhibit outward expression of the seething rage within they will find digestion disturbed. Hard physical exercise is needed to prevent the extra blood sugar doing harm in the body. Clearly, frequent and intense emotions of the anger or fright type are exhausting at any age, and are particularly bad for little children. Possibly around eight years old may be a critical time when the heart is under a strain in any case, and again in early adolescence when the heart is large though not very strong, and when the newer emotions consequent on the maturing of the sex glands are quite sufficient for individuals to cope with without any complications from these other two.

Other glands. — Overactivity of the *thyroid* gland produces a general excitability. The child is irritable, unable to relax and sleep well, unstable in all emotions. Insufficient secretion, or hypo-thyroidism, produces opposite effects. The child is insensitive, indifferent, sluggish, difficult to arouse to any enthusiasm. The *pituitary* gland energizes the tender emotions. Sympathy and kindliness are regulated by its correct functioning. The posterior portion of the pituitary gland secretes a hormone which acts as a tonic and regulator to the sex cells. Abnormal functioning of the pituitary disturbs the general maturing of the body. Anxiety states, fears, and "nervousness" may often be due to excess post-pituitary secretion. The *thymus* gland, if it does not shrink and practically cease functioning with puberty, causes the individual to retain infantile and childish characteristics. This affects the personality, retarding self-control, favoring the "inferiority complex," and predisposing towards homosexual love. The *parathyroids'* secretion assists in general control; for with insufficiency of it people exhibit extreme restlessness, great depression as well as a lack of muscle tone. The *sex glands*, so potent in the characteristic "masculine" or "feminine" emotions of the mating instinct are themselves held in check by the thymus and the pineal, and stimulated by the adrenals, thyroid, and pituitary. To the hormones secreted by them are due the coyness, bashfulness, the desire to attract and to display of the post-pubertal years.

General methods of control. — We know that the child by original nature is equipped in such a way that unlearned responses to situations occur, the accompaniments of which are the emotions. All human beings feel anger, fear, jealousy, sympathy, joy, disgust, and so on, as a matter of inherited connections. The younger the individual, the less experience has affected the individual, the more violent and unchecked will the emotion be. Children's emotions are intense, but they also tend to be more short-lived than the adult's. They need to be controlled but not eliminated; they are a precious asset for motivation, for calling out energy, and as such should be preserved and cultivated. The need is to raise them to intellectual and spiritual levels from the physical and material levels at which they first appear. The desired ends are to develop, for instance, jealousy, so that the child becomes jealous for others as well as for himself; joy, so that he is as happy over the successes of others as over his own; sympathy and kindliness, so that they are aroused by spiritual and intellectual disasters as well as by physical, and by hurt to strangers as well as to friends.

The laws of learning — exercise and effect — are instrumental in bringing about these changes. Control of emotion is brought about by the same means; but the value of analysis or the interposition of intellectual states in some way, and of the control of the expressive movements which accompany the emotion should be kept in mind. Thus we may, by the law of effect, learn not to give way to anger by finding that nothing is gained thereby, and a good deal lost. This is a slow process of gaining control, and it may be a very long time before a child discovers for himself, however careful the parents are that that is really true, that he does gain nothing by his fit of temper. Anger may be controlled by redirecting the fermenting spirits so that the energy is worked off in some rather violent exercise. Punching a bag, pitching a ball, chopping wood, "walking it off" are familiar safety valves. Or anger may be held in check by the observation of others who are angry, comparing signs of disturbance in them and in one's self; the contemplative attitude replaces the other, even a feeling of amusement may ensue. Again, analysis of the causes for anger with thoughtful attempt to remedy the conditions that have aroused it will surely disperse it. A quick diversion by a laughter-provoking joke will relieve the condition as well as the pro-verbial "soft answer." Among the physical expressions, those most readily amenable to control are the quickened breath which may be regulated and the tense muscles which may be forcibly held relaxed (just as in conquering nervousness or an impulse to give way to crying it is important to control the breath and the pitch of the voice, and to stiffen the muscles). With young children, these various distractions must be supplied from the outside. Being made to run up and down, being sent to bathe face and hands in cold water, even being plunged into cool water, drinking cold water will help some children of from three to six years of age. To be told a story, to hear singing, laughing, and other forms of mental distraction will help others. With older children their conscious co-operation in control must be sought, and the responsibility gradually shifted to them entirely.

Fear must be sublimated into prudence, caution, thrift. Anger must be transformed into forcefulness.

STUDIES OF FEAR

Situations and responses. — Fear is one of the emotions which has been most carefully studied, probably because of the recognition of the havoc it can play and its disintegrating influence on personality. It is better to speak of fears than of fear since there are so many different forms from the sudden, sharp fright to the permanent anxiety, obsession, or superstition. As children mature they learn to fear different things. From objects in the physical environment fears spread to the social environment.

Children fear blame, fear failure at school, fear ridicule. Adolescents fear they are not loved, fear in their vocational adjustments, their love affairs, their personal and social relationships generally.

Earlier studies, by Darwin, Mosso, Stanley Hall, also those by Thorndike, Watson, and others have been concerned to describe the physical reactions, the observed and reported stimuli immediately preceding. Thus, Thorndike states that fear is aroused by stimuli such as thunderstorms, reptiles, large animals approaching, certain vermin, darkness, strange persons of unfriendly mien, solitude, and probably loud or sudden noises with certain peculiar qualities. Of course, when two or more of these situations work together, *e.g.*, darkness and solitude, the fear is intensified; when some original satisfier is operating simultaneously with any one of them, the fear will be diminished, *e.g.*, candy and solitude, or the presence of other human beings when a strange person of unfriendly mien approaches. Of the responses to these situations, thirty-one of the more easily observable are listed by Thorndike.[1] Many of these are antagonistic, such as running away or remaining stock-still, therefore the responses to fear-inspiring situations differ tremendously.

Psychiatric case workers have been more interested to find the links in the chain of substituted fear objects, and so to suggest a cure. Their work has shown the futility of attempting to catalogue all separate causes of fear since their number is legion. Any object whatever, apparently, may arouse fear directly or indirectly.

Groups of causes. — We can group fears about as follows:

(1) A general hypersensitive condition associated often in first-born children with unusually difficult birth experiences — a sort of psychic injury found in cases where labor was greatly prolonged.

(2) Conditions directly traceable to poor functioning of the heart, to pulmonary tuberculosis, to malnutrition, to sub-efficient endocrine gland system.

[1] *Original Nature of Man*, p. 59.

(3) Fears conditioned in by the process described above.

(4) Fears directly taught by suggestion, imitation, or intimidation. Superstitions and some imaginary fears belong here.

(5) Fears children have learned to use as tools for getting attention or for escaping unpleasant tasks.

(6) Fears induced by poor training, especially from the over-protected, sheltered home life that prevents emotional maturing.

(7) Symbolic fears, due to an attempt to repress a fear, the result being a substitute of any sort whatever.

(8) A number of simple fears which serve to keep children from taking dangerous risks.

Remedying fears. — Obviously, prevention is better than cure. With a well-born, healthy child, carefully tended to prevent bad conditioning, well taught to discount ignorant superstitions, well trained to effective action in danger, with a happy social environment free from undue pressure to compete, free from threats, there need be no fears. Equally obviously, very few children escape forming some fears; so that the task is more often to cure what has not been prevented. No one method can do this. The first step is to analyze the cause, and it is well to begin with the physical condition of the child. Reconditioning rather than argument is necessary in many cases. Jones' experiment [1] demonstrated the value of presenting an original satisfier — food — simultaneously with the fear object — a rabbit, — with the latter at such a distance that the response with pleasure was prepotent in the double situation. Visceral reflexes in the eating response were not interrupted. With succeeding trials the rabbit could be tolerated nearer, till finally, even with touching the rabbit no negative response occurred. Care is necessary in similar procedures that the negative reaction to the fear object does not transfer to the food situation, thus "conditioning" the wrong way round. The example of other unafraid children who played with the rabbit, also helped.

The force of example is tremendous in inhibiting some fear

[1] Jones, M. C., "The elimination of children's fears," *Jo. Exp. Psy.*, v. 7, 1924.

tendencies. Confronted with novel situations, when by the law of readiness no response is ready and therefore negative, fear reactions may so easily be set up, children need a model to imitate. Every sensible parent and teacher makes use of this fact whether dealing with individual children or with the quickly contagious emotions of the crowd. Knowing what to do, how to act, may be taught more formally, as well as shown in times of emergency. Here it is especially true that to be fore-warned is to be fore-armed. Fears due to ignorance are best dealt with by direct teaching and training. Appealing to knowledge and reasoning is effective with older children in the case of (4) above. Reasoning during fright is useless. Fears traceable to (5) and (6) take a longer educative process, with much reward for attempted control. Symbolic fears need patient discovery. Attempts to recondition or to rationalize are doomed to failure in this case. The real cause behind the adopted substitute must be reached by sympathetic analysis by the trained worker; only then can suitable re-education be prescribed.

Further suggestions. — Courage in the face of physical danger can be rewarded. Indeed, even the young boys' group trains its members to admire bravery and shun cowardice. Games of skill give muscular control and consequently a feeling of security.

Ridicule and teasing should never be permitted. Far from helping a child they but aggravate the general timidity and add a social fear. To help a child laugh for himself at the fear object should be the aim.

Curiosity is an impulse antagonistic to fear reactions. It may wisely be stimulated and encouraged in new situations. The desire to be of service, protective care for others, responsibility, altruistic tendencies in general, may be invoked to overcome personal fears both of the physical and social environment. Many of our heroes have been so motivated to overcome desperate fears.

Assurance of love and appreciation, a sense of social security is as necessary for the adolescent as for the young child. This may be secured, not by sheltering either from life's difficulties, but by strengthening them to meet and overcome.

Vivid interests and a widening outlook help to prevent brooding, morbidity, and the pathological conditions in which fears so easily grow.

Fear in its crude form should certainly be a waning emotion, but fear in its modified form is necessary for the maintenance of society. Fear early becomes associated with physical pain, and becomes one of the most common weapons wielded by the adult in the control of the child. That fear of punishment, physical pain, has its place in the rearing of the child seems undeniable, for in the early days it is the only appeal that he can understand. It is equally true, however, that as the other instincts and capacities develop, this means of control should be gradually changed. Fear of disapproval, of the denial of companions, of deprivation of means of satisfying physical or mental activity, of being surpassed, of being the object of scorn of the group, each of these fears has its place until finally fear of losing one's friends, of falling short of one's ideals, of violating one's conscience, become some of the most powerful motives in the control of conduct.

PRACTICAL EXERCISES

1. How is pleasure in music provided for in the school you know best?
2. What changes in the school program since you were ten years old provide for better æsthetic development of children?
3. Examine the sixth-grade room to discover what is there to give æsthetic pleasure to the eye.
4. Visit again the home of the child selected for individual study. What is there in the home environment to cultivate good taste?
5. What can you discover in the parent-child, sibling relationships that might help or hinder good development emotionally?
6. Has your child any special fears? If so, of what? Can you and the mother trace how they arose?
   What definite plan can you suggest for curing them?

FOR DISCUSSION

1. How may training for technique in an art assist appreciation? How may it choke it?
2. By reminiscence, instance causes of childhood unhappiness. What suggestions do they offer as to dealing with children?

3. Observe a child experiencing an intense emotion. Notice the duration of the emotion and the type that succeeds. How do these compare with similar phenomena in an adult?
4. How may caution be developed without arousing fear?
5. Why is it a poor plan to try to get children to eat dinner soon after an emotional upset?
6. Give illustrations of the quick arousal of fear or anger in an individual child.
7. Give illustrations of the rapid spreading of an emotion through a crowd.
8. What is the value from the standpoint of control of the emotions in an habituated fire drill?
9. What is the danger to little children of frequent teasing which arouses anger, unhappiness, perhaps hatred?
10. How would you deal with a temper tantrum in the kindergarten?
11. Suggest wise treatment of a child who seems continually timid.
12. What advice would you give an adolescent about controlling his temper?

SELECTED REFERENCES

BERMAN, L. *The Glands Regulating Personality.* Chs. 2, 3, 10.

CRILE, G. W. *The Origin and Nature of the Emotions.*

ENG, H. *Experimental Investigations into the Emotional Life of the Child.*

GOODENOUGH, F. L. "Anger in young children." *Univ. Minn. Inst. Ch. Welfare, Mon. Series *9.*

MARSTON, L. R. "The emotions of young children." *Univ. of Iowa St. in Ch. Welfare.* v. 3 *3.

MORTON, G. F. *Childhood's Fears.*

REYNOLDS, M. M. "Negativism of pre-school children." *T. C. Cont. to Ed.* *288.

SPAULDING, E. R. "Important emotional trends in childhood." *N. Y. State Jo. of Med.*, v. 24, 1924.

STERN, W. *Psychology of Early Childhood.* Chs. 23–26, 35, 36.

VALENTINE, C. W. "The innate bases of fear." *Jo. Gen. Psy.*, v. 37, 1930.

WALSH, W. C. *The Mastery of Fear.*

CHAPTER IV

NON–SOCIAL REACTIONS

It should be borne in mind that the division suggested in this and the following chapter is an arbitrary one. Social and non-social reactions cannot be sharply defined since the situations to which the reactions are made are themselves so complex. However, for convenience in discussion it is possible to make such a division, and to treat first of those tendencies to action which manifest themselves in situations made up mostly of material objects, leaving till later those tendencies called out largely by the presence or behavior of other human beings. It would be impossible in a book of this size to discuss all these tendencies to action; therefore the following list is but a partial one, only those of importance to the educator having been chosen.

Of the non-social tendencies, the following are important: 1. General physical activity — made up of movements of gross bodily control, visual exploration and manipulation; 2. Food-getting and hunting; 3. Teasing; 4. Ownership and collecting; 5. Fighting.

GENERAL PHYSICAL ACTIVITY

Bodily movements. — The instinct of physical activity shows itself from birth on, in numerous spontaneous and involuntary movements which involve all parts of the body. During his first two years we find a child "holding up his head, sitting, standing, walking, running, stooping, jumping up and down, leaping at, crouching, lying down, rolling over, climbing, dodging, stooping to pick up, raising himself again, balancing, clinging, pushing with arms and with legs, pulling with arms, throwing, kicking, grasping," [1] and so on through an almost endless

[1] Thorndike, E. L., *Original Nature of Man*, p. 47.

60

series of movements which use all the muscles in the body. That these movements are unlearned, and the child's management of his body is a result of original tendencies seems to be the opinion of experts in child study. It is difficult to see how it could be otherwise, dependent as the human race is on original equipment for the initial impetus in all directions. The fact that it has been a common practice to speak of "teaching children to walk" is due to the imperfection of the first manifestations of these tendencies, and the gradualness of their maturing has tended to hide their instinctive nature. That opportunities for exercise and the resulting pleasure or pain of this exercise have their effect in bringing about control is undeniable, and it is the duty of the educator to furnish both; but the presence or absence of these various types of bodily movement is dependent primarily upon connections in the nervous system, and not upon teaching. In fact, the forcing of the baby to stand or walk by fond parents or proud nurses may be harmful rather than helpful. Control is dependent upon the maturing of connections between neurones whose action results in these various movements.

Provision for activity. — Two questions arise, first, is there need for fuller recognition of this tendency to general physical activity? second, is there clear evidence of the law of maturation in gaining muscular control? The first question, as to whether enough allowance is made for the strength of this tendency of physical activity, can be answered emphatically in the negative. Little children are bundles of activity, asleep or awake, and as a rule are in almost constant movement. Nerve currents which later will work themselves out in terms of mental states now result in movement. It is difficult for an adult to understand the amount of effort, of nervous energy required in young children to inhibit all the tendencies to movement which are present. One of the most exhausting things one asks them to do is to "sit still and play quietly," and yet we ask it as though it were nothing, not realizing the draft it makes on their store of energy. The kindergarten has recognized this need of the child for freedom of movement, but the primary school still falls far short in providing for this side of child nature. What society needs is primarily able-bodied, well-developed, healthy little beings, and it is by means of the use and development of this instinct that such a result is possible. To make them old men and old women before their time is not only to lose the charm and joy of childhood, but to sap the vitality of the race.

Order of maturation. — To the second of these questions we can give a decided affirmative answer. By control we mean co-ordination in the higher nerve centers permitting balanced movements, complex muscle action, the teamwork of eye-hand, ear-foot, and so on. Roughly the fact of gradual development of control has been understood in that we should not expect six-year-olds to have the co-ordination to drive an automobile, play a three manual organ, or learn the art of fencing; while steering a tricycle, playing the piano, hammering and sawing straight are possible accomplishments. An observation of children's plays shows that in the spontaneous muscle movements made then the larger muscles play a major part, — the smaller muscles within a series coming into use later; and that when movements are controlled, those involving the larger muscles within a series require less effort than do the smaller co-ordinations. A two-year-old can pick up a ball and throw it, but he cannot time his release so as to throw it in the direction in which he is looking. The infant can articulate simple sounds such as *bub, mum,* before the more difficult tongue positions for *L* and *R* can be taken. The little child learning speech finds the mouth gymnastics for such words as "breakfast," "strength" exceedingly difficult because of the timed co-ordinations necessary. Standing, walking, running, precede hopping, skipping, roller skating. Bryan,[1] in his tests of the voluntary control of the muscles of the shoulder-finger series in children from six to sixteen years of age, finds that the shoulder muscles show the

[1] Bryan, W. L., "On the development of voluntary motor ability," *A. J. P.,* v. 5, 1892.

greatest maturity and the finger co-ordination least in children of six, but that the finger muscles gain in rapidity and precision of action after nine or ten years of age.

Manipulation. — The tendency towards manipulation is another manifestation of the general instinct of physical activity. A child pulls, pats, tears, fingers, pokes, rubs, turns, rolls, squeezes, drops, picks up, waves, throws, etc., any object that permits it. His facility in the use of his fingers and his thumb in opposition to them as a matter of original nature is the explanation of man's skill and technique in all the arts and industries. These movements are as spontaneous and motiveless as the grosser bodily movements previously discussed; they are neither constructive nor destructive, although the child may learn to be either. Careful observation of the acquisition of motor control by infants and young children has yielded norms of development both in the speed of simple actions and in the complexity of co-ordination. During the second month of life the first rapid impulsive movements change to slower, repeated movements: in the third month these are watched attentively. Experimental movement with his own limbs then occupies the baby's attention much of his waking hours. Vertical arm thrusts and pushing leg movements are the most frequent. Presented with an object he fumbles it, moving the palms of the hands over it. By the third month he can feel it with the fingers and the thumb held flat, and in the fourth month with the thumb opposed. By the fifth month he can reach for and grasp that at which he looks, with both hands at first, later one hand. The first reaching — as described by Gesell, Halverson, Castner at Yale,[1] is a sweeping arm movement from above down, and from sideways to the center; this changes to the direct, linear approach. By the seventh month a one-inch cube is picked up directly, with thumb and curved fingers. A seven-millimeter pellet cannot be secured by the fingers at this age, a scooping

[1] Gesell, A., *The Mental Growth of the Pre-School Child*, pp. 75–82. Halverson, H. M., "An experimental study of prehension in infants by means of systematic cinema records," *Gen. Psy. Mon.*, v. 10, 1931.

palmar movement being needed. With this small object there is the same progression from full hand, raking means of obtaining it, through use of fingers, use of thumb closing on fingers quasi-scissors movement, to the thumb and first finger "pincer prehension" of the ten-months-old infant. Similar genetic sequences for manipulation of crayon and paper, from the first reflex, blind grasp at one month to the four-year-old's ability to copy a circle and a square have been studied, also. With plastic material, the first manipulation is to pound and roll it, that is, to use the whole fist or flat, palmar movement: later comes the molding with the finger tips. With each different kind of material used, the progression is the same — from the larger muscles to differentiated use of the smaller ones.

The practical outcome of such studies is to emphasize the value of large movements for little children, and to suggest the economy in both time and effort in the postponement of movements requiring fine co-ordinations. It also emphasizes the need of spontaneous, free exercise of all movements before the voluntary, purposive use of them. In his free play, the child should have used again and again the fine co-ordinations before he is required to make them in connection with school subjects. Many of the changes which have been so worth while in the materials used for instruction and play in the kindergarten and primary grades have been due to realization of this fact. We need more norms working out, however, for intelligent statements of requirements in school work, in physical training, and in the safeguards of industry. Children still need protection from exploitation. A standard performance for a seven-year-old is to tie a bowknot in one minute or less. Yet many children as young and younger can be, and are, trained to tie knots rapidly for hours together in oriental rug making. Their little fingers are preferred for such tasks, and for similar delicate operations in other industries, to those of fully grown workers. The resultant strain on the nervous system is manifest, even if not, as yet, adequately measured. Musical prodigies run a similar risk from the urging of ambitious parents or teachers who know little of child psychology, if fine finger co-ordination and long practice periods are demanded.

For general educational procedure the following principles are worth noting. First: large, coarse movements should precede small, fine ones. Fine co-ordinations, *i.e.*, rapid synchronized movements, or precise finger-tip control, should not be forced on young children, nor continued for long periods of time.

Second: such materials as sand, clay, blocks, heavy crayons should precede cardboard, thin pegs, fine pens.

Third: content precedes form, — doing something precedes the interest in how it is done. For example, a piece of handwork may be done with any one of three motives in mind, (*a*) to tell something, (*b*) to represent something, (*c*) to make something beautiful or perfect; and in this order the motives should be appealed to, mere technique coming last.

Fourth: originality of performance follows a variety of experiences and an increase of technique, and it should not be required until many concrete examples have been presented.

FOOD-GETTING AND HUNTING

Interest in food. — Food-getting is one of the first instincts to manifest itself. The early forms are the sucking movements and the movements of the head in seeking the breasts, the various mouth, throat, and face movements according to whether the substance tasted is sweet, sour, or bitter. As the child grows older, the reaching, grasping, and putting-in-the-mouth movements are added. These movements are quickly involved in the instinct of general physical activity and manipulation, although for about a year and a half the tendency of the baby to put everything in his mouth is a source of anxiety to the mother and nurse. Because of the civilized community in which children are born the original tendencies are soon overlaid by definite "manners" in connection with food-getting, but the interest in food is one of the chief interests of childhood and remains strong throughout life. There seems to be no valid reason why this love of good things to eat should not be appealed to as a legitimate motive in dealing with young children. It is a natural interest, one of which there is no need to be ashamed, and one of tremendous dynamic power.

The interest in pleasant tasting food seems the predominant one in early childhood. Emotional upsets are common if the flavor is disliked, and resistances are developed which send parents to the clinics for advice with a feeding problem. Later on there is anxiety about quantity, and the parent's problem becomes that of satiating the enormous appetite of a healthy, growing child. To the adolescent, social customs are so important that he will drink disagreeable things or go hungry if the current fashion so dictates.

The preparation of food becomes interesting, whether from imitation or a felt necessity it is hard to say. Little girls delight in toy cooking utensils and report the fun of "helping mother" in her more serious kitchen tasks. Boys are intrigued by crude, outdoor cooking. The appearance of food, its dainty serving, is relatively unimportant till middle adolescence, even later for boys.

Social sharing of food seems a spontaneous impulse, witness the three-year-old's offer of his cookie to people he loves. Ten-year-old boys gladly divide their good things among their own small group. Good will seems to involve attempting to feed others, or to eat with them.

Training. — Directing this interest in eating, this interest in food, involves far more than teaching table manners, desirable as that is and neglected as it is by school authorities. It is basic to our economic life, motivates the study of sciences such as agriculture, nutrition, physiology, and the like, therefore enters into vocational choice. Because of its social setting it involves self-control and therefore character training. Our earliest teaching concerns the physical skill to feed one's self, with all its substitutes of forks, etc., for grasping food directly. Later, comes the giving of knowledge to insure skill in choosing the balanced meal, the economic skill in fitting the budget to the needs of a varied group. Practice in both these should be afforded under expert supervision to both boys and girls. Socially, there are sublimations to be made in serving others first, in sharing equally, problems which are dealt with in the kindergarten period. The moral necessity of raising, making, or buying food rather than stealing it needs to be learned especially by boys between ten and fourteen years old. To deny one's self easily and happily when necessary should be part of the self-control of the mature individual. Gluttony, intemperance, drug habits evidence failure to achieve self-control. These vices are adolescent problems unless a firm foundation has been laid in childhood, directly in connection with eating and drinking, motivated by character ideals.

Hunting. — Allied with the food-getting instinct in primitive man was the hunting instinct. Thorndike describes it as follows: "To a small escaping object, man, especially if hungry, responds, apart from training, by pursuit, being satisfied when he draws nearer to it. When within pouncing distance, he pounces upon it, grasping at it. If it is not seized, he is annoyed. If it is seized, he examines, manipulates, and dismembers it, unless some contrary tendency is brought into action by its sliminess, sting, or the like. To an object of moderate size and not of offensive mien moving away from or past him man originally responds much as noted above, save that in seizing the object chased, he is likely to throw himself upon it, bear it to the ground, choke and maul it until it is completely subdued, giving then a cry of triumph." [1] Whether there are specialized forms of hunting, such as hunting for birds' nests and eggs, or inserting the fingers in small holes and crannies, is still a disputed question. Certainly crevices between boards and stones possess a fascination for many people other than little children. A sequel to hunting activity is seen in retrieving, and in the pride and pleasure taken in calling others' attention to the results of the chase. From the cat's offering on the back steps of the mouse just caught, to the mounted trophies adorning the home of the big game hunter, is a whole range of display behavior.

[1] *Op. cit.*, p. 52.

No particular need for hunting exists in our civilization, but the original tendency persists and has to find satisfaction. It is evident in many children's games, where pursuit and capture is the chief element. In adults, it is seen in the fondness of many men and some women for hunting as a sport. When the country boy satisfies the impulse by actually stalking and killing birds, snakes, rabbits, by fishing or by trapping, the city boy finds his opportunities with sparrows, pigeons, stray cats, and so on too limited, and is apt to turn his attention to chasing people, throwing stones at windows and street lights and otherwise engaging in behavior that is likely to land him in trouble socially.

Training. — The energy is here as a part of the natural equipment of every individual. It is the business of the educator to see that it gets proper opportunity for exercise in the harmless plays of childhood, and that it is diverted into such channels that in the adult it may work in the cause of justice and of service to the community. Substitute actions in games which involve hiding, chasing, throwing at a mark should be offered. Sublimated behavior such as hunting with a camera helps to awaken sympathy with the hunted, as well as to train in scientific study. Opportunities for display, on the walls, in museum cases, at special exhibits should be provided too. Further sublimations, where the hunting is mental only rather than muscular, are possible in the search through books, card catalogues, maps, and the like for that elusive piece of information.

TEASING

Impulses involved. — Teasing is a name given to behavior which combines the impulse to manipulate, curiosity, the love of being a cause, perhaps the hunting tendency. For that reason it is discussed here, though the situations provoking it are very often social. Curiosity to see what will happen inspires many an attempt at manipulation. Amusement at seeing insects wriggle, animals and humans get excited and lose their tempers, ministers to the feeling of superiority and so prolongs the action. These impulses when evoked by animals or persons unwilling or unable to protect themselves are the roots of the so-called "cruelty" in children. When it is primarily the instinct of manipulation, poking, pulling, punching, slapping, etc., manifested toward some one who does not "play back," the whole response is called teasing. Adults and pet animals who do not respond by energetic mastery suffer much at the hands of young children in this way. Older children choose other children as their victims. When the hunting is directed toward a weaker individual, it is called bullying and may be carried to great lengths by individuals of a mean nature. Teasing in moderation is thought to be good both for the one teased and the one teasing, as it tends to arouse initiative; but if exercised unduly or habitually, it is apt to degenerate into bullying. Bullying is a tendency that seems wholly bad. It is difficult to discern in it any element of good, and its uprooting, or the substitution of one of the kindlier, more helpful tendencies for it must be one of the duties of every teacher. Its persistence in adult life results in much harm and unhappiness. The brutality of the strong towards the weak, the misuse of power by governments, the refinement of cruelty shown in sarcasm and covered taunts, all are outgrowths of teasing habits carried over from childhood with no useful redirection. Some pleasure in cruelty replaces the normal satisfaction in sex behavior and so may be considered a perversion.

Redirection. — Children are not necessarily degenerate when they bully and tease others, but for the good of society these tendencies must be modified. Other things to manipulate which will bring pride in achievement will be one form of substitution. Another is to gain information which satisfies curiosity about others' actions by doing things which will excite their interest rather than their anger. This leads to the sublimation of refusing to find fun in others' discomfort. Meantime the teasee may be helped to meet others by playing back — when co-operation may ensue, or by fighting — when the question of mastery may be definitely settled, or by complete ignoring of the other's actions — which, if kept up successfully, takes all the fun away from the one who is teasing. This last method is a girl's natural defense against a boy's teasing from about eleven years old on. The first two work for children nearly the same age. The most difficult problem, particularly in the home, is to protect children from the teasing of those about three years older. This seems a gap wide enough to cause continual friction yet not wide enough to evoke sympathy very often from the older one.

ATTITUDES TOWARDS OBJECTS

Ownership. — The impulses to amass, hoard, own, and collect are closely allied. Kline, in his investigation of the instinct of ownership,[1] says that the first objects to be claimed are those instrumental in satisfying hunger; in the second group are those that administer to bodily comfort, such as "mother's lap" and a "special chair," etc.; in the third group are articles of motion and articles of dress, followed by articles used in imitative plays.

In other words, objects constantly reacted to, seen, felt, and touched habitually in connection with primal physical needs are recognized with pleasure and built into the sense of self. This tendency, which may first show by a child's claiming his bottle, his crib, his toys and clothes, develops into one of the strongest governing forces in civilized life. The mere fact of ownership or possession is enough to make one exert all one's powers to retain acquisitions. One's ingenuity is never more taxed than when desirous of possessing some object, be it article of adornment, something ministering to a hobby, a job, or a piece of information. Everything in life may be claimed; and the pursuance of "my" in any situation adds a power that is difficult to measure. It is "my" home and possessions, "my" family, "my" friends, "my" reputation and interests, "my" business concern, "my" town, "my" state, "my" country and

[1] Kline, L. W., "The psychology of ownership," found in Hall's *Aspects of Child Life.*

the same sense of possession often spreads so that it includes opinions, principles, ethics, and religion.

From one point of view the attitude towards property reflects the development of the sense of self, then. From another, it marks the moral adjustment of an individual, since traits of miserliness, honesty, and so on are involved. In somewhat the same way as children learn self from not-self they learn mine from not-mine — by conflict at the boundaries of mine and thine. At first they claim anything they like just because they want it. Very soon they meet opposition; some one else wants it too. Perhaps the strongest wins, or the slyest wins, or the noisiest, or the one who can appeal most effectively to adult intervention, or the one who can ask for it most courteously, or, most difficult to understand, the one who can prove ownership. Explicit thinking is fostered by the question to an insistent child, "Why is it yours?" Other factors may help develop the sense of others' ownership. Some one forbids touching, "Leave that alone, it's——'s, not yours." Family taboos are thus built into habits. Training differs very greatly here. In some homes there is no line of demarcation in possessions except for such obvious things as garments fitting only one person. In others, children's tendency to handle things in which they are interested has been early modified by the suggestion "Ask first if you may." Children of kindergarten level can distinguish mine and thine on the basis of acquisition by gift, or labor in construction. Further responsibility is developed by taking care of things, understanding their qualities, cleaning them, keeping them in designated places. Later, things they buy themselves with hardly earned money become specially prized. Towards goods bestowed in bulk by routine on a group, children with difficulty feel responsible. The vandalism of older children evidences a poor development both of sense of property rights of others and of their ability to identify themselves as members of a larger group. Yet, on either count, the shrubs in the park, the windows in the vacant house should not be harmed. They do not belong to the individual boy, therefore should not be touched; as a citizen he should assume group responsibility for their care.

Training needed. — We must take advantage of children's natural recognition of discovery, priority of usage, purchase, gift, manufacture, as grounds for claiming possession to help them appreciate others' ownership as well as their own. This works outward from the egocentric beginning. Having experienced the joys and anxieties, the delights and cares of ownership themselves, children have a basis wherewith to respect others' rights.

Group co-operation, and group responsibility for property must be developed as well as individual ownership.

A better knowledge of æsthetic values and scientific values will bring about other considerations than the mere legality of ownership. Such knowledge helps substitute ownership of more intangible and less concrete things. Enjoyment not through touching, but through looking, listening, memorizing, contemplating, sublimates ownership into the mental world. One's value as a citizen depends on one's possessions, not only material, but intellectual and spiritual as well. An individual must have possessions worth while, must be something worth while, before he will be much worth while to others. Pride in ownership should then be appealed to, made use of in the home and school. It is a perfectly legitimate motive, and a valuable source of power. Modification of the first crude tendency comes about as the child claims possessions of greater and greater value, from the physical and material to the spiritual, and as he learns that possessions in common are often worth more than those purely individual.

Collecting. — There is a tendency to approach any attractive object, seize and carry it off if it is not too large. At a later age, such objects are put together in some convenient place, looked at in the mass, fingered, and perhaps arranged. These objects gather value simply because they are possessed, and aimless collecting and storing of all sorts of valueless objects becomes a habit. Other tendencies, such as manipulation, curiosity, rivalry, are aroused in connection with the possessions. Burk,[1] using a questionnaire, found this tendency in evidence from six years of age through seventeen which was as far as she tested. The time of greatest prominence seems to be between nine and ten years of age when the average number of collections per child is 4.4. The thing collected seems to depend largely on the environment, the interest at first being merely to hoard something or other. The next stage involves rivalry — and the aim becomes to outstrip others in point of numbers in the collection. In the third stage, some attention is paid to arrangement and order. It is found that objects of nature precede both literary and æsthetic objects as materials for collection. Whitley,[2] using a check list of sixty items, and Lehman and Witty with a check list of 190 items found an increase in interest, stimulated by rivalry, with a maximum number of different things reported occurring at ages ten to eleven. Unbelievable quantities of things are amassed, and the larger the hoard the greater the satisfaction. Bottle tops, paper match holders, little pictures, cigar bands are favorite objects. Tin foil is sometimes collected for sale, but in general the worth perceived in the object has nothing to do with cash value. Boys are rather more interested than girls in parts of animals and in metal junk; girls, rather than boys, like pieces of cloth and colored papers. Adolescents, girls especially, like to hoard souvenirs of good times they have had, such as theater and dance programs, any miscellany reminiscent of a trip. There is also a change from the concrete to include more language items, such as jokes, quotations.

Lehman and Witty [3] suggest that mere retention of things acquired in various ways is not truly collecting if one has in mind a purposeful activity. Durost [4] considers that the term

---

[1] Burk, C. F., "The collecting instinct," *Ped. Sem.*, v. 7, 1900.
[2] Whitley, M. T., "Children's interest in collecting," *Jo. Ed. Psy.*, v. 20, 1929.
[3] Lehman and Witty, "Further studies of children's interest in collecting," *Jo. Ed. Psy.*, v. 21, 1930.
[4] Durost W. M. " Children's collecting activity in relation to social functions," *T.C. Contr. to Ed.* *535.

collection should be restricted to objects having a representative, relational value in a series. He followed a check list inquiry, the reliability of which he suspects since children are so suggestible, by a case study method including standardized interviews, with one hundred cases between ten and fourteen years old. He found that the children of superior intelligence at each age level had more collections of the better kind. By better, we infer arrangement, classification, representative values such as a museum of arts and sciences would recognize.

Use in school. — The strength of this tendency in childhood and the fact that it is still present in so many adults — witness the collections of string pieces, bottles, boxes, corks, bags, hats, etc., as well as those of hunting trophies, stamps, coins, rugs, china, art objects, etc. — suggest that the schools would do well to use this interest more. An indefinite tendency — that fact in itself gives any environmental force great power in directing it. Emphasis must be laid on the arrangement of the material and the criticism as to the value of the things collected for the purpose held in mind. Only so can we train into scientific method and utilize this tendency for constructive social work. It has been used somewhat in the intermediate grades in connection with nature study and home geography, but even there it might be used further. In the upper grades and junior high school it could be appealed to in connection with vocabulary study, either in English or a modern language, in the collection of facts of all kinds in the study of literature and history, as well as in the study of the arts and sciences. Every use of one of these original tendencies is economy, and much more can be done in this direction.

FIGHTING

Varied forms. — The instinct of fighting, pugnacity, is one of the strongest original tendencies possessed by the human race. It is supposedly stronger in men than in women, but it is present in all normal individuals. McDougall, Kirkpatrick, and Thorndike all agree that it is aroused when any other instinctive tendency is thwarted. Fighting is aroused by many different situations, and the responses must accordingly be varied. Thwarting physical activity, as when a baby's limbs are held, arouses the fighting instinct which manifests itself in a definite way. Thwarting the instinct of curiosity, of hunting, of collecting, of self-display, of mastery, or of sex in each case brings a response in terms of fighting; and that response must be different because of the difference in the stimulus. This fact makes it one of the most general as well as one of the most variable of the original responses of action. It shows itself in the very young baby in screaming, pushing away, kicking, writhing, etc. It shows itself in the older child in crying, running away from or towards, dodging, kicking, etc., and in the boy of eight or nine in the regular hand-to-hand fight, depending in each case on the cause for the particular manifestation. The attitude taken by adults towards this tendency is one of intense disapproval. Boys are put on their honor not to fight and are punished if they do. Granted that this tendency does bring much trouble both to the boy and his parents, is it wise to try to stamp it out by such means? Is it wise to stamp it out at all? McDougall says, "The instinct of pugnacity has played a part second to none in the evolution of social organization, and in the present age it operates more powerfully than any other in producing demonstrations of collective emotion and action on a great scale." [1]

Training needed. — If this is true, and there is every reason to believe it, this crude, often cruel, instinct has in it possibilities of development which make for co-operation, group spirit, and moral fiber. The social instincts are then dependent to some extent on this individualistic, non-social root. The trouble with parents and teachers often is, that they want to omit the first crude stage of the tendency and come at once to its higher levels; but on logical grounds alone, it is hard to see how, if a boy has been required to inhibit such pugnacious tendencies

[1] *Social Psychology*, p. 279.

on the physical level, he can later on fight for country or friends or principles. He has not known what it means, when thwarted, to stand for his wishes and rights; he has not known the sweets of success or the shame of defeat; he has not known what it means to suffer for the sake of gaining something that seems worth while. The door has been shut on all this opportunity when first the instinct was strong; how then can we expect him later on to fight his difficulties, take his stand for the right, to suffer for it if need be? As well expect a spoiled child who has always had his own way to be generous, or one who has never heard music to appreciate a Beethoven sonata. As in other instances already discussed, the tendency is there to be used, not to be merely suppressed. It is possible that women would not be so open to the criticism of being "lacking in honor," "of not understanding fair play," or being sneaky and underhand if this tendency had received proper treatment in childhood. Fighting, real physical combat, is a good thing for girls as well as boys, but that is only a starting point. The tendency needs modification. The child needs to learn not only to fight for his own rights, but for the rights of others; he needs to learn to be generous in the interpretation of his rights, and to submerge his interests in those of the group, — to learn co-operative pugnacity. The situation arousing the fighting response, and the response itself should pass from the physical to the spiritual level. Inhibition must be taught in connection with it so that the child learns self-control. Not disuse, nor suppression by punishment, but graded substitutions leading to sublimation is the necessary treatment.

The over-manifestation of the tendency is usually due to an environment that is not satisfying the normal demands of the growing child. Some tendencies have been continually thwarted by the conditions in which the child has spent his time, and therefore the pugnacious instinct has been aroused. True, its manifestation may be delayed because of fear, but, released from that, it appears. A schoolroom where the instincts of curiosity, love of approval, mastery, and physical activity are thwarted all day long is a hotbed for pugnacity: children released from such a room are ripe for trouble. Give the natural powers of the child opportunities for normal exercise, use a little tact in dealing with the unusually pugnacious boy, and the fighting evil will almost disappear. An eighth-grade class in a Massachusetts town had to pass judgment on the case of one of its members, continually in trouble because of his fights on the way home from school. He was a vigorous, active lad and his classmates decided he "didn't have enough to do"; so they sentenced him to punch a hay bag in the basement of the school for ten minutes every day before he went home. The boy was reformed, for the need of physical activity worked itself off before the boy met others on the way home, and therefore the temptation was removed. The same end might have been gained without the energy being wasted; but more of just such ingenuity in diagnosing is needed in dealing with all these non-social instincts if their full value is to be realized.

PRACTICAL EXERCISES

1. Observe during the recess period in the playground, for five different days. Are there evidences of teasing? If so, by the same child? Of the same child? How would you account for it?

2. Examine the toys and apparatus for the use of children in the kindergarten and primary grades, from the standpoint of which muscles they call into play. Can you suggest additional equipment that would be desirable?

3. Spend two half hours at different times in the kindergarten, or in a nursery school, or out of doors when little children are at free play. Count the occasions when physical interference starts a fight. Describe the reactions exactly.

4. Examine the high-school cafeteria from the standpoint of appeal to the interest in food (not sheer hunger). Has it any rivals in nearby drug stores, street vendors, etc.? What makes the other places attractive?

5. Look over the curriculum offered locally. What training is offered in providing and preparing food? What proportion of the children does it reach?

6. What use is made of hunting and collecting in the study projects of your fourth and fifth grades? Of the eighth and ninth?

7. For the child selected for individual study, find out
   (a) What books and toys he owns.
   (b) What pocket money he receives, if any. When?
   (c) How much he spends on candy, ice cream, etc., a week.
   (d) If he has a special place at home to keep his possessions.

FOR DISCUSSION

1. If a baby were prevented from using his hands till he was one year old what do you think would happen in his development of manipulative ability?
2. What is a good way to train children in ownership?
3. Trace the stages necessary in transforming original food-getting tendencies into table manners. How might schools help in directing this instinct?
4. Do the same, in detail, for the fighting instinct.
5. Observe instances of the fighting instinct in:
   (a) Adults in a crowd.
   (b) Young children or animals held against their will.
   (c) People when aroused by fear.
   How do the responses differ?
6. How is teasing different from play?
7. Did you make any collection as a child? If so, of what, and at what age? Why was it interesting? Has it led to anything useful?
8. Name plays and games that utilize any or all of the tendencies discussed in this chapter.
9. What are the good and bad points of fighting among boys? What games act as substitute activities? In what ways may fighting be sublimated?
10. To what social dangers does the desire to own things lead, if it is not properly directed?

SELECTED REFERENCES

Abbott, E. H. *On the Training of Parents.* Ch. 5.

Hall, G. S. *Adolescence,* v. I, pp. 353–357.

Hill and Van Alstyne. "Learning levels of the children in the nursery school with reference to the eating situation." *T. C. Bureau of Publications,* 1930.

Innskeep, A. D. *Child Adjustment.* Ch. 4.

McGinnis, E. "The acquisition and interference of motor habits in young children." *Gen. Psych. Mon. 6 *3,* 1929.

Whitley, M. T. "Children's interest in collecting." *Jo. Ed. Psych.,* v. 20, 1929.

CHAPTER V

REACTIONS TO THE SOCIAL ENVIRONMENT

In this group of the so-called social tendencies, the stimulus is the presence or behavior of some human being. A situation devoid of human beings could not be provocative of any of these responses. This was not true of the former groups. As has already been indicated, the groups overlap, some of the non-social instincts being called out by human beings, for instance, fighting. Both groups work together in building up a social community.

The social tendencies to be discussed are: (1) motherly behavior and the allied tendencies of kindliness and sympathy; (2) desire for approval, and display; (3) rivalry; (4) imitation; (5) gregariousness; (6) sex behavior.

PROTECTIVE BEHAVIOR

Motherly behavior. — Among the crude, violent, often selfish natural tendencies, protective tendencies stand out in strong relief. This group is one of the roots of humaneness; it is the source of altruism, and of the consciousness of the brotherhood of man. Only in connection with the motherly instinct is the tender emotion found, that desire to shelter that makes for the warmth and intimacy of home relations. The protective tendency is found in both men and women, though in greater strength in the latter, while the responses are different in the two sexes. To babies, women tend to respond by cuddling, handling, kissing, cooing, etc., and to babies in pain or discomfort, there is an added response of active measures for their relief. Men tend to respond to babies less by tendencies to clasp and fondle; but tendencies to watch and be interested in their play, to feed and protect them are present. Of course, this

79

general tendency to be interested in babies becomes narrowed and fixed by the possession of a baby. The maternal instinct then becomes modified by ownership, and the resulting combination is one of the strongest motives in life. Parents' love for their children may become a governing passion, overshadowing everything else. Nothing is too great to give or to bear for the sake of their children. The lives of daily self-sacrifice and denial, of longing and suffering, offered up for the sake of their children, none but parents can know. And such lives must be, in most cases, their own reward, for there seems to be no filial instinct which, in return, makes children mindful of their parents. The doll-play of very young children, boys and girls alike, has been considered in some aspects an early, gradual appearance of this instinct, though we have no evidence to show that the more inveterate doll-player makes the better parent later on. But many other tendencies are involved in doll-play, such as manipulation, fetishism, desire for companionship, dramatic representation, habitation, collecting, even bullying. The more obvious, external analogies to parental care should not mislead us into thinking it a true growth of motherly behavior.

Kindliness. — Kindliness and sympathy are more diffuse, less definite tendencies. Their source seems to be, first, the tendency to pay attention to any other human being, and to relieve hunger or pain; and second, to be satisfied with happy and contented behavior in others, and to enjoy it. Good will to men has its roots in the original nature of man. Parental love alone often becomes narrow and selfish; these two allied tendencies make for general comfort and happiness. It is natural for human beings to make others happy, and to be happier because of their happiness. In this man transcends the animals. They show the tendency to motherly behavior, often suffering death in the protection of their young; but in man we find these tendencies which lead to general community well-being very highly developed. In these we find the source of disinterested service and beneficence, and they are involved, too, in the growth and development of morals. It must be remembered, however, that these social traits grow amidst a welter of individualistic tendencies, and among other social tendencies largely selfish in their ends. It is therefore a very easy matter for them to be overlaid, choked out, or perverted to special and narrow lines.

The sight of suffering may act simply as a stimulus to curiosity, witness the crowds that have always gathered to watch public floggings, public executions, the number that stand around to look at the victims of an accident with no offer to help. Sadistic acts, actually causing pain to others, give pleasure not only to sex perverts but to many a child from the general excitement and feeling of power over weaker ones. Yet it remains a fact, in spite of the tendency to bully, that human beings shrink, at times, from the sight and realization of suffering in others, and enjoy their happiness and comfort. To retain this tendency, to stir the imagination in its service, to develop it along the lines of practical service and prevent its waste in mere effervescent sentimentality, to extend its field from the physical to the realm of the mental and spiritual is one of the most important duties of the educator.

Sympathy. — Sympathy in its first crude form is the result of reflex imitation. The baby laughs and cries, looks serious or is happy, is irritable or good tempered, according to the frame of mind of the adult. Thus at the beginning of life the mental attitudes of other people affect the child and make a difference in his own feelings. This form can hardly be called sympathy in the usual sense of the word, but along with the tendency towards kindliness it is one form of the real, conscious sympathy which comes later. Somewhere between one and four, most children show another response, also a pseudo-sympathy. They cry because the doll, the engine, or the flower is "hurt." This has been called animistic sympathy. Its presence is probably due to two reasons. In the first place, the child as a self-conscious being is not fully developed, he has not yet distinguished between the parts of his own body, and the "I" which inhabits that body. His clothes and his toys, everything he loves, he makes

part of himself, and therefore responds to the ills of these
material objects as if they were his own. This at the beginning
is not conscious personification, but lack of differentiation.
The second reason is the example of parents and nurses in such
remarks as, — "Don't kick the chair, it hurts." "Poor dolly
bumped her head on the floor," etc. Children quickly pick up
this way of talking, and it encourages this second type of sympathy. The sentimental type of nature study which gives
flowers and seeds, the wind and the rain, feelings like those of
the child, works toward the same end. This sort of thing is
not bad, only on general principles it seems very unfortunate
to do anything which encourages in the child false ideas, unless
they must of necessity be the only way of reaching the end, and
that end is worth while.

True sympathy involves the ability to be sensitive to the
situation, to understand it, to put one's self in the place of the
sufferer, and then do what may be done to relieve. The same
holds true when the sympathy is with joy. Without experience
one lacks sensitivity and ability to analyze; without imagination it is impossible to see one's self as the other — to enter
into the suffering or the joy and fully sympathize. But even
these two factors are not enough: one may have the experience,
possess imagination, but lack the interest in people which is the
necessary motive power in sympathy. Children in their cruelty
to animals lack sympathy largely because other tendencies are
for the time being stronger, or because their imagination never
makes them take the place of the animals. They lack sympathy
with the joys and sorrows of adults, and of those much more
fortunate or unfortunate than they because of lack of experience.
Adults often are lacking in sympathy because of narrowness
and selfishness; they are not interested enough in people to
care what happens to them, — their impulse towards kindliness
has been choked. This statement is especially true when there
are no signs of violent physical suffering. To keep alive the
instinct of kindliness and to develop true sympathy from the
crude roots are important for social progress and well-being.

This means giving children breadth of experience, both real and vicarious, developing their imaginations and developing interest in people by giving them opportunities to do things for real people in real situations.

DESIRE FOR APPROVAL

Man's attitude towards approval and scorn is part of his original equipment. By nature he is satisfied and made happy by approving looks, smiles, hand-touches of those about him felt to be equal or superior, or the admiring glances of inferiors, and he is made uncomfortable by scowls, frowns, derisive looks and jeers. Love, respect, or admiration for those administering the approval or the disapproval of course intensifies its effect.

Differences with maturity. — In connection with this innate desire for approval, the human being has also the tendency towards display. Every one has the tendency to "show off" in the presence of those from whom he wishes to win approval. From the "see me" of the baby, through the strut or other special gait of the adolescent to the adult who "puts the best foot first," the tendency is the natural one of winning approving responses by means of display. The power shown and the persons from whom approval is demanded or scorn avoided change as the child grows older and experience modifies his first crude reactions. At first, the display is of new things learned, new words, new tricks, or new manners; in childhood it is often physical skill or powers. It is at this latter stage that competition plays such a large part in connection with the display of various feats. In adolescence the display may include intellectual and moral qualities; it is in connection with these also that the adult tries to win approval. The persons from whom the approval is most desired are at first the adults of the immediate family, usually the mother; as the child enters the school world the opinion of the teacher becomes of first importance; with the prominence of the "gang" spirit in pre-adolescent and adolescent years, the opinion of companions of the chosen group becomes the most compelling influence in the child's life. If there is hero-worship at this time, of course the approval of the hero often becomes more valuable to the boy or girl than even what the others think. The adult seeks the approval of friends and acquaintances and society at large.

The power of the prevailing customs or traditions to hold men and women to certain lines of conduct is due largely to their fear of public scorn and love of public approval. It is a natural tendency of great power, and it needs direction rather than suppression, for in it are elements that lead to the higher development of the individual and society, elements of value and of strength. McDougall says concerning it, "For the praise and blame of our fellows, especially as expressed by the voice of public opinion, are the principal and most effective sanctions of moral conduct for the great mass of men; without them few of us would rise above the level of mere law-abidingness, the mere avoidance of acts on which legal punishment surely follows; and the strong regard for social approval and disapproval constitutes an essential stage of the progress to the higher plane of morality, the plane of obligation to an ideal of conduct." [1] It is the business of the school to see that this progression takes place, and it cannot come through the ignoring of the root motive. Appeal to love of approval is perfectly legitimate, provided both the kind of appeal and the kind of approval desired are progressive. The personal approval of the teacher for good work is a legitimate appeal for children of primary school age, but that same appeal made to high-school students is not, for they are capable of response to a higher type. It is only by means of progressive appeals that the child learns to distinguish between conduct due to the force of public opinion, and that which is an obligation to an ideal of conduct.

RIVALRY

Dynamic value. — Man, hunting or collecting or reaching out for things or trying to win approval, works more energetically when fellow creatures are doing the same things, and feels

[1] *Social Psychology*, pp. 188, 189.

keener satisfaction at success or keener disappointment at failure than when he works alone. Though this is the crude foundation upon which experience builds all the later habits of rivalry, it is noticeable that it is much easier to appeal to the interest in surpassing others in such things as sports and games, than in situations when the quality concerned is moral or intellectual. To use the instinct of rivalry in the gymnasium to get a boy to lengthen his jump is easy, but to use it in making a boy more studious or more truthful is very much more difficult.

The strength of the motive is shown by the power it has gained in its modified forms in all departments of life. It is competition which speeds up the wheels in the business world. The attitude which controls men today everywhere in the endeavor to outdo the next man in business, to make appearance, to have a better house, even to have children surpassing his — this motive is the controlling one in the lives of the majority of men and women. It appears in art and literature. Even the churches are not free from it; to send more money to missions, to have a larger congregation, to have more people join the church during a year is a positive satisfaction.

Danger of overdevelopment. — The dangers from such an attitude can be readily seen; it is working in opposition to kindliness and sympathy, and is often antagonistic to co-operation. Yet rivalry is a force of tremendous power, — a force necessary in such a complex civilization as ours to make for the best development, to weed out the useless and crown individual effort and ability with success. This end is the ideal, and it cannot be attained unless educators frankly recognize this part of the child's original equipment, realizing its value while facing at the same time the dangers of its misuse. To train a child so that the motive of rivalry will work in the higher fields of intellect and character instead of only in the field of the physical and material, is well worth while. So to train him that individual competition becomes group competition is to train for unselfishness. When the group concerned is not merely his "gang," but a larger group composed not only of friends but also of strangers, all of whom are working for a common end against another similarly constituted group, much has been done towards developing a social consciousness. But the child must be met at the level of his development. To overemphasize group work in the kindergarten and early primary grades when individual competition is so strong is contrary to the nature of the child. On the other hand, to give little or no group work in the upper primary and grammar grades at a time when the gang spirit is developing, and therefore when group competition could easily be appealed to, is wasteful. The process must be progression, from individual to group, from lower levels to higher; but the start must be made with the crude form and not at some stage far in advance. This tendency, like all the others discussed, is in the child to be used and modified, not just to be accepted, nor to be ignored.

IMITATION

Reflex. — The trend of opinion at present is to deny an instinctive basis to any of the forms of imitation, save the form known as "reflex" imitation. Man laughs, cries, runs, looks, frowns, snatches, crouches, and hunts when others do because of an original tendency. This is the crude root from which the other forms spring. That other forms, *i.e.*, "spontaneous" and "voluntary," exist is no doubt true but they are habits, learned and built up just as any other habits are learned.

As habit. — The chief reasons for denying a general instinct of imitation are three: First, it is difficult to see how the nervous system could be arranged in order to provide such an instinct; second, the higher animals, even the monkeys, prove to be lacking in any such general tendency; third, the close observers of children fail to find evidence of a general tendency to imitate.

If this point of view is correct and imitation is largely habit, then it must be governed by the same laws which control learning in general, the laws of exercise and effect. The child imitates his fellows in all sorts of ways because satisfaction has been derived from such action, not because it is an innate force. For the same reason the youth apes his elders and one nation imitates another. The force of these habits has already been pointed out. "Imitation is the prime condition of all collective mental life." Custom and tradition in all fields are but an expression of its power. Because it has been found that the imitation of the thing in vogue, no matter what it may be, brings public approval, and the violation of the prevailing custom brings scorn and criticism, man does and thinks as others of his group do and think. This tendency may be seen in politics, education, and religion, as well as in the trivial matters of dress. Young men vote as their fathers do, and show the attitude towards religious matters which is that of their family and their community. The dangers of such habits are evident; mechanically used, they make for stagnation instead of progress, for dependence and blind following instead of independence and originality.

Value of imitation. — Despite these very grave dangers, the fact of imitation is of inestimable value. It is the great conservative power by means of which the culture, inventions, ideals of each generation are passed on to the next. By means of habits of imitation the child can very much abridge the tiresome method of learning by trial and error, and can learn what his father knows in very much shorter time. It is also a great power for progress, both for the nation and the individual; for the former in that by this means the ideas and ideals of especially gifted minds come to be adopted by large numbers of people; for the latter, in that it permits him to gain a large variety of experience, and therefore to grow in originality. It is the means by which "the child is led on from the life of mere animal impulse to the life of self-control, deliberation and true volition. And it has played a similar part in the development of the human race and of society."

As a method of learning then, it is to be encouraged in all fields, — in art, in literature, in industry, in teaching, in morals, in character, imitation is well worth while. Relatively few will go to the second stage, that of constructive leadership, fewer still will think things out for themselves; the majority in all departments of life will be the followers, and all of us are followers in some fields. Well for them if in their lives they conserve the best that both the past ages and the present have to offer. For all, imitation must not be merely a means of gaining public approval by the slavish following of the present mode, but should involve conscious choice of models, should involve analysis of the method of gaining results comparable with the model in order that attainment may more nearly measure up with ideals. This use of imitation involves judgment and choice, constructive imagination and independent work. With a background of experience of imitating various models, say in music or in literature, the individual may then fairly be called upon to give his own interpretation, and to produce something original. Thus in rhythmic order, imitation is succeeded by invention, and that in turn by new and fuller imitations, and thus the scale ascends. It follows, therefore, that the work of the educator in connection with imitation is: to build habits of imitation of all kinds; to develop judgment and analysis in connection with choice of models and methods; to require a balancing of results in comparison with the model; to provide many and varied models to encourage invention, independence, originality as a result of varied imitations.

GREGARIOUSNESS

Importance for development. — In common with many of the lower animals, man is markedly gregarious. He is by nature social, responding to the presence of human beings with satisfaction and comfort, and to their absence by restlessness and discomfort. Solitude is one of the conditions he fears, and being a member of a crowd is in itself a pleasure. This desire for the presence of others shows itself in babies. Being left alone in the room will often call from the baby a cry of distress, and the adult human being seems to afford the greatest comfort to him. After babyhood, the instinct shows itself more particularly in desire for companions of the same age, although at adolescence there may be a desire for association with those older. It is also true that an adult, if left alone in a house, finds comfort in the presence of a child.

In savage communities, this instinct was necessary for the procuring of food and for protection, and from it have grown the social and community life which make for civilization and progress. It is noticeable that in general today, community of interests is the tie that binds groups together. It binds people together in the same section; it causes people of one nationality to congregate in one section of a city or state. With this tendency as the foundation, together with food-getting, hunting, and fighting activities, it is easy to see how co-operation developed; but without gregariousness bringing individuals together, making their presence a satisfaction and their absence a discomfort, it is probable that the so-called social interests would have been very slow to develop.

The strength of this instinct and its value in developing the individual through co-operation with others which it encourages make it of great importance that the child should have companions of more or less his own age. The only child, or the lonely child in a family who grows to the age of eight or nine with no playfellows of his own age, loses much that is difficult to make up later. For such a child, attendance at kindergarten and school may be the best possible help. This tendency shows itself in children during the pre-adolescent years, especially in the so-called "gang" instinct so prominent during the years ten to fifteen.

Boys' gangs. — The nature of boys' gangs and their organization have been carefully studied. The work of Sheldon, Puffer, Furfey, and Thrasher is especially well known; others, like Lee, Fiske, Forbush, describe boys' activities and give valuable suggestions for the teacher.[1] From the standpoint of social and religious workers, of the children's court, many other studies have been made, too numerous to mention here.

Thinking of age levels only we can speak of the childhood

[1] See general bibliography at the end.

gang, the early adolescent and later adolescent gang. The first of these, from seven or eight or so to twelve, is unplanned, spontaneous in origin. It meets as a like-aged play group in the street or back yards of its community. There is not usually more than a year or two difference in the ages of its members. The leader develops naturally, is not formally chosen. From eleven to seventeen years of age boys with common interests of about the same mental age level also go in groups of eight or more. The later adolescent gangs include boys from sixteen or so to nineteen. Sheldon classifies gangs according to the purposeful activity in which they engage, such as secret clubs, social clubs, predatory organizations, industrial, philanthropic organizations, athletic clubs, the last named being the most numerous. Thrasher classifies them according to the social structure they reveal, as diffused, solidified, secret, conventionalized, criminal. The diffused type, most natural with the younger boys, is comparatively simple in its activities. The loyalty of its members is not highly developed, nor does it last long. It is held together by the love of novelty, the desire to appear well, rivalry, imitation. The solidified type is the outcome of a longer development, integrated by the need to meet conflict from without. It is marked by a high degree of loyalty, its members sharing food, money, excitement, danger, blame, etc., as a unit. The secret type of gang imitates adults' societies, developing an elaborate ritual with initiations, pass words, codes, and the like. The excitement and thrill of mystery gives the group its prestige. The conventionalized type, many times fostered from the outside and constituting about one fourth of all between sixteen and eighteen years old, attempts to achieve social standing. It often organizes formally or incorporates. It meets for athletics, dancing, literary, or political purposes. The criminal type is organized for itself alone, attracts older boys who are socially unadjusted, and drifts into habitual delinquency, vice, and crime.

Psychology of the gang. — Whether loosely knit or closely organized, the like-aged, like-sexed group fills a need in the life

of boys as nothing else can between the early childhood dependence on their parents and readiness to mate and found families
of their own. In countless ways they learn independence, while
acquiring a practical understanding of democracy. Standards
of behavior evolve with regard to fair play, to property, to
physical skill; ideals of generosity, thrift, courage, honor, and
loyalty are formed. Personalities are appraised in a crude but
searching way. The boy who malingers, who is hypocritical,
mean, grouchy, cowardly, supercilious, soon finds himself unwelcome, or dropped by the gang. To make good he must learn
self-control and adjustment to the needs of the group, purposing for the group welfare.

Physical vigor and high spirits necessitate *exciting pursuits*.
Whether these are games, or plaguing people, legitimate adventure or mischief, fighting other gangs or challenging them
to athletic contests, stealing and raiding, or rendering valuable
service in keeping law and order may depend on the whim of
the moment as well as on the opportunities offered by the environment, and the degree to which the group itself is socialized
and integrated with other groups. The *imagination* may be fed
by attending the moving-picture theater, carrying on games of
the cowboy and Indian, bandit and pirate variety, poring over
the "Sunday funnies," reading together the thriller type of
story, also obscene and pornographic material. The *sense of
group self* needs attachment to an identifiable territory. A
particular street corner, a garage, the railroad freight yards,
the rented club quarters serve the city boys, where the barn,
the water hole, the wood lot, serve the rural boys. Caves in
the clay bank, the wigwam in the woods, the tree house, the
shack in the vacant lot, are witness to the boys' willingness
to build for themselves, if possible. A name for the group
objectifies the self-feeling also. Many appellations are derived from the locality where they meet, as the Wharf
Rats, the Gas House Gang, the Twentieth Street Bunch;
others symbolize certain aspirations for reputation, such as
the Tough Kids, the Red Devils, the Lilies of the Valley,

the last a sobriquet for a gang of colored boys with a sense of humor.

Gangs of older boys are found generally in the poorer sections of cities when little other social life or entertainment is available, and among those who have not the privilege of high-school clubs. The nationalities most frequently found in gangs are, in the order named, Irish, American, French, Italian, down to the Jewish.

Provision for healthy group experience. — Unfortunately the term gang connotes to many adults the criminal activities of the gangster, or, at best, the anti-social, mischievous behavior of younger boys. Consequently, attempts have been made to break up gangs wherever found, or to treat boys as separate individuals. The wise educator, recognizing the importance of group experience for children and adolescents, will help them to organize it. To attempt to ignore or suppress this tendency is the cause of much of the problems of discipline in the schools and of the juvenile delinquency which troubles the courts of the big cities. The fact that the schools, many of them, are so organized that individuals are singled out in connection with school work is the cause of much of the dissatisfaction with school in boys of eleven and twelve, as well as the cause of much of the dropping out from the sixth and seventh grades. However, recent broadening of the school duties and functions is in line with a fuller provision for the gregarious instinct in its various forms. The school playgrounds, school government, the more extended use of the school plant for clubs and societies and classes of all kinds, as well as the changes in classroom method, — all these movements help towards a fuller recognition of the child nature in the pre-adolescent years. To promote the best development needs a sympathetic understanding of the main impulses functioning in the group's actions. Games of physical contest are imperative occupations. Throwing, hitting, aiming at a mark, wrestling, climbing, digging, running, are elements that should figure in these contests. A chance to wander and explore, to see new places, have adventurous quests, should be afforded every boy. The success of the Boy Scouts and similar organizations is achieved precisely because of its appeal to the felt needs and interests of boys. Groups that are dominated by adults, or that ignore these fundamental impulses will not succeed. For the adolescent boys the many types of clubs possible in the well-administered high school open up many avenues of permanently worth while recreations and avocations. They help young people learn co-operation for other than physical pleasures. Debating and dramatic leagues enlarge opportunities for social criticism by which self-appraisal and growth in power to judge others is favored. Leadership as well as teamwork can be learned in a moral atmosphere that is positive. Similar club activities should be available for older adolescents who are not in high school or college.

Girls. — Group life is not so absorbing for girls as it is for boys. Whether this is due to innate differences, as many claim, or to the more sheltered life they lead with traditions that proscribe outdoor roaming in bands is not certain. It is obvious that the spontaneous group activities of girls from ten to sixteen differ from those of boys; also that organizations such as the Girl Scouts find the task of fostering team spirit and group loyalty difficult as compared with the work among boys. As indication that tradition has much to do with it, we note that in communities where girls have exactly the same freedom as boys they do develop group independence, witness Margaret Meade's [1] studies in New Guinea and Samoa, Kidd's [2] among the Kaffirs, even the reports that come to us of the "wild" children in Russia. As suggestion of innate difference we have the following facts. Even at the kindergarten level girls more often choose and enjoy solitary occupations such as painting and weaving, rather than floor construction games with large blocks so beloved by the boys, and which involve group action. After eleven years old girls are rather less active in their play

---

[1] *Growing Up in New Guinea.* Also *Coming of Age in Samoa.*
[2] Kidd, Dudley, *Savage Childhood.*

than boys; while their preference in active games, such as skipping rope, volley ball, later tennis, does not lead on into teamwork as do the boys' early choices of baseball and football. Girls mature earlier than boys and develop individual friendships at an age when boys are most thoroughly identified with the gang. Thereafter, girls tend to be more personal, resenting criticism, seeing little good in their opponents, finding it almost impossible to work under leaders they dislike even for the good of a group—all of which attitudes hinder the formation of the solidified type of gang, and may prevent any good club work if they survive into adult life.

What was said above of clubs in the high school applies equally well, of course, to the training desirable for girls. In the junior high-school level separate societies for boys and for girls will thrive better than mixed groups. There are too great discrepancies in physical, mental, and social maturation for real compatibility except in such fields as music, photography, etc., where differences will not be conspicuous. By sixteen or so, more kinds of clubs for boys and girls together will prosper as they both come to enjoy each other's society.

REPRODUCTIVE INSTINCT

Sex impulse. — That the sex instinct, the instinct which leads to the reproduction of the race, is one of the strongest, if not *the* strongest that man possesses, needs no emphasis. The structure of society voices its strength, while literature, art, and music are evidences of its beauty. This instinct should not be confused with the instinct of motherly behavior; the two are distinct, although they are probably related, and they exist in different degrees of development in the same individual.

Scientific analysis of the nature and development of the sex impulse has only recently been made. This fact is due to the cloak of silence and insinuation of shame that tradition has thrown about everything connected with sex, and to the difficulty of observing the stages of its development in children.

The older view was that the sex instinct became operative only in adolescence when maturity was indicated by physical signs. We know now that the presence of sexual desire is not dependent on such signs as the growth of pubic hair, erection and ejection, menstruation; also, we use the term sex instinct to apply to a wide group of phenomena, many of which appear long before puberty. The sex nature is not a thing apart from the rest of the individual; it is there all along, developing slowly at times, but continuously.

Processes occurring in two distinctly different fields combine to make up the sex impulse proper. The first set of processes go on in the physiological realm wholly, and consist of the various sensations, nerve disturbances, reflexes, secretions, and the like, which together are called the phenomena of detumescence from the root meaning of "getting smaller," in reference particularly to the glands. The second set are more in the psychic realm, and include the various attractions, fallings in love and kindred emotions, also the sentiments of disgust, shame, and modesty, especially the pats, strokings, caresses of various sorts which, taken all together make up the phenomena of contrectation, from the root word meaning "touching."

First, or neutral period. — From birth to somewhere about five years old such detumescence processes as are present are felt but vaguely with little sex consciousness or localized sensations except in pathological cases. Interest is directed towards the genitals by the training received in bowel and bladder control, and the emphasis placed on cleanliness. Attitudes are set towards modesty; childish curiosity concerning sex differences, or adult versus child bodily form is enhanced or satisfied by the particular sort of family customs in bedroom and bathroom behavior. The love emotions are called out by the adults' physical ministrations, especially those connected with food, and by the endearments offered. The nurse, the mother, becomes the first love object, apart from children's own bodies. Jealousy is frequently aroused by the arrival of the next baby who now requires the greater share of the mother's attention.

Undifferentiated period. — This begins anywhere from five to seven years old and lasts till puberty. Detumescent processes are still impossible because of the immature body; but uniquely pleasurable sensations become localized in the sex organs. Various tendencies may appear which need careful watching lest they harden into habits and develop into perversions later on. Among these may be mentioned exhibitionism, masturbation, skatophilia, mutual malpractice with either sex including masochistic and sadistic acts. Curiosity, love of novel experiences and of sensations for their own sake, combined with manipulation are quite sufficient to account for the easy start of bad habits, especially if a feeling of shame and a tendency to secretiveness are fostered by an unwise atmosphere of concealment and suppression on the part of the adults.

During this period the contrectation impulses frequently become very marked; children form strong attachments for other children or for adults of either sex, sometimes even for animals, but there may be quite a succession of these objects of affection. These impulses are expressed by taking every chance to see, be with, touch, kiss, or embrace the person who is for the time being the one beloved, or even, in a sort of fetishism, any article belonging to, or touched by that one.

In the two years or so just preceding puberty there is an actual dislike for like-aged members of the opposite sex as shown by their infrequent play together, the active seeking of same sexed groups, the opprobrious language used by boys and girls of each other, and the type hero that is admired. On the whole, this is a homosexual period as contrasted with the auto-sexual love of the little child, and the heterosexual love of the adult.

Developmental period. — This begins with puberty and lasts roughly till eighteen or twenty. There is great individual variation in the time of the beginning of these stages just as there is in the time of the onset of puberty; but, as in the latter, girls are apt to be a year or two ahead of boys of the same age. The sex glands themselves may be stimulated to action in four ways, by physical causes, normal or abnormal, by emotional states, by imagined situations. Comparison with the lachrymal and salivary glands may be helpful. For instance, cold wind, or inflammation of the nasal membranes will bring tears. Emotions of grief, hilarity, etc., or imagined tragedies in the storybook will start crying, too. Food in the mouth, biting the tongue will cause saliva to flow; anger, or the imagined taste of lemons will also induce salivation. Similarly, on the physical side, the normal sexual act, or mechanical stimulation or inflammation and irritation of adjacent parts will bring detumescent processes. The emotions peculiar to sex, also violent dread, or imagined erotic scenes will induce them, too.

This fact, of the fourfold excitability of the sex system is a new problem with which adolescents must deal. Eventually, as stated before, detumescence and contrectation impulses will be felt together; but it is quite possible for them to be experienced apart for a long time. Thus, nocturnal emissions on the one hand, prolonged séances of mere caresses on the other, illustrate their independence. Another possibility is that the two may occur simultaneously but are not understood as related. Thus the coincidence in adolescence of a rush of affection and of an involuntary orgasm may come as a complete surprise to the individual experiencing it.

This lack of understanding could only occur when the adolescent has not been well instructed; the psychic shock of it may be considerable.

Girls. — The contrectation impulses are shown, usually, first for members of the same sex. They have a "best friend," from whom they are inseparable, or a "crush" for an older woman. Their adoration shifts from one to another, however, a few months to a couple of years being the longest usual time for the same love object to hold the devotion. Romantic dreams, blind jealousy mingled with passionate devotion often produce most erratic conduct, from slavish imitation to outbursts of wild display. Cases of "calf-love" and "crushes" are illustrations of these complexes. All this does not mean to imply that every case of enthusiastic friendship is a manifestation of the sex instinct, but that, very frequently, the incompletely developed instinct does show itself for a while in this form. In the genuine, sex-dominated loves, however, there may be lacking every simultaneous, localized sex-feeling proper, especially any conscious connection for the individual with physical changes and processes; though sometimes the keen desire for close proximity leads to undesirable practices, not to say real risks. The opposite sex becomes attractive in the form of some one rather older. The screen idol, the young religious teacher, curate, priest, or what not, are recipients of a great deal of young feminine devotion. Up to sixteen or seventeen there is little discriminative love worship. The maiden enjoys the feel of being in love with a love idol of her own creation believed by her to be incarnated in the love object for the time being. The mate, if chosen now, is scarcely the one the mature young woman would select as co-parent. In later adolescence her affections are more likely to center around a male of more nearly the same age, and explorations of each other's personalities begin in real earnest. Meantime she is sex conscious, blushes easily, is coy and bold by turns, is tremendously interested in hair, jewelry, clothes, perfumes, and cosmetics. A never failing theme of interest is what he said, what I said, and what he said.

Some girls pass at once, with puberty, from the homosexual stage to being "boy crazy." Early absorption in sex dulls the interest in general cultural improvement, in school studies, in social affairs generally. Early marriage is deprecated on the eugenic grounds that the better babies are not born of very young mothers. It is ill-advised on economic grounds, since young people are as a rule not in a position to support themselves and possible offspring, and so the parental generation becomes doubly responsible. It is undesirable on social grounds since further education of the girl is usually halted, and wider interests atrophied. In most oriental countries these grounds for objection count for less, and early marriage is, for girls, the rule. In this country we find older customs persisting among some of our immigrant population as well as in our more primitive communities. The legal minimum age at which a girl may marry is still twelve years old in a quarter of our states, and fourteen years in nine more. The census of 1920 showed 18,388 girls of fifteen or under who were wives, and over 800 more who were widowed or divorced. The conditions behind these facts show conflict with school attendance laws, and with child welfare laws, and constitute a civic rather than an individual adolescent problem.

Otherwise, our tendency to defer marriage till long after there is physical capacity for reproduction has intensified, if not created, what is connoted in the phrase "the adolescent problem" for both boys and girls. The solutions offered by society and those arrived at, hit or miss fashion, by the young people themselves, are not always in agreement.

Boys. — Boys maintain their hostile attitude to the other sex longer than girls do, as they mature later. Their extremely bashful, sex-conscious, girl-shy period is likely to come around sixteen. A usual development shows four phases. First is a romantic, idealistic devotion, the "first love" which can be so delicately beautiful, but which is so often spoiled by the teasing which a boy meets. Next is the flirting, display stage, coincident with what has been aptly termed the tie and sock age. It is characterized by display of strength, skill, ability to spend, color in clothes, daredeviltry, in short all the qualities felt to be overwhelmingly attractive to the female. After this comes more serious falling in love, but without sex experience. The love object may be a girl slightly younger, a woman five or six years older or even a dozen years or more his senior. These love affairs are brief in duration but intense while they last. A fourth phase is bisexual relationship, either illicit free experimentation, or with a prostitute, in either case with none of the responsibility that the legalized relationship would bring. These phases presage the complete adult experiences, are a series of separated steps in preparation for courtship and marriage. Thus, the first foreshadows the emotional approach, the second is the introduction to the more serious tactics of courtship. The third permits a trial of mutual compatibility of tastes, is a real try-out of personality; the fourth reassures the boy of his potency in the sexual act. It is seldom that the mate the more mature young man selects has been a partner in any one of these separated preparatory steps.

SEX EDUCATION

Failure to progress from the infantile through the undifferentiated stage may involve abnormal psychic tendencies in adult life such as fetishism, sexual anæsthesia, homosexuality, and the like even though in mild forms. It is necessary, therefore, to recognize the significance of the period of childhood for the training of healthy-minded, really moral adults. We must not make the mistake of supposing we can ignore sexuality, so vital to the social welfare, in the years before the obvious signs of maturity are present.

Training. — As implied above, training is begun from infancy, whether mothers realize it or not, by the physical habits established, by the emotional attitudes induced, by the conversations that take place. In addition, a permanent dislike for one sex or the other may be conditioned into young children by unhappy relationships with either parent. Further, their first understanding of home making, of married life, of parental function, which will influence their later expectations, comes from what they see exemplified around them. It is not well for children to share the parents' bedroom after they are two years old, indeed after one year old according to some authorities.

With older children, on the physical side undue activity of the instinct is prevented by encouraging much physical outdoor exercise, by not allowing them to sleep with others nor to be too warmly covered in bed, nor to stay long in bed after they are awake; by seeing to it that the genitals are kept absolutely clean, and that the clothing is not tight, by not allowing the handling of the parts by the child nor by any one else; by being on the watch to eliminate corporal punishment, bicycle or horseback riding, gymnastic exercise such as vaulting or pole climbing if any sex excitement results. On the mental side, care must be taken that the attitude toward all sex matters is not that of shame, nor of mystery, nor that of frivolity, nor vulgar familiarity, but one of wholesome, dignified frankness; that they form no impure associations with such matters, due to bad companions or books or pictures; that ideals of purity, of reverence for parents, of the sacredness and use of the sex function be built up from the beginning. The habit of self-control with regard to eating is important. To have indulged appetite at any time and in any way desired is a bad precedent for the adolescent's idea of self-control with regard to the sex appetite.

New habits of physical care must be formed with puberty. Many-sided interests must be stimulated, with a chance for creative activity along congenial lines — this as a safeguard against preoccupation with sex, and as an outlet for energy. Opportunity for contact with the opposite sex under sympathetic supervision is vital. The etiquette and best *mores* of the social group must be habituated through practice, with all their implications in ethics, chivalry, and scientific knowledge. Shared interests in music, literature, hobbies, must be discovered as well as in recreations; co-operation in constructive social work of some kind is much to be desired. The varied vocational activities of married life should be considered along with other vocations, and training in home making given both sexes.

Instruction. — It must be remembered that the question does not involve a choice of giving or withholding certain information; children get it anyway. The question is rather, shall it come from a reliable source in a way to establish confidence and sympathy, with sacred and beautiful associations, or shall it come from companions on the street, perverted, untrue, and with coarse and brutal associations? It is wisest to answer children's questions frankly and truthfully so far as their age will permit understanding. It should also be borne in mind that the instruction should be positive and constructive, dealing with the normal and leading to high ideals and principles, not negative with the emphasis on perversion, and the need of avoiding disease.

The first questions, usually about four years old, refer to anatomical puzzles, those before eight to the origin of babies. Fathers have a unique opportunity on the occasion of the mother's pregnancy to discuss with their young sons the meaning of the condition and the responsibility it entails on all in the family. Galloway [1] found that few fathers had taken advantage of this home situation to foster wholesome attitudes in the children, and share with them the inspiration to reverent chivalry which the mother's needs present. The earlier the facts are known the more they are taken as matters of course rather than matters of exciting, shocking mystery. There is no special reason for teaching about reproductive processes from the standpoint of botany rather than from that of human interest. Much will depend on the immediate surroundings. Children in rural sections, on farms, have plentiful illustrations of life processes where city children's observations may be confined to dogs, cats, and sparrows. Pet animals, for instance rabbits that breed so often, offer many points of interest about which children will ask questions. Good teaching implies directed observation, and interpretation in terms of family life, of the necessity of care for offspring, of the sacredness of the life principle.

Before twelve, enlightenment regarding the changes to be expected must be effected, and in the next few years each sex needs to be taught about the other's nature and needs, both from the hygienic and the social point of view. Knowledge of the dangers of venereal disease must be included in the teens. The legal, civic safeguards of the marriage relationship should be intelligently discussed, the facts, again, interpreted in their social setting rather than merely for individual convenience. The study of heredity, of eugenics, helps orient the older adolescent's personal problems.

[1] Galloway, T. W., *The Father and His Boy.*

The teacher's duty. — First of all, we should not think of sex as a separable aspect of a child's development, nor of sex education as a few biological facts to be taught in a few weeks' time. Rather it is a continuous guidance from babyhood to adult status, a part of character education that relates the individual's actions and attitudes to society in view of his relationship to the generation immediately preceding and immediately succeeding him. Obviously then, from the nursery school teacher to the college dean, the professional worker's share in sex education is distributed over all the ages of development.

Second, teachers must be thoroughly well informed themselves. Ignorance of biological science is ridiculous for any adult, of state laws reprehensible for any citizen, for the teacher doubly so. Yet Davenport [1] found normal school students, soon to be teachers, in need of instruction about the most elementary facts even of personal hygiene. How are such people fit to be trusted with the education of children? The teacher's knowledge should include the history of the family as well as child and adolescent psychology. For guiding individual children a teacher should know the facts regarding sex development, should know the precautions to be taken to prevent undue excitement, and should know the signs of abnormality so that medical advice could be given to a child when needed. She should be ready to give necessary information to the child if the parents will not, or cannot; and she should realize, especially if her work is with an ignorant class of people, that it is part of her duty in connection with mothers' and fathers' meetings often to give them facts in this line and always to raise their ideals, and make them realize their responsibility.

The school instruction gives children a vocabulary, often sadly needed, with which to refer to physiological facts. It may utilize equipment which the home cannot supply such as the microscope, the moving picture. The school can give courses in care of the sick, in home management, in social dancing,

---

[1] Davenport, Isabel, *Salvaging of American Girlhood.*

all of which interpret home and sex relationship very definitely to the adolescent. The discussions of the novel, of the drama in the literature courses, of the place of woman in different nations at different epochs which appear in our high-school work help orient the thinking.

Not all teachers are called upon to give sex instruction. Bigelow [1] instances five types of people who are not qualified as teachers along these lines: (1) those who cannot talk calmly and dispassionately on the topic; (2) those with abnormal outlook on life, who are too readily influenced by psychopathic literature; (3) insufficiently informed people, who tend to stress the abnormal in their presentation because of hasty preparation; (4) people who are pessimistic as a result of unfortunate personal experiences; (5) those of flippant attitude and questionable ethical behavior who cannot command the respect of their pupils. School teachers of nature study, biology, literature, and civics have opportunities not only of giving knowledge but of creating the right attitude to the facts. Playground directors, the gymnasium teacher, the school nurse, the physician may all add to the knowledge along different lines and watch over the formation of good habits. Club leaders, pastors, social directors find still another avenue of approach and field for training. It is the function of all in contact with children and young people to train good habits in them, to interpret cold facts, to inspire to a life of efficiency, social adaptation, and ethical beauty.

PRACTICAL EXERCISES

1. Spend two half hours, at different times, in intensive observation of one child four to six years of age, recording all that he does in that period. Analyze this behavior into expressions of the various instincts treated in this and the preceding chapter. Note particularly the situations arousing responses of fighting, hoarding, teasing, kindliness, display.
2. Visit a meeting of a Boy Scout or Girl Scout organization if feasible. How does it make provision for the various tendencies discussed in the last two chapters?

[1] Bigelow, Maurice, *Sex Education*, pp. 115–116.

3. For your individual child — find out from the mother what questions he has asked about the origin of life, about sex differences, about marriage, etc., and how they have been answered.
4. Find out from your State Board of Health what exhibits, including motion pictures, are available for sex education in the high school.
5. What help can the American Social Hygiene Association give your local community?
6. Consider your home making, biology, English, physical education courses from the standpoint of their contribution to sound knowledge and attitude towards social hygiene.
7. Collect a bibliography on sex education useful for study in parents' clubs.

FOR DISCUSSION

1. What means may be taken to develop kindliness and sympathy in children?
2. Show how desire for approval may be utilized to motivate school work in the third grade, in the eighth grade. To influence moral conduct in the kindergarten, the fifth grade, the high school.
3. Suggest methods of training that will change personal rivalry into group rivalry.
4. Point out some disadvantages in fashions, customs, precedents, moral tone, etc., that come from imitation. How may the force be made an advantage in these matters?
5. How could gang loyalty be directed into civic loyalty and utilized in community service?
6. What does a boy miss in the way of character development who is not a member of a gang?
7. Which tendencies in particular have been misdirected in the case of the criminal gangster?
8. What is the difference between sex instruction and sex education in (*a*) aim, (*b*) method, (*c*) subject matter?
9. Give some reasons for information, or training, or both, with regard to sex in the first five years of life, the next nine or ten years, the later teens. How can social and religious organizations help in this matter?

SELECTED REFERENCES

ANTHONY, JOSEPH. *The Gang.*
CLEVELAND, E. "If parents only knew." *Children,* 1927.
DENNET, M. W. *The Sex Education of Children.*
DE SCHWEINITZ. *Growing Up.*
FISKE, G. W. *Boy Life and Self Government.*

Furfey, P. H. *The Gang Age.*

Gruenberg, B. *High Schools and Sex Education.*

Lee, J. *Play in Education.* Chs. 40, 41.

Moll, A. *The Sexual Life of the Child.* Chs. 1, 7, 9.

Seagrave, M. "Causes underlying sex delinquency in young girls." *Jo. Soc. Hyg.*, v. 12, 1926.

Stopes, M. C. *Sex and the Young.*

Stowell, W. L. *Sex for Parents and Teachers.*

Thrasher, F. M. *The Gang.*

CHAPTER VI

PLAY LIFE

The play behavior of children is so obvious and universal a phenomenon that it has attracted much attention from philosophers and educators. Childhood is the playtime of life. Children seem quite willing to devote all their waking time and energy to play, provided this tendency has not been inhibited by some environmental condition. To play is as much a part of their original nature as to eat, or to sleep. Just what is the source in original nature has been discussed for years. Why do children play, and why do they play in just the ways they do? Several theories have been advanced, each containing something of value, none, perhaps, being a completely satisfactory explanation.

THEORIES OF PLAY

Excess energy. — One well-known theory, crystallized from earlier philosophies by Schiller and by Spencer, suggests that energy stored up in excess of immediate needs finds outlet in useless exercise. Because of superfluous energy children play. It is doubtless true that healthy, rested children play better than sick, tired ones; but both animals and children play when sick, play till exhausted, recommence play before any excess can be stored up. Granted that, in the absence of economic needs children's whole energies may be directed into play, this theory does not account for the particular forms taken by play, nor for the fact that development of play activities follows a certain sequence irrespective of environment.

Preparation for life. — Groos,[1] who studied play in both young animals and in children, thinks that in the various plays

[1] Groos, Karl, *The Play of Man.*

children practice the forms of activity that they will later need and upon which their struggle for existence may depend; that such practice is necessary for the future perfection of the various activities, and that development of the individual depends on it.   No doubt in some instances, especially if one considers primitive man, there is some such correspondence; but in most cases the preparatory effect of the various games is hard to trace.   For instance, it might seem valuable to children of uncivilized races to indulge as they do in the running, catching games, because the adult savage depends largely on his agility and strength for his existence; but for what do these plays prepare a civilized child? — For catching a street car perhaps, or getting out of the way of an automobile.   The preparation, if there is one, must be taken in a very general sense, for no close correspondence can be found.

Atavistic theory. — This has been most strongly held by Stanley Hall; it is, indeed, but a special application of the recapitulation theory, and subject to the same criticisms.   He says "I regard play as the motor habits and spirit of the past of the race, persisting in the present, as rudimentary functions sometimes of and always akin to rudimentary organs.   The best index and guide to the stated activities of adults in past ages is found in the instinctive, untaught and non-imitative plays of children which are the most spontaneous and exact expressions of their motor needs. . . .   Thus we rehearse the activities of our ancestors, back we know not how far, and repeat their life work in summative and adumbrated ways." [1] Theoretically, scientists do not believe that human nature has undergone such definite and well-marked changes due to the stages of culture through which it has passed.   Practically, it is difficult on this theory to explain why boys like to go swimming and to live in caves at the same age, or why it is that children enjoy playing with toy boats and trains before they want a bow and arrow, or why the favorite toy of most girls under nine is the doll.   That there are common elements to be

[1] Hall, *Youth*, p. 74.

found in the plays of all children, whether civilized or primitive, there can be no question, but the explanation is probably not the one Hall supports.

Catharsis. — This doctrine explains play as a harmless outlet for tendencies of which individuals need to rid themselves. Thus, football can relieve boys of their pugnacious impulses. True, our task is often to direct energies now resulting in mischief and anti-social acts into safe and social channels; but it is a question whether the joyous thrill of playing hold-up man with toy pistols at the age of eight or ten renders it less likely or more likely that the boy will continue that particular form of excitement and domination at eighteen.

Relaxation, recreation. — Play is thought of as any activity permitting the higher brain centers — presumably overstrained by concentrated work — to rest. Patrick [1] has recently re-expressed this older theory. Of course we agree that change of occupation is often restful, when it uses less energy, less attention, or is pleasanter than the preceding one. Also, muscles cramped from work during sedentary work find welcome recreation in exercise. But we have no proof that the higher brain centers fatigue any more quickly than the others.

Rivalry. — McDougall [2] considers children's play as due to the premature ripening of the instincts. For him, the essence of play is rivalry. He says, "A motive that may co-operate with others in almost all games, and which among ourselves is seldom altogether lacking, is the desire to get the better of others, to emulate, to excel. This motive plays an important part, not only in games, but in many of the most serious activities of life, to which it gives an additional zest. . . . But wherever it enters in, it is recognized that it imparts something of a playful character to the activity." But rivalry does not enter into many of the plays of children. Some plays, the make-believe plays, the doll-plays, and the play of an infant are noticeably lacking in such an element. Moreover, the presence of rivalry when two

---

[1] Patrick, C. T. W., *The Psychology of Relaxation.*
[2] McDougall, *Social Psychology*, pp. 112–113.

individuals or corporations are fighting for the upper hand by no means changes their activity into a playful one. If carried out fully, this suggestion would involve a differentiation of each instinct into two, — one the serious form, and the other the playful form which is always accompanied by the spirit of rivalry, and this does not seem to be true. It seems impossible, then, to take this theory as a full explanation of the play impulse, although of course it has an element of truth in it.

Compensation. — From the psychiatric school of thought comes the emphasis on the compensatory value of play. It is described by Robinson [1] as the biological resolution of a conflict. It is obvious that many imaginative plays satisfy the motive of escape from humdrum reality; that novel reading, attendance at prize fights, ball games, moving pictures allow passive, vicarious enjoyment as compensation for lack of firsthand adventure. But not all play can be interpreted in this way.

Biologic need. — Appleton advanced a theory stating that play is dependent on the structure of the body, and that the activity is of such character as will satisfy the needs of the growing body. "With the infant, the head or arm muscles being strongest, control the somatic type of play, together with the developing sense organs of the nervous system and the brain. Sensations, coming through the sheen of light, the shake of the rattle, the throwing of the ball, are his mental toys and his delight. Later, when stronger muscles co-operate in stronger and more complex movements and when further brain development makes perception and apperception possible, activity of the whole body is the somatic type, while mentally imagination, volition and imitation, become his toys. And so we hear, 'Tell me a story,' and see, a little later, the story epitomized in dramatic representation. . . . Is it not significant that whatever the type of play may be, it just keeps pace with the type of somatic growth? And does not the impulse to exercise these

---

[1] Robinson, E. S., "A concept of compensation and its psychological setting," *Jo. Abn. Psy.*, v. 17, 1923.

growing parts furnish all the explanation that is needed for the existence of the play activity?" [1]

This accounts for sequential forms of childhood play but hardly for adult play activities.

Other terms. — The idea of self-realization is emphasized by Claparède,[2] of freedom from conflict and motive-satisfying by Taylor and Curti.[3] Though real contributions to our thinking, the all-inclusiveness of these explanations depends rather on their vagueness. Also, they seem to connote a directed, conscious purpose in play which is not always present, nor true of the youngest children.

To sum up: we may never achieve one thoroughly satisfactory answer as to why we play, nor what play really "is," though each of these explanations offered has suggestions of value. Dewey reminds us that activity is the essence of life; so that play activity needs no apologetic as such, though the varied forms it takes should be studied in the light of the conditions producing them.

COMMON USAGE OF TERMS

Play is complex. — "Play" describes the functioning of an organism in situations not stamped with the socio-economic need which would lead us to call it work. It is what we *want* to do. The state of maturity of the organism determines the sequence of the forms of functioning. Conditions in the environment, and the organism's immediate adjustment to them determine the actual forms. The law of readiness determines the kind of play engaged in at different periods. Thus, running and chasing is not a feature of play under eighteen months, nor dramatic representation under three years, nor competition under six or seven, nor language games much before ten, nor social dancing with the other sex till about fifteen. Similarly, the rattle that pleases the baby is ignored later, the woolly

---

[1] Appleton, *A Comparative Study of the Play Activities of Adult Savages and Civilized Children*, p. 77.
[2] *Experimental Pedagogy and the Psychology of the Child.*
[3] Curti, M. W., *Child Psychology*, pp. 359–371.

lamb on wheels dragged down the street by the two-year-old would disgust the nine-year-old, the eight-year-old's doll no longer interests the fourteen-year-old.   The law of exercise controls the tendencies so that experience and learning quickly modify what in the play or work was the outcome of original nature.   The law of effect also enters in to determine the length of time children will play; their persistence till skill is acquired in roller skating, top-spinning, pitching ball, hopscotch, and whatnot, above all, makes the occupation, for them, play rather than work.

Amusement, games, sport. — Several forms of enjoyment are included under the general name play.   There is amusement, which presupposes a somewhat passive attitude on the part of the person enjoying: thus, we amuse children by showing them pictures, telling them stories, taking them to a conjurer's performance.   Games are characterized sometimes by the use of dramatic imagination to a definite end, chiefly by the presence of rules of varying degrees of complexity, the element of competition, frequently by a limitation of the number who may participate.   For example, we have games of charades, cross-tag, dominoes, going to Jerusalem, checkers, croquet, football, and the like.   Sport rather connotes athletics out of doors, often with contest against physical nature, such as swimming, boating, races, though it may mean games, such as polo, golf, or "indoor sports," such as volley ball.   Sport is play made into work, as are also hobbies.   This terminology obviously overlaps to some extent; but with these subtracted, the term play is reserved for the free play of very young children, for random, unattended-to movements, such as the nervous occupation of a lecturer's hands, or for some activity less definitely organized and regulated than is a game, such as "playing" horse, Indian, dolls.   There is no sharp line of division in the use of the terms.

Play, work, and drudgery. — Of more significance is our thought of all forms of play as distinct from work or drudgery. The difference here is not primarily one of the kind of activity, but one of attitude.   No given activity can arbitrarily be placed in either class. Given the same elements present in the nervous system but a primitive environment with its urgent physical needs, the probability is that the responses of action would not be called play because of the service they would render. As Thorndike says, "If infants from a year to three years of age lived in such a community as a human settlement seems likely to have been twenty-five thousand years ago, their restless examination of small objects would perhaps seem as utilitarian as their father's hunting." [1] In many instances, because of the protection and care of the parents, because of the difference between primitive and civilized society, because of the complexity of the environment, children respond in ways not immediately useful, and we say they play. For example, we call it playing when ten-year-olds have a pillow fight or a game of chase, when they model a snow-man or build a bridge or a dam across a small stream; but were the opponents really inimical, the plastic material clay, the country in danger of a flood we should consider the activities work. So, too, very small differences in the situation are sometimes big enough to call out different responses. A bottle given a hungry baby will stimulate the food-taking responses; given to the same baby when satisfied may stimulate manipulation and vocalization. In the latter case we should call it playing but not in the former; not that the baby has two sets of responses, one serious and the other playful, but that the slight difference in his physiological condition makes him respond in the first case so that we recognize the economic need, and in the second so that we do not. The need exists for the baby each time, but in different form.

Listening to a concert, working problems in mathematics, sewing or painting, attending a reception, playing a game of chess, taking a walk, working in the garden, — any one of these may be work of the hardest kind to one person and the most delightful play to another. This difference in attitude is caused by the difference in certain characteristics of the activity. When the activity is considered as work, it is being engaged in, not for

[1] *Original Nature of Man,* p. 146.

its own sake, but because of some result worth while, only to be reached by means of the given activity. The purpose of the worker is found outside of the activity in the result beyond. When the activity seems play to the individual, the process itself seems worth while; he is concerned only with the activity, that in itself satisfies him. The same result may be obtained as in the former case, but it is not the most important thing to the one engaged in the activity. When it is work, the process is merely a means to a desirable end, but when it is play the two are fused, and the process with its result seem desirable. For example, the boys who were paid to clear the potato patch of potato bugs found it most disagreeable work at first, and did it only to secure the money or escape the punishment for disobedience, or both. But when the competition and make-believe elements were introduced by some bright spirit, and the potato bugs became pearls and each boy tried to get the largest collection, — then the money received in payment was no longer the largest factor, but the process itself became of absorbing interest.

The work attitude is brought about because the activity in question for some reason is not adapted to the individual's capacity at the moment it is indulged in. This lack of adaptation may be due to fatigue; often some occupation begun with zest becomes drudgery before it is completed because of the fatigue occasioned. A child who usually considers his gymnasium period as play may, because of the late hours of the night before, find it hard work. Lack of particular ability may be the cause of the lack of adaptation. Music, or art, or handwork, or athletics may always be work for certain children simply because they lack ability along these lines. Sometimes the lack of adaptation is due to the fact that the activity has been planned by an adult who has not taken into proper consideration the stage of development of the child. When this occurs, the activity being beyond his stage of development, calling for powers and tendencies not yet ripe, or, as is sometimes the case, calling for tendencies which have matured, to be used in no new way, the process satisfies no need on the part of the child. The only motive he can have in the pursuance of it is to satisfy the adult from whom the initiative has come, who has planned the activity. Under these conditions it is impossible for the child to throw himself wholly into the task, his attention is divided between the process and the end, and divided attention is always accompanied by strain. Were the activity suited to the child, if it called out some developing power, the process and end would not be disparate but a logical whole, and the attention therefore of a unified, concentrated type.

To sum up, the attitude rather than the occupation determines whether a person is at play, work, or drudgery. Play means a feeling of freedom, presence or absence of a conscious purpose, enjoyment of the procedure for its own sake, a varied and rather wide range of activity, adaptation to ability and stage of development, immediate attention. Work means action directed by one's self or others, a conscious purpose in the result to be attained whether or not there is enjoyment of the procedure, a fairly narrow range and variety of activity, possible lack of complete adaptation to the individual, probably derived attention. Drudgery connotes that the work is imposed by another, that the purpose is forgotten or so remote as not to motivate — in any case the purpose is not within the present procedure — there is frequently much repetition of a narrow range of activity, probably little adaptation to the individual, most likely forced attention.

Fusion of play and work. — In life situations there is not always the sharp distinction between play, work, and drudgery here suggested; but at the extremes we find these characteristics. Fully to enjoy some play entails work; to realize one's purpose in either work or play may involve some drudgery. Of immense value is the fact that children in their free, social play learn the necessity of work and sometimes put in a good deal of attentive, persevering effort to achieve the desired end. For example, some little girls want to play tea party; but before they do they must wash the tea set, go out to pick some berries, and lay the table.

In another setting this might be work, but when felt as a necessary preparation to the play it is done with much of the play spirit. Some boys anxious to figure as the band in a military parade will carefully practice the technique of the mouth organ, drum, whistle, or other chosen noise-maker in a way that would rejoice the heart of a teacher.

Significance of the play spirit. — So long as the school organization is as it is, and so long as civilized ideals hold sway, work and even drudgery must have a place in the education of every child, but when possible the play spirit must be encouraged, be planned for if results worth while educationally are to be obtained. For it must be remembered that the play spirit appears whenever activities are suited to the individual's capacity and stage of development, and in themselves satisfy a need.

In emphasizing the need of the play spirit in education two facts must be borne in mind. First, that the play spirit is not synonymous with the free physical activities of the child. It is much broader. It is not confined to any type of activity, nor to any age. It is characteristic of the intellectual responses just as truly as of the physical; imagination, observation, judgment, and reasoning are used in play. The constructive and æsthetic arts with their fusion of the physical, intellectual, and emotional factors are often characterized by the same spirit. In our thinking of play we have been prone to think of the earliest manifestations of it in the field of physical activity principally, and thereby have neglected the more important features. Any activity engaged in primarily for its own sake, which is in itself satisfying, is characterized by the play spirit. The second fact to be borne in mind is that play does not mean being amused, and it is not synonymous with aimlessness, and lack of results. Again, the error has been committed of taking the first immature manifestations to be the earnest for all. Think how much of time and energy a ten-year-old spends on his play, — how his resources of ingenuity, imitation, tact, judgment, perseverance, are all taxed. And think, too, of the results he gets, the ends he attains. In play, as we shall see, children evolve a task idea. They feel a responsibility to complete, to achieve, to produce results that shall be satisfying æsthetically, practically. So, too, in games, the feeling of responsibility to others may be very highly developed. Here, then, is the very opposite of aimlessness.

FACTORS INFLUENCING PLAY

Tradition. — Many folkplays are handed down by one generation of children to another without any direct teaching by adults. Some such are very ancient, their origin lost in the mists of antiquity. City children from the lower economic levels know more of these than children from the upper levels who probably have more adult contacts and control in their play periods. Different countries, different nations, and races have their own reservoir of folk material in play as well as in story from which their children are supplied. In spite of these differences there is considerable psychological resemblance, as studies of Chinese, Persian, Kaffir, Samoan children show. Some religions have traditions of their own influencing play. They may deny the right of children to play after certain ages. Chinese girls and Russian-Jewish boys have been specially limited this way. Some forms of play may be taboo for one sex, as is frequently true among primitive people — or for all, as for example playing cards, dancing, going to the theater. Play itself may be frowned upon, or forbidden on certain days. Conversely, religious pageants, festivals, ceremonials offer opportunity for dramatic participation by adults and children alike.

Topography, climate, season, fashion. — Whether children live in the mountains, by large bodies of water, by small streams, or dry plains makes a difference in the outdoor sports they will enjoy; so too with the presence of wooded areas, rocks, sand. All of these contrast with the concrete paving and brick walls of the city child's environment, or the back yards, lawns, and quieter streets of the suburban dweller. As an extreme instance of the effect of climate, it is obvious that snow and ice sports are unknown in warmer latitudes. For some children they are seasonal affairs, as are bathing and boating. Marbles, kite-flying, jumping rope, football, bonfire making, use of fireworks are fairly closely tied up with seasonal traditions. Unexplained fads and fashions sweep over communities, too, introducing new games, reviving old ones.

Space, companions, time. — Plays that are largely physical, which include running, chasing, throwing, jumping, swinging, as well as the various ball games need space in which to be played. Crowded city streets offer no inducements and the law forbids their use as playgrounds. Consequently the bodies of children in most slum districts suffer for want of legitimate exercise. Plays which involve numbers, which necessitate group work and teamwork, also need space. Lacking a place for such games the characters and mental alertness of children suffer. The opportunities for the development of honesty, of generosity, of co-operation, of sacrificing individual pleasure for the good of the majority are lessened; all these and many more of the characteristics most worth while in adults are poorly developed, simply because the children did not have a place to play. Opportunities in the way of playgrounds more or less well equipped are absolutely necessary for the rich development of childhood. Later on, it is equally important that youth should learn the use of the school buildings, club rooms, etc. Play does not cease with childhood though the character of it changes.

On the other hand, some country boys who have all the space needed have not enough playmates of suitable age and strength to form the two teams of size desirable for some of our ball games. Children from homes of economic stress may lack time to play; likewise those from homes of wealth where their time is so closely budgeted and supervised that there is practically none left for free choice in play equipment.

Equipment, toys. — Toys and play materials are necessary to bring out some features of play. They are partly aids to physical development, partly aids to the imagination, partly agencies to perfect craftsmanship. Without play materials children have a starved, stunted life. True, they show ingenuity in the poor slum districts by using ashes, dirt, paper, and stick refuse, but in both their fiction and construction play they miss a great deal that children more happily provided for learn easily.

Toys may be thought of essentially as things with capabilities of movement. Examples of those that incite the whole body to movement are such as kiddy cars, hockey sticks and pucks, horizontal bars, and other gymnastic equipment. Those facilitating speed in movement are such things as sleds, roller skates, automobiles, gliders. Inviting skill and grace are some of the above, also canoes, skis, balls. Those that give power over distance may be illustrated by sling shots, flash mirrors, radios. Examples of those that move in surprising ways, that seem to defy gravity, are jack-in-the-box, tops, magnets, soap bubbles, kites. Movement and noise are interestingly combined in the rattle, toy drum, firecrackers. Small models of objects adults use, which can be moved in countless ways, are doll houses and furniture, laundry sets, trains, etc. Plastic materials, clay, sand, blocks, erector outfits, textile materials, cardboard, wood, and so on are some of the most important play materials.

Mechanical toys, those that do everything themselves once they are wound up, are seldom chosen spontaneously at any age. After the first amusement at its antics has passed the interest changes either to discovering what makes it work — this from boys, mostly — or to using the object in a more complex imaginative game. Better a simple toy that will stand manipulation and investigation than the complicated machinery that gets out of order if not delicately handled. The "do with" toys that permit child activity, and invite construction or fiction plays are the type most profitable to select.

Social maturity. — Very little children do not play together, though the presence of other children, or of adults may stimulate them to greater activity. Contacts with others in the nursery school age are transient. Two or three children may play with similar toys, but even in the kindergarten there is more individualistic play in company with other children than real play with them. All through life this pleasure in *solitary play* can keep up, but other types are also enjoyed. The first group play is in a loose organization. Either imaginative plays, or construction plays — especially among boys — call for reciprocity in action, and so three, four, or five children are drawn together. The older children may also permit younger ones to share in more active games. The numbers required are undefined, very few rules exist, if any, there is no definite goal to win. Tag is a good illustration of this sort of *undefined group* game, just as are such occupations as playing house, telling stories, athletic stunts. This form, too, persists through life, and is specially likely to occur when large groups of people, strange to each other, meet for a brief time. The next step in advance, seen from nine years old on is the *double group* game. Here, since competition and rivalry are strong factors, participants try to match sides evenly for strength and numbers before beginning. There is a definite goal, and more or less complex rules. Prisoner's base, charades, tug of war illustrate this form. The difference in group consciousness with these is that children must learn to evaluate each other's abilities in the light of the aim of the occupation, which is not necessary for the undefined group type.

A fourth type, the *pair, or double pair*, develops in middle childhood too. Checkers, bridge, tennis are examples of this, with very different requirements of mental or physical activity. It differs from two or four children just playing together just as a pair of anything differs from a couple. There is opposed action, a strong feeling for partnership, a control of all movement in the light of the others' behavior. The fifth type, the *team game* proper is appreciated in and around puberty. Hockey, football, basket ball are examples of this. True, smaller children play with footballs, hockey sticks, play at baseball; but their play is a practice of the individual skills that are needed in the game, and, so far as the group feeling is concerned, they are either an aggregation of units or a quarrelsome group of the double group type. The team proper is a close knit organization, each member having his own, differentiated responsibilities which he must carry out with constant reference to the movements of all others. Self-sacrifice may be in order for the good of the group. Adolescence is the time when several varieties of team games are intensely enjoyed.

Age differences. — The order of this development is away from mere physical and sensory activity towards that involving more of the intellectual factors; away from the individualistic towards the social and competitive. Besides this change in the forms used in play, there are other changes of equal importance, especially in the complexity of the activity. The early plays are comparatively simple, but as the child grows older the plays are more complex. This change results in greater organization and the plays become games, with rules which must be carried out by all the participants. The increasing complexity and organization of the plays necessitate the introduction of elements of work within the activity as means to an end.

Roughly, the kinds of play enjoyed at different ages are as follows: during infancy sensory and perceptual plays predominate, with the developing tendencies to general physical activity, locomotion, manipulation, and vocalization. The responses are crude and, at first, seem almost the result of random movements. Before seven, children engage in play rather than play games; it is pre-eminently the toy age, with imitation and imagination as new developing factors. From seven to ten play is decreasingly solitary, increasingly competitive, involving much physical exercise such as running, jumping, throwing, hitting, climbing, also quieter manipulation, more sustained group dramatization, collecting and hoarding. From nine to twelve or so the greatest variety of games is played; for to the tendencies already functioning is added more general mental activity helped out by wider information, shown in guessing games, wider reading, the interest in language. Abilities are developed by rivalry in ball play, swimming, construction work, jumping the rope, doll-dressmaking, the use of words and the like, while there is an added love of more passive movements such as swinging. The rise of the gang spirit, inciting to greater possibilities of adventure, is one of the most important tendencies of this pubescent age. In the teens doll-play, chasing, imitative, and mere make-believe games decline, whereas rivalry, teamwork, games of chance, rhythmic movement, athletics of all sorts gain in favor. Now is the time of highly organized activity, and of the elimination of many earlier forms of imaginative play. Adolescent boys are more fond of running games than are girls, specialize on fewer, organize better, play intellectual games, and games of chance less. There seems a craving for tests of endurance in the later adolescent years. The hardest feats, the most dangerous sports, the hazards calling for extremes of strength and skill are eagerly undertaken by the eighteen- and nineteen-year-olds. The change from level to level is a very gradual one, and the difference is not so much in the incorporation of new elements as in the change of emphasis on those already present.

STUDIES OF PLAY

Extensive observation. — Studies of this type fall roughly into three classes: (1) those made on young children in a more or less controlled environment, (2) studies by single observers, usually in large cities, (3) recreational surveys.

Examples of the first are by Hetzer, Van Alstyne, Bott,[1] Bridges, Farwell, Garrison.[1] The findings disclose that raw material toys (blocks, sand, clay, etc.), are most enjoyed by little children, whereas pattern toys (peg and board, colored cardboard, beads) are neglected, and that mechanical toys have little if any value. Between two and six there is a rise of interest in balls, crayons, blocks. Even very little boys are more interested in construction play with blocks than are girls, and choose active plays with a wagon, dump truck, trains of cars more often than girls do. Girls are more interested than boys in household and doll materials, clay, crayons, and choose more sedentary occupations, such as with small cubes, scissors,

[1] See bibliography at the end of the volume.

wooden animals. Paper and cardboard construction is not often chosen by either sex. All need help in the correct use of materials. Girls more than boys need to be definitely shown the way to successful manipulation; boys' social contacts more often present problems. The greatest length of time little children willingly spend in one chosen occupation varies from six minutes at four years old to about an hour — this last if it is a favorite, absorbing play. The average number of different things played with in a forty-five minute period changes from five at two years old to twenty-nine at five and a half. Only two or three materials are played with 10 per cent of the time or more; most materials are played with less than 5 per cent of the time. Little talking to other children occurs. At two and a half about 90 per cent of children play individually, and at five and a half over 70 per cent.

Examples of the second sort of study are by Hetzer in Vienna, Chase [1] in New York City; examples of the third, made by numerous observers in various cities and towns, are the Ipswich Report, the California Inquiry, the Cleveland Survey, the Report of the Committee on Street Play carried on in twenty cities of sixteen different states.[2] Valuable for the purposes these observations served, *e.g.*, estimating the need of play space and play supervisors, they can touch only one sort of play life, and fail to reach much that is significant for child development. Some of the findings from them are that scarcely any construction play takes place in the streets, and that little opportunity for the creative attitude arises. Between five and eleven years old about one fifth of the children engage in group play. The youngest ones may watch or join the group but do not participate. After three years old they will imitate the older ones, but do not really take part; after four they are able to imitate sequences of action, and seem to enjoy very definite directions as to where, when, and how to move in the

[1] Chase, J. H., "Street games of New York City," *Ped. Sem.*, v. 12, 1905.
[2] Reeves, W. R., "Report of commission on street play," *Jo. Ed. Soc.*, v. 24, 1931.

game. From seven to ten seem the most important years for learning group games, for getting the function pleasure from social groupings. After ten, there is considerably more freedom of movement within the group, and, once the general aim of the group play has been defined, a more creative, fiction pleasure develops. Boys are rather in advance of girls in their social reactions. Between eleven and thirteen the percentage of girls observed joining in group play dropped to around six, one symptom of the pre-pubertal anti-social phase. With boys, this shows in the ages thirteen to fifteen.

Reeves, summarizing the observations in twenty cities, stresses the amount of idle, disorganized fooling that goes on. Two thirds of the children were boys between six and fifteen years old. Of the average of 40 per cent of children seen really playing, very few engaged in organized games. About a hundred and fifty different kinds of games were seen, ball games of some sort being most popular; basket ball and pass ball were two organized, team games found. The list of most popular games given by Chase in an earlier study of one city does not agree with this composite finding.

Questionnaire and check list. — Monroe [1] and Croswell, [2] inspired by Stanley Hall, made extensive studies by the questionnaire method. McGhee [3] presented a list of activities from which children were asked to check their favorites. Altogether, over nineteen thousand children between six and eighteen years old were included in these studies. The results were analyzed. Findings show the popularity of ball games, and games involving running and chasing. Both co-operation and rivalry were stronger among boys than among girls. Girls play fewer running games at all ages than boys, and fewer after nine or ten years old. Interest in games of chance rises rapidly after ten, with girls.

[1] Monroe, W. S., "Play interests of children," *Amer. Ed. Rev.*, v. 4, 1899.
[2] Croswell, T. R., "Amusements of Worcester school children," *Ped. Sem.*, v. 6, 1899.
[3] McGhee, Z., "Play life of some South Carolina children," *Ped. Sem.*, v. 7, 1900.

The most thorough study by the check list technique is that made by Lehman and Witty [1] in 1923–1926. Their Play Quiz consists of two hundred items from which children from the third grade up checked those they had played during the preceding week. Over twenty-four thousand returns were received from rural and city children, at different seasons of the year. In addition, seventeen hundred younger children were investigated by the oral method of mentioning favorite games at home and at school.

These large numbers offset those limitations inherent in the method which are due to children's suggestibility and inaccuracy in reporting. They do not gauge the intensity of interest by the frequency or persistence of any child in a certain play occupation, nor do they analyze the quality of the play as an observer can do.

The study confirmed the boys' greater love of competition, of active, vigorous games, of organized games. Girls showed up as more individualistic, less active, playing language games and reading more often than boys. Below the third grade playing house, playing school, and playing with dolls ranked as the favorite occupations for girls, playing ball for boys. A greater variety of games was checked between eight and one half and ten and one half, when also the largest sex differences were found. Older subjects gradually ceased checking such games as tag, hiding and finding things, ring games, and mere imitative games. Changes in play interests were very gradual, however. The curve of loss of interest of boys in playing cowboy, and of girls in playing with dolls follows almost exactly the curve of physiological age and pubescence. Individual differences were very great, and more important than age or seasonal differences. Children of superior mental age, the gifted children, indulged in relatively more solitary plays, especially reading, while those of lower mental age, the duller ones, avoided reading and were more dependent on participation in group plays. Country boys under ten reported fewer different activities

[1] Lehman and Witty, *The Psychology of Play Activities.*

than city boys of the same age, a condition that was reversed in the older ages. Rural boys were less mature in their play interests, particularly with regard to group games. Children in the fifth and sixth grades who reported fewest play activities with other children were ranked highest by their teachers in industry, self-confidence, perseverance, dependability, and ambition, while those reporting plays requiring more social participation were ranked lowest by their teachers in those same traits, but highest in personal attractiveness.

FUNCTION, FICTION, FACTUM SEQUENCES

Movements. — Pleasure in the various sensory qualities experienced in muscle exercise has been termed function pleasure by Charlotte Bühler. *Function* play is characteristic of young infants' movements as they get acquainted with their bodies. Later, the joys of coasting, swinging, just running and shouting, are of this function type. It is our first approach to new means of locomotion provided the skill requisite is not too difficult to learn. So, too, when mastery is gained, in skating, rapid driving in automobiles, surf-board riding, etc., function pleasure persists through life.

As early as the third month this pure functional exercise begins to change. When babies see and attend to their movements, repeat them more slowly, the stage of self-imitation has set in. Before the end of the first year babies can imitate simple movements made by others, such as shaking the head, pounding, drumming, vocal cadences in pitch. During the second year, around eighteen months old, a further change takes place. The ability to walk and to steer a "kiddy car" has opened new avenues of function play. Exploration and mastery of space have proceeded rapidly; also, in acquisition of language, sounds have acquired symbolic meaning. Then, and not till then, movements with objects take on symbolic meaning too; *fiction* play is possible. The kiddy car becomes an automobile, the child on hands and knees is transformed into a barking dog. Fiction play is imitative at first, later creative. Rhythmic plays are invented, stunts are devised, combined into a circus play. Gradually this too gives way to the interest in *the result* of movement. Skill is sought in marksmanship, in ball throwing, grace is found desirable in skating, good form in dancing and so on, and the *third stage* is reached.

Materials. — The same changes occur with toys and play objects. At first toys are simply objects for *function* pleasure. They are all treated alike, lifted, banged, sucked, dropped, and so on. With the acquisition of sound symbols in speech toys too are perceived as things-in-themselves, with differing possibilities. *Fiction* play is possible. This is always imitative before it is creative, a point the significance of which seems to have escaped many educational philosophers. A doll is perceived as a re-presentation, and the first imaginative play re-presents scenes in which children themselves have been participants. The doll is kissed, wrapped up, laid to sleep, put in a wagon and wheeled around. Two blocks pushed along are a "choochoo" car. Children play house, school, car conductor, grocery store, traffic policeman. Following the imitative phase of fiction play comes the creative, when fancy no longer copies and mimics so faithfully, but combines in new relationships, adds details, changes forms, and invents situations. Plays are composed. The richer the background of factual knowledge and of observed and imitated behavior the more material there is for creative imagination to use. As pure symbolism gives way to a desire for *similarity to reality*, the *third stage of factum play* with objects has arrived.

Construction play. — A similar sequence is clearly seen here. At first there is mere fumbling manipulation, or watching others' activity. Build a tower of blocks for babies, and all they want is to knock it down and watch it being built again. About eighteen months old they will pause to regard the result, to contemplate the finished effect. This consciousness of product appears first in observing the action of others, later is transferred to the products of their own activity. Between eighteen and twenty-three months Bühler found about two thirds of all babies thus showing perception of product, and by three years old all of them. Once this relationship of activity and finished appearance is sensed the attitude to play materials changes. No longer is it "idle play," it is a creative work idea. This preponderance of construction play over fiction play comes between four and five years old for most children.

The factum play itself, the clear idea of result, shows three phases. For instance, in playing with blocks they start to build by adding block to block in a one-dimensional way, either flat or vertically. Next they build in two or three dimensions in exploratory fashion, no plan in mind, just building to see what will happen. (1) On regarding the finished product they will name it. (2) Next comes the phase of having an idea during the process of building, born of the imagined resemblance noted. (3) Last of all comes the definite stating of an aim before beginning the activity. This last is the work idea.

This sequence may be noted with each new kind of material. For instance, in drawing, after the first aimless scribbling movements (mere function pleasure) comes the imitative movement and localized scribble of the fiction stage. (1) The naming of the observed product comes next. "See, this is a man I've made." (2) Next comes naming while drawing as new fancied resemblances catch the attention. "I guess this is going to be a kite; no it's a butterfly." (3) Last comes the goal idea well conceived, "I'm going to draw a house." At three years old no goal idea is present; at four, about one third of the children name their drawing beforehand, at five 80 per cent of them, by six all of them. In building, however, this work idea is present for practically all by three years old. In clay, sand, and similar material, 90 per cent of them reach the pre-plan stage between five and six. Along with this preconceived plan is the intensity of the drive to complete, to achieve. "I *must* build," "I *must* get it finished" is heard. The task idea, the feeling of responsibility, is there, with all that that involves ethically.

This is the factum stage, looked at in another light. The product matters. The building must have windows, a firm roof;

the wheels must work, the boat must sail. The craftsman has
evolved. By six, then, with the work idea, and the task idea
present, children are ready for the more formal instruction
of school which stresses achievement of results, quality of
product, practicality and excellence of workmanship. There is
gradual development here. At first a bare scheme of a thing,
with the main features prominent, is produced. An increasing
desire for reality, shown markedly from eight years old on,
leads to better attention to detail, to observation of the structure
of objects. Mere outside appearance no longer pleases them,
they strive to re-create the details of inner parts. Boys develop
earlier than girls in this respect. While girls are still satisfied
with approximate resemblance to the model in what they make
boys show interest in the mechanics involved, reason practically
as to how things work and toil very earnestly at their own
crafts. The need to make their own products efficient becomes
increasingly intense after eleven years old. Girls' degree of
interest in this requirement is considerably lower as well as
slower in developing. A fifteen-year-old girl is about on the
level of a ten- to eleven-year-old boy in the feeling of responsibility in craftsmanship.

Language. — Similar stages can be traced in wholly different
fields. For instance, the interest in language is shown *function-
ally* as infants enjoy the sounds they make, and as little children
talk along just for the exercise of talking. Gradually the *fiction*
or tool use of language supersedes the first. Stories are told,
new words and their relationships are studied. Here, too, the
imitative phase precedes the inventive. The first stories copy
pretty faithfully what they have heard; later, details are deliberately changed and new situations created. At about eleven
years or later an invented language is intriguing. This is mostly
imitative, in that the mother tongue is disguised or trans-
literated. Many never pass to the truly creative phase of
language play. The third, *factum* stage, that of achievement, is
reached when adolescents are careful to select the best words to
express the exact meaning, when the balance and style of the

whole composition assume importance. Again, in this factum stage, the preconceived goal is not the first phase. Too many of us still write it down and then read to see how it will sound, or develop the argument as we go along rather than plan from the beginning.

Social relationships. — Here too the same sequent stages are seen. (*a*. Function.) Pleasure in merely being together comes first. The shared occupations are quite casual, no purpose, no organization develops. Personality possibilities are explored. (*b*. Fiction.) A group consciousness arises, a leader emerges, and simultaneous directed group action occurs. This, too, is imitative at first. The club's name may be highly imaginative but its pursuits are not original. At this point development ceases in many groups. Gangs and clubs exist for all ages primarily to minister to their own functional pleasure with a bare scheme of organization and merely imitative occupations. Some go further. The group mind invents something interestingly new for the club to do — still as a self-contained unit. (*c*. Factum.) The more serious-minded groups conceive a responsibility in their occupations, make not the club's existence their aim and object, but the club's achievement. They conceive a goal, a product worth while in itself, not just for the sake of the club. This goal may be more clearly defined while the group works, or, in well-seasoned groups, be predetermined. The group organizes into a team, integrates or federates with other groups, and perhaps makes a contribution to human progress in a larger unit.

EDUCATIONAL IMPLICATIONS

Health values. — Active plays are indispensable for muscle development. From the infants' kickings and stretchings, through the trotting about, bending and stooping of little children, the running, jumping, throwing games of middle and later childhood to the endurance feats of adolescent athletes, the stimulation to growth by exercise is obvious. The lungs, too, get a chance for better functioning from the more active games as well as from the shouting that so inevitably accompanies them. Crippled, blind children suffer in their physical development not only directly, because of their handicap, but indirectly for lack of the rapid, hard exercise of co-ordinated muscles which the normal child so easily indulges in. The needs of the individual child must not be overlooked in our mass planning for physical play. For all, skill and grace may be fostered as ideals.

Information values. — Since first-hand contact with things offers the best opportunity for discovering their physical properties, it is clear that the exploratory plays and manipulative activities of little children are of great importance in gaining knowledge. Criticism of their activities while they are still in the early functional pleasure stage with some new material, is not helpful. Later, in the construction plays and in hobbies, there is endless opportunity for creative ingenuity to express itself. To avoid fruitless, scattered miscellanies we need to direct children's observations to the principles behind the facts, the relationships and scientific laws which await discovery and use. The reading interests alone tap a vast field of information. Here the teacher's privilege is obvious.

Social values. — Before ten years old the need to be generous, to be brave, to play fair, has been vividly experienced in social play. Loyalty to the group, how to be a good sport, are priceless lessons in character training, learned through doing rather than from moral homilies. Adolescents find problems to solve in playing the team, in winning or losing gracefully and courteously as well as honorably. Prejudices of caste, race, religion tend to be forgotten in the common effort towards a goal on the playground. A nation with a democratic ideal must help its younger generation exemplify that ideal in its happiest activities.

In general. — In their play children learn to observe quickly, to judge, to weigh values, to pick out essentials, to give close attention; they learn the value of co-operation, to recognize the rights of others as well as to insist on their own being recognized; they learn the meaning of freedom through law; they learn the value and function of work and the joy of accomplishment. No wonder that play is regarded by many as the most important educational factor of them all. A child who does not play not only misses much of the joy of childhood, but he can never be a fully developed adult. He will lack in many of the qualities most worth while because many of the avenues of growth were unused and neglected during the most plastic period of his life.

Supervision, wise and unwise. — Supervision and direction of play offer another opportunity although of a different character. Not only must there be nothing to inhibit the development of an inborn tendency, but often such a tendency needs stimulating. The wise guidance and suggestion of an adult will often furnish opportunities which the children, if left to themselves, would never have discovered. Such supervision will also conserve the nature of individual children, in some cases protecting them from themselves, in others encouraging them to fresh endeavors. The social, intellectual, and moral elements are more likely to be stressed and encouraged if there is supervision than otherwise. The children are not allowed to play on a lower level of development when they are ready for a higher. The possibility of work in play is made much of, although the relative value of the two is emphasized. Wise supervision, of course, does not force but only suggests and encourages.

Valuable as supervision is, not all play should be supervised. Complete freedom is handicapped by the presence of an adult. When play is supervised there are some serious dangers which must be avoided if it is to be a truly educational factor. All these dangers grow out of the fact that adults do not in the first place fully understand the nature and value of play, or in the second place do not study closely enough the stage of development of the children they are supervising. As a result, it is often the case that the teacher or supervisor introduces plays for which the children are not ready. It is difficult for the supervisor not to emphasize the intellectual factors along the line, and all ages of children are not equally ready for that phase of play. Another danger is that the supervisor will push the complex, organized game before the children are ready for it. The simple plays, without many rules, quickly played and easily changed, must come first. Perhaps the greatest danger of all in supervised play is that the initiative will come from the adult instead of from the child. When this is true, even though children seek the direction and guidance, one of the greatest values of play is gone. The initiative, the motive force must come from the children if their play is to them really natural. When there is too much direction the essential character of the activity may be changed for the children, and what in form is play may be work; when this happens, the value of both play and work is diminished. The very fact that the supervisor or teacher is an adult, and that the players are children, makes educative supervision very difficult. Adults must efface themselves more, they must play the rôle of observers more effectively, the doctrine of "hands off" must be applied more often in dealing with children both in their work and in their play if they are to reap the full benefit of their activity.

PRACTICAL EXERCISES

1. Observe the neighborhood closely for about a quarter of a mile square in a city, more in the suburbs or country. Enumerate the facilities and conditions for play such as, (*a*) space; (*b*) topography, including slopes, gutters, vacant lots, sand, clay or rock, trees and grass, steps, area railings, low walls, etc.; (*c*) physical safety, such as conditions after dark, amount of traffic, street railways; (*d*) moral suggestions, such as number of saloons, churches, libraries, moving-picture theaters, overcrowded living conditions; (*e*) points of interest to children, such as toy and candy stores, fire engine houses, garages, fire hydrants, building going on, exposed fruit stalls, etc.

  Make a map, if time allows, and enter these features.

2. In the neighborhood you surveyed spend a total of from three to six hours at different times, in periods not shorter than ten minutes, at various times of day, to observe the play activity going on. Take advantage also of the school playground, back yards that can be seen from a window, and other places where children congregate. Take notes as you observe, without attracting the children's attention. Enter the time of day, the date, the weather conditions, the special topographical

conditions. Count the children of each size. Give their appropriate ages.
State exactly what they are doing. Be on the lookout for imaginative
games, for traditional games, for quiet, sedentary games if any. Note
the incidence of quarrels. Distinguish carefully games of the double
group type from the true team game.

Symbols in C.	Q.	quiet,	A.	active
	M.	moderate,		
in D.	Sk.	interest in skill	R.	repetition
	S.	sensory enjoyment	Rh.	rhythm
	Con.	constructive interest	A.	æsthetic interest
	Cp.	competition	L.	language interest
	D.	dramatic imagination	P.	problem solving
	Ch.	chasing		
in E.	I	individual	II	undefined group
	III	double group	IV	pair or double pair
			V	organized team

Compare your record with those of others. What do they show about
children's interests?

Do your results confirm Reeves, in that about 60 per cent are not
playing, just idling? Do they confirm Hetzer, that very few girls participate in group play? What differences do you find in the poorest
section of the district observed?

Activity described	A size, sex	B age	C physical	D intellectual	E social
Digging in dirt, making mud pies	3 g.	4 or 5	M.	S. Con. D.	II
Roller skating	2 g. 3 b.	7 to 11	A.	Sk. S.	I
Baseball and bats	7 b.	9 or 10	A.	Sk. Cp.	III
Cross-tag	2 b. 6 g.	8 ?	A.	Ch. Cp.	II
Cross word puzzle	1 g.	12	Q.	L. P.	I
Mumbly peg	2 b.	9?	M.	Sk. Cp. P.	IV
Hopscotch	5 g.	8 to 10	M.	Sk. Cp.	II

Analyze the activities seen from three points of view, the physical, intellectual, social. State whether the physical aspect was active, moderately active, or quiet. Estimate which of the following intellectual features made the play enjoyable: interest in developing skill, pure sensory enjoyment, construction interest, competition, dramatic imagination, rhythm, æsthetic interest, language interest, puzzle or problem solving, chasing and being chased.

From the social point of view analyze into individualistic, undefined group, double group, pair or double pair, organized team.

Organize and tabulate your findings from the several days' observation according to the sample record on page 134.

3. Visit a nursery school or kindergarten. (*a*) Count the children present. (*b*) Make a diagram of the room, locating play apparatus. (*c*) Record the occupations of the children. (*d*) Ten minutes later record them again. Repeat this for four or five successive records, tabulating as shown below. (*e*) Note any real play groups, not simply children playing individually at the same thing as others near. How long do any such groups maintain themselves? (*f*) Describe any beginnings of a fight. What caused it? (*g*) Describe any instance of spontaneous help given by one child to another. (*h*) What sex differences do you note? (*i*) Check the proportions of function pleasure play, fiction play, factum play, by numbers of children recorded at each 15-minute interval. (*j*) What educative leads for information, for skill, arose? (*k*) What social adjustment problems occurred?

TWENTY-FIVE CHILDREN

Occupations	10 a. m.		10.15		10.30	
Individual carpentry	3 b.	2 g.	2 b.	1 g.	1 b.	1 g.
Group with large floor blocks	4. b.		3 b.			
Doll-play, bed, carriage		3 g.		4 g.		2 g.
Toys at sand table	2 b.		1 b.		2 b.	3 g.
Watching rabbit	2 b.			1 g.	1 b.	
Painting at an easel	1 b.	1 g.	2 b.	1 g.		1 g.
Pasting, cutting pictures	1 b.	3 g.	1 b.	3 g.	2 b.	4 g.
Crayon work		1 g.	1 b.		1 b.	
Imaginative play, toy telephone		1 g.		2 g.		
Painting clay bowls previously made					4 b.	1 g.
Dragging toys on floor			2 b.		1 b.	
Looking at pictures		1 g.	1 b.		1 b.	

4. Make an individual observation on a selected child in the same environment (on another visit if possible). (a) Having diagrammed the floor, trace the child's movements during a continuous 15-minute period; checking off each minute. (b) Describe the occupation as minutely as possible, commenting on dexterity, general body balance, distractibility, perseverance. (c) How many times does the child seek contact with other children? (d) Describe the social attitude as aggressive, passive, imitative, resistive, etc. Repeat for another 15-minute period an hour later. Repeat another day. What does this disclose about the child?

5. Make a similar observation to that suggested in 3 above, out of doors in a play space for little children.

6. Make out a list of sixty or more plays and games you enjoyed from as far back as you remember up to eighteen years of age. Arrange them in a list according to the age at which you played them. Tabulate as for question 2 above. How do your results agree with the facts brought out in the chapter? What special factors influenced your play as a child?

7. Give the Lehman and Witty Play Quiz to children in the fifth grade or above. If intelligence test results are available compare the ten highest I.Q. children with the ten lowest for (a) number of items checked, (b) type of activity from the standpoint of social participation. How do the results compare with the findings of Lehman and Witty?

8. What additional play facilities would you suggest are needed in the district in which you observed for 1 and 2 above?

9. Visit a large toy store during its pre-Christmas display. List such articles as you would advise parents to get for children under three, under seven, seven to ten, ten to thirteen, in the early teens.

FOR DISCUSSION

1. What does a teacher mean by saying "Stop playing now, and get to work," or "You haven't worked at this, you've only played"?

2. Is following a hobby play or work? Why?

3. Describe and illustrate the attention characterizing play, drudgery.

4. How would you bring the play spirit into a task children are likely to consider drudgery?

5. What is the chief significance of the work idea, the task idea seen in construction play?

6. What are the mental health values of play, and the educational implications therefrom?

7. Discuss these statements: — Competition as a motive is an ineffectual appeal at the kindergarten level. Girls' choices of games offer fewer opportunities for social learning than do boys'. A child who has not

arrived at the work idea in his construction play by six years old is likely to be retarded in his moral growth.

8. Schwendener finds that third-grade children spontaneously play a very few, only, of the games taught them in their gymnastic periods during the first three grades. What might this suggest?

SELECTED REFERENCES

ADDAMS, J. *The Spirit of Youth and the City Street.* Pages 51–106.

BLANCHARD, P. *The Child and Society.* Chs. 5, 8.

BOTT, H. "Observation of play activities in a nursery school." *Gen. Psy. Mon.*, v. 4 *1.

BUSH AND RIGBY. "The play hour." *Psych. Clinic*, v. 18, 1929.

HALL, G. S. *Youth.* Ch. 6.

HULSON, E. L. "Block constructions of four-year-old children." *Jo. Juv. Res.*, v. 14 *3, 1930.

KNIGHT, H. R. *Play and Recreation in a Town of 6000.*

LEE, J. *Play in Education.* Ch. 11.

LEHMAN AND WITTY. *The Psychology of Play Activities.*

LEHMAN AND WITTY. "A study of play in relation to pubescence." *Jo. Soc. Psych.*, v. 1, 1930.

STERN, W. *Psychology of Early Childhood.* Chs. 19–26.

VAN ALSTYNE, D. *Play Behavior and Choice of Play Materials of Pre-School Children.*

CHAPTER VII

ATTENTION AS BASIC TO LEARNING

ATTENTION-GIVING

Satisfyingness. — The roots of the conduct and feelings of man have been found in his original equipment in terms of neurone connections and neurone behavior-series which in definite situations are ready to act. Not only are there neurone connections in terms of the reflex arcs that make possible the reaching, fighting behavior of man, but there are also synapses between the sensory neurones and ganglia in the nerve centers whose action gives rise to sensations of all kinds. To experience sensations and have things happen in consciousness is, in and of itself, satisfying to man; to see and hear and feel things happening in the physical world brings satisfaction, but to be the cause of such happenings is still keener joy. Further, because consciousness, or mental life is felt as worth while for its own sake man has gone far in the field of intellectual attainment. So far as present opinion goes, it is in the possession of this love of general mental activity that man so far surpasses the lower animals. Consciousness in them merely plays the part of adapting physical responses to physical situations, and is worth while, satisfying to them as soon as it performs that function; whereas in man it not only connects mental states which serve as situations with mental states which are responses, but that process in and of itself, apart from the results, is satisfying.

Original stimuli. — Attention is the fundamental tendency which leads to other mental states. As a matter of original nature, man has the tendency to prolong certain situations, and of disposing himself to be more effectively impressed by them. The situations to which he thus responds are those originally

138

interesting, and his attitude toward them is that of attention. The situations to which, because of original equipment, he gives this interest and attention seem to be intense stimuli, such as strong blasts of wind, sharp pains, sudden stimuli which make sharp changes, such as loud noises coming in the midst of quiet, strange, or unusual stimuli, rhythmic or cadenced rather than monotonous stimuli, moving objects, recurrent even if faint sense perceptions, stimuli that act as signals of organic needs and "situations to which he has further tendencies to respond as by flight, repulsion, play and the like." The tendencies of visual exploration, vocalization, and manipulation alone offer an almost infinite variety of situations. The situations which progressively attract and hold the attention differ with the age and sex of the child, and it is these changes and differences that it is important for the educator to understand.

Terms used. — The psychology of attention has almost a vocabulary of its own which it may be well to review. Describing the object of interest we contrast *sensory* with *intellectual* attention. Describing the intrinsic value or secondary value of an object of interest we contrast *immediate* with *derived* attention. Describing the feeling tone we contrast *active or voluntary or forced*, all involving conscious effort, with *passive or non-voluntary*, or *free, spontaneous*. Describing the extent of the field attended to we speak of the *distribution* of attention. Describing the number of lines that can be handled by rapid shifts of attention we speak of the *division* of attention. By *span* is meant the number of stimuli that can be grasped when presented successively, such as numbers read aloud or shown. By *range* is meant the number grasped — usually by visual perception — when presented simultaneously. By *duration* is meant the length of time attention is sustained to the same object.

Individual differences. — Though we may be chiefly concerned in pointing out the differences in attention-giving which maturity and training bring, yet certain predominant types have been supposedly recognized among children as well as among adults. Thus, we notice differences in division of attention, from the so-called "single track mind" to the individual who easily keeps several activities in control with no nervous excitement. We can distinguish the *fixating* type, of sharp focus and narrow distribution who is slow to adapt, from the *fluctuating* type of roving attention, wider distribution, and quick adaptation. There are some children who, once started on a piece of work are distracted and confused by repeated directions and reminders; one direction at the outset is sufficient for them. They are referred to as the *static* sort. More frequent are those whose performance is held to a greater steadiness by repeated directions and requests to attend. We call these *dynamic*.

Pathology of attention. — Inability to cease attending to one train of thought tends towards obsession, which is symptomatic of abnormal mental health. Delusions, fixed ideas are other samples of morbid attention. When expressed in behavior governed by dominating, unreasonable impulses, we speak of a "compulsion." Conversely, inability to concentrate, a flighty wandering from one topic to another may indicate, not simply immaturity, but an acute emotional tension, or a certain class of mental illness. In either case the child should have expert diagnosis and help. More frequent is a state of dawdling indecision of many adolescents which may be explained by unwillingness to attend to an idea somewhat disagreeable in its requirements of ultimate action. If during childhood the habit of giving active attention on demand has not been formed, the adolescent will probably experience difficulty in attending long enough to an idea to reach a decision to act counter to habit, or to persist in an unattractive course of behavior.

DIFFERENCES BETWEEN ADULTS AND CHILDREN

In type of attention. — The attention of the child is primarily of the sensory type; that of the adult is more largely intellectual. The little child's world consists relatively of sense impressions and movements, which serve as the chief stimulants of attention. The root of intellectual attention is, of course, in the satisfyingness of mental activity; but even here the stimulus for these connections is for many years a sensory one. Observe a child and an adult out for a walk. The child is alive to seemingly every sense stimulus; seeing, hearing, the feeling of different movements, smelling, tasting (if allowed), handling, — while the adult is conscious of something in his surroundings, but much more absorbed in the connections, images, associations, and memories which each sense impression calls up. The practical outcome of this difference is evident. The starting point for habits of attention is in the sensory field. Ideas as concepts and abstractions become capable of holding the attention only as they are the outgrowth of experience in perceptual form; and this development is a very gradual process.

In ability to give voluntary attention. — Perhaps the most vital difference in attention as the individual passes from childhood to adulthood is the increased power to stand the strain of effort in connection with the act of attention. Some acts of attention are spontaneous. The object of attention appeals to the individual's consciousness, either for its own sake or because of some value attaching to it, in such a way that it satisfies him. There is, as Dewey puts it, an identification between the individual and his object of thought, because it satisfies some need. On the other hand, there is the type of attention which is forced. The object does not identify itself with some intrinsic need, but because of duty, or social pressure, or ideals, the individual feels he must attend, despite the effort involved. There is division, not unity, in the conscious state. A child lacks power to give forced attention, to stand the strain of effort involved and to attend in spite of it. Probably this lack of power is due both to physiological reasons and lack of practice. The natural, childlike form of attention is the spontaneous; forced attention comes, if at all, with age and training.

In breadth of field. — Children and adults also differ in the breadth of the field, the number of lines along which attention is freely given. The child's attention is more omnivorous than that of the adult. He seems to attend to anything that is novel until the novelty wears off, and as he is a newcomer lacking experience, everything is new to him. He is at the mercy of his impulses, and each one opens up a field of attention. For the adult with his broader experience, most of the everyday things have lost their novelty, and his power of concentration, due as it is to knowledge and habits, serves to lessen the number of things to which it is necessary to attend. Adults are bound by their habits; they have lost the characteristic which in childhood is so charming, that of being interested in everything. True, they accomplish more, delve deeper because of this power, but they have also narrowed their field of attention. Every habit, every interest, while it is an aid in the field to which it applies, is also a limitation. This breadth of interest and attention on the part of the child is of the utmost value and significance, educationally. Because of it, the actual interests and habits which are fixed, which are selected from the mass and made permanent, becoming the foundations of character and conduct and giving the bias to life, — these are determined by the environment and training. All nature does is to provide the fund of tendencies toward attention in all sorts of lines; education must do the rest. The effect of the narrowing of interests and attention due to this very habit-formation must be borne in mind; because of it, the teacher must see to it that Herbart's "many-sided interest" becomes a fact in the life of each child. Broad and manifold interests developed in childhood are the cure for narrowness and bigotry in adult life.

In distribution, span, and range. — Tested under laboratory conditions we find the range at six years old to be 2 or 3, by fourteen 5, where in the adult it is 4 to 6. The span at six years is 4 or 5, at eleven to twelve is 5 or 6, at fourteen 6 to 8, where the average adult span is 8. Of course this increase occurs as a matter both of growth and of training, though the small effect of practice in the function seems to point to inner growth as the chief factor in bringing about the change. This narrowness of the attention-range may account for some of the difficulty that young children have in reading long words.

In giving directions, in dictating words, teachers should take into account the size of the span or range for the age they are dealing with.

The unit thus grasped may be simple or may itself be complex. Thus, where only six unrelated letters could be attended to, grasped, and correctly reported, once group those letters in meaningful ways and six familiar words could as easily be given. If words are grouped, six well-known phrases could be grasped. The chief difference, then, is not so much the length of the span or range as the detailed complexity, and the understanding of the unit involved. As children relate impressions into meaningful wholes their apperceptive grasp increases; and as they organize and systematize their ideas so their attention is facilitated. One psychological law is that only one object of thought can be in the focus of attention at any one instant of time. This is true for all ages, but for the adult the "object" may be a whole system; and the many relationships involved, the conditions which must obtain, the most important associations, — all these may be in the margin and color the focal point, whereas with a child, few of such connections can be held. With him, it is one fact, one object, one condition, rather bare and unadorned. Any one accustomed to deal with children knows how difficult it is for them to carry in mind more than one point at a time. Ask them in nature study to notice color and form, and attention is given to either one or the other, not to both; in geography, if they are asked to determine the occupations of people in a certain section by a consideration of the climatic conditions, and of the land forms, they are very likely to work through with just one condition in mind, unable to grasp the complex situation.

The first requisite in developing power in attending to a system of thought as a whole is that the teacher shall know, first, the child's limitations, and second, just how complex is the situation. If she knows that the thing to which she is calling attention involves just so many relationships, she will not be nearly so likely to ask the impossible of the child, and

in consequence to bring about confusion and disorder.   The
process must be a very gradual one; at first, each thing is learned
almost alone and thoroughly before it is brought into a complex
situation as an element; later, as power increases, the number
of elements or relationships may be increased.

Another cause for the difference in distribution of attention
is the lack, in the child, of many mechanical habits.   An adult
can use eyes, hands, and feet in running his machine, smoke,
listen to a conversation and criticize it mentally all at the same
time.   Another can read the music and words of a song, get the
meaning, use voice with artistic effect, use hands and feet in
the piano accompaniment and still attend to the way the audience is listening.   The adult does many things at the same time,
and therefore apparently has a wider range of attention because
several of them are mechanical habits, such as need no special
attention except to start them or to overcome an obstacle of
some kind.   But with the little child the things we adults do so
easily are matters of serious attention and effort, and very
seldom can more than one thing be done at a time.   If in reading
he pays attention to the pronunciation of the words, or the
holding of his book, or the inflection and accent, he loses the
meaning; and if the meaning is in the focus of attention, the
others suffer.   If in composition work attention is given to
"good writing," the content suffers.   If in arithmetic the numer-
ical combinations have to be thought about, or the form in
which the work is put on paper, the problem involved may be
entirely lost sight of.   If the child is talking of something he
saw or heard, the hands which should have been busy sewing,
or chopping wood, or washing dishes, or fastening buttons are
idle.   Attention can be given only to one thing at a time; any
number of mechanical operations may be carried on at the same
time, but only one that requires thought.   Progress is made,
then, as operations are made mechanical; and the faster this
occurs the better for the fundamental operations in all lines of
work.   Here again it behooves the teacher to analyze the situation, to know just what she is requiring of the child, and

then to remember that nothing becomes mechanical without much attention, drill, and practice, even at the cost of possible monotony.   Because the adult has for so many years done so many things mechanically, he has forgotten that once he had to learn to do those very things, and that learning took, for the time, his full attention.

In concentration, perseverance, and duration. — The child on the average does not get so deep into his subject as the adult does.   He is more likely to be distracted by disturbances of any kind than is a mature adult.   No matter how deeply absorbed or interested he may apparently be in play or work, he still is "all ears and all eyes" as compared with the adult.   A word spoken, a sound in the street, a movement made, and his attention flashes to the distraction.   Of course, this is not always true; he can become absorbed, deeply absorbed in his play, but that is not the usual state of affairs as hour after hour he occupies himself with all sorts of things; nor can such absorption be compared in depth to that of the adult engaged in some interesting occupation, lost to the world, forgetting his meals, engagements, to whom "the house could burn down, he would not know it" might apply.   Children unquestionably lack the power of concentrated attention which characterizes the average adult.

Since distractibility may be used as a measure of concentration, attempts have been made to count the number of effective distractions to which children respond while engaged in interesting play.   The interruptions were the ordinary kind occurring in a playroom such as a person entering the room, speaking to an adult near.   Between two and three years old 90 per cent of all such distractions were effective, that is, the child looked up, or listened, stopping his play meanwhile. Between three and four 84 per cent were effective, between four and five 72 per cent, between five and six 53 per cent.   The children were least distracted from the kind of play in which they were most likely to persevere.   In the fourth year the greatest improvement in ability to concentrate was seen.

Closely allied to concentration is the duration of an act of attention. Even when no distraction occurs, a child very soon tires of one occupation, or one line of interest. His attention wanders, flitting from one thing to another, dwelling on each for but a moment.

Bott,[1] studying nursery school children where they had entire freedom in choice of play material and occupation reports the average length of time spent with one kind of material. At two years old this was 2.5 minutes, varying from 1 to 7.5 At three years old the average was 4.7 minutes, varying from 1 to 12 minutes. At four years old the average was 5.6 minutes, varying from 1 to 14 minutes. Materials such as puzzles, which challenged mental activity, engaged them longer than a toy such as the hobby horse. Mechanical toys were least attended to. Beyrl [2] reports the average maximum duration of attention, or perseverance, among sixty children, ten of each age from one to six under experimental conditions where only three choices of play material were possible. From six months to one year old this maximum was 14½ minutes: between one and two 21 minutes, between two and three 27 minutes, between three and four 50 minutes, between four and five 83 minutes, between five and six 96 minutes. Building with blocks was the most absorbing interest till three years old, and sorting objects by color between three and five.

Even the pre-school age child, then, is able to concentrate attention, and finds it easy to sustain attention when varied problem activity is initiated by himself. This principle holds throughout. Older children, like ourselves, attend to that which promises new developments, which has changing relationships, and lose interest in unvarying, mechanical, routine procedures. Looked at in another way, the chief cause for both the lack of concentration and the shortness of the period of attention is the poverty of mental content. Since attention cannot be held

[1] Bott, H., "Observation of play activities in a nursery school," *Gen. Psy. Mon.*, v. 4, *1, 1928.
[2] Beyrl, F., " Konzentration und Ausdauer im frühen Kindesalten," *Zeitschr. f. Psych.*, v. 107, 1928.

on the same object for more than a few seconds, the object must change or the line of thought develop, if either is to hold the attention. Because of his want of experience and knowledge, the child has few associations in connection with any one situation, he sees but few possibilities, and consequently he soon exhausts the situation, whether it be mental or physical. He cannot continue to attend to it for very long because he comes to the end of his material. Power comes with age because of the added possibilities each situation possesses, just as a matter of mere experience; but increase of power is hastened if associations, facts, relations are definitely made in lines where attention is desired. The more knowledge an individual has in any line, other things being equal, the greater is the probability both of the depth of his attention and the length of the period of attention. This is clearly seen in watching children study. Left to themselves they read over the lesson, once, twice, or more times, and that is the end of it; they have come to the end of their resources, there is nothing left in the material so far as they can see, and their attention wanders. The value of various suggestions and questions in connection with their study is evident, if merely as a means of holding attention to the material for a longer period of time. Another practical application of these facts is its bearing on the length of school periods. The younger the child the shorter the period; the less in any given subject you can call on the child's experience the shorter the period. The length of period, therefore, must vary not only with the age of the child but also with the character and newness of the subject.

Not only will experience and knowledge of a subject increase the power of concentration and the length of the attention period, but practice in attending also plays a large part. The child who has never been required to attend for more than fifteen or twenty minutes consecutively, despite the presence of all the necessary conditions, finds it very difficult to do so. Adults in general have so fixed their habits of attention through mere usage that one hour, two hours and a half, or some other length of time is their "working period," at the end of which they become restless, their attention wanders, and their time of good work is over. Habit is a large factor here as elsewhere; and if power is desired, if rapid progress is economical, then a habit of protracted attention-giving must be formed by the application of the laws of learning, exercise, and effect.

SUGGESTIONS FOR TEACHERS

Attention and learning. — Though it is not true that nothing is learned without attention, yet it is clear that attention favors clearness of perception and therefore is a fundamental condition of correct and rapid learning where sense organs are involved. We know, too, that a physical adaptation of posture with a certain muscular tenseness is associated with greater alertness mentally to sensory stimuli. Teachers are justified in objecting to slouching, to limp leaning against supports when concentrated attention perceptually is desired.

Attention reduces the time taken to memorize, and helps prevent errors in the repetitions necessary to memorization. Training given in good methods of this type of learning will include directing critical attention to testing and appraising the correctness of reproduction as well as to the meaning of what is learned. That such training is often neglected, especially by music teachers, may be inferred from the errorful, inattentive practicing many children do. In reasoning processes, attention must be given to noticing likenesses and differences so that valid comparisons and abstractions will be made. The goal idea is so often forgotten as attention shifts to irrelevant by-paths that care must be given to scrutinizing attentively the pertinence of each suggestion offered.

Inattention. — When teachers complain — as they most frequently do — that children are inattentive, they do not mean that the children are giving no attention at all to anything. That would be impossible, so long as they were awake. They are attending to something other than that which is the responsibility of the moment. The rival attraction may be some *sensory stimulus*, such as the heat of the room, feelings of fatigue, the grimace Ann is making, the many visual and auditory distractions probable in a roomful of busy people. Individual trains of *thought* may have superior pulling power, for instance the adventure daydream, so much more attractive than the history discussion. The *social* situation on the playground, interrupted by schoolroom routine, may be of more vital interest than the Latin translation. An *emotional* condition is more personal and absorbing than the mathematics problem. Even with the best methods of "identification of the self through action, with some object or idea" which is the explanation of the interest that compels attention, there is always the chance in a large group that those not the leaders will lose interest and shift attention. Change, in the sense of development, opportunity for mental as well as muscular manipulation, helps sustain attention.

Value of active attention. — The value of forcing attention has been much discussed. Only when attention is freely given can it be easily sustained, it is true. So long as it is forced, part of the energy is used in keeping one's self at the task; and this added fact, that this effort is so taxing that forced attention can be held for only a few seconds at a time, makes it impossible to do work of vital worth when this type of attention alone is employed. The work that counts in the world, the work that discovers new principles, makes new applications, touches the emotions of men and women is always done by free attention.

However, the spontaneous attention of little children is closely connected with their immediate needs. Their very egocentric impulses, if exclusively directing the attention, would not fit individuals for the responsibilities of participation in the social life of civilization. Children do not look forward to remote ends, nor deny themselves now to reap greater benefits later, nor suffer individual privation in order that the group may profit; this comes partly with maturity, partly by very definite training in attention-giving. Ability to give attention to other than transitory stimuli on intellectual and ideal levels must be habituated. This involves learning to sustain attention in spite of pleasant distractions, learning to attend promptly instead of wasting time attending to one's own feelings of dislike for the task.

Effort and interest. — One of the greatest mistakes education has made has been to lose sight of the relation to each other of these two. The old education believed in the value of effort for its own sake; whatever was hard was therefore considered good. From the very character of the type, though, this cannot be true for itself alone; forced attention accomplishes no result, it but opens the door to possibilities which spontaneous attention left to itself could ignore. On the other hand, soft pedagogy gives a fictitious value to that only which is pleasurable, and counts effort, therefore, as harmful and valueless. The truth lies between the two. We must recognize forced attention as a means to an end, as a stepping stone from the level of impulse to the level of judgment, from the level of individual interest to that of social well-being. Because of the recognition of the peculiar value of forced attention, the need for motivation is evident. For the child to desire an end that is valuable to him, and then to realize that the path to it involves the effort of forced attention, is to give the true value to the means, and also to train the child in the power of standing the strain when the end makes it worth while. This sort of training fits him for life's demands, gives him perspective, helps him to judge values. The child who, keenly desiring to build a boat that will float, feels his need of the knowledge of certain measurements, and, despite the effort needed, sets about learning them; the child who, desirous of making her mother a Christmas present, finds it does not look pretty because her stitches are too large, and so practices making small stitches although it is an effort to do so; children who find that it pays not to spend every penny as it comes because later they can buy something they really want, although the waiting and denying themselves are unpleasant, children such as these are learning the true value of effort, and are forming habits which make for strong characters.

Incentives and attention. — Spontaneous attention to things that are most worth while may be gained by other means, as well as by forced attention. Activities of all kinds derive value if they are closely associated with or involve the activity of one of the original satisfiers. As James points out, the interest involved then spreads over and imparts its impetus and character to the material with which it is associated. Derived interests of this kind involve spontaneous attention. Sometimes the incentive may later be dropped, and the interest thus started continue. More often, incentives of some kind are needed all through life. There are multitudes of things to which the adult gives spontaneous attention, not because they are of value in themselves but because of some value attached to them. This must necessarily be true because of the make-up of human nature.

An incentive of low level is fear. The time-honored caricature of the teacher's function as punisher witnesses the frequency of the appeal to that incentive. Fear of failure, fear of disappointing family expectations if low grades are reported are other goads to attention. Display and rivalry are often effective means to sustaining attention.

Emulation, the example of one's friends has awakened many an interest for all of us, and is one of the most dependable ways of gaining and holding attention. Pride in achievement may be used at all ages, and suggests the careful grading of tasks to the abilities that are present. Pleasure in æsthetic fitness is a valuable incentive, and familiar to all good teachers. A sense of social responsibility, of "duty" is a potent incentive with increasing maturity.

Curiosity and attention are bound up together, and the facts usually referred to by the term "curiosity" probably are the tendencies of manipulation, visual exploration, and general mental activity. There is probably no separate and distinct instinct of curiosity. These other tendencies have already been discussed, and all that need be said here is to emphasize once more that children do not have to be cajoled into thinking;

mental activity is its own reward. The cajolery and the incentives are necessary when the nature of the child and the requirements of society come into conflict and the conflict is more often an imagined than a real one. If teachers would only make use of the rich fund of interests actually present, instead of substituting for them formal and artificial requirements and incentives, child nature would be preserved and education proceed apace.

The suggestions here would be, in so far as incentives are necessary: (1) choose those natural to the child's stage of development, work with nature, always making use of what is there; (2) choose those most natural to the subject to which the attention is desired; (3) choose those that will appeal to the greatest number; (4) choose those that are permanent, *i.e.*, will be found in life situations, as well as school situations; (5) choose the highest that will work.

To develop from the original tendencies to attention habits of sustained, concentrated, and spontaneous attention to the things in life that satisfy best the wants of the individual and the race; to cultivate the power to stand the strain of effort to situations where the end is worth while and this is the best means of attaining it; to make use of the instinctive interests in gaining derived values for things of fundamental importance in themselves but for the time being of no value to the individual; — these objective ends make up the latter-day problem in education.

PRACTICAL EXERCISES

1. Repeat an observation similar to that suggested on page 17 using a four- or five-year-old child as subject. Choose a time of free play. Arrange your paper to keep a record of continuity of occupation and number and duration of distractions. Use six 10-minute intervals. Students should preferably work in pairs, checking their records on the same child for accuracy. Records for ten different children, both sexes, should be made.

    How do the results compare with Bott's findings? Beyrl's?
2. During a study hour period in the seventh or eighth grade observe one pupil continuously. Have paper prepared as above to record duration

of work time, number and duration of distractions. Notice particularly the character of concentration in the first 10 minutes, and what it shows of the length of "warming up" period. Results of some dozen students' observations should be compared.

3. In the library where tenth- and eleventh-grade pupils work make a similar observation.
4. Criticize your own study habits from the standpoint of rapid settling to work, liability to interruption, ability to resume after interruption, ability to keep a goal in mind.

FOR DISCUSSION

1. Pool the results of the exercises above. What do they indicate as to individual differences? Age differences? How may habits of attention-giving be improved?
2. By what do you judge that a child is paying attention?
3. What does a teacher mean when she says, "You must learn to pay attention"?
4. Why do such things as flapping window shades, a person turning to use the blackboard, a different pitch of voice, attract children's attention?
5. What means would you take to help children "learn" to attend?
6. What is the value of having children assume attitudes of attention in the classroom?
7. Illustrate the psychological and the practical difference between gaining attention and sustaining it?

SELECTED REFERENCES

BOTT, H. "Observation of play activities in a nursery school." *Gen. Psy. Mon.*, v. 4 *1.

COLVIN, S. S. *The Learning Process.* Pages 251–270.

DEWEY, J. *Interest and Effort in Education.*

HUNTER, W. S. "The delayed reaction in a child." *Psych. Rev.*, v. 24, 1917.

MEUMANN, E. *The Psychology of Learning.* Pages 174–179.

PILLSBURY, W. B. *Education as the Psychologist Sees It.* Ch. 8.

CHAPTER VIII

LEARNING ABOUT THE PHYSICAL ENVIRONMENT

The human being is equipped by original nature with certain tendencies in terms of connections between sense organs and certain brain centers whose action results in the mental state of sense perception. The structure of these sense organs, together with the delicacy of the connections between them and the brain, determines to what situation the individual will be sensitive, and what sensations will be aroused. The eye is sensitive only to certain vibrations of ether; at each end of the spectrum are vibrations of which the human race is unconscious. Insects are sensitive to musical tones to which the human ear is insensitive. Dogs respond constantly to slight differences in odors which it is impossible for human noses to detect. Original nature sets limits within which sense perception must be developed, if it is developed at all.

PHYSIOLOGICAL CONDITIONS OF PERCEPTION

Sense organs. — At birth the sense organs themselves are at different levels of perfection. We note reactions within the first few days which indicate sensitiveness to differences in temperature, to light, to pressure which we should call pain, to hunger, to sound, to odors, to tastes, and so on. These reactions are very simple; the eyes, for instance, do not move coordinately, though the pupillary reflex to light is present. From the first stare, the eyes learn to focus on an object by the fifth week, and to follow a moving object, first in the horizontal direction, then in the vertical, after six weeks. Thus the mere fact of physical growth and control enables the infant to perceive better. All the sense organs are perfected in the

154

first two years; so that development of perception which occurs during school life is due to other causes.

General psychology as well as common observation emphasizes the fact that all knowledge is dependent upon sense perception, and all learning is conditioned by it. If this type of experience is so valuable, obviously the first thing in the education of children along this line is to be sure that the organs of sense are in a condition to be affected by the stimuli presented. Defects of eyes or ears have been found to mean a handicap to the child of such a far-reaching nature that detection and correction of such defects is one of the primary duties of school officers. Extreme defect in either of these senses has caused children to be considered stupid and even mentally defective, when the only trouble was inadequate sense organs.

Eye defects. — The percentage of defective eyes among school children is very large, but the exact figures will vary with the kind and delicacy of the test used. Some investigators have found only 19 per cent having defective eyes, others, at some ages, as many as 92 per cent. The most common defect, also that definitely increasing with age, but fortunately easy to discover, is *myopia*, or shortsightedness. This defect is due to a too long diameter of the eyeball from front to back causing the light rays to focus in front of the retina. The opposite condition — too short an eyeball with the rays brought to focus behind the retina — produces *hyperopia*, or farsightedness. Here there may be no loss of acuity of vision, and with some effort the eye may be forced to do the work required of it; but this, so far from being a benefit, as some people imagine, will, if uncorrected by convex lenses, induce a fatigued condition of the ciliary muscle which regulates the accommodation of the eye. A third defect, known as *astigmatism*, is due to uneven curvature of the cornea or perhaps of the lens of the eye itself. Here too there is danger of constant strain on muscles which may result in reflex disturbances of a serious nature. These last two types of defect are not usually discovered by the ordinary tests of vision applied in the schools since they are

designed to test acuity. Consequently, children possessing
them may go on year after year using up their energy, perhaps
breaking down their nervous systems in the mere effort to see.

There are other eye defects shown in lack of balance or control in some of the six muscles that move the eyes in their sockets.
The most serious is squint, *strabismus* or "cross eyes," which
generally results from excessive hyperopia in one eye causing it
to be gradually disused, therefore turned in or out. As the
double vision thus experienced is confusing, the child soon
comes to disregard the retinal image of the squinting eye; this
further aggravates the trouble, since power to focus and to
move is lost in time, from disuse. Prompt and early treatment
is of the highest importance if vision is to be retained. As
muscle strain in the eyes may result from the less easily detected hyperopia and astigmatism teachers should be on the
watch for symptoms in children such as frowning, smarting or
watery eyes, complaints of blurred print, bad posture over work.
Reflex symptoms exist too, such as headache, particularly in
the frontal region, perhaps nausea or other forms of indigestion,
neurasthenia, motor disturbances, and general emotional
instability.

Another, rather different eye defect is that of *color-blindness*
found in about 4 per cent of boys and less than 1 per cent of
girls. Red-green blindness is the most common form. It may
be in one eye or in both, and therefore may go unsuspected till
a careful test is made. It is congenital and incurable, though
children may learn to recognize some reds or greens by means
of differences in brightness.

Ear defects. — Defective hearing is not so serious in its
results on the nervous system of the child as is eyestrain, but,
when it exists, it interferes with the development of perceptions
and therefore of knowledge. A number of investigators find
about 20 per cent of school children defective in one or both
ears. Such children frequently show an imperfect language development, and, because they fail to get much of the instruction
in the schoolroom, are apt to be considered dull and get retarded

in school progress. From being partly shut off from the play of normal children, they are in danger of growing up "queer," anti-social, bad-tempered, subnormal physically and abnormal emotionally. Once the condition is detected the cause of deafness should be sought for by the physician. Sometimes the removal of tonsils and adenoids will secure relief; but if treatment will not effect a cure, deaf children need to be taught by special methods, therefore, for a time at least, segregated.

It is evident from these facts that the two senses of sight and hearing must be carefully tested by experts who understand the dangers and the handicaps that various types of defects cause, if children's health is to be preserved and their physical equipment be such as will make possible the accumulation of a fund of clear, accurate sense impressions.

MENTAL CONDITIONS OF DEVELOPMENT OF PERCEPTION

Sheer awareness. — The kind of mental life aroused at first by the action of all sorts of stimuli can only be guessed at. Nothing like our consciousness of things, of qualities, of relationships can be present. It probably is not very dissimilar from the low level of mental action felt sometimes in a slow awakening from sleep or recovery from anæsthesia — without its sophisticated self-consciousness and efforts to remember, of course — where a diffused feeling of warmth and well-being, or pain and cold, quite unlocalized, appears as a simple satisfier or annoyer. Sounds impinge on consciousness in a dislocated, meaningless, noisy way; vague appeals to vision occur, with shape and distance unintelligible, mere dark and light long preceding color.

The Gestalt school of psychologists would describe a perception as a quality emerging from a uniform background. We should in any case face the task of observing the reactions infants make.

Selective attention. — We can note the serial order of integrated reactions to sense stimuli. Newborn infants respond negatively, that is, they shrink from almost any stimulus, evi-

dencing the hypersensitivity of the sense organs and neurones.
Gradually they learn to bear stimuli, and begin to give them
attention. They are in the stage of mastering them. Once so
mastered, the duration of attention to any particular stimulus
is lessened. For instance, in the third month the attention is
longest to single sounds of different quality. By the eighth
month simple sounds are no longer so interesting, but attention
is given to series of sounds in melody. Between three and four
months is the greatest duration of gaze to single colored lights,
though there has been active turning towards them in the
second month. In the first three months of life, then, infants
pass from enduring sense stimuli to showing active interest in
them. As shown elsewhere, the span and range of attention
increase with age, and this alone favors perceptual learning.
So long as the attention is uncertain, wandering, and superficial,
flitting with great rapidity from this to that, pausing nowhere
for more than a few seconds, objects, as such, make but a hazy,
incomplete, and often inaccurate impression. To get clear outlines, definite and accurate qualities, the attention must be
caught and held. Defective attention, such as a "scatterbrain"
has, for instance, results in deficiency in sense perception.

Co-ordination. — A third mental condition of perception is
the co-ordinating of different sensory experiences. The development is brought about by the repeated action, and varied inter-
action of the different sense organs. When a baby handles his
rattle the tactile and muscular senses in hand and arm are
stimulated; when he shakes it, the sense of hearing as well,
and the sense of sight as his hand comes within the line of
vision; as he hits himself with it the tactile sense in other parts
of the body is aroused; as he puts it in his mouth further tactile,
perhaps gustatory sensations occur, but the object may have
disappeared from sight. When some one else shakes the rattle
before him, some, but not all of the sensations are repeated.
When other objects that do not rattle are grasped there is
another grouping of simultaneous stimuli. The rattle may be
pink, hard, and smooth, the ball pink, soft, and fuzzy, the toy

lamb white, soft, fuzzy but of a different shape — and so on through the endless combinations of appeal to different sense organs, or to different qualities sensed by the same organ. If his rattle stimulated only the sense of touch, and that always in the same way, it is doubtful whether anything more than indeterminate sensation could result from that stimulation. But because the rattle stimulates more than one sense organ simultaneously, and never stimulates them in just the same way, the result in consciousness is the feeling of "thinghood," or perception. In order, then, for definiteness to result from confusion, a world of "things" from chaotic sense feelings, experience must afford conditions of the simultaneous and varied stimulation of several sense organs by the same object. To the extent that this kind of experience is lacking or limited must the development of perception be handicapped.

Better analysis. — Perception is by vague wholes at first. Some reaction is made to an object, and is habituated. Other objects roughly similar will stimulate the same response till discrimination of details is forced. The general pattern suffices for adults to recognize familiar words not clearly seen; this same process of reaction to wholes, called syncretism, is still more true of children who have not yet learned to observe and interpret small features of objects as cues for different reactions. As curiosity, or unfortunate results of wrong reactions, or the skill of the teacher in inviting comparisons, or other causes focus their attention on details, they are able to understand things in the physical world about them more clearly by analysis.

Grasping of relationships. — Children often react to some one part of an object exclusively, not understanding its relatedness to the whole. Spatial relationships will be ignored or confused when they set out to represent an object by drawing it or making it in miniature. The detail that has struck their fancy — that has necessitated reaction — may be exaggeratedly large; thus, teeth in a human face, the handle on a door are given undue prominence by four- and five-year-olds. Rhythmic relationships are similarly distorted by much older children

in reproduction of music forms, by their interest in some one
detail to the ignoring of others equally important to the composition.

Decrease in subjective reference. — Growing out of their
own needs in reaction children interpret everything at first only
as related to themselves. They are egocentric, and perceive
things as emotionally of significance rather than as objectively
related. A chair is to sit on, or adequate for the gymnastic
impulses of the moment rather than an article of furniture made
thus and so, or a period piece. Music that is familiar and enjoyed
may be rendered crescendo, accelerando, fortissimo regardless
of the intensity and time relationships for which its artistic unity
calls. Very gradually do these personal interpretations of the
physical world give way to the scientific attitude of objectivity.

PERCEPTION IN SPECIFIC FIELDS

Brightness, color, form. — Differences in brightness are
reacted to by six months of age. Between that and one year
reds and yellows are discriminated. Blue and green are confused
for a longer period according to several investigators. Between
three and five or six years old children seem more attentive to
color as attributes of objects than to mere form. For instance,
in the type of test devised by Katz [1] and repeated by Brian and
Goodenough [2] in this country a child is given, say, a blue cube
and a yellow sphere, then a yellow cube with the task to match
it. He will choose like-colored objects or like-colored surface
forms. Decroly and Descoudres [3] require matching a series of
sixteen pictures by form and color, or sixteen all alike in form
but to be matched by color. The latter task takes longer between two and one-half and six years, indicating the difficulty
in that type of learning, and the absorbed degree of attention.
As between color and simple form, then, color is more intriguing
as an attribute to be attended to and learned at this age.

[1] Stern, W., *Psychology of Early Childhood*, ch. 29.
[2] Brian and Goodenough, "The relative potency of color and form perception
at different ages," *Jo. Exp. Psy.*, v. 12, 1929.
[3] Stern, W., *op. cit.*, pp. 196–198.

(Forms of solids are perceived by touching as well as by looking, therefore have had the advantage, since color can be perceived by vision alone. Further, color is of no such importance to the two-year-old as is reaction to form; therefore the task of learning it is deferred.) Further experimentation in this field has been extremely scanty and not well planned, since form and position have been greatly complicated while the color problem has been left relatively simple. For instance, in scoring for a norm in matching eight pictures for color combinations or object combinations, there were only two color variables but four object variables. With the former, four and one-half-year-old children did as well as 7-year-old children with the latter. Matching for eight different arm positions of a human form is almost too difficult for eight-year-olds.

Sound. — In pitch discrimination of sounds individual differences seem greater than age differences. Seashore [1] thinks such discrimination is an innate, basic capacity, slightly if at all improvable by practice. Children of ten years old can be given his test in groups; below that age it is better to give individual tests to insure real understanding of the directions, especially the terms *higher, lower,* used in connection with pitch. Tests with tuning forks, adapted to the attention span and fatigue limit of young children may reveal even at five years old the relative status of a child in ability to discriminate pitch accurately. McGinnis [2] reports successful work with children of nursery school age in pitch and intensity of sound discrimination. Kwalwasser and Dykema [3] include discrimination of quality of musical sounds in their battery of ten tests, and obtain excellent scores from some young children, as well as a great variation in score at all ages. Where improvement takes place in score on these tests it is not in the physiological ability to hear, but in the greater maturity of attention, better understanding, development of taste, better ability to compare.

[1] Seashore, C., *The Psychology of Musical Talent.*
[2] McGinnis, E., "Seashore's measures of musical ability applied to children of pre-school age," *A. J. P.*, v. 40, 1928.
[3] Victor Records, 302–306, K–D Music Tests, *Manual of Directions.*

Needless to say, evidence of sense discrimination, whether in color, pitch, musical quality or anything else, should not be confused with ability to name in words the differences felt, or to use correctly any verbal series of terms.

Other fields. — In *perception of weight*, it is probable that there is not much change with age, and that practice has comparatively little effect on the power of discrimination. In *skin sensitivity* the consensus of opinion is that children are much more sensitive than adults, and that practice improves the capacity enormously. This experimental evidence is borne out by the fact that in some industries where delicacy of touch and fineness of discrimination are necessary, such as the knotting required in making oriental rugs, children have been in great demand.

As to *space perception* there are very decided differences of opinion, because little adequate extensive study has been made. Apparently there is a trial and error adjustment to space as infants learn to grasp, to creep, to walk, which may, however, be as much a learning process of muscle co-ordination, and of eyes' and muscles' co-operation as of sheer visual perception of space. As the infant's locomotive powers improve he gets continual practice in muscular adjustment to space and seldom, by two and a half years old, makes any great miscalculation of distance.

DIFFERENCES BETWEEN CHILDREN AND ADULTS

The development which takes place in sense perception from infancy to adult life is due to several causes. Physical growth provides for the perfection of the sense organs and their neural connections. A rich and widening environment provides the conditions for the consciousness of objects to be evolved. Changes in mental maturity result in greater ability to compare, analyze, and remember the sense data. Practice gives better discrimination and interpretation in all departments of sense perception.

Lack in richness of detail. — The chief differences between the sense perception of adults and of children grow out of these facts of development. In general, children lack in richness, in definiteness, and in detail of sense perceptions. Despite the fact that there have been tremendous strides during the first few years, still, the ignorance and lack of observation of the common everyday objects by children of school age are appalling. G. Stanley Hall [1] long ago drew our attention to the fact that six-year-old children entering school did not know facts about many things in the environment which teachers and makers of textbooks had rather taken for granted they would understand. It is hard to believe that 53 per cent of Boston school children tested had never seen a sunset, 30 per cent never saw clouds and 55 per cent were ignorant of the source of wooden things; and yet when a high-school graduate believed that apples were dug from the ground as are potatoes, and a youth that had lived all his life on a farm could not tell how a horse lies down, and a country girl did not know a robin, one begins to realize how much observation is lacking.

Huff [2] has made a similar investigation among children of a poor social environment, of chronological ages six to sixteen, of somewhat inferior average intelligence. The same marked ignorance was found. He points out that descriptive writing, calling upon children to construct visual images, not only is disliked, but is of no value if perceptual experience has not preceded it. Where home or school care had been taken to give children first-hand acquaintance with things, to stimulate their curiosity and answer their questions, they made a high score on his tests. Otherwise there was no noticeably higher score with increased chronological age.

Difference in amount of cue. — Another striking difference between the perceptions of children and adults is the difference in the amount of stimulus necessary to call up a percept. The child at the beginning needs a large amount of stimulus, and needs it to be given in just the same way in order that the per-

---

[1] "The contents of children's minds on entering school," *Ped. Sem.*, v. 1, 1891.
[2] Huff, R. L., "Percept content of school children's minds," *Ped. Sem.*, v. 34, 1927.

ception be of the same object. Mother in a different dress, or
appearing suddenly in new surroundings may not be recognized,
and certainly it is a long time before mother is perceived by just
seeing the back of her head, her silhouette in the distance, or
her walk. The older the individual, the greater his experience
with the situation, the less the amount of stimulus needed to
call up the percept. This fact of mental development is particularly noticeable in connection with reading. The child needs
to read every word in order to get the meaning of the sentence,
every sentence in order to get the paragraph, whereas for the
mature individual the important word or two in the sentence,
or the topic sentences in the paragraph are enough to furnish
the sensory clue to a full perception. It takes time for the
child to evolve his types or standards in connection with perception. As he accomplishes this end, fewer and fewer characteristics, less and less of sense stimulation is necessary for him to
proceed.

Power of mind's set. — A third difference between children
and adults in their perception lies in the power of "mind's set,"
or the passing mental content to determine the percept. Every
one is influenced by the state of mind he is in as to what he
will think in the next few minutes, and a previous mood is a
strong factor in determining his point of view. We all tend to
see or hear or feel what we expect; but the child, because of
the characteristics of his attention, is even more influenced
by the passing mental state. Two important practical precepts grow out of this fact. In the first place, it is very necessary that with a child the aim of the work be kept very clearly
in mind; he should know very definitely what he is to look
for or to do if results worth while are to be obtained. In the
second place, new material in any line should not be given
until the child has had time to warm up, to adapt himself to
the new line of work.

Cause of illusions. — Because of the strength of the passing
mental content, children are more subject than adults to one
type of illusion. A child in the dentist's chair is hurt long before

the instruments have touched his tooth. Sent to watch for father, he sees him several times before father arrives. Having talked about the bluebird, he sees the flush of its wing and hears its call when it may be only a robin. If he is told by some one whom he loves or respects that such and such a thing is there, the normal child of seven or eight will see it or hear it. The suggestibility of children under ten has been proven by experiments in many fields, but every teacher has evidence of it day after day in her own classroom as children see and hear and feel what the questions or talk have suggested. On the other hand, children are probably freer than adults from illusions dependent on habitual interpretation of phenomena. The adult, while reading rapidly, is more likely than the child to overlook a misprint in spelling in a word familiar to both, or is sure he read the name of his destination on the front of the street car yet finds himself up the wrong avenue, or fails to hear the transposition, omission, mispronunciation, or whatnot in a time-honored quotation which sends the child into mirthful convulsions. It is because of this difference that a child is sometimes called more literal than the adult. If his mind is not very much taken up with something, if it is not "set" in a certain direction by suggestion or aim, he is likely to see the facts as they are, whereas the adult may be influenced by life habits into a misinterpretation.

TRAINING IN PERCEPTION

Varied first hand contacts. — The first step in sense training is to make sure that the sense organs are in proper condition. Not only must these be in good shape in order for proper perception to be developed, but children need training in the methods of learning through their senses. It is through the action of the sense organs that all the mental stuff comes from which is built the world of knowledge, of imagination, of reason. It is fundamental to intellect, to character, and to conduct. Limitation of experience in this field, or incorrectness of perception, must result in a lack of some kind in the more complex realms of mental life. All this is known intellectually by teachers and educators, but it is far from being a conviction with them. Far too little time and thought and preparation are given to the refining and enriching of the sensory experience of children. Yet much of this is needed if the child is to enter into and possess the world of things. He must be given time to touch, look at, listen to, feel, lift, perhaps smell and taste, many objects. In nature study he must learn to perceive form, color, number, relative size, position by looking, touching, pulling apart, feeling the texture, getting possibly the temperature, odor, and taste. In music he must have tones of varying pitch, intensity, duration; he must hear the difference between a note sounded on piano, cornet, violin, organ, flute, human voice of different qualities; he must feel the effect of groups of successive or simultaneous tones with all possible variations again of pitch, intensity, duration, rhythm, and color value before he has what we call an "ear" that is cultivated. In spelling he must look at, pronounce, write, and listen to the letters, syllables, and words. In a cooking lesson, amount, color, proportion, texture, space arrangement, distance must be tested by eyes and hands, while ears as well as nose may help judge processes before taste sits in judgment. The hands must acquire skill in movements such as kneading, egg-beating, and this depends on discrimination of cutaneous and kinæsthetic sensations. All this needs careful planning by the teacher. Left to themselves children's percepts are hazy, incomplete, and inaccurate. Definite provision and preparation are necessary if the perceptual growth of children is to be what it should be. With all its faults, the Montessori system has done much in once more calling attention to the need for more training in sense perception and discrimination, especially to the gain to the very little child in using touch and movement to help out the eye judgment.

The whole question of so-called sense training or observation lessons is bound up not only with the facts of perception, but also with those of attention, memory, and the formation of concepts. It is convenient, however, to treat of it at this point rather than later.

Types of observation. — Observation may be of three kinds, according to Meumann: [1] (1) *inquiring, or purposeful,* to which one comes prepared with varied points of view and definitely directed attention. The act of perceiving may be either leisurely, as in looking at a picture or specimen, or momentary, as in watching an event in rapid progress, or listening for a sound. In the latter case the attention is more highly concentrated, and after-images and immediate memory are relatively more important; (2) *non-purposive,* surprised, forced upon one by some sudden occurrence in the environment; (3) *purposive,* but passively expectant, in which one is definitely attentive, open to any and all impressions, to which one comes with no points of view clearly in mind. In speaking of sense training, we usually mean the first or purposeful type. In this the function of attention is firstly, to hold in mind the "goal-idea"; secondly, to increase the clearness to the sense organs and to consciousness of the details observed; thirdly, to fixate in memory the things noted; fourthly, to assist in classifying or analyzing one's impression.

Individual differences in perception. — People differ in their ability to concentrate their attention and to resist distraction. The changes in children as they grow older in their power of attending will make a difference in their capacity to observe. People differ, again, in the amount perceived and in the speed with which they can reproduce what was presented; therefore as children's span and range of attention increase we may expect improvement in the amount and accuracy of their observing. People differ also in their habit of using the first or the third type of observation. The first is productive of definite, but sometimes prejudiced results in a narrow field; the third may be vague in intent and method, wide in scope and serves well as a preliminary stage in a new field of inquiry, revealing lines of interest that may be followed up by using the first type

[1] Meumann, E., *The Psychology of Learning,* chs. 3, 4.

of observation. Children need systematic training if they are to be habituated to the method of the first type, and accomplish ends worth while. People differ further in their suggestibility under questioning that follows the act of perception. Children under twelve are much more suggestible than are adults, therefore their reports of perceptual experiences are likely to be more inaccurate the more they are interrogated with "leading" questions. Another difference is to be noted between the subjective observer, who is misled by his expectancy, his imagination, and his interpretations, and the objective observer, who readily distinguishes what is actually perceived from what might be subjectively added. This difference in type is found among children too, though their fluctuating attention and intensity of interest may make them less consistently of one type. Girls are more subjective than boys.

Improvement in observation. — In general, natural ability to observe improves steadily up to about fifteen years of age. Spontaneous descriptions of perceptual experiences double in amount between the ages of seven and fourteen, according to Stern,[1] and nearly triple between seven and nineteen. When pressed by questioning further facts are remembered and reported on, but after fourteen years of age no improvement in the total amount thus described is found.

Children of different ages observe by different categories, if we can judge by the items they will freely report or ignore. Just as in describing a picture, so also in observing stationary objects or events occurring, we may notice sequent stages of enumeration or naming, of interest in action, of attention to spatial, temporal, causal relationships. Not till after twelve years old does there come, spontaneously, the qualitative analysis of objects presented. Girls will tell better about persons, boys about things, a distinction that comes out also in the noticing of color. Boys are more accurate in their reports than are girls, but narrower in their range. Accuracy increases with age and practice, though here again the sexes develop differ-

[1] Stern, W., *Beiträge zur Psychologie des Aussage.*

ently — the boys improving most during the years seven to ten, the girls from ten to fourteen. Training to observe by different categories, such as number, color, form, has an immediate but probably not permanent effect if the category used is in advance of that which is natural to the age.

Teaching suggestions. — Some applications of these facts would be: first, since the feeling of certainty is no measure of real accuracy of memory, children should be trained to rely more on repeating the sense impression and comparing their memory directly with the perceptual experience. This habit of "taking another look" is much needed in spelling and accidence for the establishment of correct usage, and is invaluable as verification in science work. Second, since children lack many controlling ideas by which to systematize their observation, it is important to arouse their interest, direct their attention, suggest an aim or "goal-idea," and teach them the value and method of use of such ideas rather than proceeding in haphazard fashion. Third, as accuracy can be improved by training while the amount noted depends more directly on the age of the child, emphasis should be laid on attention and verification. Overquestioning on the memory of the material presented will not assist the quantity recalled very much; indeed, the high suggestibility of children makes this last a doubtful expedient at best.

All through childhood continual contact with things of all kinds is necessary. Consider the value of excursions, museums, factories, nature study, handwork, elementary science, duties about the home, in the school, on the street, which involve dealing with the World of Things. This should be followed by the testing of the perceptions acquired, at first under the direction of the teacher. Also situations must be arranged that encourage free, spontaneous observation on the part of the child, first in one field and then in another. In all this training, it must be constantly borne in mind that there is no faculty of observation or perception that can be trained for usefulness by a course of arbitrarily arranged material. If observation of people is needed, training in that line must be given; if of nature, the training must be with that material; if of foodstuffs, or dress materials, or musical tones, or words, or qualities, or relationships, in each case the training must be definite and particular. Further, training the eye to perceive will not, cannot train the fingers; they must be trained, their power developed by their own activity. There is no mysterious transfer of power from one sense department to another. Every level of achievement reached comes as the result of some definite activity, and the fingers have been much neglected in the development of perception. The very fact that in childhood the sense of touch is so delicate should stir teachers to make the best use of it at that time, not only in handling objects, but in responding to texture and to pressure. The muscle sense which, combined as it often is with the tactual, gives the true feeling of a thing, also needs special training in the perception of form and contour. Nor need the sense of smell, decadent as it is, be neglected.

In connection with this matter of training, Dewey says, "No number of object lessons, got up *as* object lessons for the sake of giving information, can afford even the shadow of a substitute for acquaintance with the plants and animals of the farm and garden, acquired through actual living among them and caring for them. No training of sense organs in school, introduced for the sake of training, can begin to compete with the alertness and fullness of sense — life that comes through daily intimacy and interest in familiar occupations." [1] Although the country offers the best opportunities to develop perceptions in connection with the natural world, yet the city, the great field of industry, of the result of man's labor and invention, offers measureless opportunities for development along different lines. No matter where the child is living, material is there, — living, vital material, to which the child is constantly reacting. It is the duty of the teacher to take these life situations, and in connection with the reactions which

[1] *School and Society*, p. 24.

naturally take place to develop perceptions which are clear, correct, and adequate, to see to it that they are as numerous and rich as possible, and to supply material or motive when either is lacking; for upon the material gathered from sense perception will depend all future growth and development.

PRACTICAL EXERCISES

1. Make Experiment 10 exactly as directed on pages 169 to 172 of Goodenough's *Experimental Child Study*.
2. Spend 15 minutes in each of three or four classrooms noting indications of defective vision or hearing among the children. Verify by consulting the teacher for names of the children suspected and by looking up such records as the school keeps of each child's physical condition.
3. Find out who has charge of examining children for sense defects, (1) in the rural districts nearest you, (2) for the high-school population.
4. Get specimens of the physical report cards used in the city or county where you live.
5. Have a short selection played on a victrola five or six times.
    Attend the first time to the melody.
    Attend the second time to the rhythm.
    Attend the third time to the quality of the sounds.
    Attend the fourth time to the alterations in tempo (if any) or extremes of pitch.
    Attend the fifth time to the harmony.
    Attend the sixth time to the thoughts or images suggested.
    Notice how different your attention feels each time. In which case did you get the least result? Why? What does this suggest?

FOR DISCUSSION

1. How does the method used in the early teaching of Helen Keller, or of deaf-mutes, illustrate the growth of perception from sensation?
2. What is the difference in attention when one looks, looks at, or looks for? Or listens, listens to, listens for?
3. What is the fault in teaching as follows: giving fifth-grade children a map saying "Study that for next time"? Announcing that "I want you to listen while this is played and then tell me what you notice"?
4. Mention cases where touching and manipulating objects are of great assistance in helping correct perception.
5. What have the facts about children's perceptions and ideas derived therefrom to suggest for educational method?

SELECTED REFERENCES

BALDWIN AND STECHER. *The Psychology of the Pre-School Child.* Pages 115–134.

BRIAN AND GOODENOUGH. "The relative potency of color and form perception at different ages." *Jo. Exp. Psych.*, v. 12, 1929.

HALL, G. S. "The contents of children's minds on entering school," in *Aspects of Child Life.*

HUFF, R. L. "Percept content of school children's minds." *Ped. Sem.*, v. 34, 1927.

KOFFKA, K. *The Growth of the Mind.* Pages 125–142.

STERN, W. *Psychology of Early Childhood.* Ch. 29.

WHIPPLE, G. M. *Manual of Mental and Physical Tests.* Ch. 8.

CHAPTER IX

MEMORY

TERMS USED IN DISCUSSING MEMORY

Impressionability. — The term "memory" has been used to refer to several different kinds of mental processes, but in its most general use it refers to the fact that a situation tends to evoke the mental response with which it has previously been connected.

The physiological basis for this fact is found in the modifiability of the synapses in the cortex. A connection once made leaves its influence on the synapses involved, and, as will be discussed in connection with habit-forming, this greater impressionability and modifiability of the synapses produces in man a power of learning, a memory far above that of the lower animals. Good and poor memories find their ultimate explanation in this plasticity of synapses. They are a result of the physiological structure, a gift of original nature.

Recognition or recall. — Memory means more than the ability to take on or retain impressions. It involves the power to reinstate any action with or without stimuli from perceptual sources, the power to "bring back to mind" facts once learned whether or not a cue is present to the senses or is offered in words. The ease of this reinstatement depends greatly on this presence or absence of outside help. *Recognition* is comparatively simple. To recognize a melody, a picture, a quotation, implies that there is now a perceptual presentation to which the pupil responds by a feeling of familiarity. It is called for in questions of the multiple choice variety where the pupil is told to check the correct answer out of several suggested; for example: The capital of Montana is — Butte, Billings, Helena,

173

Grand Rapids. *Recall* is relatively more difficult. Independent effort is required to sing the melody, describe the picture, give the quotation with no assistance from without. It would be required were the above question in the form, The capital of Montana is —?

Immediate memory and retention. — To distinguish further between the different usages of the term, it may stand for *immediate* memory, that is, the reproduction of material without any appreciable time interval between the impression and the expression; and *retention,* indicating the power to reproduce material after a considerable interval, varying from hours to months, has elapsed. It is important to notice in which of the two senses the term "memory" is being used; for the development is quite unlike in the two abilities, as is also the difference between children and adults. Many authors use the expression "memorizing" when discussing immediate memory, since rote memorizing for laboratory purposes has usually been tested immediately. Naturally, for schoolroom purposes, a teacher's use of the same expression by no means coincides with the experimenter's idea of mere immediate reproduction.

Retention may be measured by noting after how long a time since learning an accurate response may still be given. Or, keeping the time elapsed constant, the measure may be the percentage of the original learning which persists. Either of these is more like the ordinary schoolroom procedure, where the amount correct is used as a measure of a child's memory, even though the time elapsing since the original learning is not taken into account. The third way of measuring in experimental procedures is to note the decreased time it requires to relearn anything compared with the time — or number of repetitions— originally required for one correct response.

Obliviscence, reminiscence. — We speak of forgetting, or obliviscence, to refer to the fact that the strength of a connection weakens through disuse. This is usually measured inversely by the per cent of the amount originally reproduced which is retained and recalled after fixed intervals of time, as in measuring retention. Reminiscence, in the technical sense, refers to the curious fact noted by Ballard that young children, after a 2 to 4 day interval often recall more of a poem, etc., learned than they were able to reproduce immediately after having learned it.

Memory proper. — This denotes the ability to recall events of one's own personal life in distinction from the schoolroom meaning of memory for objective facts, or of muscle skills. It is the peculiar property of the individual's own recall rather than the common knowledge of associated facts. Thus, one child would remember his automobile trip through Montana, while another remembers the circumstances under which he first learned anything about the geography of Montana. It is these subjective phenomena which keep a person one individual from infancy to old age in spite of profound changes in his physical and mental make-up. It is the sort with which psychiatrists particularly deal. Though it, too, is subject to ordinary obliviscence, yet occurrences of unusual, persistent or prolonged forgetting may indicate an emotional complex which is the root of psychic disorder.

MEMORY FOR VARIED MATERIAL

Memory for place and position. — One of the most fundamental facts remembered, which is demonstrated in the learning of lower animals, is that of space orientation. Thus, before cats learn which type of action will release them from a puzzle box they remember the place where to work in order to escape. Whatever perceptual guides are most potent, sight, feel, or odor, it is a fact that associations of space are primitive data in the learning process. Accordingly, it is interesting to note this form of memory development in infants and young children, whether tested immediately or after a delay between impression and recollection.

Gesell [1] finds that at six months old over 65 per cent of infants, having been interested in playing with a spoon, evi-

---

[1] Gesell, A., *Mental Growth of the Pre-School Child*, pp. 368–369.

dence awareness of its disappearance if it is dropped over the edge of the table. Fewer than half of them will definitely look for it; but by nine months old over 90 per cent look for it. Hiding a cube under an inverted cup in plain view of an attentive infant is another laboratory test. At nine months most babies manage to lift the cup, and by twelve months 86 per cent secure the cube.

Wislitsky [1] hid a toy under a box while the child was watching, distracted him with play for varying intervals, then noted if recollection was evidenced by seeking the toy or could be stimulated by asking the child for it. At nine months there was success after 1½ minutes distraction, at eleven months after 2½ minutes, at two years after 17 minutes. Bühler,[2] in her baby tests, shows a box with a toy in it. After a standard interval of three minutes the box is shown again without the toy. At ten months old an infant should evidence surprise at the absence of the toy, or definitely seek for it.

Further complications in the experiment are introduced when there are two or three boxes, cups, plates, etc., under one of which the test object is hidden, or when more than one test object is used. During the second year more than two objects can be remembered, by twenty-four months three objects, by four years five objects, by six years ten objects, in each case after a standard interval of five minutes. Skalet,[3] using sixty children between the ages of three and a half and five and a half, hiding a cookie under one of three plates, found an even chance of correct response after a 15-day-interval. By the age of school entrance, then, teachers may well expect ready learning and easy remembering of where things are kept, as a basis for habits of orderliness they wish to form.

Memory for pitch, etc. — In spite of our long history of music teaching we have almost no valid and reliable definite knowledge of the growth of ability to remember melodies,

[1] Quoted by Ch. Bühler.
[2] Bühler, C., *The First Year of Life.*
[3] Skalet, M., "The significance of delayed reactions in young children," *Comp. Psy. Mon.*, v. 7, *4, 1931.

rhythms, harmonies and so on. For brief pitch patterns, unmelodic in the sense that they suggest no key relationship, the Seashore [1] norms show that 75 per cent of fifth-grade children answer two thirds of his "tonal memory" test correctly, and 75 per cent of eighth-grade pupils answer three quarters of it. This ability is directly related to attention-span, in that the younger children seldom succeed with more than four units in a sequence, the others seldom attain success with a sequence six units in length. For teaching purposes, the teacher must discover by the trial and error method how many repetitions of a musical phrase are necessary before children of a given grade can reproduce it correctly. Also the teacher must find out by practical experience what degree of difficulty in length or complexity in a musical selection it is reasonable to expect of an average group of pupils of a certain age or grade.

Memory for visual material. — Silhouettes of animals have been shown to pre-school age children, and, after varying intervals of time, they were required to identify which form they had seen from a group of six or eight forms. Skalet [2] experimented thus with individual children by the recognition method, to test retention. Less than half the responses were correct with a 3-day interval, though there were great individual differences. With geometrical forms the task was harder; with unfamiliar, unnamable forms, from two to six hours delay gave more accurate responses than longer intervals. The correlation between this ability and mental age was significantly high.

Lee,[3] using 310 subjects with an age range of eight to sixteen and a 24-hour standard interval, found also that pictures were recognized and recalled better than were geometrical forms. Ability to recall improved with age more than did recognition.

Clearly, even in these experiments the language factor may have been an important element. Even memory for place, in

---

[1] *Manual of Instructions and Interpretations for Measures of Musical Talent.*
[2] *Op. cit.*
[3] Lee, A. L., "An experimental study of retention and its relation to intelligence," *Psy. Mon.*, v. 34, *4, 1925.

all but the young infants who did not yet talk, may have been reinforced by ability to verbalize. In the older experimental work on children's memories, whether tested by recognition or recall, whether immediate recall or delayed, very little distinction was made between verbal and non-verbal material.

Memory for mixed types of material. — Memory for different types of material has been described, emphasized, and tested by Binet, Meumann, Netschajeff, Lobsien, Pohlmann, and others. Unfortunately the nomenclature is apt to be confusing — for instance: auditory impressions were given of a series of different sorts of sounds, such as clapping, whistling, stamping; or of words meaning sounds, such as music, song; or digits were spoken rather than presented in series to the eye, and any one of these things may be meant when speaking of "auditory memory." However, there is no guarantee that material presented to any one sense organ is remembered in corresponding imagery, so that "memory for auditory presentations" would be a more accurate way of expressing the facts. Moreover, to write a description of a sound heard, as in the first series described above, is not the same sort of thing as making a similar series of sounds one's self, as is demanded in a music test, nor is it so simple as writing down a series of numerals heard rather than seen.

With these precautions in mind we may accept the findings of Smedley [1] that auditory memory develops rapidly up to about fourteen years of age and but slowly afterwards, while visual memory seems to develop up to about fifteen or sixteen years of age. Before nine, auditory memory is stronger than visual.

Gates [2] found that for college students visual presentation brought superior results to auditory. This illustrates the strength of the reading habits formed. Possibly, were an unselected group of eighteen- to twenty-year-olds tested, rather

[1] Smedley, F., *Report, Dept. Child Study and Pedagogic Investigation* (Chicago public schools), *3, 1900.
[2] Gates, A. I., "The mnemonic span for visual and auditory digits, *Jo. Exp. Psy.*, 1916.

than subjects selected for power to survive a bookish education, as great superiority for visual over auditory presentation might not be shown. The years ten to twelve are specially favorable, the period fourteen to fifteen specially unfavorable for development. Girls are better than boys during the ages eleven to fourteen, and usually reproduce more of the material, though with less accuracy in the order, than boys.

Narasaki [1] found girls superior to boys in all sorts of memory material. Other investigators confirm this fact, whether it is immediate or delayed reproduction that is required. Other sex differences are as follows: "With boys the memory for objects is first developed, then words of visual content, words of auditory content, sounds, terms denoting tactual and motor experiences, numbers, abstract conceptions, and, lastly, emotional terms; with girls, the order is words of visual content, objects, sounds, numbers, abstract conceptions, words of auditory content, terms denoting tactual and motor experiences, and emotional terms." [2]

Meaningfulness of words. — Norsworthy [3] found at all ages from eight to sixteen that the score in reproducing lists of related words was higher than in reproducing unrelated words. Between ten and twelve years old the difference was greater for boys than for girls. Lee [4] found that written lists of words representing common objects were better remembered than lists of nonsense syllables or than series of geometric forms. He tested both immediate recall and reproduction after a day's interval.

It should be noted that children's memory for a series of words denoting emotions, such as joy, sorrow, hope, care, is poor. Naturally, to them this is a series of abstract terms more remote from their normal vocabulary than the corresponding adjectives would be. It is not surprising, therefore, considering

[1] Narasaki, A., "Sex differences in the mentality of children," *Philosophical Studies*, v. 8, *3.
[2] Rusk, R. R., *Introduction to Experimental Education*, p. 82.
[3] Norsworthy, N., *The Psychology of Mentally Deficient Children*.
[4] *Op. cit.*

the late development of memory of abstract terms, that children should do poorly with lists of this type. What is really amazing is that the investigators, on such a foundation, should have based a statement that children below fourteen possess a very poor memory for emotions. If we could induce a series of actual emotions in the children, or arouse them even in imagination, testing by normal bodily expression or "acting out," we should probably find a very different state of affairs. Certainly children's emotions are keen enough, and this very intensity serves to recall experiences after long periods of time; but we need a more refined test before accepting at face value any conclusion such as that stated above, and so frequently quoted.

Verbal or logical memory. — The memory for ideas conveyed in words is, of course, all important for higher thinking of all sorts. As such it has been tested chiefly by seeing how long a sentence can be repeated, word for word, after one hearing, or how much of the substance of a paragraph can be reproduced immediately after one presentation. Thus, at three a child should be able to repeat accurately a sentence such as *The dog runs after the cat.* At four: — *When the train passes you will hear the whistle blow.* At six: — *Walter had a fine time on his vacation. He went fishing every day.* At ten: — *It is nearly half past one o'clock; the house is very quiet and the cat has gone to sleep.* At sixteen: — *Yesterday I saw a pretty little dog in the street. It had curly brown hair, short legs, and a long tail.* These are samples from the standardized series of the intelligence scale. At ten, also, a paragraph of fifty-three words is read by the child, who should be able to reproduce eight ideas out of the twenty-one details it contains. Before twelve years old concrete words are better remembered than are abstract terms, and, as might be expected, memory for objects seen is better, and develops earlier, than memory for words or numbers.

Foster [1] experimented with a species of completion test, using pre-school age children as subjects. Short stories were told

---

[1] Foster, J. C., "Verbal memory in the pre-school child," *Ped. Sem.* and *Jo. Gen. Psy.*, v. 35, 1928.

over as many as ten times. After the first presentation a pause was made at key places to give opportunity for the child to supply the next words. By the fourth or fifth repetition of the story all the children began to participate thus, and by the tenth repetition could give, on the average, from 20 to 28 words — mostly the ideas conveyed in nouns and verbs — according to the story. This method might well be extended with older children since it tests a point very practically useful.

Especially we should welcome norms for different ages for retention of verbal material. The facts are too confused with regard to depth of interest, methods of teaching, individual differences, degree of difficulty of the material, for the factors of age and length of retention to have been disentangled as yet. Re-examinations in school subject matter after an interval of time in which there has been no direct instruction show a large amount of obliviscence or a small amount of retention, which-ever way one wants to look at it. That high-school pupils fail to recall much that they supposedly learned in the grades is no news to the teacher, any more than the fact that as adults we have forgotten much of the history, Latin, and other material not in constant use. There are few exact measurements of this inability to recall. Layton,[1] testing high-school students, found that after one year's interval of no teaching, about one third of the knowledge of elementary algebra was retained.

DIFFERENCES BETWEEN CHILDREN AND ADULTS

Learning capacity. — Contrary to popular opinion, adults can memorize better than children can. Children fall far below adults in their power of immediate memory. All the experi-mental evidence goes to show that there is a gradual improve-ment in this ability up to about fifteen years of age, roughly just at or after puberty. Some investigators think the period of most rapid improvement comes between thirteen and sixteen. After this there is relative stability which Thorndike,[2] consider-

[1] Layton, E. T., "The persistence of learning in elementary algebra," *Jo. Ed. Psy.*, v. 23, 1932.

[2] *Adult Learning*, pp. 159–165.

ing all the evidence together, thinks lasts till about forty years old. He places the high peak of learning ability somewhere between twenty and twenty-five.

Retention. — The facts concerning permanent memory tend to bear out the common impression that children have better memories than adults. It is probable that what on the ground of theory one would suppose to be true, is really true; namely that the retentive power of children is greater than that of adults. Although retentiveness is weak during the first four years it improves steadily up to about twelve years old or perhaps slightly later; after that, both ability and accuracy in retention fall off. So that although children forget more than adults do, as is proved by the conditions of immediate memory, the material that survives the process of obliviscence is retained longer than the same material by the adult. Combining the facts of immediate memory and retention, then, a child of ten would not learn so easily as an adult of twenty-five for an immediate test of memory, would forget more during the first twenty minutes following the memorizing, but would keep better to the next day or next week whatever survived this first forgetting period. Whatever may be the factors that account for this difference, greater interest, greater plasticity, fewer mental processes going on, or fewer facts already fixed in memory, the fact still remains that what one gets in childhood is more likely to remain than what is fixed at any other time in life. In old age, or sickness, it is the more lately acquired associations of maturity which are the first to fade or become inaccurate; those made in childhood persist. The recent work of the Freudian school tends to emphasize this fact, though rather from the point of view of the force of early impressions tinged with any emotion or excitement.

Desultory versus logical memory. — Two factors which condition the recall of a fact are the depth of the impression, and the number of associations or cues which it has. When memory depends primarily on the first factor it is likely to be of the desultory type, whereas an emphasis on the second factor results in logical memory. The adult's tends to be of the logical type, while that of children is more of the desultory type. The memory for related ideas improves steadily up to thirteen or fourteen, so that a larger proportion of the associations in the child's mind is of the desultory sort than in the adult's mind. It seems almost impossible for an adult to hold in memory a fact when there is not much to hang it to, no relationships or reasons that will serve as cues, whereas such facts seem simply "to stick" in the minds of most children. This being true, it behooves the educator to take advantage of this tendency and to fix in children's minds certain more or less isolated facts, such as modern language vocabularies, equivalents in mathematics, names in geography, symbols in chemistry and physics and spelling. Wessely affirms that "vocabularies (Latin-German) are reproduced more accurately at the expiration of one to four weeks when learned by twelve-year-old, than when learned by fifteen-year-old S's." [1] This is a strong argument for beginning modern languages in the grammar grades; and when one realizes that it is from ten to twelve that children become so very much interested in secret languages, dog Latin, etc., the motive for such work is supported. As this type depends primarily on the depth of the impression for the power of recall, it is necessary that the impression be made as intense as possible by use of appeals to native attention and instinctive interests. On the other hand, the fact that logical memory develops with age offers many opportunities for training. There is no question that logical memory is the more efficient type in the long run, although desultory memory is of value to all people sometimes, and for certain professions is an absolute necessity. The development and training of logical memory is one of the means of developing children's thinking power, and from another point of view it is an essential element in all thinking.

Accuracy of reports. — The general characteristics of the memory of children have been shown in interesting and con-

[1] Summarized by Whipple, *Manual of Mental and Physical Tests*, p. 376.

crete form in the study of testimony and report. The lack of capacity which children show in these lines is caused not only by their defects of memory, but also by the inaccuracies of attention and perception which have already been discussed, by the inadequate action of their imaginations, and by the fact that they do not tend to put into words what they observe. Whipple in summing up the various experimental results says, "The reports of children are in every way inferior to those of adults; the range is small, the inaccuracy large, and, since the assurance is high, the warranted assurance and reliability of assurance are both very low. During the ages 7 to 18 years, the range, especially the range of knowledge, increases as much as 50 per cent, but the accuracy, save in the deposition, does not increase as rapidly (20 per cent). This development of capacity to report is not continuous, but is characterized by rapid modification at the age of puberty. The one factor that more than any other is responsible for the poor reports of children is their excessive suggestibility, especially in the years before puberty." [1] Inaccuracy increases with the length of time elapsing between the occurrence and the reporting, and with the number of times the incident has been described. It is also true that a report may be absolutely inaccurate in some of its details and accurate in others.

These facts are of practical value in dealing with children in connection with school situations. Both teachers and parents must recognize that with the best of intentions, children's reports of what happens in the school, on the playground, and on the streets, cannot be accepted at their face value, — and the younger the child the more this is true. Much of the trouble arising between parents and school authorities could be avoided, if they both could be convinced of these facts. It should also be borne in mind that the child is often not conscious of falsification, is not lying in any sense of the term. Such inaccuracies must occur under certain conditions because of the incomplete mental development. The parents and teachers themselves

[1] *Op. cit.*, p. 306.

gave such inadequate and false reports in childhood. The danger of using questions with young children to get at the truth of an occurrence is also made clear by these investigations. Every question contains a suggestion; and before puberty, when the children are so suggestible, it is almost impossible for them to withstand the force of the suggestion offered. This is true not only when occurrences requiring discipline are subjected to questioning, but when the doings of the child or his family, excursions, visits to museums and art galleries, or even the material in a textbook, are asked about. Of course, this does not mean that questions should never be used; but it does mean that the questions should be most carefully framed, and that some other means should be resorted to as well, in order to make sure of the truth or accuracy of the reports.

WAYS OF MEMORIZING

Distributed or continuous method. — The value of distributed, rather than continuous periods of learning is obviously important in the case of young children, because of the characteristics of their attention. The younger the children the greater should be the number of brief periods. For primary children it is certainly better to have a subject twice a day, than to concentrate the same number of minutes into one period. For grammar-grade children it is better to have a subject for a shorter time every day than to have three long periods a week. For high-school students, a double period once a week is an uneconomical allotment of time. Not only do the characteristics of attention involving interest and fatigue make this distribution advisable, but the fact that with impressions of equal strength those formed earlier are less adversely affected by time adds another reason. Besides this value of the aging of associations and the extra opportunities for recall, the facts of repetition and correlation suggest that a month's short, intensive course, not followed by a related course, is little likely to produce good results. The twenty or more crowded lessons, isolated from other similar material, would be better remembered if spread over a longer period with more opportunities for cross-associations, wider range of relationships, and recall at longer intervals. At the other extreme of undesirability is the course of thirty lessons spread over an entire school year, with a large fraction of each period, and therefore of the total teaching time, spent on renewing contact with the subject matter, "warming up" as it is called. However, it must be borne in mind that both the character of the minds taught and the character of the material must determine the length and frequency of learning periods. Too long periods may induce a lack of attention if there is monotony in dealing with mechanical processes or material very nearly mastered, or they will involve fatigue with young children; too brief periods may not allow for orientation in meaningful or new material, nor for those children who warm up slowly. Too frequent periods may prevent logical synthesis and may train in cramming methods; too infrequent periods may result in dissipated interest and effort and in shaky habit formation. As to the intervals between the periods, experiment shows that these should be small at first when dealing with new phases of subject matter, and should gradually lengthen as the periods themselves perhaps decrease in length. Thus, a new topic may occupy the whole of Monday's lesson-period, two thirds of Tuesday's, one half of Wednesday's, one third of Friday's, take one fourth the time the next Monday, be briefly reviewed the following Thursday or Friday.

Repetition, concentration, or recall. — Given something to learn, it is natural for the child to adopt the method of repetition in order to fix it. He will repeat the material over and over again mechanically, but it is probable that his attention is on something else after the first few repetitions. This state of affairs obviously results in waste of time and energy, also the lesson often remains unlearned, and bad habits of study are being formed. And yet, this is the natural method; on the surface the easiest. Telling a child to "concentrate his attention" has little or no effect. Some motive must be supplied, for it is essential that children from the beginning learn to work while they work. There is no royal road to the accomplishment of this end, — so much depends on the individual child; the teacher's ingenuity must find the best means of appeal. To limit the number of repetitions allowed for the memorization of the poem or the spelling lesson, or to limit the amount of time which may be put on a given lesson, are incentives to concentration, and of course an appeal to the instinct of rivalry always brings results. No matter what the means used, children must be taught to abandon the poorer method in favor of the better.

In many cases, even repetition with concentration is not efficient as a method of learning. In much of the school work the object is to get the meaning of the material, and not to learn it by rote. This method of repetition and concentration emphasizes only serial connections; there is no opportunity to break the material up into meaning units, no encouragement to form cross-associations. The connections being formed are not those that will be used when the material is called for. For example, in studying from a book a boy is making connections between the sensory neurones of his eyes, and certain associative neurones aroused by paragraph after paragraph as he reads. But in the classroom the stimulus will probably be auditory — some question by the teacher — which will require a breaking across of all the serial connections formed and the selecting of one small fact in other relationships. If in his study, the boy has prepared for nothing of the kind, his answer will come with hesitation or perhaps he will "know it but not be able to say it." He has not formed connections in the way in which they will be used. The same thing holds when the stimulus is some life situation, and the child must recall from within the answer, with no sense cue, and no series of related associations as aids. It is necessary, therefore, that children be taught how to memorize, and how to learn. Not only must they learn to concentrate, but in their study they must form the habits of recalling from within, of asking themselves questions and reorganizing the material.

Expression. — Even when it is rote memory, experiments have shown better results when the study involved recall from within rather than sheer repetition or impressions. Gates,[1] for instance, showed in a memorization experiment the superiority of using from one half to three fifths of the total learning time in endeavors to "recite" or reproduce, to the method of mere dependence on repetition of the impression by rereading. This, of course, is one further illustration of the importance of learning material in the way it will be used.

Whole or part method. — Laboratory experiments have shown that the whole method of learning is better than the part method in rote memory work, that for instance, better results are obtained in memorizing a poem if it is studied as a whole instead of stanza by stanza. General psychology makes clear the reasons for this result, and because of these reasons we should expect the whole method to be the better for children. In actual school practice, however, serious difficulties have been met with in the application of the method. Colvin sums them up under three heads.[2] In the first place, children are discouraged because when they spend a given period of study on a selection as a whole, at the close of it none of the selection is above the memory threshold, they seem to have accomplished nothing. In the second place, some parts of the material are more difficult to learn than others, and therefore it may be that many repetitions of the whole memory material are needed for the sake of these few difficult passages. In the third place, it is rather hard to practice recall when the whole method is used. The younger the children the more serious these difficulties become, but they are not insurmountable. If the length of the selection to be memorized is adapted to the age of the children, and they are warned of the first difficulty and incited to work so hard that at the end of the second or third period of study they will know most of the selection, discouragement then will not be serious enough to be a hindrance. Because of the second difficulty, it has been found advisable to adopt a combination

---

[1] Gates, A. I., "Recitation as a factor in memorizing," *Arch. of Psy.*, v. 40, 1917.

[2] Colvin, *The Learning Process*, p. 161.

of the whole and part methods. When by the whole method, the selection has been well enough learned for the difficult parts to stand out, these may be mastered by the part method, and a return made to the whole method for a completion of the learning. So far as the third difficulty is concerned, the only thing to do is to encourage recall by all possible methods.

Colvin summarizes a compromise method thus: "Select material of reasonable length for one period of study; go over it carefully and slowly for purposes of orientation; repeat this until the general nature of the material is clearly understood, then increase the tempo. Continue to learn by the whole method until the majority of the material is raised above the threshold of memory. Next, strengthen the weak associations; . . . then go over the whole again till it is fixed. It is desirable to raise all the elements considerably beyond the threshold of memory. During the learning period practice recall; also, allow several minutes after the actual learning is finished for recalling and fixing the associations already formed. . . . Relearn the material on several succeeding days."[1]

SUGGESTIONS FOR THE TEACHER

Overlearning. — The fact that immediate memory is comparatively poor in childhood makes it imperative that measures be taken to insure the retention of the material beyond the most active period of obliviscence. The value of "overlearning" for purposes of recall needs to be impressed on teachers and students. To be able to repeat a thing once without error, though it may satisfy a laboratory requirement, does not argue a memory of it in the sense of probable accurate retention. The correctness may be a matter of chance as every learner discovers when "trying once more." Consequently, children should be encouraged to learn till they can repeat material at least twice running without error, which will entail a much greater number of repetitions and efforts to recall.

The fact that so much of what is learned in school is forgotten

[1] *Op. cit.*, p. 175.

below the level of recall even one year later has been used to support an argument something as follows. "Why waste time teaching pupils so much that they will forget in any case? Why not concentrate on teaching thoroughly just what will be remembered, say one fourth to one third of the present amount, and so save time and energy?" Without answering this argument from the standpoint of the impossibility of determining ten years in advance an individual's particular needs, or the special items he would recall or forget, the reply from the psychology of memory would be as follows. (1) If pupils forget two thirds of the total learned and were taught only one third as much as now they would retain $\frac{1}{3}$ of $\frac{1}{3}$, or $\frac{1}{9}$, and that, probably, of a very commonplace character. (2) The fact that information cannot be recalled does not mean it is wholly forgotten, as the decreased time to relearn it proves. This revivability of bonds of knowledge, of skills, makes people much more likely to be readily interested in many fields, to be intelligently sympathetic with the leaders of thought, to be socially responsive.

Rate of learning and retention. — It has been customary for teachers to regard with suspicion the child who learns his lesson in very much less time than the rest of the class need. Recent experiments with both children and adults as subjects prove conclusively that the quick learner is not the quick forgetter. Children who learn quickly retain more on the average than those who learn slowly, both as tested by immediate and permanent memory. It is very important that all those dealing with children bear this fact in mind. The quick learner, whose work is looked upon with suspicion, and who is sent back to it again and again, is not only developing an emotional attitude of dislike or indifference for the subject and sometimes even for the school, but he is forming bad habits of work. He is learning not to put his best work into his study, not to work at his highest speed, because it "doesn't pay." He forms habits of half-hearted work of divided attention, and the teacher is to blame. Many children of bright minds and quick memories may thus have been almost ruined for their best work, just because their ability was not given full rating, was not accepted at face value. Of course, all children have to be taught to test themselves when they are studying, and to know when they can reproduce reliably, and not to stop just short of the threshold of recall but rather to go a little beyond. All children need this training, but the quick learner does not need it any more than the slow learner. More individual instruction, less formality in school programs, will be demanded, more variety in material offered; but such changes are essential to the development and saving of the quickest minds.

Variation in sense appeal. — Smedley and Pohlmann [1] have investigated the type of presentation most effective in memory work with children; they agree that combined appeal is more powerful than appeal through any one sense. The order is probably auditory-visual-articulatory; auditory-visual; auditory-visual-hand-motor; visual or auditory (depending on the age). From these results it is evident that writing is not always an aid to memorizing. After the act of writing has become mechanical it will probably serve as an aid. The method of having children in the lower grades write their tables or the poem as a help to memorization is probably wasteful; but to hear, see, and say the material is the best means of impressing it.

The value of motion pictures to demonstrate geographical facts, biological facts, industrial processes, and the like which could not otherwise be presented visually, is evident. Here again, teachers must not be content with visual impressions alone but should utilize oral explanation, class discussion, pupil reaction in any suitable form to insure not only understanding but such expression and recall as will assist retention.

It has been found that rhythm is an aid in learning; with young children the interest in rhythm and the tendency to respond in rhythmic terms are strong. Not nearly enough use

---

[1] " Experimentelle Beiträge zur Lehre vom Gedächtniss," *Zeit. für Psychologie*, v. 44, 1907.

has been made of this fact. The energy here, the interest already provided by the child's nature, has been proved an aid; and yet teachers in general neglect it, and use artificial devices to catch the attention and insure the fixing of facts.

Present status of memory work in school. — At the present time, memory work in the school is at a discount. In many quarters it is considered "old fashioned," and "unpedagogical" to require children to memorize, and the work of children in the higher grades and in the high school is suffering from just this lack of a foundation of essentials in terms of memory. Memory is necessary in all learning, as has already been pointed out; information, knowledge depend upon it. It is also indispensable in constructive imagination and thinking of all grades. With sense perception it forms the foundation upon which all advanced mental work of a more complex and inventive nature must build. Incompleteness or inaccuracy in either of these fundamental factors results in serious difficulties later.

The discredit and contumely which is heaped upon memory is due largely to two causes, first, a realization that "memory work" as an end in itself is a low aim. Remembering is but a tool in the service of recombinations of ideas. Second, there is a healthy reaction against the dead, formal methods that used to be employed. There is no doubt that the memory training of the past fell short in both of these directions. Mere memory work even of the logical type will not prepare a child to meet efficiently life situations; but because this fact is true, to go to the other extreme, and require little or no memorization is absurd — it makes impossible the realization of the very aim in favor of which memory work has been discarded. Present-day education, in its desire for independence of thought, originality of belief, and freedom of conduct, is in danger of inducing a foolish lack of dependence on facts, a cheerful belief in pseudo-originality which ignores the achievements of the past, and erratic conduct free from co-ordination by verification, and from automatic regulation. Knowledge as well as habits of all kinds, must be present in the child's mind if he is to make any progress in independent work, and this is only accomplished by memorizing, and often by drill.

This does not mean that the former barrenness of rote memorization need be adopted. Logical memory, the fixing of meanings and relationships should receive greater emphasis than mere ability to give accurate verbal reproductions. While the vocational needs of the actor and the musician may call for rote memorization of long selections, scores of other vocations require the remembering of desultory facts — the names and prices of commodities, name of person and achievement, name for a sound recognized, name for a thing seen, pairs of facts of all sorts. Number combinations for computation work and letter combinations for spelling words when writing are needed by everybody, and nothing else than absolute accuracy should be the aim of memory drill in these two universally necessary fields.

The material chosen to be learned must take into account the present needs and interests of children as well as the ultimate aims of education. The methods employed must allow for the transfer of training value as well as for the immediate use. The motivation used must be suited to the age of the pupils. For older ones we may well stress the greater independence and versatility that comes from good retention and practiced recall. The social value of good immediate memory may be pointed out as it enables us to receive and act upon directions, to acknowledge introductions, to be informed upon topics of conversation of current interest socially, and so on. Children need to have aroused in them a desire to improve in various kinds of memory, and to be given standards by means of which such improvement is to be judged. What they need is not less memory training, but more of a different, and more effective kind. Accuracy in memory needs special stress. They must not tolerate 75 per cent accuracy about information any more than a bank would permit 75 per cent accuracy in its bookkeeping, or a scientist in his statement of facts. Greater insistence on the professional standards required need application in the everyday experience of reporting events. Some absurdities of rumors might thus be prevented.

PRACTICAL EXERCISES

1. Arrange to have a ten-year-old child memorize out loud for you. Explain that you want to find out exactly what children do as they learn by heart; and that you want everything, thinking, practicing, trying out, etc., to be done out loud. Arrange a quiet place for your subject and yourself alone. Supply him with a copy of a poem 4 or 5 stanzas long, 4 lines to a stanza. For yourself, have a copy prepared with all 4 lines written continuously across the long side of the paper. Follow his performance with underlining, using these symbols.

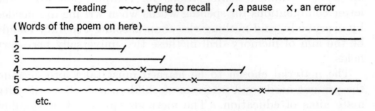

————, reading   〜〜〜, trying to recall   /, a pause   ×, an error

(Words of the poem on here)

etc.

Also annotate to indicate (*a*) general method of whole or part attack; (*b*) pauses filled with getting the meaning, imagery, comments, etc.; (*c*) rapidity or acceleration of repetitions. Analyze carefully afterwards, for report and comparison with others' results.

2. In October, repeat with a sixth- or eighth- or eleventh-grade class an examination on subject matter in science, history, or geography which they took in May in the previous grade. Compare the two sets of papers for measure of retention.

FOR DISCUSSION

1. What do the results of Exercise 1 demonstrate?
2. How would you teach children of that age to memorize the selection you used?
3. For what sort of subject matter would it help most to write it out?
4. Would writing the melody of a song assist in its memorization?
5. What do the results of Exercise 2 illustrate?
6. Given a musical composition memorized in childhood, one in the teens, one in the early twenties, which is likely to be most easily revived in the thirties? Why?

7. Supposing the methods taken to memorize were equally good in each case, who would take longer (or require more repetitions), a nine-year-old or an adult, to fixate: (*a*) the spelling of a word in a foreign language, (*b*) a piece of music, (*c*) a prose paragraph of interest? Why?

8. Of a class of twenty-six fifth-grade children, after looking at a list of words during ten minutes that they were visible on the blackboard, writing each twice, hearing each pronounced and spelled anywhere from 7 to 15 times, nine made one or more errors during a written test. What does this suggest as to (*a*) any risk of overlearning? (*b*) probable difference with twenty-six adults? (*c*) methods of memorizing spelling?

9. What facts from the psychology of children's memories explain why grammar is a difficult study for most of them?

10. Suggest several reasons for the ability of some people to memorize quickly.

11. What are the advantages and disadvantages of "six weeks in astronomy" for a first-year high-school science course?

12. Illustrate the use of rhythm in helping to fix facts for children.

13. Illustrate the method of recall in connection with memorizing
    (*a*) a foreign vocabulary,
    (*b*) a piece of prose,
    (*c*) formulæ in trigonometry, algebra, or chemistry,
    (*d*) the substance of a dozen pages of a history textbook.

14. What is the mistake made by the kindergarten teacher who asks "Which story that I've told you this month would you like to hear again?"

SELECTED REFERENCES

BROOKS AND BASSETT. "The retention of American history in the junior high school." *Jo. Ed. Res.*, v. 18, 1928.

EIKENBERRY, D. H. "Permanence of high school learning." *Jo. Ed. Psych.*, v. 14, 1923.

FOSTER, J. C. "Verbal memory in the pre-school child." *Ped. Sem.* and *Jo. Gen. Psych.*, v. 25, 1928.

LEE, A. L. "An experimental study of retention and its relation to intelligence." *Psych. Monog.*, v. 34 *4, 1925.

THORNDIKE, E. L. "The permanence of school learning." *Sch. and Soc.*, v. 15, 1922.

WHIPPLE, G. M. *Manual of Mental and Physical Tests.* Pages 365–403.

CHAPTER X

LEARNING AS HABIT FORMING

CHILDHOOD AND HABIT-FORMATION

Importance of habits. — There is no subject of child psychology more important than that of habit-formation. It is the element that gives character to the individual life, for character after all must be defined in terms of one's habitual modes of response. Since habit makes up so large a part of life no work can be more important for a teacher, for a school system, for any and all of the educational forces than that of making efficient the factor responsible for so much of the activities of the human race. The teacher's fundamental duty is that of habit-formation; for only so can she make possible the activities leading to independence and originality. This fact was pointed out in connection with memory, which is habit-formation in the realm of mental states; but it needs to be emphasized again and again. Not too many habits, but too few is the danger that teachers must avoid. Having too few habits results in insufficiency of control, in lack of material, in narrowness of conduct and thought. To have the wrong habits, whether in skills, in study, in hygiene, in emotional or in social reactions, means to restrict and hamper the individual's development. It may well spell tragedy not only for him but for those with whom he comes in contact. The main purpose of child-training is to fix effective, valuable habits of all sorts. The greater the number of good habits that an individual possesses in all fields, — thought, feeling, conduct, — the more efficient will he be, especially if among them is found the habit of forming new habits.

Physiological basis of habit. — Though we know of no specific neural pathways involved in such a habit as putting on one's shoes, still less in a complex study habit such as making an outline of a long selection read, yet it is clear that every habit depends upon the ability of the nervous system to establish functional contact at a series of synapses so that responses of a predictable sort will be made to certain situations. Habits depend also upon a characteristic of physiological structures to become permanently modified by what happens to them. This characteristic has been generally called "plasticity." Man above all other animals possesses this something, and children are characterized by it to an extreme degree. Plasticity means the power of neurones to be sensitive to what happens to them, and to be changed permanently thereby. This fact of the plasticity of the connections, together with the richness both as to number and variety of man's original equipment, accounts for his supremacy over all animals in power to learn. If either factor were less perfect than it is, there would result decreased educability. A lessening of the richness and complexity of the responses grouped under such heads as manipulation, vocalization, attention, mental control, would enormously change his power of learning. If the nervous system were less impressionable, or were less permanently affected, the same result would ensue. Both the multiplicity of neural connections and the plasticity of such connections are necessary to explain the difference between man and the lower animals in respect to learning; for learning has always to do with the modification of some definite response of thought, feeling, or action.

Variation in plasticity. — Three questions arise in connection with this characteristic of plasticity: (1) are all bonds equally modifiable? (2) is this plasticity equal at all ages? (3) are some bonds more open to modification at certain ages than at others? Taking these three questions in order, all bonds are not equally modifiable; those controlling the physiological and reflex operations are but slightly modifiable. Such responses as those connected with fear, food-getting, and mastery are less modifiable than those connected with vocalization, manipulation, and attention; but all in this group are more modifiable than those in the first group. With regard to permanence of the modification, it seems probable that those bonds made up of sensori-motor connections hold the effects of modification longer than those connections which are sensori-associative, or associative-associative. In other words, learning which results in such habits as skating, swimming, sewing, piano playing, typewriting, will probably be more permanent than learning which results in memory of historical facts, or poetry, knowledge of geometry, or linguistic skill.

Second, plasticity is not equal at all ages; childhood is the most plastic period. The discussion of the retentive power in children is an illustration of this point. Much has been made of this fact, and the value of childhood from the standpoint of learning has received much attention. Without doubt all that has been urged for it is true, but on the other hand, the resulting implication, and in some cases doctrine, that habits can be formed only with difficulty after one is twenty-five and only as a miracle after thirty-five, is untrue to the facts. In the laboratory experiments with adults when the conditions were the best, modification was always noted, and in some cases very great improvement took place. Of course, there are all sorts of individual differences here as elsewhere, but the facts point to a much longer period of learning than has commonly been accepted. Thorndike [1] summarizes the findings of several investigators to show that in speed and efficiency of learning there is improvement up to the age of twenty-two, at least, even though sheer retentiveness may not increase after fourteen or fifteen. The richer complex of habits already available, of nerve co-ordinations already established, facilitates the learning process so that at eighteen people do better than at eight, for instance.

In the third place, as a matter of mere inner growth, it seems to be true that certain neurone-systems are more susceptible of modification at certain times than at others. It is a generally accepted fact that the finger dexterity and supple-

[1] *Adult Learning.*

ness required in musical technique must be acquired in childhood; accent in speaking another language is much more easily
acquired in childhood than later, also the skill of the acrobat
or tumbler must be developed during the early years. These
and many other facts point to the conclusion that physical
learning comes most easily in early childhood. Such habits as
these, however, depend upon the plasticity of muscles, sinews,
bones rather than on the nervous system alone as study habits
may do.

Maturity and habit forming. — These facts have important
practical bearings. The great plasticity of the period of infancy
and early childhood must result in the formation of habits.
Whether the parents know it or not, whether the teacher realizes it or not, the very nature of the child's nervous system
necessitates learning. It is affected by all that happens to it,
and something is happening every minute of the day. For the
young child the *emotional* tone of the environment is one of the
most important influences in his education. Because of the
force of reflex imitation working with this factor of plasticity,
the emotional attitudes of those by whom he is surrounded
leave their impress on the child. Before he has lived thirty
months his disposition is formed; he is becoming irritable,
quick-tempered, moody, or sunny and cheerful, timid or well
poised, just which, however, being determined to a larger extent
than people realize by the natures of the adults surrounding
him, — and this all unconscious to himself, simply as a result
of the modifiability of his neurones. The habit clinics to which
children are brought for remedial treatment find it necessary,
in about four fifths of the cases, to deal primarily with the
parents' attitudes and methods of dealing with the children.

In the field of *social adaptation* this same fact of early environment is particularly important. Certain sorts of responses
towards other people, such as methods adopted to gain attention,
certain ways of accepting success or failure, are now habituated so firmly that a child's personality or disposition may be
permanently molded. On the other hand, if retraining becomes

necessary the earlier it is undertaken the greater is its probable
chance of success. The teacher of children of nursery school age
has a better opportunity to correct faults than has the primary
grades teacher, or even the kindergarten teacher. All need to
understand the home conditions, especially the parent-child
relationship, if they would interpret the child from the behavior
patterns they see already formed. In the field of *morals and
manners*, the same element makes itself felt. The old adage —
"Let a child run until he is six and you never catch him" —
is a recognition of the far-reaching effects of the habits formed
in this period. The further facts that criminals show a delinquent
career beginning at ten or younger, and that if a child is a
proved delinquent by the age of ten it is difficult to change his
social habits, reinforce the importance of the right environment
for the early years.

It was noted above that not only is the plasticity greatest in
early childhood, but that it is greater in lines of *muscular* habits
than it will ever be again, and further, that sensori-motor bonds
are retained longer than any other kind; therefore, without any
doubt, the years before nine are pre-eminently the ones in which
to establish good physical habits. The hygienic habits of eating
and sleeping at regular periods, of evacuation; habits of cleanliness and tidiness; habits of posture, carriage of the body, and
of walking; habits of pronunciation, both of the mother tongue
and modern languages; habits of the use of tools and implements.

This does not mean that adolescents can be careless of posture
and so on. Obviously the constant changes in relation of size
of limbs and strength of muscles necessitate continual readjustment of controls. When full growth is reached, say at eighteen
or so, is an important period for perfecting and establishing
habits of gait and carriage as any one handling recruits for the
army and navy knows full well. It would be poor economy
from every point of view to defer physical training until sixteen
years of age, however. We do not expect skilled artisans at nine
years old, either; but unless hand training is included early and

constantly we know that dexterous manipulation is exceedingly hard to acquire in later childhood, let alone that the personality suffers from a sort of bias.

For *hygiene habits, physical skill habits, craftsmanship,* the period of early and middle childhood is exceedingly important, just as for emotional habits the earliest years of all are significant. If the habits are good, the child has made a splendid beginning in the race of life, he has capital the benefit of which he will feel as the years pass; if the habits are bad ones, just the reverse will be true, and it must be one or the other. Children in these early years cannot help forming habits; for, as has been said before, it is the nature of their nervous systems to be modifiable.

Study habits. — What we think of as study habits are included mostly in three large areas of human activity, (1) that of attentive, thoughtful observation of objective phenomena, (2) the technique of using language and all its tools such as books, maps, blue prints, calculating machines, filing systems, libraries, etc., (3) that of organized thinking. This last involves habits of weighing values of facts in the light of the immediate purpose, habits of comparing and contrasting facts so as to interpret relationships, habits of checking and verifying, and deferring belief in statements till verification is possible. The extremely poor behavior of so many adults in this third field may be due, not so much to lack of ability, as to lack of training in good thinking habits.

In the first field mentioned, beginnings are made with the simple nature study work in nursery school, kindergarten and first grade. It is well that this precedes learning to read, so that there is opportunity to emphasize the value of direct, first-hand information rather than reliance on books. About the second-grade level, at seven and a half to eight years old, which is an important turning point in several respects, stress should be laid on exactitude of observation. We do not discuss how many legs a spider has, we count them. We do not wonder in which direction the wind is blowing, we find out. No habits of guess work can be permitted when it is a question of accurate space, quantity, rhythm, color discrimination. (Note that this is not a matter of skill or crudity in reproducing, but in observing.) Here both artist and scientist need a foundation of precise rather than vague knowledge; and habits for acquiring this must be in process of formation by eight years of age.

In the second field above clearly there are hierarchies of habits. We may begin by stimulating interest and care in the handling of books by the use of picture books at three and four years old. The language habits of reading, spelling, writing, computation, traditionally occupy the years six to ten. The poor results shown may be due in part to the fact that scientific analysis of the habits involved had not till recently been undertaken nor the results made known. Today, however, studies of the psychology of the elementary school subjects, for example Thorndike's [1] in arithmetic, Gates' [2] in reading, are available so that teachers can know just what habits have to be formed, and what is to be avoided. Once the basal skills are automatic comes the time for intensive training in summarizing, outlining, expanding, rearranging, whether in reading or in writing. Besides this we have to form habits of use of the various devices invented to further business life, scientific, literary research. The school trains in the use of maps, dictionaries, encyclopedias, indices, in the upper grades, and, with the co-operation of the librarian helps pupils of junior high-school age to intelligent use of our many arrangements for classifying information and rendering it readily accessible. In this respect the children in our small towns and rural sections are frequently at a disadvantage in the materials provided for efficient techniques.

Habit-formation in the third field of study, that of organization of thinking, needs more attention than it has received. Any purposeful thinking gives opportunity to criticize the pertinency of suggestions made. Whatever the topic studied there is need to relate it to other knowledge, to illustrate it, to

[1] *The Psychology of Arithmetic.*   [2] *The Improvement of Reading.*

see its implications for human life today; and this means habits of looking for likenesses, differences, causes, conditions, and so on. Children under twelve should not be expected to react thus with abstract material; but they greatly need practice in these respects with concrete material. Any type of work, not only the mathematical problem, but spelling, craftsmanship, the laboratory experiment, the assemblage of data for debate, requires the habit of checking and verifying. Perhaps the ordinary citizen needs, more than the habit of verifying his own work, the habit of withholding belief in, and especially of refraining from repeating, facts told him orally until there has been demonstrable proof of their veracity. What untold misery could be spared, what senseless, superstitious reports could be stifled were this habit firmly rooted by constant practice since middle childhood in the characters of our population.

CONDITIONS OF HABIT FORMING

Associative shifting. — The simplest cases of forming bonds between stimuli and reactions are illustrated by the process called conditioning. As Pavlov, John Watson [1] and others have demonstrated by the conditioned reflex, given a bond already existing, such as the response salivation to the stimulus sight-and-smell-of-food, another stimulus, such as hearing-a-bell-ring can be supplied simultaneously with the old stimulus till, with repetition, the response comes to be linked to the new stimulus alone. In the case of emotional reactions the response of starting-with-fear, made originally to the sudden, loud sound, can be linked to a new stimulus, such as the sight or feel of a furry animal, provided the two stimuli are presented at the same time. On a higher level than that of glandular, visceral reflexes, taken care of through the autonomic nervous system, the same principle of the shifting of bonds works. For instance, a child already responds by saying "cat" to the stimulus seeing-a-picture-of-a-cat. The teacher presents a picture and the printed word

[1] Watson and Rayner, "Conditioned emotional reactions," *Jo. Exp. Psy.*, v. 3, 1920.

simultaneously; the response is made. Soon the picture is omitted, and the new stimulus alone is potent to elicit the response.

Thought of in another way, variations can be gradually introduced in a complex neurone activity provided part of such activity pattern is already familiar. Thus, a new response can be linked to an old situation just as well as having an old response to a new situation. In teaching a foreign language, the new sounding words are given orally while the teacher suits the action to the word. The pupil is led to make the new response in saying the Latin, German, Spanish, French, etc., while he sees and thinks of a familiar situation. In this way habits at any level may become initiated.

Law of effect. — No habit can be formed without a response of some description, though all responses are not made automatic, as habits. Whether a response is repeated or not upon the second, tenth, fiftieth repetition of the stimulus depends on (1) whether the result was satisfying or not, (2) the degree of pleasantness or unpleasantness attaching to the whole complex. Extreme degrees of feeling tone promote rapid learning. Thus, one acute experience of fright, pain, humiliation, may be sufficient to prevent repetition of an action, where ten mildly unpleasant penalties serially encountered might not insure desistence. Conversely, one greatly pleasing effect upon self-esteem may bring a sure and certain repetition of an act where dozens of mild, well-worn expressions of approval are of little avail. The facts are complicated here by the actual difficulty of the habit to be learned, also by individual differences in emotional susceptibility, age differences in the appeal of specific rewards and pains.

As for pleasure versus pain, both laboratory experiments and ordinary social experience demonstrate that the latter may teach what not to do, but does not teach what the correct reaction is except by a process of elimination. Pleasure has the selective advantage of strengthening that bond which leads to the correct reaction. In habituating techniques, in mechanizing spelling, computation, in building moral personalities, this difference is peculiarly significant.

Law of exercise. — Use, frequency, repetition, drill, are other terms used to refer to the fact that many reactions cannot be habituated, in the sense of being made with a minimum of directive attention, unless there is plentiful practice. Some writers have taken pains to point out the ineffectiveness of mere repetition to insure habituation, illustrating by such occurrences as animals learning the method of escape from a puzzle box after the less frequent repetition of the correct reaction rather than by the greater frequency of incorrect reactions. Also they remind us that children forced to repeat certain kinds of behavior scores of times do not evidence persistence of habit bonds. This emphasizes the truth that repetition alone, without attention, without intention, without satisfaction attached, may be useless. But to go to the other extreme and preach the doctrine that repetition is unnecessary is absurd, as any tennis player, actor, stenographer, social worker could testify. Attentive practice, willing co-operation in exercise is what is needed.

Motivation. — Both to initiate a habit and to sustain interest in practicing it, motivation is necessary. By this we mean anticipation of feelings of pleasantness or unpleasantness, recollection of such, or actual occurrence of such during attempts to react correctly. It may be part of the situation externally — as when the pleasure of seeing a glittering object precedes the baby's reaching for it. The imagination may play a large part in determining the forcefulness of motives when they are not inherent in the physical situation. Curiosity, fear of failure, the pleasure of anticipated ownership, the promise of promotion, the hope of social approval are samples of powerful motives commonly operating to stimulate behavior. Recollection of previous successes, of æsthetic enjoyment will induce renewed effort. The present fun of competition will speed up action and call out much energy, though it may distract attention from the critical evaluation of the reactions made.

Teachers must allow for the intense, yet short-lived emotions of childhood when seeking for suitable motives to supply, and for satisfying results to be brought about so that they are felt in direct connection with the desired response. Also, in cases of exercise of undesirable tendencies in spite of disagreeable effects, the situation should be analyzed further, and counter attractions set up.

Knowledge of goal. — Many habits are " picked up " unawares, by simple imitation of the most frequent model — as in intonation, accent, phraseology — or by vague though satisfactory relief following an impulse — as in biting the lips. For the great majority, however, of the processes which teachers wish to habituate in pupils attention must be centered on the aim to be achieved in order to facilitate criticism of the progress made. Any suitable means, such as explanation in words, demonstration in action, by completed model, must be utilized to give the learner a clear idea of what is expected. Here again, the psychology of the special subject matter will indicate valuable means as well as safeguard the teacher against artificial devices, "crutches" that have been proved valueless.

Transferability of training. — What was said above concerning the variability possible, provided some part of the complex activity pattern is already familiar, should reinforce the idea that the younger the child, and the fewer habit patterns he has, the less transfer there can be. Training a reaction in one situation will not transfer it to another, totally different situation. Thus, because a child puts away his toys in the kindergarten before going home does not teach him to put toys away at home before going to bed. Nor will pupils who draw neat graphs for the algebra teacher necessarily hand in neat drawings in the biology lesson. Emphasis must be laid on the similarity of methods or of subject matter, or of desirability of the ideal in the two situations in order to draw the learner's attention to the possibility of using old habits as far as possible. Correlation of subject matter, a reminder at the opportune moment of how things are done on other occasions, is constantly needed. Knowledge must be called upon to function in directing a multiplicity of acts if we would secure flexibility and adaptability. Thus, similarities in syntax or in derivation in two different languages may be noticed by a few pupils, but should be pointed out. Geographical knowledge should be called on in several sorts of social studies; the ability to state that heat coagulates albumen should function when washing plates sticky with egg.

Above all, when the only connection between habits is an abstract classification, no transfer need be expected with children too young to deal with abstractions. In conduct habits "courtesy" might mean to respond to the situation *being-handed-something* by saying thank you: or to respond to the situation *somebody-trying-to-pass-me* by stepping aside; or to respond to the situation *being-greeted-by-a-lady* by raising one's hat. The total activity pattern is so different that the only possibility of transfer could be through the appreciation of the ideal inspiring all of them. Meanwhile, the habits must be thought of as specific, and taught each for itself.

THE LABORATORY AND THE SCHOOLROOM

Working for improvement. — The business of education is not merely to form habits, but to raise them to their highest level of efficiency; therefore, the psychology of improvement of habits is very important. That this need of improvement is not kept clearly in mind by teachers is shown by the low level of efficiency of the most common habits despite the great possibilities of improvement in them. All the work that has been done in experimental laboratories and elsewhere on all forms of practice experiments points to the same conclusion, *i.e.*, that all functions are capable of improvement, and most of them enormously so. There are four reasons for this striking difference between the improvement in habits in ordinary school practice, and under experimental conditions.

Consciousness of definite goal. — One is that the factors upon which improvement depends are more carefully planned for in the laboratory than in school. In the practice experiments, the

improvement worked for is always very definite and clear;
it is adding, or striking a dot, or memorizing words, or typewriting by the sight method. There is no confusion in the
subject's mind as to just what he is to do. It is not a big general sort of task such as "to do better work in arithmetic,"
or "to present neater papers in English," — but one or two
factors involved in this complex task are analyzed out, focused
in the mind of the subject, and worked for. Hence the improvement. The aim must be definite, and must be held clearly in
mind, if children are to improve. The chief trouble is that
teachers have not considered their work from this point of
view. They often do not have clearly in their own minds just
what habits of responses in terms of thought, feeling, or action
they are working for in any given subject, much less having
it clearly defined for any given lesson. The children, therefore,
cannot improve very fast or very much.

Speedy working of law of effect. — A second reason is that
the law of effect plays its part immediately in these practice
experiments. The subject knows when he is doing well or ill.
There is no difficulty in making the connection between the
satisfaction or the discomfort and the bonds concerned, hence
the effect is felt at its full strength. This condition is often not
allowed for in school, — the child works at "something" but
when it is just "something," the satisfyingness of the result
cannot attach to anything very definitely. And besides, as
has already been pointed out, it is too often true that the child
is left in ignorance of the result, and therefore the law of effect
plays no part.

Desire to improve. — A third very important factor in all
improvement is that the idea of improvement itself must be
prominent in the mind of the worker. It is not enough to have
as an aim, to learn to add, or to toss a ball into the basket, or
to spell, but in each case it must be also to add faster than
yesterday, to make a basket from various positions, or to have
more words right, or learn them in a shorter time. Improvement in itself must be a conscious aim, yet conditions are such

that children in their learning seldom have more than a very
indefinite feeling that, of course, they are supposed to do better;
and this is true often because they do not know when they improve or how much. It is not safe for teachers to think that
children know when they improve. They do not, — even those
in the upper grammar grades do not. Their standards of what
is excellent are not clearly defined, and their power of analyzing
their own work and comparing it with a standard is undeveloped.
They need help along these very lines; and the only way to
give it is to be sure that the amount of improvement, or the
lack of it, is very clear in the child's mind.

Our many standardized achievement tests offer a ready means
of clarifying to a child just how good his work is. Scales of
penmanship can be displayed so that objective evidence of
standards in quality and speed is available. Charts and graphs
of individual and class progress can easily be arranged and
prove very stimulating.

Interest in work. — A fourth factor, which would seem hardly
to need mentioning theoretically, yet which may be woefully
neglected, is that of interest. Somehow or other, if improvement
is to be steady the work must seem worth while to the child,
it must satisfy some need of his, he must be interested in it.
In the practice of the experimental laboratory this interest is
present and helps to account for the results. Sometimes it is
the novelty of the experiment that attracts, sometimes it is the
desire to see how much one can do, sometimes it is the joy of
beating some one else, and sometimes it is the realization that
improvement along this line will materially aid in some work
itself interesting; whatever the reason, the general rule is that
improvement comes most rapidly when the whole of the child
or subject is in the endeavor. It is almost pitiful when going
into any classroom and starting one of these experiments, to
see the vim and eagerness with which the children set to work.
More of this same energy could be called upon in connection
with the ordinary school work if some of the characteristics of
the practice experiment were incorporated in it.

The practice curve. — Two characteristics of the practice curve are important for students of child psychology, — the rapid rise at the beginning, and the presence of plateaus. It is true that the improvement at the beginning of many practice series is very rapid, and the newer the work the more rapid the improvement. Of course this means that children's gain at first in a new subject or phase of it is very marked. This is dangerous, in that it offers a temptation to go so fast in the learning process in the early stages that the material gained or the skill acquired is only just over the threshold of learning, is not fixed firmly enough to serve as a foundation for the next higher level of habits. The unwisdom of such procedure is shown in the unnecessary frequency and length of the plateaus which occur later. It is absolutely necessary for efficient and economical learning that the foundation be well laid, that the elementary habits be made automatic before the complex work that soon appears is attempted. Teachers must allow for and even encourage overlearning in the early stages if they wish to avoid the discouragement of the plateaus later.

These plateaus, or places where there seems to be no progress, themselves offer a problem. They seem to depend chiefly on two conditions: first, the lack of automatization of elementary habits, which has already been mentioned; and second, the loss of interest. When one of these pauses in progress occurs it is highly necessary for the teacher to overcome it as soon as possible, for it is one of the most fruitful sources of discouragement. In order to overcome it the teacher must know to which of the above-mentioned causes it is due, for her method of dealing with it would vary as the cause. If it is due to lack of automatization, the cure would, of course, be found in review; the onward progress would have to cease for the time, and the old work be taken up once more from ever-varying points of view, with interesting drills until the necessary automatism in response is acquired. On the other hand, if the pause is due to monotony and loss of interest, the cure might be found in an added spurt in the forward movement, or an entire cessation of the work for

the time being, or in appealing to other interests, or in adding
incentives. In any case, the method used would depend upon
the cause of the plateaus. With adults it may be safe to leave
the diagnosing of the trouble to the person concerned, but with
children that certainly is impossible. They are probably not
conscious of the lack of improvement, and they are certainly
not capable of ascertaining the cause. This duty must rest
on the teacher, and it is not an easy one by any means.
The fact remains, however, that with care and alertness on
her part, the number of these hindrances to steady improvement can be materially lessened, and the amount of time
spent on the plateaus which do occur can be considerably
diminished.

Muscular skill. — It has been pointed out by those who have
investigated the acquisition and improvement of acts of skill
when the responses are complex, that changes in method which
are effective in bringing about improvement are at first hit
upon unconsciously, but that their ultimate usefulness depends
upon their being made conscious. This method of trying this
and that in a blind effort to solve the situation is the animal
method of learning, the simple trial and success method, and
it seems to be fundamental and indispensable in all learning
which involves physical skill. Explaining to a child how to do
something is useless in the early stages; only after he has made
the co-ordination, done the act in some fashion or other, has
the telling any content for him at all. This suggests the need
of much more experimentation method, much more "trial and
success" in the learning of little children, and in the beginning
stages of any learning involving muscular responses, even with
adults. After the learner has attempted some responses by his
own initiative, the suggestions of a teacher would be useful.
True, if left to himself, he might in time stumble on a good
method; but waiting for each learner to do so is not only lacking
in economy, but runs the risk of forming bad habits. It is the
business of the teacher to watch a child's endeavors, and at
the opportune moment to suggest valuable changes in his

method. Given in that way, suggestions are more likely to be effective, but given preceding any movements they are meaningless. The explanation to a child of the value of holding his pencil, or his needle, or his plane, or his bat just so, has no content for him until he has attempted to do it; the suggestion will then have an apperceptive basis, and the reasonableness of it is more likely to be clear by comparison. Teachers must not be afraid to let children try things out for themselves. Of course, the danger of the bad effects of a wrong start must be guarded against by a close watchfulness; but trial and success with selection of the best variation of response is the only way to bring about effective and steady improvement.

Another fact in connection with this type of learning must be borne in mind. Although suggestions of change of method may be possible in the early stages, still a time comes when the act is so complete that words are meaningless; no one can tell how to improve. It must be left to the individual to stumble upon the necessary change, but the teacher can be of help in bringing the change to attention at once, instead of letting it pass perhaps to be lost, or at least with no greater chance of its occurring again rather than any other variation. There comes a time in throwing a ball when a certain suppleness is necessary; in dancing, when an added element of ease must come if the slide is to be graceful; in singing when a fullness of tone is needed; and in painting when a certain lightness of touch conditions the smooth, even laying-on of the wash. No amount of telling how to hold the ball or bend the wrist, of how to hold the body or move the feet, of how to place the voice or open the throat, or of how to hold the brush, will bring the desired result. It must come of itself. But if a watchful teacher is there to say, "There now you have it, — that is the right quality of tone," "That is what you have been working for," attention is immediately attracted to the right response, and it is made more likely to reoccur because of the satisfyingness attached to the commendation.

Laws of exercise and effect. — From these two general laws two practical precepts have been evolved: "Form habits as they will be used," and "Reward good impulses." These seem almost too obvious to merit discussion; yet it is true that no laws or precepts are more often overlooked in dealing with children than just these. For example, though habits come only by repetition and exercise of the learner's own nerves and muscles, yet many parents and teachers seem to expect them to come by magic. Of course they would not admit this, but what else explains their expectations and customs? Instead of seeing to it that children *form habits*, they rest content with mere exhortations or expositions. Mothers expect little girls to be polite with no further training than an exasperated "Don't be so rude!" can give; teachers suppose that children will be able to add 3 plus 12 because they know 12 plus 3. Children are told how to hold pencils or needles, how to use a plane or a paint brush, how to throw a ball or produce a legato touch on the piano, and then adults are impatient when they do not do these things from the mere telling. As though nerve connections used from ear to associative center would bring about automatism from motor center to hand.

As bad as these violations of "form habits . . ." is the ignoring of the rest of that maxim, ". . . *as they will be used.*" Much time is given to oral spelling and reading, to written language and arithmetic, to composition in art and music, whereas ordinary life situations call for written spelling, silent reading, oral language, mental arithmetic, appreciation in art, rendition of others' music hundreds of times as often as for the activities mentioned. Then, too, children are drilled in serial habits, such as repeating tables of weights and measures, multiplication tables, principal parts of verbs, declensions and conjugations, lists of dates, and the like, when the connections needed in ordinary usage are not these at all but paired facts possibly, or a response to one fact by itself. A serial habit of this type not only omits to form a habit that is to be used, but it is a distinct hindrance to the early stages of the formation of the needed habits.

For any desired habit we cannot trust to mere repetition; it must be repetition *with satisfactory results.* Neutral consequences or unpleasant accompaniments will not succeed in establishing a habit. Children must not be expected to learn their spelling words by repeating them over and over again to themselves with no different result to their consciousness when they repeat correctly from what they experience when they repeat incorrectly. Practice will not make perfect unless satisfaction follows the variations that are in the direction of the ideal. Good impulses must be definitely rewarded, and undesirable impulses must fail of achieving satisfaction. Too often this maxim is violated by such practices as granting children their requests if they tease long enough, paying attention to troublesome children and those who are trying to "show off," while ignoring the good, well-behaved ones. Other misuses of the law of effect are such customs as giving children poetry or Bible passages to memorize as a punishment, exaggerating the value of a promised reward, forgetting to comment on an improvement, quoting a child's impudence in front of him as though it were commendable, and the like. In line with these are the schoolroom customs of scoring only the mistakes in composition, drawing, or music, and of giving misspelled words and incorrect syntax for correction; only in these cases the wrong form of the habit is encouraged by emphasizing it to the exclusion of the right forms.

With young children the responsibility of providing opportunity for exercise, and of making sure that satisfactory results follow effective exercise, rests on the adult, either teacher or parent. Many of the habits which it is worth while for children to form seem to them to be of no value, and therefore, of their own accord, they do not exercise them. Some one to whom their value is evident must provide the opportunities. It is also true that the younger the child the more often must the reward come from without. The aim of the teacher, of course, is so to arrange the situations that the activity itself shall bring its own reward; but that cannot always be the result, and incentives and rewards of various kinds have to be resorted to. The teacher will show her ingenuity and probably secure results if she uses the original satisfiers in connection with the formation of the habit. With little children this satisfaction, whatever it may be, should follow immediately the activity it is supposed to reward. It would be unsafe to defer rewarding a child of five for good pronunciation or clean hands until the close of school; and similarly to keep a child of seven waiting for his reward for the correct holding of his pen or any other habit until the end of the week or month would be foolish. In either case, the child will, of course, be delighted with his pleasure; but the point is that it is not closely enough connected with the working of the particular synapsis to help fix the right discharge.

Importance of precedent. — The facts concerning the greater plasticity of the earlier years of a child's life as compared with the later apply also to any period in habit-formation when compared with any later period. The particular set or bent given by the first few responses to a situation have a much greater effect than the same number at any later period; hence, the emotional effect of the first responses at the beginning of any habit-formation series is particularly important, and more so for children than for adults. This is true whether the habits be motor, intellectual, or emotional. And yet how often this fact is ignored in dealing with children in the home and in school. It is the first few days in the new class that are so influential in determining the discipline, the attitude towards the work, and towards the teacher; and yet how many teachers say that "it takes a week to settle down," not at all realizing the importance of the beginning weeks for habit. The same thing holds true in beginning a new subject, or in meeting a new friend; it is the first impressions that count for so much. Again, how often it is true that the habits allowed to be formed at the

beginning, or in the early stages, are absolutely wrong; and
these are most difficult to change. Children at first accustomed
to having each sentence occupy one line form the habit of
moving their eyes in accordance with that arrangement, and
therefore find it most difficult to change to the habit of picking
up the sentence on the next line and reading smoothly. When
in the early stages of reading children have been allowed to
pronounce each word to themselves, it is troublesome to break
the habit when for the sake of rapid reading it is necessary. To
how many children geometry has been a most tiresome and
difficult subject because, in dealing with the first few proposi-
tions, the habit of memorizing them was formed. In the primary and early grammar grades "studying" to the child meant
memorizing, and that sort of studying brought satisfactory
results; hence when that sort will not satisfy the conditions,
and teachers in the upper grammar grades and the high school
try to teach them what the studying really means, they find
it most difficult, because of the "set" given by these early
habits. The time to begin to teach a child how to study a book
by other methods as well as rote memorizing is in the primary
grades when he first begins to use books.

Slogans for the teacher. — Much of the above may be condensed into brief reminders, about as follows:

See that the pupils react; don't preach to them. A habit is a
    definite action, therefore talking in abstract terms, espe-
    cially to young children, or about ethical habits, is useless.

See that the pupils know exactly what to aim for.

Appeal to the best motive that will work.

Secure their intelligent co-operation in the necessary drill.

Contrive satisfying results for the right reactions.

See that it is the right reaction that gets rewarded.

See that nothing pleasurable is connected with the wrong
    reaction.

Arrange for success in the early stages of practice by gradu-
    ating the difficulty of the task.

Secure correct responses from the beginning.

Allow sufficient time for practice, and frequent opportunity.
Center the pupil's attention on definite improvement.
Recognize improvement as objectively and as soon as possible.
Analyze causes of lack of improvement, or failure.
Train in methods of objective self-criticism.
Guard against fatigue, carelessness, loss of interest.
For any habit a pupil is to form he should be able to say —
   1. This is what I am to do.
   2. I want to do it.
   3. I have done it.
   4. This is why I succeeded.
Form the basal habits first, the less frequently used ones later.
Do not teach habits that must later be changed.
Do not passively expect training to transfer; work for it.
Analyze the causes for undesirable habits you find already
   formed in a pupil. They are there because they bring
   satisfaction. The preferred reaction you wish to substitute
   must be made more attractive than the old one.

PRACTICAL EXERCISES

1. Observe first- and second-grade children while writing, and then
   illustrate each of these points made by James:
      Habit saves time.
      Habit simplifies movements.
      Habit lessens fatigue.
      Habit diminishes the constant attention with which the act is
      performed.
      Habit makes movements more accurate.
2. Review the results of observations made on distractability during study
   periods.

FOR DISCUSSION

1. Explain from the standpoint of habit forming the following: —
      An ounce of prevention is worth a pound of cure.
      Well begun is half done.
      As the twig is bent the tree is inclined.
2. Will learning to use the waste paper basket in the schoolroom teach
   picnic parties not to disfigure the countryside with litter? Could it?
   How?

3. Why is close supervision advisable in the early stages of habit forming?
4. Describe in physiological terms the risk of allowing exceptions when breaking an undesirable habit.
5. Why would it be poor training to have forty children take turns in being monitor for one day each?
6. Why are boys "willing to take the whipping if we can get the swim"?
7. Explain the unwisdom of assigning homework on a new principle in algebra before it is understood.
8. Should the strongest incentives be used at the beginning or at the plateau stage of a habit? Why?
9. What would be the value of definite lessons in table manners? How could they be planned so as to "form habits as they will be used"? In what ways does the high-school quick-lunch counter violate this precept?
10. Make a list of hygienic habits in the formation of which the teacher and home can co-operate.
11. How would you arrange to "reward good impulses" so as to have children form the habit of truth-telling?
12. What is the danger to a child, from the standpoint of habit-formation, of too early specializing in a vocation?
13. What means would you take, other than assigning school grades, to make progress aimed for and evident in such habits as: technique of piano playing; looking for the topic of a lesson assignment; careful observation in nature study work; the use of references, encyclopedias, Poole's index, etc.; outlining and summarizing?
14. Make a list of thirty or more specific, concrete directions you would give to replace the abstract one, "Be neat in your work about the laboratory."
15. What is the value to the teacher of thus analyzing a standard or an activity?
16. Considering the facts of transfer of training, of what value in sex education is knowledge, and microscope study of cell division, and embryology? Knowledge of the laws of heredity? At what age might such knowledge be expected to have a personal appeal in control of behavior?

SELECTED REFERENCES

BLANTON AND BLANTON. *Child Guidance*. Ch. 13.
JAMES, W. *Talks to Teachers*. Ch. 8.
MORGAN, J. J. B. *Child Psychology*. Pages 113–121.
STILLMAN, B. W. *Training Children to Study*.
THOM, D. A. *Everyday Problems of the Everyday Child*.

CHAPTER XI

IMAGINATION

KINDS OF IMAGERY

Reproductive. — One school of psychologists refuses to acknowledge the existence of images of any sort since the evidence rests upon introspection, the validity of which, as a method, they deny. Most of us feel quite confident that we do see in our "mind's eye," or hear in our mind's ear, and so on, representations of experiences originally perceptual; and we think we can understand others' reports of similar mental states. They are a more or less vivid form of memory image, *concrete* in nature. We speak of them as auditory, visual, olfactory, gustatory, kinæsthetic, and so on. They seem, from children's descriptions and reactions, to be present as early as between two and three years old.

Different from these are the physical phenomena known as *after-images*. The retina behaves so that after staring at a brightly illuminated object we "see," floating in space or projected on a blank surface, the object in complementary colors. This discovery is one usually of great interest to children.

Different again are the *eidetic* images, rarely found in adults but demonstrable by experimental procedures in a fair number of pre-pubertal children. The eidetic child is able to see again with extraordinary clearness an object once viewed, and to describe in this image details which he cannot recall by ordinary methods, which he does not even understand. This image can be projected on a suitable surface permitting the experimenter to measure it, match it for color, and otherwise deal with it objectively. This ability seems to have no correlation with intelligence. The other form of reproductive image is the *verbal*. Thus the thought of a violin may be accompanied not by an image of the instrument's appearance, sound or feel, but by the image of the word as printed, heard, or spoken by oneself. The thought of abstractions which cannot be perceptually encountered, for instance the idea of "antithesis," of "philosophical," "administration," is apt to be accompanied by a verbal image, if any. Pausing over the idea may favor some fleeting scheme of kinæsthetic imagery, or visualized action which illustrates the idea; but the more rapidly we think the less time there is for dealing with images of any kind.

Mention may be made here of a special sort of image having to do with number or time concepts. About 2 per cent, apparently, of people, report having from early childhood a way of visualizing the numbers from 1 to 100 in three-dimensional space, with bends at the tens, sometimes at 12. They also "see" a week or a year in some peculiar symbolic form such as a colored circle, an endless chain running round a sprocket. Unfortunately, such people tend to travel about in their number forms, so to speak, when computing, and find themselves hampered in speed in consequence.

Productive imagery. — This is the sort generally spoken of as imagination. It deals, not with past wholes but with old elements combined in new ways. One form is the *constructive* image, originating to illustrate ideas presented in some detail from without, and verifying itself by comparison with reality. Thus, a child is asked to fetch from the second shelf from the top the book in a red cover that is third from the left. He possibly constructs imagery as he listens, and its correctness can soon be checked. In geometry, the pupil draws triangles and tangents as directed, or imagines them drawn and foresees the consequences. The laboratory directions in physics, or the cooking recipe probably stimulate this sort of imaging in visual or kinæsthetic form. The printed music page suggests constructive auditory images which can be speedily verified by performance. The imagery illustrating the story or the historical account would also be termed constructive.

The *creative* image has no immediate outside source, nor does it so frequently involve the mediation of language. At the wish of the individual fancy is let loose to weave any kind of pattern preferred, with any degree of emotional coloring. No verification is demanded, especially in the daydream type; but in the socially oriented creative imagination some plausibility is desirable.

DIFFERENCES BETWEEN CHILDREN AND ADULTS

In kind of images used. — *Children visualize more.* — It is probable that in childhood the proportion of visual images is greater than at any other time. This fact, however, which used to be considered of great practical importance, is of little value, and this for two reasons: first, experimental psychology has shown that the type of image depends not on the individual, but on the material, on the extent to which purpose is involved, and on the presence of difficulties. An individual cannot be classed as being of the visual type, for instance, for the reason that though when imagining people he may visualize, when his images deal with words they may be auditory-motor, when flowers are the subject they may be olfactory. Likewise, though in passive imagery the visual type may predominate, in active imagery some other type may take the lead. The old idea that people are divided rather distinctly into "types" is being replaced by the opinion that individuals of a fixed type are rare, whereas those of the mixed type are the most frequent. This is as true of children as it is of adults, even though the greater proportion of visual images in childhood remains a fact.

The second reason for the change of attitude regarding the importance of imaginative types is found in the fact that the sense department through which the material is received, and that in terms of which it is recalled, need not be the same. Thus one may depend on one's eyes for the clearest, most effective percepts, and yet in recalling the situation use auditory images, as in memorizing music. Or one may listen to a description given orally, construct visual images to illustrate it, and recall in terms of those same visual images. Or one may learn by making movements, as in dancing or producing a certain speaking or singing tone when visual and auditory percepts play a secondary part, and the imagery may be almost entirely lacking so far as terms of recall are concerned. The old advice to the teacher, to discover what type of imagery a child used in his thinking, was given in order that she might present perceptual stimuli in corresponding terms; but since the percept and image need not so correspond, the reason for the advice does not hold. She need not present visual stimuli for those who use visual images, nor auditory percepts for those who use auditory imagery, and so on. What is important, however, is that a sufficient number of varied perceptual appeals be made, with strict attention on the part of the learner, so that the memory may be good and the response accurate. So far as the imagery is concerned it may be present or not, be vivid more or less, may correspond with or differ from the percept in kind; it makes very little difference so long as the results reached by the child are correct. The presence of one or another type may be of interest in theoretical psychology, but has no practical bearing on the kind of perceptual presentation used by the teacher for a whole class. Occasionally the tendency to a mistake may be traced to the form of imagery a child has employed; for instance, a spelling confusion such as "proceed" with "precede" is probably due to a lack of visual imagery, and a contraction such as "adaption" for "adaptation" to a lack of auditory imagery.

Children use concrete imagery more. — Another difference between children and adults, one which is of much more importance, is that between the object and word type of imagery. Experiments seem to prove that children tend to think in terms of objects, whereas adults are more inclined to use words. To a child the thought of a tree or a house or a book is a picture of the object; the thought of the Pilgrims' Chorus or E-flat is the melody or the note. To an adult, the thought of any of these is more likely to occur in terms of words, — the actual object itself not appearing in consciousness. The value of the verbal-images as opposed to the object-images from the stand-point of economy of time and energy, of definiteness and accuracy, and of retention, has been demonstrated in all fields. Of course, it is the only type of image available in dealing with abstract subjects; and its efficiency in constructive work, even in the arts and literature, has been testified to by workers in each of these fields.

Differences in vividness of imagery. — Not only do children and adults differ in the kind of imagery which they use, but also in the vividness of that imagery. The images of children seem to be more vivid, more intense, than those of adults. So true is this that there is a time in the mental life of little children when it is difficult, and sometimes impossible for them to distinguish between memory images and the images of imagination. In some children the confusion goes even further, and they cannot distinguish between percepts and images. Both types of confusion occur when children are young, generally between three and six years of age, and can be explained on physiological grounds. The chief difference between these mental states is a difference in the kind and in the number of associations with each. In the early years children have few associations with any of them, and consequently are likely to mistake any one of them for either of the others. They lack definite criteria by which to judge either the actuality of occurrences or the possibility of their fancies; moreover, their proneness to illusory errors, their extreme credulity, their ready suggestibility, combined with their newly discovered power of "being a cause," mentally make, in very truth, the "wish the father to the thought," *i.e.*, the assertion the generator of belief in the fact. When through experience children get accustomed to find certain sorts of sensory elements present with their percept of, say, a dog, they will not so readily mistake an image, which lacks these elements, for a percept. Further, the knowledge of possibilities which comes with experience will help to differentiate these several mental states. For instance, when a child learns, not by mere telling but by lack of sensory elements, that lions do not live under little boys' beds, the feeling-of-lion-under-the-bed will be much less real, much more readily recognized as an image of the productive type.

Differences in amount of imagery. — One other difference between children and adults in their images is a natural outgrowth of the differences already discussed, and that is the differences as to amount. It is certainly true that children have more of the concrete kind of imagery than adults, and the probability is that in total amount they excel the adult. The higher types of mental states which are so important in thinking are later in development than the image. The adult's thinking is full of feelings of relationship, meanings, and judgments, whereas that of the little child is made up almost entirely of images. The rich flood of imagery possessed by children has its drawbacks. One cannot get very far with that type of mental stuff; the other more subtle and far-reaching mental states must be developed.

Changes with age. — Without doubt, the reproductive is the fundamental and earlier type. There is little possibility that children under three can use any but this kind, and even after that age the plays of the kindergarten and primary school child are largely reproductive and imitative. Andrews,[1] experimenting with over one hundred pre-school children, found increasing quantities of reproductive images with age. The creative type of image was at its height during the third and fourth years. At this period the imagination is characterized by the fairy-tale element, its disregard of the possible. It is fantastic, and the flights of fancy in which children of this age indulge are comparable only to the night dreams of adults. As they grow older, between ten and thirteen perhaps, most children become more matter of fact. Their productive imagery loses its fanciful characteristics and becomes more bound by the laws of the possible. The imagery of children of this age is more practical, of value as it accomplishes results; it still has a

[1] Andrews, E. G., "The development of imagination in the pre-school child," *Univ. Iowa St.*, v. 3, *4, 1930.

large share in their plays, but it tends to be more purposeful. It is objective rather than subjective, realistic rather than fanciful.

Struve,[1] using three creative and interpretative tests with young adolescent subjects found significant individual differences in type of imagination. Some reactions, comparable to those of little children in handling perceptual stimuli, were merely enumeration and tabulation in sequence of all the imaginative suggestions that came to them. Other reactions related the various items into a coherent whole. The majority of girls did one or the other of these two things. Other subjects, and these were more often boys, gave response of piecing together in sequence a fantastic or plausible invention; or the reaction was to produce a complex whole at once without attention first to one detail, then to another. The themes interesting to girls were personal and domestic; those interesting to boys were largely fighting adventures.

During adolescence, a new element is added in the intensity of the emotional life of that period. The imagery now takes on many of the characteristics of the first period, though the content of the imagery is different; it is no longer of the fairy-tale type, but has to do with the youths' and maidens' own doings, ambitions, accomplishments, and plans. It is highly subjective, for the adolescents always hold the center of the stage in their dreams. The element of fancy, and the joy in the imagery for its own sake make it like the early period rather than the intermediate one, but it may be termed idealistic, since persons and human relationships are of prime concern rather than mere miraculous occurrences. This is pre-eminently the age for daydreaming. True, it appears earlier, especially with sensitive, lonely children, but at this age almost all indulge in it. Investigations emphasize the frequency and the absorbing power of this type of mental life. As the period of adolescence passes, the swing of the pendulum is again away

[1] Struve, K., "Typische Abslaufsformen des Deutens bei 14 bis 15 jährigen Schulkindern," *Zeit. f. angew. Psy.*, v. 37, 1930.

from the fanciful, emotional type of imagination to the practical. The adolescent type now passes altogether with most people, though some individuals never grow away from it at all; yet the average adult is so pressed upon by the demands of a practical world that his imagery, to fill his need, must measure up to the requirements of life.

Symbolism. — We saw, in discussing play with materials, the three stages of function pleasure, fiction pleasure, factum pleasure. The fiction play occurs only after an object is conceived as a symbol, and this involves an act of imagination. After the mere physical and perceptual pleasure of placing blocks end to end or gaining skill in piling them, the child discovers a resemblance, in miniature, to a sidewalk, a gateway, a tower, and straightway his imagination invests the thing-that-is with a new identity. Nothing need be itself alone any more; it can stand for that which it resembles. Any thing can be transformed by the magic wand artifice, any action may represent other actions. Thus the uninspiring task of washing dishes becomes the adventure of rescuing shipwrecked passengers from a soap-and-watery fate. The rugs to be beaten can be conceived as the enemy awaiting onslaught. Used in this way, the exercise of imagination acts as a compensation, an escape from the less pleasant realities to the enchanted world of have-it-as-I-please, a process which has both values and dangers. Roughly, the development in understanding symbols is about as follows. During the first half of the second year of life a *sound* is understood as symbol *for a thing;* a word re-presents an object. After this, but not before, a *visual* presentation, a picture, is recognized as symbol *of a thing.* Next, one *concrete thing* is used as symbol *of another, i.e.,* a toy is used in dramatic fashion. Next, a concrete *thing* is taken as symbolic of *a personality.* For instance, when drawing, the symbol of a hat indicates a man; in acting, the paper helmet transforms the wearer into the fireman, or the king. At about this point the school's tradition may interrupt the natural course of development. It introduces *visual symbols for sound* *symbols* as it teaches reading, colored signals *for action* in crossing streets, and encounters special difficulty with visual symbols for abstract number concepts. Among themselves, the *concrete thing*, as a badge or emblem comes to symbolize *group personality*, as does also the gang's name for itself. With the invention of secret languages *words* stand for *other words;* and with the appreciation of puns, and double meanings word symbols become still more flexible. Metaphors, parables, fables, and the like are not adequately interpreted before twelve years old, nor is the situation in a complex picture well imagined.

VALUES OF IMAGERY

Enjoyment. — The most obvious value of imagery is in the sheer pleasure it affords. By its means we find it possible to live over again scenes that were enjoyable and so to prolong their pleasure. Future experiences may also be anticipated in imagination and great delight found in planning and picturing details. For childhood plans these images are probably concrete; for more mature organizing, the verbal image, the vague scheme may be all that precedes the orderly outline at last set down in writing.

Social sharing of interest in descriptions of concrete things is facilitated by vividness of imagery. Conversation is more fluent when there is a background of wealth of imagery to lend color to the language. Appreciation of others' narrative and descriptive powers is heightened by images constructed to accompany their discourse and by the ability to understand such symbolic phrases as they use. Wit, humor, even slang, depends upon a seizing of relationships. People devoid of imagination are proverbially slow in seeing a joke that is not expressed in crude, concrete form. Delicate shades of meaning, metaphors, similes, fables, parables, and the like are apprehended more readily, it would seem, by those who report plentiful imagery.

Sympathy. — Much tactlessness may be explained by the lack of imagination of how other people feel, how they might react. Conversely, ability to put one's self in the other's place involves imagination. We saw how the "empathy" of the first dramatic plays develops this function. Reading, theater attendance encourages it further. The interest of children about the fourth grade and up in stories of people in other lands, other times, depends largely on the play of imagery, stimulated as it is by pictures, curios, and descriptions. Appeals to philanthropy are based on the emotional reactions of people whose imaginations can be stirred. For effective sympathy, that connotes co-operation and understanding assistance, imagination must be directed towards living rather than fictitious characters. Here again, without a basis of fact in perceptual, concrete experience, imagination may go very far astray.

Creative work. — By means of imagination one is able to invent marvels in machinery, or aëroplanes, or costumes; one may revolutionize the world of philosophy, or find the cure for all social ills; one may control the forces of nature or convert nations, — one creates new worlds. All thinking, all invention, all progress depends on this power of reconstructing the old into a new thing. Craftsmanship, artistic creation, literary and music composition, invention, mental manipulation of the scientific sort utilize the creative imagination appropriate to the material. Here is one of the most inspiring channels in which it may function, also one of the safest, from the standpoint of mental hygiene.

MISUSE OF IMAGINATION

Lies. — In young children the confusion of percept and image may result in conduct which, while normal, is certainly questionable. One consequence is seen in the so-called "white lies," the kind of falsification which makes children tell such big tales of what happened in school, on the street, at play, at home. This has been already spoken of in connection with the lack of accuracy in children's reports. Looking back on an imperfectly observed perceptual experience we all tend to mix our suppositions of what occurred with what actually took place. With retelling, the story grows, particularly in the direction of the things we would like to have had happen. Little children do all this and more; they can escape contemplating any disagreeable part of the recollection by "pretending" it didn't happen, or they can intensify the excitement by magnifying it. Their preference, like the veritable fairy wand, so changes the outlines of events and emotions, so colors them that the disguise is complete for them and all but impenetrable for the adult. Thus, as seven-year-old D— was walking along a road bordered by a fenced pasture, a mild-mannered cow lifted her head and looked at the child, causing a little trepidation. D— first told of several cows that came to the fence, later that they followed her the length of the fence "roaring," later that a bull and lots of cows ran after her while she threw stones at them, still later that she had been in the field, was chased by a bull and at least fifty cows till she escaped over the fence and routed them by pelting with large stones.

It should be emphasized again that children are not deliberately telling lies, they either really think thus and so happened, or dwell so much on what they wish had occurred that there comes to be no difference in their minds between the world of fact and the world of make-believe. After all, this realm of "have it as you wish," this world of play is so much the more important and vital to little children that why should they not give the adult the benefit of it when he seems interested and begins asking questions? Scolding or punishing for this kind of lying is unfair to the children and does not get at the root of the difficulty. They must be taught the difference between the real and the fancied without detracting from the charm of the latter. Of course, the training which is taking place at this time in perception will help along this line. Requiring children to check up their stories by the actual facts when this is possible is the logical way to bring home to them the difference. One obstacle in clearing up this confusion lies in the fact that so little opportunity is given children of using their constructive imagination under supervision, so that they do not grow accustomed to labeling one kind of thing true, and another false. If parents and teachers would ask children to tell make-believe stories and happenings, and then to tell "true" ones, and do the same themselves, not only would there be built up in the children's minds standards by means of which they could judge the real and the make-believe, but they would also be having experience in judging between the two. Added to this they would be having the joy of telling a big story and seeing the amazement of the hearers; — both are legitimate delights of childhood which, because of the matter-of-fact point of view of the adult, are not indulged enough. The romancing of little children cannot be ignored because it may become a habit and continue when the original cause of it has passed; on the other hand, children cannot be held accountable for a confusion, the necessary accompaniment of a certain stage of growth, which will gradually disappear as the mental states concerned become properly differentiated.

Night fears. — Another result of the confusion between percepts and images is seen in many of the night fears of young children. Fears have already been discussed, but it must be emphasized at this point that many of these night fears are due to the confusion now described. They may readily believe that there is a giant in the corner of the room, or that the witch on her broomstick is coming in at the window. Adults little know the terrors children suffer, especially sensitive, imaginative children. If they would stop to consider how they would feel, especially in the dark, if they could not distinguish between the world of fact and of fancy, they would have a clearer conception of what children must feel. One way to prevent this type of fear is not to allow children to be frightened. Once thoroughly alarmed, and the child will recall and recall the emotion in connection with all sorts of things. The need of avoiding material which could serve as a center for the emotion is evident. Children should not be allowed to hear stories or see moving pictures which have present any element of the horrible, or fear-inspiring. In this connection it must be remembered that what is "the horrible" to a child is not that which is horrible to the adult because of a difference in content; likewise what frightens the child when it is recalled, is often nothing that frightened at the time of telling, or may be nothing frightful in itself. The manner of telling the story, the emotional attitude of the teller which calls out the same emotional response in the children, is often more important than the mere content of the story. It is a great temptation to the good story-teller to use her power so that her listeners are hanging breathless and sometimes trembling on her words. It seems harmless enough, the children respond with a shriek of joy as the story ends, they may play it all over again in their free time; but at night, alone in the dark, what was thrilling in the daylight with companions about may become a source of exquisite terror. These facts should be borne in mind both in selecting the myths, fairy tales, and stories which children hear, and in the manner of telling them.

Imaginary companions. — Still a third result of the confusion of percepts and images is the creation of imaginary companions. The presence in a child's life of imaginary companions is very much more common than has been supposed. It is perhaps the continuation of the animistic tendency, only now it is an image that is endowed with life. These companions usually appear between three and four years of age or even earlier, the time when children are experiencing this confusion between mental states, and the time when they are becoming acquainted with their different selves. It is usually a lonely child that develops these play companions, and they become to him more real than his living playmates. The little girl who, when shopping with her mother, began to cry violently and could not be comforted until her mother discovered that she had sat down on a stool upon which the child's imaginary companion was seated so that the child was sure she was killed, is an illustration of how real such companions are, and also suggests some of the difficulties that may arise if this sort of thing is carried too far. Very few children retain these after eight or nine years of age, as they gradually fade away under the influence of more vital companionship with other children who are congenial. In general the tendency to indulge in these play-fellows is harmless; however, if it is carried to an extreme by young children or if it is continued up into adolescence, harm may result. Children who play continually with an imaginary companion lose all the give and take that comes with living children; they get no training in considering the rights of others, nor in co-operation, and it is very easy to form the habit of shifting the blame whenever anything goes wrong to the shoulders of this imaginary companion. All of this hinders the best social and moral development. If the play is continued into adolescence there is danger of becoming reserved and morbid, and losing the perspective as to real values.

In productive imagery. — One of the dangers of the pressure brought to bear upon children to "be creative" is analogous to that ensuing if they were turned loose to do good muscular work without any intake of nourishment for those muscles, supposing that exercise alone would bring development. Crea-tive imagination does not grow by exercise alone. Human beings do not create by mere fiat in a void. Where we used to say "no impression without expression," we now run the risk of looking for expression without impression. But imagination, if it is to reach its highest development, must be given oppor-tunity to develop and material to feed upon, it must be stimu-lated and directed. Imagination, to be healthy, must be rooted in facts, plenty of them, must continually draw from them, assimilate and resynthesize them.

In inventive work a period of exploration of the possibilities of materials comes first with rather close imitation of known forms, adapting and trying out the changes and the new com-binations till greater freedom in creation is gained, and, in the light of critical appraisal of results, a new art form, a new machine, etc., is produced. This critical appraisal requires a training in the standards of appreciation of beauty, of truth, of humor, of feasibility, of social acceptability, of ethics, or in whatever field the creative impulse is expressing itself. To encourage children in the belief they have produced something beautiful or worth while just because they have enjoyed the act of creation is not only absurd it is harmful.

Possible dangers in adolescent period. — The period of adolescence is the most critical in its possibilities and, at the same time, the most difficult to handle. The imaginings of adolescents are more absorbing, take more thought and energy than at any other time, and may become more vivid to them than the real environment in which they are living. The importance of getting the practical, constructive imagination started well in the period just preceding is partly due to the fact that now it may continue to be used to drain off some of the energy which might be used in morbid lines. Kept healthy by plenty of outside interests, physical exercise, companionship, and the satisfying of questions that the physical development of the period must bring into the foreground of consciousness, the imagination of this time is the motive force of ideals, is the root of appreciation of the beautiful in art, music, and literature. But it is also true that because of the strength of the interest in the opposite sex, there is a tendency for it to be directed into morbid channels instead of developing along healthful lines. Imagination allowed to run riot in unknown or erotic channels first stimulates desire, and later incites to action. It is all-important here, as earlier, that the material upon which the imagination feeds should be wholesome and suitable. The books read in the teens are an immeasurable force in directing the imagination. It is useless and wasteful to try to starve it out by giving only material of scientific character. Adolescents should have romance, love stories, adventure, stories of reconstruction, and poetry, but they should all be good, — good not from the standpoint of the need of the adult, but from the standpoint of the need of the adolescent. The danger in this age of leading two lives, the outside one with which parents and teachers are acquainted, and a very different inside one, — not necessarily bad, but egotistic, emotional, and imaginative, —

is increased by the sensitiveness of adolescents, and their fear of being laughed at if they give the keys of this inner life to any adult. In the sympathy and understanding of a wise adult, however, lies safety for the development of the unstable, intense, imaginative, emotional life of the teens. Once inside the doors of this reserve, the power of the trusted adult to mold and direct is almost limitless. The sympathetic approach must be largely an individual matter. The aim must be to keep alive in adolescents the belief in their own power, while shifting the limelight from their own doings to that of others; to take the imaginings from the field of fancy and build them into ideals; to bring about a balance between the inside life and the life of conduct; and at the same time to retain much of the fertility and power of the imagination for use in the playtime of maturity.

Living in unreality. — The general danger at any age, but coming to a climax in adolescence, is that of substituting an imaginary world for the real one. Using imagination as a compensation for thwarting, as a refuge from the disagreeable, the child who is non-aggressive, timid, introvert, finds it increasingly easy to slip away from ought-to-believe into make-believe and there to stay. The more healthy-minded use these compensations and refuges to be sure, but return refreshed from the recreation of the daydream, the novel, the theater to actual life. When this world of fancy and have-it-as-I-please becomes preferred to all others the individual is unlikely to make good social adjustments. In extreme cases we find people altogether shut in to a world of their own creation and so ineffective in consequence that they have to be cared for in a mental hospital.

Imagination, then, cannot be safely used for selfish enjoyment alone. It must create for others, and find expression in some line or other. Also, it must lead back into realities.

TRAINING NEEDED

In verbal imagery. — It would seem part of the business of teachers to replace the less effectual object-image of children

by the much more useful word-image. But teachers are prone
to object to hurrying this process on the ground that the object-
image is necessarily fundamental, and there is danger that the
children will get words without content. In the first place,
it has yet to be proved that the object-image is necessarily
fundamental; *e.g.*, smell and temperature images are notably
rare; in the second place, the word-image should get its content
not from the inaccurate, unreliable object-image, but from
direct perceptual experience. The word "horse" in a child's
thought has meaning in proportion as it has been directly connected with sensory experiences of the object, not through the
mediation of an object-image of the animal. To use object-
images only is the mark of an immature mind. They may add
a richness of color in certain fields of appreciation, and there
they should be called into play; but in the field of thought they
should be replaced as quickly as possible by verbal images.
This practice would mean two things: a broadening of sense
experience and a direct connection of words with it, and more
extended and definite training in thinking in terms of language.
Children's ability to think is dependent on language. Age
helps, but training can do much to give meaning to the word-
images, increase the thinking vocabulary, and give control to
the manipulation of these images.

In connection with the extended use by adults of words
and symbols for all sorts of concrete experiences of varying
degrees of complexity and richness, has arisen the question
as to whether the mind in its thinking does not go one step
further, and think without using images, at least without using
anything that could be classed under the usual term "image."
From the standpoint of child psychology the dispute offers
some practical suggestions. The well-trained mind not only
replaces object by verbal images, but gets on with a minimum
of these. Kinæsthetic forms, such as a mental gesture with
the hands, or a lifting of the eyebrows may convey meanings
such as clarification or doubtful hesitancy. Even without these,
the feeling of being attracted to, or repelled from a certain

course of action or line of thought, with mere fleeting snatches of phrases, may be found to play a large part in logical thinking.

Now this sort of thinking is worth while for the same reason that the word-image is more worth while than the object-image; *i.e.*, it is economical. If so, it is the teacher's duty to develop more of this type of wordless thinking in children. An analogous type of training is done in connection with perception, when one characteristic is enough to arouse the full percept, and when children are asked to "skim" a paragraph or a book, and get the meaning. They are asked by the help of a few of the important words, a feeling of the drift of the paragraph, to get the essentials without wasting the time to get a clear percept of all the words. In thinking we need more of the same kind of training, and it can be done only by limiting the time allowed and insisting on some kind of answer. To give children several alternatives and demand a choice with reasons almost immediately forces them, simply by the exigencies of the case, to do thinking of the type we have been considering. With the facts in hand in history, to prophesy what the ruler, or the congress, or the inventor did, without being given time to work out the details reduces the verbal images used to mere schema. In arithmetic, the plan followed by good teachers of asking the children to estimate or "guess" the answer to the problem before solving it gives training along this same line. This is not the place to discuss the value of this method from the standpoint of training children to think; but any thoughtful person must realize that not only are the children getting training in the use of efficient tools, but in the process of thinking also. Of course, in all this process, care must be taken that it is true thinking, and not "guessing" in the ordinary use of the term that is taking place. If, however, children are required to abide by the choice they have made, or to find out what did actually happen, or to check up the correct answer with their prophecy, and then be asked for a criticism of this forecast, the work will be placed on a safe basis, and random, unsupported guessing will be abandoned.

Training the imagination. — No more need be said at this time of the value of the reproductive image. The productive type, however, offers a new element of the utmost importance. It is one of the most precious abilities of the human race, and should be developed and fostered by all the means at the command of education. Upon the wealth and fertility of the imaginative power man must depend for all the suggestions that will make this world other than it is.

In the period from four to eight, the stories, fairy tales, and myths offer material for children's creative imagination to work on. They fill a very definite need of children's nature at this time, and should certainly be given them. The lack of knowledge of physical laws and of the ways of the world, and the tendency towards animism make the material offered by the myth and fairy tale not only acceptable, but necessary for a full growth. At no other time in life will this material be as vital or as satisfying as at this period. The dangers of overindulging the fancy will largely be corrected by the training in sense perception and observation that comes at this time. Not only should they be given the material to feed the imagination, but the tendency to construct which is present should be made use of. Children of seven or eight are very willing to tell stories drawn from their imaginations, and this willingness should be encouraged. Not only is opportunity offered to develop productive thinking in the realm of fancy, but the opportunities for the training in the use of words and real language in general are great.

During the next few years, when in school the emphasis is being laid on facts, when children in their own development are passing through a period of readjustment, when retention is almost at its maximum and the suggestibility is less than before, it comes about that the mere fanciful element is replaced by a more practical one. This is the time to encourage constructive imagination in connection with handwork projects, or geography; here is the opportunity to teach simple geometry, art structure, and physics. Children are willing now to plan and then test their plans by putting them into execution. Earlier, they had neither the power nor the patience; later their imaginings are of such a character that this sort of thing is almost impossible.

Use of symbols. — It was customary in the conservative school of kindergartners to use symbols to teach great truths. For instance, the sphere was used to represent unity, and the doctrine was that the child in playing with the ball or sphere must absorb something of that meaning. The knight of the Middle Ages is the symbol for bravery, and in playing the plays of the knight the child is supposed to get an ideal of bravery, something with meaning. Religious teaching is full of examples of the same supposition. The earlier discussion of symbolism should show that such teachings are folly, based on lack of understanding of the development of a child's mind. Symbols are used only after direct personal experience of the thing symbolized, not before. Children do not possess abstract truths, nor generalizations; how then could a symbol call them to mind or stand for them? They are the product of much teaching and experience, and are characteristic of the philosophical adult mind. Even those teachers who use such symbols may have themselves but a faint glimmering of what the abstractions they stand for really are. The parables of the New Testament made no such mistake in their appeal to the hearers as many a zealous Sunday School teacher does today. To use something outside of a child's experience, something strange and new, in order to teach an unknown truth is incomprehensible, he has content for neither. Certainly such a use of symbols violates the law of apperception. Children use symbols only for known experiences, and those symbols must be as nearly like the thing represented as possible; that is all that is possible for the child mind to grasp. This does not at all mean that such material and plays may not have a value; but if so, that does not lie in their power to teach great truths.

Dramatization. — Dramatization is the working out by the child of his constructive images in terms of action. Dramatic play occurs first with objects, that is, with toys as soon as their symbolism is perceived. After this, personalities are changed about. "You be the little girl and I'll be the mother," says the child to the parent. Familiar people around such as the mailman, the grocer, are imitated, and thereby, by the process called empathy, the child feels himself into new spheres of interest in purposing. Imagery concerns itself with the emotions, the words and actions seen. By the kindergarten period dramatic games with one another are enjoyed, with some slight help from dolls, toys, and object symbols. By the eight- or nine-year-old level these can be dispensed with in the co-operative dramatic game which involves much running about. Opposing military forces, for instance, can point their fingers and shout "Bang bang" as they creep from ambush upon the foe. However, when objects are used, they must resemble reality very greatly, to satisfy the eight- to ten-year-old.

When stories are told to children there are no percepts to be reproduced later in dramatic play, only such constructive images, probably visual, as they form for themselves while listening. The problem later is to act from source material in image form rather than in perceptual form. This explains the development of ability to dramatize stories heard later than that of dramatizing scenes in which children have been participants or observers. It is folly, then, to tell a new story to children of kindergarten age level and expect them to be enthusiastic immediately about the teacher's suggestion of acting it. They may need six to twenty narrations before they have "material" enough to re-present. Even at the third-grade level it is clear that, whether due to attention-span, or lack of knowledge of detail, or to lack of constructive imagination, or to hesitancy about expression, new stories are but poorly dealt with at the first attempt to act them out. Yet in this very fact of progress from the vague, poorly understood original to the appreciative interpretation rich in details, lies the educative value of dramatization. Working out a constructive image in terms of action necessitates a clearing up of hazy parts, a working out of details, thereby making the idea more clear and definite. It organizes the imagination by developing a perspective, and making clear the need of emphasizing essentials. It helps to make clear the difference between the imagined and the real. It adds a richness to the thought content by its arousal of an emotional background. It develops co-operation, initiative, self-confidence, and the use of language, and is an aid to memory.

All this, if properly used, is a means to an end. But too often the means becomes the end. The teacher wants a finished product, and therefore the planning of details and the work of interpretation is hers, if not entirely, at least so much so through suggestion, that what might have been of great developmental value becomes a trivial performance in which an inexcusable amount of time and energy is wasted. Because its true function has been lost to sight and presentation has become an end in itself, the children who do it best are those chosen to do it, instead of the work being given to those who need the development in any of the above-mentioned ways. It should also be remembered that the very ease with which the emotional element is aroused by dramatization brings with it a danger. An emotion aroused by the part a child takes may react unfavorably on his character, or he may form the habit of allowing the real emotions, whose function is to inspire conduct, to wear themselves out in acting. For the majority of children these are not grave dangers; but if the dramatization is overdone, for the highly emotional, sensitive child who has a tendency to act, some such effects may be produced. This is especially true if the continual urging of the teacher is to "throw yourself into your part," "lose yourself in it." To be used effectively, the teacher must keep in mind both the function of dramatization in the whole scheme of development, and the nature of the children with whom she is dealing.

For adolescents, dramatization is an invaluable experience. They are passing through a period of wondering what their real personalities are, and of endeavoring to be like first one, then another, in bewildering succession. In the play there is an opportunity to experiment, legitimately, with different characters. Then again, many faults of carriage, of enunciation, bad manners, gaucheries, can be directly corrected for stage requirements where the most tactful, indirect suggestion has failed to operate. In the third place, creative expression is afforded in so many different lines in staging a play that it provides teamwork for the most varied interests. A pageant, especially, offers such wide opportunity for social and artistic development that one could wish it an inevitable experience for every adolescent.

That imagination is valuable is evident, but all kinds are not equally valuable, nor valuable for the same purpose. The schools must discriminate and cultivate the different types at their proper time, and in their proper place. The most crying need is for greater emphasis on constructive, verbal imagination, for that is the type upon which thinking depends; but at the same time, individual differences must not be lost sight of, and a capacity for rich, concrete imagery in connection with art and literature should be developed for the sake of its appreciative and interpretative value. If it is true that "Imagination has the power to alter the face of the world, to bridge distance, to annihilate time; like an alchemist, it can transmute, refine, transform; like the artist it is skillful to glorify and to enrich. On the moral side of life, it knows how to comfort and encourage, to inspire and control, to animate, and to rejoice," then every child in our schools needs it trained and developed that he may reap these rich benefits. But before this desired end can be reached, teachers must recognize its importance for life, and not merely for enjoyment, and devote much more time and thought to plans for its development.

PRACTICAL EXERCISES

1. Recall your own adolescent daydreams. Write out a brief description. How do they illustrate the points described in this chapter? Were they much influenced by books you read, people you met?
2. Collect illustrations of symbols used in teaching that might well be postponed for the reasons here discussed.

3. Observe for half an hour to an hour each the free play of (*a*) children under seven, (*b*) children of nine to twelve. Into how many of their games does dramatic imagination enter?
4. Get a six-year-old and a ten-year-old to tell you a story. Note whether one is fanciful and the other realistic.
5. Observe dramatic play of six-year-olds and of ten-year-olds. How do they differ in (*a*) source and kind of material dramatized? (*b*) spontaneous use of dialogue?

FOR DISCUSSION

1. In what way might social development be retarded because of having an imaginary companion?
2. Suggest methods to use to help little children distinguish between fact and fancy.
3. Just what is involved in "being creative"?
4. Are there children under your observation who seem in danger of misusing the imagination in any of the ways described? What can be done about it?
5. What should be the teacher's aim in calling for dramatization in the first two grades?
6. For what sort of school subjects are concrete images valuable? For what are verbal images preferable?
7. What school subjects train constructive imagination? Creative imagination?
8. Compare results of Exercises 4 and 5, above. What conclusions do you draw as to changes in imagination with age?

SELECTED REFERENCES

ANDREWS, E. G. "The development of imagination in the preschool child." *Univ. Iowa St.*, v. 3 *4.
KLÜVER, H. "Studies on the eidetic type, and on eidetic imagery." *Psych. Bull.*, v. 25, 1928.
LEE, J. *Play in Education.* Chs. 17, 18.
PRUETTE, J. "What's happening in the daydreams of the adolescent girl?" *Jo. Soc. Hyg.*, v. 10, 1924.
STERN, W. *Psychology of Early Childhood.* Chs. 19, 20, 24.
TANNER, E. *The Child.* Ch. 9.

CHAPTER XII

LANGUAGE DEVELOPMENT

ACQUISITION OF THE MOTHER TONGUE

Functions of language. — We may distinguish three functions of language, that of *stimulating others to action*, that of *self-expression*, that of *symbolic or representative* use. Animals use cries in the first two ways; and the more intelligent species, trained to work with mankind, arrive at the point of understanding meanings in sounds and gestures used by us. They do not themselves use sounds in representative fashion; only human beings employ a sound as a symbol for a thing. It is of great importance, then, to note a child's ability in reaching this third level of functioning, for with it comes the possibility of communicating thought and therefore of all human culture.

Prerequisites. — Physically, it is necessary, first, that the speech mechanisms such as the lips, palate, vocal cords are present and in normal condition. Ability to hear is essential; a congenitally deaf child does not talk, but has to undergo very special training. Second, a certain maturity of growth is necessary, with co-ordination of the different muscles and neural connections involved in talking. Psychically, the first prerequisite is a playful use of the speech mechanisms with voluntary imitation of sounds heard. The second is mental maturity to the point of connecting sounds with the meaning of objects and situations.

Early stages of learning. — These are qualitative, overlapping as to age limits rather than being discrete chronologically. At first there is a simple *reflex*, such as the birth cry and the expressive sounds of the first few weeks. The primitive squall is differentiated into special cries denoting hunger, pain,

243

anger, etc. By the process of conditioning the second function of language appears, so that by the third month the infant makes effective use of his various cries. Next comes *vocal play*, at first of the impulsive sort; for instance a cooing, babbling sound after feeding expresses satisfaction. By six months old this becomes an experimental play with sound, the true third stage of *babbling*. This differs from impulsive play in that it is deliberately imitative of sounds heard, is purposeful, for self-entertainment. It is also social, since the infant responds to others' advances by increased vocalization. The fourth stage is reached when the infant *understands a few words* as used by others though he does not imitate the sound at the same moment. The fifth, or truly *expressive* stage, is the important discovery of the naming value of the sounds he himself makes. Sometime in the last quarter of the first year this stage is commonly reached.

Kinds of sounds made. — At first only open vowels are heard, the squalling cry of a, ah, u, or ue being easily produced by the simple opening of the mouth. As the lips, trained in the act of sucking, sometimes close during vocalization the sounds are modified by the addition of *labials* (m, b, p), this in the third or fourth week. Next come the *gutturals* (k, hard g) produced by action at the back of the tongue as in swallowing. In the second month we hear these, also *nasals* (n, ng) as the tongue clings to the roof of the mouth. When the teeth begin to erupt and the tongue tip explores them and the gums immediately in front, the *dentals* (d, t) are possible. By the time the babbling stage is reached, then, the baby has a large repertoire of syllables with which to play built from all the possible combinations and permutations of vowels and these four types of consonantal sounds alone. Here is the root stock of universal baby language. From this, by the efforts of adults around, specific meanings are attached to sounds. By pleased acceptance of such duplicated syllables as ma ma, go go, nu nu, de de, as referring to special people or objects the family teach the baby to "speak" Chinese, German, Greek, or English, as the case may be. The various languages emerge from this root stock of vocalizations by means of the laws of exercise and effect. The sound-person, sound-object connections are fixed for the child by the behavior of those in his environment.

Sequent stages. — The first use of single words is in reference to the child's own relation to persons, objects, and activities. Desires and emotions are not distinguished from the naming function. These words are "sentence" words, the exact meaning of which is helped out by tone and gesture. Thus "ite" may mean That is the light, Look at the light, The light has been turned on, etc. Commands, requests, identifications are conveyed by intonation. For six months or more these one word sentences are all the infant uses, though he understands considerably more of what is said to him, and may, in his vocal play, utter long strings of sounds with cadences very faithfully copying the conversations he hears. The few words he does gain are either natural symbols from the sounds associated with the object such as tic toc, bow wow, or the conventional symbols gained by direct imitation of others' usage. Between eighteen and twenty-four months comes the understanding of the representative function of speech, the discovery that everything has a name. With that comes a rapid increase in true vocabulary, and the first combining of two words in a meaningful way into a sentence. The question "what" as referring to objects and activities also appears. Very soon the three word sentence is used. The word order is quite plastic; the meanings are there as a whole and are expressed in chance array. The feeling for order is acquired gradually from the contact with the Chinese, German, Greek, English example heard. The emotional type of expression is replaced by the declarative statement describing activities being performed, things being looked at. As memory develops, the telling function follows the pure naming. Things previously seen, actions already in the past are described, absent objects are asked for. Words themselves begin to be inflected, especially for past tense and plurals. The pronouns *I* and *you* occur more frequently than any other naming words in all recorded utterances between two and a half and five years old.

The question "when" appears, and "what is" in asking for the meaning of words themselves, lastly the question "why." This is particularly noticeable about three years old, though here again the age range is very variable. Gradually the sentences lengthen and are filled out with modifying words. More adverbs, adjectives, prepositions, and conjunctions are used with the fundamental stock of nouns and verbs. Next comes the complex sentence with its dependent clauses. Words such as "because" and "if" generally introduce these subordinate clauses. Inflections for comparison are mastered about the same time; and a slight need for the future tense is felt in making plans and programs. Thus by five years old we see a practically completed stage of the ability to use the mother tongue.

With entrance to school most children's attention is given to the mastery of visual language, and the growth of word and sentence usage orally is less marked. After eight years old there is again a more rapid increase in vocabulary and in the power of expression both oral and written. As facility is gained in the manual act of writing the style of composition improves. From the short, simple sentence, or the series of phrases introduced by an unvarying "and," the ten-year-old passes to longer, better balanced complex sentences in his writing.

OBSTACLES IN DEVELOPMENT

Poor environment. — The findings of Descoudres[1] and of Hetzer as to the retardation in speech development of children from poor homes is corroborated to a slight degree by studies in Scotland and in this country. Thus, both in age of beginning to talk and in average size of vocabulary those children are superior whose parents use good English and who talk to them, rewarding their efforts and directing their learning. The educational status of the mother is more influential than that of the father on the progress young children make. Obviously, children who

[1] Descoudres, A., *Le développement de l'enfant de deux à sept ans.*

have poor models for pronunciation, syntax, and phraseology will form bad habits at an early age, the correcting of which is often a long and troublesome job.

Divided attention. — The plateau stages in vocabulary acquisition may be accounted for on the ground of preoccupation with other problems. For instance, from eleven to fifteen or sixteen months the infant is beginning to walk. If the physical difficulties of balance become too engrossing he may cease his word learning. Similar halts have been seen when a child has to become accustomed to a new physical environment. If new personalities are simultaneously encountered, particularly those with whom he does not feel at ease. a child may be checked in his talking progress. Hull [1] reports an interference in talking during the stage of learning voluntary control of the bladder. Restriction in the use of the hands may delay speech.

Handedness and speech. — There is evidence that a forced change from natural left-handedness, or sinistrality, to right-handed usage, or dextrality, especially in the matter of writing, may affect speech in unfortunate ways. A hesitation, a fumbling sort of muscle co-ordination may ensue, or stuttering and stammering. This does not mean that every case of stammering can be traced to this, there are other possible causes. Nor does it mean that all attempts to force a change of hand usage will bring about speech difficulty. Since hand preference is shown before speech proper begins, it is likely that the earlier the training for change is begun the less probable is it that bad results will follow. Parson [2] reports successful training in right-hand writing for sinistrals in Elizabeth, N. J., over a four-year-period with no observed resultant speech difficulty. But we have too many clinic cases of speech troubles in which we can discover an original sinistrality overlaid by dextral training for us to ignore the connection. Further, if such children are allowed to use the preferred hand without interference the speech improves. Cases

[1] Hull and Hull, "Parallel learning curves of an infant in vocabulary and in voluntary control of the bladder," *Ped. Sem.*, v. 26, 1919.
[2] Parson, B. S., *Left-Handedness.*

of mirror writing, inverted reading such as *d* for *b*, *was* for *saw*, are traceable to the different sighting and eye movements of a natural sinistral, and to the confused eye-hand co-ordinations brought about by a forced change. These need individual study and diagnosis with special remedial treatment, frequently in the form of tracing with the hand while reading letters and words.

In general, the advice would be, if a change is desired begin it early. When visual and written language must be learned start with large symbols, with crayon and blackboard work for large movements. If any speech interference is noted allow the child to use whichever hand he prefers for writing.

Pronunciation difficulties. — Mechanical problems in unusual positions of the tongue and lips retard some children. The sounds of *l*, *r*, *f*, *th* involve trouble for many, as indeed they do for foreigners. Lazy habits of substituting *p* for *f*, *d v* or *f* for *th*, *w* for *r* need careful correction and much drill in enunciation. A short upper lip favors the production of *m* and *b* by bringing the lower lip to the upper teeth only. Uneven front teeth, incorrect placing of the tongue, being tongue tied, all act to blur the *s* sound. Combinations of consonants requiring a rapid shift of mouth position also cause difficulty. Thus a little child finds words like *breakfast, grandmother, shriek, Christmas* hard to pronounce. This inadequate mouth gymnastics accounts for transpositions such as *efalant* for elephant, *waps* for wasp, *medness* for medicine, also for assimilations, example *gaggie* for grannie, *goggy* for doggy.

Many early mispronunciations are accounted for by the fact that the models heard are so poor. In rapid adult speech unaccented syllables are elided; the child omits them, clips beginnings and endings, dovetails words. Thus *c'in* for machine, *tocky* for stocking, *s'own* for sit down. Beyond that is the influence of the dialect or the vowel sounds continually heard. Later, when poor habits have become fixed, it is extremely difficult to redirect attention to the peculiar sounds made, and to set up new ear-voice co-ordinations. Teachers know the long struggles to correct *goil* for girl, *li'dy* for lady, *hurree* for hurry, *co'se* for course, *ile* or *erl* for oil, *idear* for idea, *comin'* for coming, and other typical regional errors. Even when the better usage is well habituated the adult may, in moments of emotional stress, revert to the earlier learned sound productions.

LANGUAGE AND INTELLIGENCE

Age of beginning to talk. — This ability is considerably influenced by the general state of health, and by the control of standing and walking, and by the advance in the use of the hands. Even with normally healthy infants there is a range of variation in the time when talking begins, from 9 to 25 months. Though early use of language may be looked upon as a good sign of mentality, delayed use need not be symptomatic of lack of intelligence. The average age has been considered 14 to 15 months; but Gesell gives two words as a norm for 12 months. Comparing feeble-minded children with normal the age range for the former, taking all degrees of feeble-mindedness together, is from 12 to 156 months, with an average of 34 months. Hetzer and Reindorf, with studies of sixty-five children, found that those in a good environment, that is where they are talked to frequently by educated people, show a superiority of 6 months over children from a poor environment. Whether this is not due in part to the probability of superior intellectual endowment is not clear.

Size of vocabulary. — This is very generally used as an index of mental age. Gesell [1] gives norms of 2 words at 12 months, 4 at 15 months, 5 or more at 18 months. Earlier studies, largely by superior parents on their own children, gave higher numbers than this, such as 9 words at 12 months, over 500 at 24 months. Hetzer [2] found as maximum vocabulary of children from the "good" homes 49 words at 15 months, 91 at 18 months, 216 at 24 months as against 1, 4, and 27 respectively for children from the "poor" environment.

Up to two years old it is a comparatively easy task to register

---

[1] Gesell, A., *The Mental Growth of the Pre-School Child.*
[2] Hetzer, H., *Kindheit und Armut.*

all the words a child can use. After that age the vocabulary increases so rapidly that complete recording is practically impossible. A few investigators, such as Bateman, Beyer, Mateer, Nice, the Whipples, the Brandenburgs [1] have attempted to transcribe the entire list of utterances of older individual children during specified days. For extensive tests on larger numbers of children the method of sampling and estimating is necessary. Representative words are carefully listed and conversation so arranged that the child is led to use or explain them. Descoudres in Geneva has thus devised standard language tests for children of kindergarten age. Madorah Smith [2] at Iowa University investigated by a somewhat similar procedure of her own 273 children from 8 months to 6 years old. She gives a correlation of .69 between a language score and mental age on the Binet scale. The average size vocabulary she found to be 3 words at one year, 272 at two, 896 at three, 1540 at four, 2072 at five, 2562 at six. Girls, until three, are more precocious in vocabulary acquisition but later than that the boys catch up.

In the Terman tests for intelligence children of school age are asked the meanings of words in standard lists. The total vocabulary is estimated from the proportion correctly understood. A presumed total of 3600 is the norm for the eight-year level, 5400 for ten, 7200 for twelve, 9000 for fourteen. A wide knowledge of words, then, enters as a large factor into the score which represents age achievement for any child tested in his mother tongue.

Bilingualism. — Studies on a few individual children from bilingual homes indicate that even in the very early stages the two vocabularies, then pronunciation and syntax may be kept apart. This is probably more likely to be the case when the two parents always address the child in different languages, or when the parents speak one tongue and the servants another. Here then is easy opportunity to habituate different thought systems. More intensive studies of this situation are needed. Whether

[1] See *Ped. Sem.*, vols. 16, 24, 26.
[2] Smith, M. E., *Univ. of Iowa St. Ch. Welf.*, v. 3, *5, 1926.

or not it is an advantage to have two words for one thing, and whether vocabulary may not be doubled at the expense of clear thinking has been suggested by Saer [1] and by Frank Smith.[2] In extensive tests on Welsh and English speaking school children Smith found the progress of monoglots between eight and eleven years of age superior to that of bilinguals in power of expression, choice of vocabulary and accuracy of thought. Saer found the monoglots' period of most rapid increase in vocabulary to be between eight and eleven, the bilinguals' after ten years old. There was a higher range of I.Q.'s for the monoglot children; and higher averages of intelligence among university students from monoglot than from bilingual homes.

LANGUAGE AND THINKING

Words and ideas. — According to John Watson's interpretation thinking does not go on apart from language. Ideas are verbalized, symbolized reactions to the world of objects. The infant is "conditioned" into substituting sound symbols for perceptual experiences with things, and develops ideas only as he learns to manipulate these sound symbols. By language, Watson would include internal, silent speech and incipient movements of all sorts. Thoughts, then, are simply verbalized acts. Among these, the finer distinction between ideas and mere emotional impulses would get lost.

More popularly we speak of words as expressing thoughts, of thought being clarified by being put into words, of the value of finding the right words for the idea. By thoughts we might mean memories of perceptual experiences, single concepts, simple judgments, sequences of imaginary construction, intentions, or the reasoning out of imaginary construction, intentions, or the reasoning out of problems. Certainly, we can follow a little child's thinking ability fairly easily for the simple reason that he talks incessantly. By noting his use of language we can

[1] Saer, D. J., "The effect of bilingualism on intelligence," *Br. Jo. Psy.*, v. 14, 1923.
[2] Smith, F., "Bilingualism and mental development," *Br. Jo. Psy.*, v. 13, 1923.

trace his growth of feelings of relationship, his memory span, his methods of association. Later on, by far the greater portion of the "mental" testing of a child over three years is through the medium of language. True, there are picture tests, spatial, color, form, and size problems, tests for mechanical ability, and so on, but in general we seek to discover facts about memory, imagination, and reasoning through language responses. Thus, in the Terman intelligence tests we find color naming, counting, sentence repetition among the requisites for the younger years; and with older children we investigate the ability to describe differences and to define first concrete, then abstract terms.

We grade children in school largely by their progress in dealing with the mother tongue in visual form, and by the highly symbolized language of number. We teach them to read for informational content, for directions for action, for recall. They must note details, or skim for the main idea; they must understand factors and conditions and be able to predict the outcome. They must be able to analyze, summarize, expand, rearrange. They must learn symbols for maps and for musical sounds. Reading, then, involves much more than word recognition, or even sentence and paragraph comprehension. Efficient thinking is tested by the ability to manipulate different sorts of symbols, visual as well as oral, and by the manipulation of larger co-ordinated units of such symbols.

Interest in language. — This is shown in a variety of ways. We have noted the question as to word meanings, sometime between two and three years of age. As the stock of words increases a child will practice saying them, apparently for the pleasure of the sound of odd combinations or the feel of them in the mouth, as a little boy put it. By the kindergarten age the joys of rhyming words, perhaps of alliteration, have been discovered so that a new sort of vocal play is frequently heard. The interest in spoken language is somewhat overshadowed for awhile by the new problems of learning to read; but by eight there is generally a delight in simple play of word meanings, as in conundrums and puns. Alphabet games are enjoyed too, where guessing requires thinking of words beginning with designated letters.

As reading and writing become tools rather than skill problems, interest is awakened in manipulating language in new ways. Rebus writing and word puzzles are tackled not only in a passive way, they are constructed. Visual symbols for numbers and for musical sounds may be played with. Songs, stories, poems may be composed for the pure fun of it. Many teachers are now alive to the value of developing this spontaneous music and poetry creation of pre-adolescent children. Somewhere around puberty a new use of words as symbols is found. Just as the infant from twelve to twenty months gains insight into sounds as symbols for perceptual things, so now there is developed an appreciation of sounds and visual signs as representations for other words, for abstract ideas, for mere relationships. Some are overwhelmed by the thought that "everything stands for something else" as one girl put it. She became quite suspicious of double meanings in even the simplest expressions. Parabolic sayings, figures of speech are now really apprehended, enjoyed, and experimented with.

Another form of language interest, prominent between eleven and fourteen, is the construction of a secret code. The oral forms generally employ a scheme of added prefixes to the mother tongue, or inversion of syllables, or transposition of letters. The written forms are most often simple transliterations into secret symbols. This is more nearly a disguise then, not a real invention. As such it is clearly of importance to the gang. Occasionally we find a child who invents a language for its intrinsic interest. It is then more elaborate with syntax rules of its own.

In early and middle adolescence there is for some a pleasure in collecting quotations, slogans, mottoes, jokes, and so on. Now, too, the various forms of literary composition awaken interest for study and imitation. Appreciation of fine differences in shades of meaning is deepened. Wider acquaintance with different languages invites comparison of sentence structure, of word roots, of colloquialisms. The finer rhythms of stylistic prose are sensed. Choice passages will be marked for reference, not merely for thought content but for beautiful expression, and real literary criticism is evolved. Letter and diary writing may evidence very determined efforts for better style. The school paper is a felt necessity for the ambition of seeing oneself in print; it provides an outlet for the very diverse gifts of authors and editors.

The emotional stresses of adolescence are reflected in what has been appropriately called "slanguage." This evidences a certain wit and humorous grasp of relationships in its highly symbolized expressions. These, and strings of superlatives are pressed into use so constantly that, to the adult listener, a meaningless monotony is the chief result. Too long an habituation to slang really thwarts progress in the appreciation of the finer points of meanings inherent in the mother tongue. A vocabulary enriched by much good reading and practiced orally in debates, dramatics, and other forms will safeguard adolescents from paucity of expression and inability to talk without slang which is so regrettable in the uncultured adult.

Interest in reading. — A request to be taught to read is frequently made at an early age by children of superior mentality. In many cases they seem to teach themselves with very little adult assistance. They learn more new words per year than do children of average intelligence, and take fewer repetitions to learn any new word.

With the mastery of the printed form of language we can follow the changing intellectual interests by the *type of reading* most often engaged in. Terman and Lima [1] found that around eight or nine years comes the peak of interest in fairy tales for most children, continuing longer for girls than for boys. Parallel with this fantasy is found the interest in reality. Stories of child life in other lands win favor, also books of travel, and the realistic, informational kind of nature study. After ten

[1] Terman and Lima, *Children's Reading*.

many myths, legends, and hero tales are read, the adventure element preponderating. By twelve there is a very general interest in biography provided the emphasis is on action rather than on character analysis. Boys are attracted to description of inventions, machines, scientific discoveries; girls seldom are, preferring stories of home and school life. Books such as *Treasure Island* are popular with both sexes. After twelve the girls' earlier maturity shows in their liking for the romance theme in adult fiction, and in their enjoyment of poetry; boys do not, as yet, find these interesting. From fourteen on, though boys' hobbies and mechanical inventiveness sway their choice more than the sentimental leanings of the girls, yet individual differences come to supersede sex differences. After sixteen the reading taste is practically the adult's. Essays, character studies, philosophical treatises are not generally chosen before late adolescence.

Gates [1] found that in the first three grades narratives are preferred to informational reading in the proportion of about 3 to 1. Elements of surprise, liveliness, a definite plot, direct discourse, the introduction of animals, humor within their grasp, *i.e.*, funniness of incident rather than play upon words, are all factors that hold interest in the younger grades. Taking the first five grades together tales of fancy headed the list of preferences, with "thrillers" and grotesque stories second. In the eleventh and twelfth grades the rank order was fanciful fiction, tales of familiar, family relationships, thrillers. At the college level the rank was wit and humor, thrillers, familiar life situations. In all stages informational reading came last on the list.

The *amount of reading* done correlates highly with mental ability. Terman [2] found that his group of gifted children read from two and a half to four times as many books during a two months' period as did the control group. They also read less of the typical "juvenile" fiction, less emotional fiction, more

[1] Gates, A. T., *Interest and Ability in Reading.*
[2] Terman, L. M., *Genetic Studies of Genius.*

informational fiction, more fairy tales, more nature stories and science, more history, biography, and travel. Subnormal and dull children read very little without constant urging, and they develop few different reading tastes. Books must be chosen for them. Bright children generally show a catholicity of taste, and, with free browsing privileges in a good library, will surprise, even shock adults by the omnivorousness displayed.

Language as revealing interests. — Many studies have been made of the topics of conversation among younger children. McCarthy [1] recorded fifty consecutive utterances of any one of thirty-one nursery school age children. She noted about 12 per cent of questions. The toys and present activities evoked most of the sayings. Rugg's [2] study of kindergarten age children found 40 per cent self-assertive utterances, 10 per cent questions, 6 per cent language experimentation, about 0.25 per cent self-depreciation. Older children, studied by Zyve [3] in the more formal situation of the third-grade discussion period, talked about their play at home, about auto trips they had taken, about animals, about things they were making at school. Miscellaneous topics occupied about 12 per cent of the time and were on the increase through the school year. Thus the interests are still egocentric though the talking itself is less so than at an earlier age.

The most extensive and long continued studies of this sort have been made by Piaget. [4] The younger children talk, at first, continuously. They talk about and to their toys, describe their own actions as they perform them, exclaim, comment, affirm with little waiting for others' comments, no interchange of thought or conversation in the real sense, though they may enjoy an audience. This egocentric talking he analyzes into three categories, (1) echolalic repetition, (2) single monologue,

[1] McCarthy, D. A., *Univ. Minn. Inst. Ch. Welf. Mon. Series *4.*

[2] Rugg, *et al.*, "Studies in child personality," *Jo. Ed. Psy.*, v. 20, 1919.

[3] Zyve, C. I., "Conversations among children," *Teachers College Record*, v. 29, 1927.

[4] Piaget, J., *Language and Thought of the Child.*

(3) collective monologue in which children are affected by the presence of others but do not consider them, nor their point of view. The socialized talking is analyzed into (4) remarks adapted to the others' viewpoint, (5) criticisms of others, (6) orders and requests, (7) questions, and (8) answers. By taking the number of utterances of the first three categories as compared with the total number of the first seven, thus

$$\frac{1+2+3}{1+2+3+4+5+6+7}$$

Piaget arrives at a measure which he calls the index of egocentrism. This is high till five years old, decreases with age till by seven and one half to eight there is a real social interchange of thought in the conversation.

About 12 to 15 per cent of all remarks of children three to five years old are questions, indeed, this is sometimes called the age of questions. *What is*, referring both to things and to the meaning of words, *when, where*, and *why* are in constant use. The *why* reveals interest in people's motives or in explanation of their actions far more often than interest in cause. The use of why in long strings of questions will very speedily baffle the would-be-helpful adult. Questioning may degenerate into nonsense, or appear as a sort of mania, the child not stopping for any answers. One little girl, recently arrived at the "why" stage, burst open her aunt's bedroom door early in the morning, put her head in, said "Why?" and went out immediately.

Controlled studies of older children's conversations are not available; but by casual observation it is apparent that descriptions of other than personal concerns enter late and slowly as topics of interest. Dwelling on relationships with other people, what he said, what she said, how I felt, evince the adolescents' romantic and emotional trends. Plans for the future, ideals, enterprises are discussed increasingly. After seventeen or so there is, for the more intelligent at least and among those stimulated by higher education, group discussion of philosophic, religious, scientific, and literary themes. Roughly it might be said that just as the verb usage goes through the sequent stages of present tense, past tense, future tense, so the conversation interests center at first around present occupations and perceptual surroundings. By middle and later childhood the emphasis is shifted somewhat to past activities, possessions, and skills. By adolescence there is a further shift to more coherent consideration of the future, together with absorption in the self's standing with other selves, and, still later, interest in abstract ideas as entities in themselves.

DRAWING AS A LANGUAGE

Function. — Drawing may have three different purposes or functions. The first is to *tell something*, to give information. Here the conveying of an idea is more important than either visual realism or any æsthetic consideration. The story picture, a produce map, an anatomical diagram are examples of such drawings. A second function is *to develop an effect that will be pleasing* to the eye. Ornament, decoration, the production of beauty in color, line, and composition belong here. A third function is *to represent* an object. Accuracy in observation and the technique of perspective are involved in carrying out this function. Children are motivated by these purposes in the order given. Not infrequently they relinquish all attempts to draw when the technical difficulties of faithful representation become evident.

Stages of development. — The first may be called the *scribble* stage. Children under eighteen months make mere imitative movements with no regard for the result produced by the crayon on the paper. The second stage is called *localized scribble*, because here children pause to contemplate the effect of their markings and, if asked about them, will point more or less consistently to parts which are named head, feet, etc. Third, they arrive at a stage of *logical realism* in which the imagination is the only limit, as well as being the driving power. This period is most characteristic of early childhood and has been more studied than any other. Later, anywhere from seven and one half to ten comes the stage of *visual realism* when the third function becomes the main motive. If the spontaneity of the earlier years can survive the disappointment of finding that their products do not correspond with the visual world around, then a renewal of interest may be seen in early or middle adolescence in the art of drawing. Otherwise the ability to draw may never develop beyond a typical ten-year-old level.

Characteristics of the third stage. — The mental attitude here is egocentric, as oral language also reveals. Drawing is indeed a second language at this time. Children *draw from within*, giving a linear description of what they mean and what interests them. Thus we see exaggerated detail, pictures of sounds, of the wind, as well as of boats, airplanes, cars, animals, and people. They pay no attention to a model if one is supplied but draw from their own consciousness what they know is there. Thus they may supply the leg of the rider on the far side of the horse, or both eyes on a face supposedly in profile. The picture tells a story; so the house is drawn, and then some action going on inside. What matter if the adult criticizes these diaphanous effects? Generally they talk as they draw; and since this running commentary is frequently necessary for a sympathetic understanding of the artist and his product it is well to take down what is said in explanation. "Here's the house — and here's where you go in the door — and here's the elevator — and you push the bell — and then you go up." The total effect is that of a huge elevator bell button basal to a lattice work elevator dominating a transparent front wall. Another characteristic is the habitual *use of certain symbols* such as a hat and a pipe for a man, smoke from a house chimney, special circles and loops for hands. So conventional do some of these become that it is not unusual to see the preferred form of human face or leg used as an animal's parts.

Another important fact is that at first children think, and draw, *in parts*, adding piece to piece. For instance, in drawing a horse an ovaloid loop is made for the head, a larger loop touching the first represents the body. Lines or loops, any number, added at any place to the second loop, are the legs. A tail is attached too. It takes a far more mature child to draw one line completely round the outline, having thought the whole animal from the start.

The *interest in ornamentation* begins to function in this stage as well as the story-telling interest. Many buttons decorate the humans' clothing. Curtains and shade pulls adorn the house windows. A passion for details in bricks or in flower gardens appears. There is a riot in the use of many-colored crayons. Girls surpass boys in this.

Gradually the third function or purpose is felt. Desire to draw "my" house or some special child necessitates the inclusion of recognizable features. Children begin to question how they really look, and to be critical of their productions. The attempt to illustrate stories with action in a landscape brings the problem of representing space. Children begin to wonder how that is done. For awhile the logic realism prevails. Thus, trees on the near side of a stream would have their tops in the water if drawn in the usual upright manner. But since children know the tops point away from the stream they may so draw them, or, to the adults' interpretation, upside down. Asked to draw a table from a model before them they will make the top rectangular since they know its shape, though of course the view they really get is anything but that. For many the difficulty of translating a three-dimensional world into a two-dimensional medium becomes too great. Some find the transition to representation facilitated by copying a flat drawing, particularly since in the art of writing prescribed flat models have been copied many times and the outcome criticized for its likeness to the original.

Drawing as revealing interests. — A great many extensive studies have been made. The best known are by Maitland in California, reported by Lukens,[1] by Ivanoff in Switzerland, re-

[1] Lukens, H. T., "Children's drawings in early years," *Ped. Sem.*, 1896–97.

ported by Katzaroff,[1] and by the International Kindergarten Union in thirty-four cities of the United States, reported by McCarty.[2] It is found that the human figure is drawn more frequently than anything else up to ten years old, and in adult form more often than in child form. Houses, trees, furniture, cars, boats, airplanes, animals are favorites too. Boys will, more often than girls, draw men, flags, boats, automobiles. Girls, more often than boys, draw children and babies, flowers, furniture and decorative designs. This last interest may be the only one to survive into the teens except for the specially talented child. Older boys like to attempt caricature. They find a use for working drawings in connection with their construction projects.

Drawing and intelligence. — In the first three stages the sequence of development is so well known, and, in the third stage progress is so clearly marked by typical details that it has been a comparatively simple matter to arrange a scale by which to judge a child's maturity in general. Instances of this definite sequence are as follows. In drawing a house a square is an earlier form than that with the addition of gable ends. Line drawings precede mass. Single lines are used for the limbs of animals and humans before loops are. In drawing the human form legs are drawn from the head before a body is indicated. Body and arms are shown before a neck is included. Heels, eyebrows, jointed limbs, the correct number of fingers are late additions. Full face precedes profile. In profile drawings the feet are turned before the body, and so on.

From intimate knowledge of this progression a specimen of a spontaneous drawing of a man may be compared with the typical drawing for the chronological age and a rating be given in terms of mental age. Gesell includes this test in his battery of tests for younger children. In clinic work it is a quick method of preliminary investigation. Disregarding artistic standards,

---

[1] Katzaroff, M. E., "Qu'est ce que les enfants dessinent?" *Arch. de Psy.*, v. 9, 1910.

[2] McCarty, S. A., *Children's Drawings.*

and using fifty-one points of definite progression by age Good-enough has devised a rating scale suitable for use with children up to eight or ten years old, and especially good for those handicapped by deafness or a foreign language.

The ability to copy is also used in a series of intelligence tests since here too the progress is sharply distinguishable. Children can imitate some one drawing a vertical stroke before they can imitate a horizontal stroke. Given a completed model to copy, a circle can be drawn before a square, this about four years old. An oblique cross is more difficult than one in the upright position. A diamond, with its four oblique lines is far harder to copy, and is part of the test at the seven-year level.

Feeble-minded children are characteristically retarded in their drawing development. Psychopathic children show curious combinations of mature and primitive characteristics in one and the same drawing. Sometimes there is extreme attention to certain details with inexplicable omissions of important items. Superior children vindicate themselves when judged by these developmental scales; but that must not be taken to mean that children of high I.Q. are necessarily good in drawing from the artistic point of view. One cannot predict excellence in artistic work from knowledge of mental superiority. Artistic gifts as such seem to exist fairly independently of intelligence; that is, the special endowment may be found with widely differing degrees of mentality. We note, however, less creative work from those of inferior intelligence even though they may learn to copy well.

It is rare to find unusual ability in drawing or painting before puberty; whereas musically gifted children are discoverable at an early age.

PRACTICAL EXERCISES

1. Study the English compositions of fifth-grade children from the standpoint of length of sentences, complex sentences.
2. In the sixth grade, secure a transcript from memory of "My country 'tis of thee." Apart from misspellings, what misinterpretation of language is evident?

3. Observe a four-year-old in a free play situation with other children present. Record everything he says for 50 consecutive utterances. Analyze afterwards for the egocentric index as described in this chapter.
4. If there are any children available from bilingual homes to whom individual Terman tests have been given, study the records of their performance on such tests as require language usage or comprehension, as compared with their performance in other tests.
5. Familiarize yourself with the method of scoring drawings as standardized by Goodenough (see below). Ask a child under seven to draw a man — the very best man he can make. Score it, as directed. Compare with the mental age found by any other tests the school has given.
6. Ask four ten-year-olds, four twelve-year-olds, two boys and two girls in each case, what books they have read this last month. What magazines they like to read and why.
7. Visit the children's room of a public library, spending about two hours there. Sketch the floor plan to indicate the location of different types of books such as fairy tales, adventure series, history, nature study, etc. Watch boys' and girls' choices at different ages, counting the number of children. Consult the librarian, when she is not too busy, as to what is in greatest demand.
8. What children in each room in the school have a speech defect?

FOR DISCUSSION

1. All the above exercises should be discussed. The results of 3 and 6, if made by a dozen or more students, should yield material that can be treated statistically and graphically. How do the findings of 3 compare with those of Piaget? of Rugg? How do those of 6 and 7 compare with those of Terman and Lima?
2. What risk is run by teaching little children songs and poems orally?
3. What plays and games help enlarge the vocabulary?
4. Argue for and against beginning the study of another language than the mother tongue at four years old. At eight years old. In the seventh grade.
5. Did you ever use a secret language as a child? Of what kind?

SELECTED REFERENCES

DOLCH, E. W. "Grade vocabularies." *Jo. Ed. Res.*, v. 16, 1927.
GOODENOUGH, F. L. *Measurement of Intelligence by Drawings*.
GRANT and WHITE. "A study of children's choices of reading." *T. C. Record*, 1925.

McCarthy, D. A. *The Language Development of the Pre-School Child.*

McCarty, S. A. *Children's Drawings.*

Piaget, J. *The Language and Thought of the Child.*

Raubicheck, Davis, and Carll. *Voice and Speech Problems.*

Saer, D. J. "The effect of bilingualism on intelligence." *Brit. Jo. Psych.,* v. 14, 1923.

Smith, M. E. "An investigation of the development of the sentence and the extent of the vocabulary of young children." *Univ. of Iowa St. in Ch. Welf.,* v. 3 *5.

Stern, W. *Psychology of Early Childhood.* Chs. 8, 11.

Strayer, L. C. "Language and growth." *Gen. Psych. Monog.,* v. 8 *3, 1930.

Terman and Lima. *Children's Reading.*

CHAPTER XIII

THINKING AND REASONING

Of all the various powers that man is heir to, his power of thinking is the most important. It is most important because it explains man's position in the animal scale. Because of it he reigns supreme in the world of nature, farthest removed from the animal type of mind. That man has this power is just as much a matter of original nature as that he sees or moves. It is just as much dependent on structure as seeing is dependent on the presence of an eye and its nerves; but as thinking is more complex than mere seeing, so the structures upon which it depends are more complex and numerous than are those of the eye. In fact, thinking involves and requires the full equipment of the human being. Thinking is not a characteristic merely of the adult. As Dewey defines thinking, — "A matter of following up and testing the conclusions suggested by the facts and events of life," it may be observed in even an infant. Noticing that the back and front views of people, though so different, yet mean the same person — wondering over the appearing and disappearing of objects and people behind furniture, through doors, in boxes and drawers, in the delightful game of peek-a-boo — puzzling over the metamorphoses of people by clothing — these and many other similar daily experiences are stimuli to thought, in the sense of feeling relationships, for a baby under twelve months. With the acquisition of language individual feelings of meaning are clarified and simple judgments expressed.

HOW IDEAS DEVELOP

Kinds of ideas. — Mental activity consists in re-presenting things, in becoming aware of the connections and relations between them, in being able to refer to them, in managing them symbolically. We should therefore be interested to trace the development of ideas of different sorts and to observe how children use these ideas to solve problems.

Ideas may be classified as *individual, general,* or *abstract,* for example, this horse, horses, equine. Of these the individual meanings develop first. The baby, by the laws of association comes to react in a definite way to stimuli of sight, touch, perhaps the words of others, before he begins to use speech himself. He also gives evidence of recognition of objects, of color perception, of reactions to space relationships, even of memory for absent objects. Even thus early, then, ideas of a specific sort are present.

Growth of general, or class ideas. — The development of a general idea from individual meanings may occur on a very simple level. Thus, a child was accustomed to go to her high chair ready for a meal on the direction "Get into your chair." On her second birthday she was given a red kindergarten table and a couple of small chairs to match. She was invited to sit in her new chair — and ran to the high chair at once. Further invitation with reassurance produced a wondering look from one chair to the other. "This is your chair too; this is your little chair, that is your high chair." Reaction followed, with much enjoyment from sitting in the new chair. Next day, with appropriate adjectives and gestures the comparison was again made with the additional "This is mother's chair." On succeeding days her attention was drawn to the various specimens of dining room chair, overstuffed upholstered chair, cane seated chair, hard kitchen chair, always with the remark "this is a chair too," with plenty of time for scrutiny. At the end of a week she would respond readily to the request "Show me a chair, another chair, another chair." Thus she had a general idea of chairs, or a chair; though, not having yet encountered a rocking chair, a dentist's chair, a Pullman chair, the idea is not as complete as it may be later.

Similarly, a child progresses from the individual idea of

mother as being the name of one person to a more general idea by hearing other children call other women mother. When the cat has kittens and the mother bird is observed feeding its young the mother idea will be enlarged. It may still include the notion that babies and children are the only ones to have mothers. When grandmother comes and his own adults address her as mother the idea is still further developed. Thus by encountering many examples, alike in one essential but differing in the total complex of details the general or class idea is built up by a process of comparison contrast, analysis. This process goes on continually in childhood, adolescence, and adult life. The analysis is seldom well or explicitly made by younger children; instead, the best-fitting type of reaction is singled out and habituated in thought. Thus, a chair is conclusively described as "to sit on," a knife is "to cut," a potato is "to eat" at five years old.

Abstract ideas. — These evolve in the same way, by noting qualities inherent in perceptual experiences, characteristics in common between ideas of any level. The woolly coat is soft, so is the ice cream, and mother's cheek and the kitten's fur and the bath-mat to bare feet; while the floor is hard, and bones and teeth, and the spoon and the buttons on the coat. Softness becomes an idea by itself. By observing the things all mothers do and the characteristic relationships involved in their attitudes the abstract ideas of motherliness, motherhood, come into being, and later on, of maternity, mother country, alma mater, and so on.

Asked to describe such abstractions a child at first offers examples only. "That pillow is soft." Up to eleven or twelve years old there is very narrow, specific content for such ideas as pity, justice, salvation. An occasion may be cited when the word was used. Thus, "She hurt herself it was a pity." Justice is a statue with a blindfold on; it is a justice of the peace; it is doing to the other fellow what he did to you. Salvation is the Salvation Army. Charity is giving what you don't want to the poor. The first-hand experience behind these replies can be readily inferred. Not that a ten-year-old cannot feel a specific injustice to himself, nor is he incapable of pity; he cannot think and talk of them in a detached way.

Feelings of relationship. — Because of the need for muscular reactions, ideas of *quality and space* based on objective learning are developed early. Ideas of *time* are more difficult since perceptions through eyes, ears, and hands do not help much. Time to do so and so is understood; but many of our expressions are puzzling to the five- and six-year-old. Consider the idioms time passes, time is up, we have time, behind time, on time, a hard time, a bad time, beating time, telling time, three times, lost time, making time. Where does time go to? How does the clock keep time? If the sun makes time for us, isn't there any time when it is dark? Does that elusive tomorrow ever come? If it will be winter time when the snow comes how confusing when there is no snow.

Meumann thinks that all complex time concepts such as last spring, day before yesterday, a month ago, are quite unintelligible to a six-year-old. Arithmetic books to the contrary, the eight-year-old's day is from waking time till dark, containing a varying, indefinite number of hours. Not till nine or more birthdays have passed does a child begin to regard a year as other than a wonderfully long period, and to date events in his past either with any great accuracy, or over long intervals. Still less is there any impersonal chronological sense to prevent nine-year-olds thinking of Abraham, King Arthur, George Washington as probable contemporaries, though living in different countries. After ten there is better orientation in time, helped by increasing use of numbers and wider reading.

Feelings of *likeness and difference* arising from perceptual comparisons naturally appear earlier than those existing in the functions of things. Also, if the child's own reactions are involved the comparison is easier than if two things, related to each other but not to him are to be considered. Thus, oranges and apples can be usefully compared when bees and flies cannot. Questions in the Terman intelligence tests calling for differences between a stone and an egg should be satisfactorily answered at seven years old, that of the likeness between wood and coal, iron and silver by eight. The difference between a president and a king may not be well stated before fourteen, nor between abstractions such as poverty and misery, character and reputation till sixteen.

Relationships involved in humor. — A feeling for the incongruous is basal to a sense of humor. By studying what children consider funny will indicate, then, what feelings of relationship are already developed. Charlotte Bühler finds children between two and three years old able to appreciate the joke of being offered a cookie and having it withdrawn, while the adult speaks pleasantly. They also begin little teasing tricks of fooling other people at this period. In the nursery school age frequent laughter is provoked by the surprise or slight shock element in their own sequence of actions. Part of the fun of dressing up in adult clothing may be due to the feeling of disproportion, just as daddy wearing baby's hat is sure to provoke mirth.

Tested by pictures, the habitual space relationships function earliest. Thus, three- and four-year-olds are amused at disproportionate or impossible parts. A very large person riding a tiny animal, furniture with human legs and feet, would be sensed as ridiculous. When the humor necessitates interpretation of the future situation resulting from actions depicted, it takes older children to grasp it. Thus a man shown cutting off the branch on which he is seated is regarded with interest but no appreciation. When asked to draw something funny the same sequence is seen, first disproportion, next inventive combinations, later situations in action. If the picture is symbolic it is rare to find pre-adolescents understanding the wit. Children who were tested by having to describe and explain cartoons were found by Shaffer [1] unable to feel the force of the hidden meaning much before eleven years old.

When the joke is mediated through language wholly, chil-

[1] Shaffer, L. F., "Children's interpretations of cartoons," *T. C. Cont. Ed.*, *429.

dren's memory and imagination are called on heavily, and they may easily fail to grasp the idea that is so funny to the adult. Just because they laugh when older people do at the conclusion of an anecdote is no evidence that they see the point. They are apt to be too literal; or else some irrelevant, superficial relationship has caught the attention. Thus, the joke in the exclamation "tremendous" made by the window broken by the falling tree is explained as consisting in the fact that the window could not really talk. In the standard intelligence tests the ability to tell what is absurd in the statement that the road goes downhill all the way to the city and downhill all the way home is placed at the ten-year level. An acceptable interpretation of fables such as the milkmaid's plans is not expected before twelve years old. With the young adolescents' better grasp of abstractions and deepening interest in social relationships, the sense of humor can function on a new plane.

LITTLE CHILDREN'S IDEAS

Ideas of number. — As Thorndike has shown,[1] a number, such as 3, may have four different meanings. It may be a *series* idea; 3 is more than 2, comes before 4 in counting. It may be a *group* idea, a collection of 3 things. It may be a *ratio* meaning in size, space, time, or amount relationships, such as a 3 inch stick, a 3 pint bowl. It may be a *relational meaning*, it is one quarter of 12, the cube root of 27, 8 less than 11, and so on. Little children of nursery and kindergarten age learn to repeat a series of words in counting, but do not necessarily know numbers in the first sense above. Words like forty, a hundred, a million may be used to express "ever so many" with, naturally, no clear idea of their meaning in any of the above ways. Real counting is built up from auditory perceptual experiences mixed with visual, and is achieved by the age of four for numbers up to 4 or 5.

The group idea seems more difficult, and at first is confused with the series idea. Thus, a child may not know he has four

[1] *The Psychology of Arithmetic.*

blocks or five fingers though he has just counted them. The word "four" is felt as a name for the last one counted, is, indeed, an ordinal number rather than a cardinal. By using differently arranged groups the collective idea of fourness, five-ness, is built up. As in other tests the form of question "How many are here, are here . . ." is harder than the form "Show me four dots, three dots." The relational and ratio ideas of number are rarely learned before school days begin, except that the word "half" may be understood.

The work in the first two years of school consists chiefly in correcting wrong ideas of counting and developing these four distinctly different ideas of number. This must be done in connection with perceptual problems at first, admitting of im-mediate verification: later comes work with imagined concrete material, then with abstract numbers themselves. Over-drill in counting may be responsible for some of the visual num-ber forms which a fair percentage of older children and adults report, and which slow down the processes of addition and sub-traction. Little advantage has been taken of children's early facility in memorizing rhythmic material to teach multiplication tables by sound before the attempt to rationalize them. Scholas-tic experiments with this might be as fruitful for teaching methods as research work in the process of learning to read has proved.

Ideas of the world about them. — Piaget,[1] from the work of himself and his intensively trained collaborators in questioning younger children about their notions of the origins of such things as the sun, trees, stones, their ideas of what it is to be alive, finds two important tendencies of the little child's mind. One is *animism*, the other *artificialism*. They ascribe conscious-ness, life, purpose, emotions to all sorts of things at first. A little later, movement, especially spontaneous movement, is taken as a criterion of life. Still later, life is confined in their idea to plants and animals. Bubi Scupin, who was studied

[1] Piaget, J., *The Child's Conception of the World. The Child's Conception of Physical Causality.*

intensively under Stern's guidance, showed these three stages
very clearly. The percentage of all his anthropomorphic statements was calculated and observed to decrease to 20 per cent
by his sixth year. Many children do not seem to have arrived
securely at the third stage till nearly eleven years old, according
to Piaget.

The tendency to artificialism was remarked by Sully [1] also.
Thus, some men made a big ball of stone which went up in the
air like a balloon and became the sun or moon. God takes water
from the sink and throws it down to make rain. The lake is a
big hole made by men digging. The river came by men pouring
water on the ground. Seeds are made by the shopkeeper even
though they are planted and grow into trees. People make
stones. Replies of this sort are common up to seven or eight
years old, after which better knowledge from directed observation leads to more natural explanations.

Ideas of God. — One constituent in the God idea develops
from the *early relationship to the parents*. The infant's physical
dependence habituates an emotional attitude of confident ex-
pectation. So far as two-year-olds are concerned, the parents
order their lives in all details, are the source of food, of authority, are all powerful, all wise, yet unknowable; in other words,
their parents are their gods. Sooner or later children realize that
parents are not so infallible, not so absolute as they had previously supposed. Father cannot do something, he makes a
mistake, mother does not know — and the resulting mental
or emotional confusion has been termed the first great crisis
in their development. The implicit faith has been freed, however, and may be reattached to a concept of God towards whom
the attitude will be very similar to that of the little child towards
his parents.

Another constituent is the *artificialism* tendency described
above. A master workman is frequently posited, responsible for
things in nature, who is himself very large and clever and
strong. Such ideas are found in the absence of any direct

[1] *Studies of Childhood.*

teaching. The third constituent is, of course, *what children pick up* from the words and attitudes of others, or from books and pictures. In the large percentage of children in this country who receive no religious instruction it would be interesting to discover the further content of the idea. Unfortunately, investigations have been carried on usually with the minority of children under some systematic scheme of teaching. With the former group, chance contacts with oral or printed references will mold the idea, which probably will not be critically examined till the adolescent period. With the latter group indoctrination is usually accompanied with some emotional atmosphere. Thus we can find ten-year-olds violently partisan in atheistic statements, six-year-olds delightedly assured of a species of beneficent magic worker, fourteen-year-old girls in ecstasy over the thought of a heavenly bridegroom, remorseful eight-year-olds afraid of a vengeful spy, sixteen- or eighteen-year-olds in reverent wonder over some marvel in biology, and so on. One thing is clear. No matter what idea the adults try to impart children will, according to their stage of maturity, construct their own. The anthropomorphism of the earlier years, reinforced by the pronoun *he* and perhaps by pictures, predisposes them to the visual image of a large man, probably with a long white beard, living "up" somewhere. A (Catholic) six-year-old explained that they kept God in a box in church and took him out in a procession sometimes. A (Jewish) eight-year-old said God was a ball of fire.

Questions about the omnipresence of deity are plentiful up to eight or nine years old. As generalizations and abstractions are better grasped the God idea undergoes characteristic development with many synchronous inconsistencies. Conflicting ideas may present an acute problem in middle or later adolescence.

METHODS OF THINKING

Three levels. — Thinking as problem solving may occur on the level of *concrete, specific ideas,* or *class ideas,* or in *relational* *systems* of ideas. The first implies *thinking about objects* which are present to the senses. They present a problem in some way; some new feature is observed, some failure to function in the expected manner sets a child thinking. There will be manipulative experimentation of the trial and accidental success order. The child tries to find out how to build his blocks securely, why the wheels do or will not go round. Construction problems in shop work and many that arise in play require this sort of thinking. Memory and imagination help here, since by recalling experiences with similar objects and by foreseeing new arrangements of parts a solution of the problem is more easily found. Many exercises in geometry call for this type of mental process.

The second level of thinking implies the *discovery and use of class ideas*, of principles, laws, and the like rather than perceptual comparison of concrete material. Generalizations have been aptly termed the tools of thought. It is obvious that the more perfect the tools the more efficient work the mind can do. These tools are fashioned by the process of induction, in which elements common to many individual cases are abstracted and formulated into a definition, a rule, a law. Henceforth, the broader meaning of the concept is applicable to new situations. When so used the thinking is deductive, in which a problem concerning a particular case is solved by identifying it with some known principle, classifying it under some category already familiar in its implications. Thus ideas of adverbs, of peninsulas, of three-part song form are built inductively from the examination of many instances of each. The decision that this word is an adverb, that this land is a peninsula, this composition is in three-part form is made deductively.

The third level is that of *systematization and integration*. Though it is useless to try to classify knowledge unless there is a reasonable amount there to start with, it is equally true that facts however well memorized and understood as things-in-themselves do not function in the most helpful way unless they are organized into meaningful relationships. The child who has skill in multiplying and dividing may fail in solving arithmetic problems if he cannot see when to employ either of these processes. Good observation in nature study work is worth while for its own sake; but relating the facts so observed is necessary for a science of botany, zoölogy, etc.

Judgments combine ideas. — Simple *analytic* judgments state explicitly some fact observed, *e.g.*, Your dress is brown. This box is heavier than that one. *Synthetic* judgments relate knowledge in new ways and involve the various feelings of relationship from the simpler sort of quantity and space, through those of similarity, genus species, time, to condition and result and purpose.

DIFFERENCES BETWEEN THE THINKING OF ADULTS AND THAT OF CHILDREN

Children think less than adults do. — It has been customary to assert that children do not think so often as adults, that the amount of thinking done by children in a day is less than the amount done by adults in the same length of time. There are three principal reasons for this difference. First: the *character of the adjustments necessary to young children is predominantly mechanical.* They have to learn to control the various parts of their bodies, to talk, to use the common tools and utensils. Their mental life centers largely in the sensory sphere, their conduct is controlled by impulse. In the field of imagination, the spontaneous, uncontrolled type holds sway. Children must possess a fund of free ideas, of percepts and images, of responses of conduct, before much thinking, in the sense of control and testing of such reactions, is possible. Much of children's time and energy must be given to acquiring the mental stuff necessary to thinking. Children think less often than adults partly because more of their time has necessarily to be given to mechanical processes of acquiring material for higher kinds of thinking.

The second reason for the fact that children think less often than do adults, and from an educational point of view a more important one, is that *the tendency* is not stimulated, *is even inhibited by their environment.* Problems are not allowed to arise in the child's world, or if they do they are immediately solved by overanxious or careless adults. Toys lost or broken are allowed so to remain or are replaced depending on the mood or the ability of the adults; but in how few cases are the children allowed, with help, to solve the problem thus occasioned? They get no spending money at all, or else having some, are told just what to do with it, or are allowed to spend it with no guidance. They are told what to do, are shown how to do things. They are shielded and protected, and made to imitate and conform until the natural spontaneous tendency to think is well-nigh killed through disuse. That both the power and the inclination to think exist in children at an early age is shown by their reactions in free play when the overzealous adult is out of the way; then, in the stimulating environment of other children or even of their own world of fancy, little children see problems and solve them in greater abundance than adults dream, unless they have watched with the motto, "Hands off." Wherever the environment presents problems, the frequency of reflective consciousness increases. Children think as little as they do partly because adults will not give them opportunity to do it more often.

A third reason for this lack is the fact that *discomfort is actually made to follow the exhibition of the tendency.* That may seem to most people a preposterous statement, but a little reflection will prove its truth. Tendencies to think are nipped in the bud because they are troublesome to manage. Consider the hundreds of questions normal, healthy children of four will ask in a day with the effect that before long the adults, having reached their limit of knowledge, or of nervous energy, tell the children to stop asking questions, or to keep quiet; with the result that not only do most children stop asking questions, but they also stop thinking questions. Of course, it is true that sometimes children ask questions without either expecting or wanting answers merely to hold the adult's attention if possible; but this happens comparatively seldom with most children, and can easily be discouraged. It is no easy task to answer a child's questions, and a still more difficult one to answer them in such a way that thought is stimulated still further; and yet not to do so is to inhibit one of the most necessary phases in the development of a thoughtful man or woman.

Not only is the asking of questions discouraged, but children's attempts to think things out for themselves are often greeted with shouts of laughter by older members of the family, and are repeated to others in the children's presence with such exclamations, as, "Is not that funny?" "How do you suppose she ever got that idea?" "How do children get such queer notions?" The effect of such an attitude on sensitive children is disastrous. To have their honest attempts to answer the questions experience puts to them held up to ridicule, or even commented on and exclaimed over, takes away their self-confidence; children soon give up such attempts, and simply sink back with an "I don't know," or come to depend absolutely on adults, or later on books, for the answers which at one time they were ready and anxious to try to find for themselves.

Similarly, when they experiment at manipulation of things, their efforts meet the same kind of discouragement. Of course many of the experiments turn out wrong, bringing results that the children had not dreamed of; they, in consequence, are considered "naughty" and "troublesome." The children of a surgeon who, hearing much of operations of all kinds, cut open the hens, emptied their crops and carefully sewed them up again to see if they would live, would in most cases receive such a punishment that all desire for experiment would be absolutely killed. The actions of the child who tears up the cushion to see if there are real feathers inside, or who sets the water pitcher out-of-doors in zero weather to see if the water will freeze and crack it, or who tries to walk backwards downstairs and gets a bad fall, or who takes the clock apart to see if he can put it together again, — these, and hundreds of other honest attempts to test knowledge and power, are condemned by the short-sighted adult as deliberate mischief making, and punishment is meted out to the investigator. And how many teachers dread the "original," "curious" child — the one who always has another question to ask, or who always has another way to suggest, or who is always popping up in unexpected circumstances. Yet these are the very signs of the characteristic which in theory we are striving to cultivate — independent thinking power. No, in practice it is the unobtrusive, quiet child, who "stays put," who receives with ready mind all that is given him and never objects, who does what is expected of him in the usual way, — he it is who gets the rewards; and consequently the large majority of children soon moderate in their zeal to do and to think, for it is human nature to take the road that brings least discomfort.

Children's thinking is inaccurate. — The second great difference between the thinking of children and that of adults is in the accuracy of the results. Children are more likely to make mistakes, to reach incorrect conclusions than adults are.

There are several reasons why this must necessarily be so. In the first place, their *supply of facts is not adequate*. Children lack experience, they do not possess much of the knowledge adults have, and therefore, when they try to think things out, although their thinking processes may be perfect, their conclusions may be incorrect because the crucial fact, the one upon which the solution hangs, is missing. The child who vigorously tugged at his mother's hair, and when expostulated with said it did not hurt dolly, lacked the knowledge of the difference between people and dolls. Time and time again the thinking of children in arithmetic, geography, and the other school subjects is inaccurate, simply because of the lack of data. Without facts and experience thinking is impossible, and the larger the amount of data the greater the possibilities of thinking.

In the second place, *the material they do possess is apt to be inaccurate* and not well understood. The tendency of children to be careless and inaccurate in their observations was pointed out in connection with the development of perception. Thus the premises from which they reason are often false or incorrect, and therefore when these are used in their thinking of course incorrect conclusions are unescapable. Feelings of meaning, especially abstractions and concepts, feelings of logical relationships, that is, of cause and effect, of co-ordination, or subordination, of concession and so on; judgments of the explicit type which, replacing the unreliable image, are more permanent and at the same time show reflective results, — all these are necessary before thinking can be carried far, and to successful conclusions. These in children are imperfect, undeveloped, the very thinking itself is necessary to develop them; and so long as this is true their thinking must be inaccurate, for the tools with which they are working are not adapted to the use to which they are putting them. They are not reliable enough, nor are they all of the kind to carry on the process of thinking efficiently.

In the third place, *the character of children's attention makes accurate thinking difficult.* Thinking requires that the problem be held clearly in mind, and that the material offered be accepted or rejected in accordance with its bearing on the question at hand. Now this selective activity requires concentrated, sustained attention to ideals. Children's attention, as has already been noted, tends to lack in concentration and to be easily distracted; and these characteristics are the more marked when the attention is given not to perceptual objects but to ideas. Children may have all the data necessary to solve a given problem and have it in the most usable form, and yet reach an incorrect solution merely because they could not hold attention to the question long enough and clearly enough to make use of what they have. How often a teacher finds that after a few minutes of work some of the children have absolutely lost sight of the problem, and are going along in a haphazard way with, of course, the inevitable result, — a wrong answer. So long as this tendency is strong in children, their thinking must be correspondingly inaccurate.

In the fourth place, their thinking is inaccurate because *they lack systematization of ideas.* They juxtapose rather than organize their judgments, and are content with logic-tight compartments of thought. The connecting element between their ideas is mere propinquity, or a superficial likeness, even a verbal resemblance. Not till middle adolescence is there any great need felt for consistency in a point of view, or any distress at conflicting ideas of a general or abstract kind.

In the fifth place *their type of association is that of association by wholes* rather than by contrast and similarity which might favor analysis. Thorndike's [1] study of errors made by sixth-grade children in answering questions about a paragraph of reading material shows how frequently one word may dominate their thinking, excluding any real understanding of the separate elements of the ideas involved. Their failure was due, not to lack of memory, or lack of organization nearly so much as to lack of analytic understanding of the sentences. Mental activity of this undifferentiated type can go but a little way toward solving a problem.

In the sixth place, *children lack a critical attitude*, and hence often go astray in their thinking. This lack of criticism works in two ways: because of it, children accept some minor, unimportant element as the essential one in the problem, and also they fail to weigh and test their results. In most thinking, the key to the problem depends upon the substitution of some part, element, or aspect of the situation for the whole situation. The element selected will, of course, determine the course of association, and therefore the answer. To pick out the right element from among the many offered requires keen discrimination, a valuing of the element from the standpoint of the problem; in short, it requires a critical weighing of the respective merits of all the possibilities offered. This children do not do, partly because from lack of experience with the various elements of the material offered they do not know which is the essential condition, but also partly because they have not the attitude of criticism towards what is offered. The child who, having been accustomed to hearing stories told her at bedtime, asks to be put to bed in the morning, in order to have stories told,

---

[1] "Reading as reasoning," *Jo. Ed. Psy.*, v. 8, 1917.

is a case in point. An unimportant element is selected as the essential one, and hence the result of the thinking is incorrect. The same defect is illustrated by children who, having been taught addition by the use of sticks, and subtraction by the use of beans, always added when sticks were given, and subtracted when beans were distributed, irrespective of what the problem called for. This lack of a critical attitude is manifested again in the attitude of children towards their results. They tend to accept them without any further consideration, whereas an inspection of the result in the light of the problem, or testing of the result to see if it would work, would often show that it could not possibly be correct. Older children and adults, because they are more critical, save themselves from accepting something totally wrong as the right solution; but this tendency is not characteristic of the young child's mind.

These six reasons for inaccurate thinking on the part of children overlap in several instances. They are interrelated so that defective action of one type often involves others; however, they are more or less independent causes of mistakes, and in training each one must be reckoned with.

Children's problems are different. — Another difference between children and adults in their thinking is in the character of data used. In adult life, thinking is done in connection with problems that have a direct bearing on the well-being of the individual, or his family, or the community at large. It is in connection with business problems, or questions of politics, or religion, or social conditions, that adults are called upon to think. The results of this thinking are fairly evident and very often valuable in a practical way. We make this adjustment, are successful in this way or that, get along in the world, deal with people, propound a new theory, suggest means for social betterment, publish a book, or perfect an invention, and in each case, something of value from the standpoint of the world at large is accomplished. In childhood all this is different. Children's thinking is done largely in connection with their play; their little problems are often unknown to adults or thought to be trivial and pointless if known. They apparently accomplish nothing worth noticing as a result of their thinking. Of what account is it that a child, as a result of his own thinking, has found out the quickest way to get dressed in the morning, or how he can beat Johnny in getting to school, or how the doll's eyes work, or which is the best spot to fish in? The average adult ignores all such thinking as not worthy of the name. This is but another of the countless instances of the unfairness and shortsightedness of adults in dealing with children, when they consider worthless any data, processes, and results that are unworthy of adult thinking. Of course such an attitude is manifestly unfair. Children cannot be judged by the same standards as adults in any sphere of thought or conduct. Thinking of the type illustrated is just as valuable, just as significant, just as difficult for the child as the more abstract and complex variety is for the adult.

No abrupt change at adolescence. — The fact that much of the childish thinking has been ignored because of the triviality of the situations occasioning it is one origin for the theory that at adolescence comes an awakening of the thinking powers. Childhood has been designated as the unreflective period, and adolescence talked of as if at thirteen or fourteen thinking power and reasoning suddenly developed. The truth of the matter probably is, that in the adolescent period the problems dealt with are similar to the problems confronting the adult, and therefore receive recognition. There is no experimental evidence to show that there is a sudden birth of thinking power at this time. In fact, all the evidence goes to show that it is a gradual development beginning in early childhood, and continuing to maturity, — not necessarily a regular growth, but a continuous one. Another reason for the prevalence of the theory is that in the adolescent period, because of the aggressiveness of youth, more freedom is allowed, and therefore more opportunities for problems arise with the resulting attempt at solution. The difference in actual power between the little child and the youth is thus exaggerated by environmental conditions.

CHARACTERISTICS OF CHILDREN'S THINKING

Egocentricism. — Thinking at first is largely a matter of desire. Little children, though they are curious and ask questions about things about them enjoy their world of imagination so much that their beliefs may be said to be dominated by their wishes. Their construction play, however, brings them into contact with the resistances of reality. They are not concerned with the use of words to prove a point or to convince any one else, but chiefly to move others to action or to express their own feelings and intentions. They show no ability to change from the egocentric point of view to that of another, nor to see relationships in their absolute sense. Thus, six-year-old Philip will tell you he has a brother John, but deny that John has a brother. He may know his own left and right hands, but will be confused in pointing to the left hand of some one opposite to him. Tested with three objects side by side, the middle one cannot be thought of as on the left of one yet on the right of another.

Juxtaposition. — Because of this weak sensing of relationships their judgments are strung along together, juxtaposed rather than connected by implication. There is little use of "because" and none at all of "therefore." Piaget, in listening to the spontaneous conversation of little children with each other found that "because" occurred in less than 2 per cent of their utterances up to four years old, in less than 5 per cent at seven years old. No case of reasoning occurred in 10,000 consecutive remarks, and no generalizations, though there were plenty of contradictions.

Syncretism. — Yet there is probably a vague feeling that all things do belong together somehow. They have been seen or heard together; if perceived together why not conceived together? Any one thing can be explained by any other, or by any detail attended to, a peculiarity of thought process Piaget calls syncretism. Just as they perceive vague wholes in the concrete world about them, so they apperceive the verbal statements of others by this same process. They suppose they understand when all they get is a hazy feeling of the whole, patterned after the rhythm of the sentence, perhaps, and emotionally colored by some special word. Difficult words they ignore, the better known ones they connect into some sort of schema from the general context, much as we do when getting the "drift" of a page or two in a language with which we are not very familiar. Verbal analogies may cause them to make many mistakes. Children feel they understand the words adults use much better than they really do, as can easily be discovered when they are questioned about separate items, or are asked to connect the words in new ways. The reception has been syncretistic; but there has been no explicit understanding, no ability to use the new terms in communication of thought to others.

Between six and seven, about the first-grade level, the relationship of part and whole, the meanings of *some, all, any,* function in their reasoning well enough to enable children to solve simple problems. Causal and logical relationships are not well understood, however, and if pressed for explanations, young children are most likely to invent one. After seven there is less confusion, and more different sorts of relationships can be analyzed.

Tested by control materials including a magnet, well known optical illusions, some trick toys, about 30 per cent of six-year-olds made a genuine effort to explain what they observed. Less than half these explanations had any basis in fact or reality, however; the rest were of the imaginative, fairy-tale or magic sort. About two thirds of the seven-year-olds' explanations were realistic, and almost all given by nine-year-olds. Tested with a queer looking contrivance left in the classroom with no remarks made by the experimenter, the seven-year-olds showed simple curiosity in their questions about it, the eight-year-olds began to ask about its various parts, the nine-year-olds attempted realistic explanations of its parts while the ten-year-olds seemed to sense the thing as a related whole and tried to explain it as a unitary object.

Lack of argument. — When we test single judgments and children's progress in combining judgments to form an argument, we find that even up to ten and eleven, though their vocabulary increases amazingly, they have very crude ways of thinking. Without rigid training they do not form the habit of checking results because they feel little need of so doing. The will to believe or the desire to dominate others functions much earlier and more insistently than the wish to prove a fact by logical demonstration. Need for demonstration is felt only in a social setting, and is the result of argument and the need to convince others. With better observation of the material world the nine- and ten-year-olds' realism is shifted to their reasoning about concrete ideas. They will not admit premises in which they do not believe even for purposes of argument. Thus, the suggestion "Supposing dogs had three tails, then if five dogs were here we should have fifteen tails," is met by a flat denial of the possibility of the first statement, without any consideration of the logic based on the assumption.

The term *although* appears in spontaneous conversation among themselves by ten years old, words like *therefore, since,* about eleven or twelve, indicating a felt need for logical justification. However, an argument among eleven-year-olds is largely a crescendo reiteration of statements till, literally, words fail them — and the thinking behind the words — and they have recourse to blows or other emotional ways of dealing with the situation. In early adolescence, too, there is more heat in the debate than the cold, clear light of logic. Proof may still be by assertion; belief is often swayed by personal likes and dislikes.

TRAINING IN THINKING

The lines this training should take are, as has been suggested, to see that children do meet problems, that we refrain from doing for them what they may be encouraged to do for themselves. Further, we must not only present problems of interest to children, but realize that results which are trivial to us are dignified and worthy to them. Then, from sympathy with children's need for knowledge, answer their questions simply, truthfully, yet tentatively, as a stimulus rather than a check to further thought. More, their investigations must be regarded not as malicious offenses but as, possibly misguided, laboratory experiments. Space and safeguarded opportunities for activities are needed more than reprimands or penalties. Then, copious fact-finding, together with the scope for varied and immediate contact with things, in themselves supply a greater range and accuracy of data from which to reason along higher lines; but especially when dealing with abstract problems, assistance must be given in the form of constant reminders of the point at issue, suggestions for systematizing ideas, criticisms of the relevancy of thoughts as they occur. Drill will be needed in analysis, in picking out the significant part of the whole situation, in testing the results of thinking, especially in forming the habit of supporting conclusions by stating explicitly the premises from which they are derived.

PRACTICAL EXERCISES

1. Try the following, orally and individually, for children under nine, taking down all they say as they try to decide. Make hektograph copies for class use in the fourth grade and above.

   (a) Some of the men in the town of Newberg are Italians. All the Italians from the town of Newberg were killed in the war. Are there any men left in Newberg? —————

   (b) John is taller than Fred. John is shorter than Robert. Who is the shortest? —————

   (c) A cow is to a calf as a cat is to a —————
   A nose is to the face as a handle is to a —————
   Beef is to meat as roses are to —————

   (d) Ann is older than Margaret. Ann is younger than Louise. Who is the oldest? —————

   (e) Fill in these sentences to make good sense.
   I am not hungry because—————
   It is hot today although—————
   The man fell in the street because—————
   John has lost his pen, therefore—————
   I took my umbrella today although—————
   Alice was hurt, therefore—————

Mother will punish him unless————————

We lost our way because————————

He did not get wet in spite of the fact that————————

She will not win the game unless————————

He is ill (sick), therefore————————

The man can see in spite of the fact that————————

2. What is the value of exercises such as the following for children in the fourth, fifth, and sixth grades? (They are taken from Bonser's monograph on "The Reasoning Ability of Children.")

Directions. As quickly as you can, make these sentences correct by drawing a line through the wrong word where two words occur, one above the other.

Iron is $\frac{\text{softer}}{\text{harder}}$ than wood.

Shadows are $\frac{\text{shorter}}{\text{longer}}$ in summer than in winter.

Anything that floats is $\frac{\text{heavier}}{\text{lighter}}$ than water.

Oranges are $\frac{\text{more}}{\text{less}}$ sweet than lemons.

Among these reasons why horses are better than cattle for driving and working animals, check those which you think are good reasons.

1. Horses are more intelligent than cattle.
2. Cattle are not so tall as horses.
3. Horses like corn, oats, and hay.
4. Horses are much more active and walk faster than cattle.
5. Cattle are extensively used for food.
6. Horses are much more beautiful and graceful than cattle.
7. The skins of horses are sometimes made into gloves.
8. Horses are more easily trained and controlled than cattle.
9. President Roosevelt likes to ride on horseback.
10. Horses have more rapid and varied gaits than cattle.

FOR DISCUSSION

1. Pool the results from the exercise above. How do they illustrate
    (a) special sorts of difficulties in thinking, *e.g.*, the undistributed middle.
    (b) inability to deal with abstract relationships.
    (c) age changes in ability to deal logically with language.

2. Analyze and explain the processes of thinking which lie behind the following. (They are taken from Brown's "Study of children's reasoning," in *Ped. Sem.*, v. 2.)

   (a) Age 1 yr. 8 mo. After visiting a bald grandfather, child renamed a doll whose hair had come off "Grandpa."

   (b) 2 yr. 8 mo. F. saw the moon when it was full, later in its first quarter, thought her little brother had been meddling with it.

   (c) 3 yr. G. planted a dime in the garden expecting to be rich when it grew.

   (d) 3 yr. When H.'s father overslept one day she asked if it was Sunday morning.

   (e) 3 yr. 8 mo. L. criticized her aunt's method of darning, "Oo ain't darnin' . . . right at all; my mamma puts 'em on a darner."

   (f) 4 yr. "I would like to go out in the rain and get bigger, 'cause the rain makes you grow."

   (g) 5 yr. On seeing a crooked tree, "See that tree sitting down."

   (h) 5 yr. 8 mo. Referring to the ownership of gray eyes, "You are getting to be an old woman."

   (i) 5 yr. B. heard the noise of frying pork and simultaneously the cat crying, and reported later that they were frying the cat's tail.

   (j) 7 yr. E. turned over the picture of a girl "to see if her dress was buttoned in the back."

   (k) 7 yr. 8 mo. X. watching black smoke rising from a mill chimney stack said it would rain next day, for "black smoke makes black clouds, and that's the ones that rains."

   (l) 9 yr. Bethlehem is judged near the equator, because the mother is pictured wearing a lace dress, which would be worn only where it is hot.

   (m) 10 yr. 9 mo. Child thought it would be colder riding than walking "because you are higher up in the air."

   (n) 12 yr. 3 mo. F. buried his kitten in a very shallow grave because he had heard that cats have nine lives and "if his cat came to life he didn't want it to smother."

3. What school subjects offer most constant opportunities for training in reasoning?

4. What special training value for thinking is there in the constructive activities of manual training, garment making, cookery, shop work, etc.?

5. How may training in reasoning be made of moral value?

6. Study the reasoning tests in Burt's collection, or the group intelligence tests of whatever sort are accessible. Notice the age level at which they are successfully dealt with. Can you explain why children younger than the "norm" fail on them?

7. How would you help a retarded child who still clings to his anthropomorphic and artificialist ideas at ten years old?
8. In what subject matter besides arithmetic should we train children to use checks, proofs, verification?
9. What habits need to be formed in connection with reasoning?
10. Why is it more difficult to teach pupils to think than to teach them to memorize?

SELECTED REFERENCES

ALPERT, A. "The solving of problem situations by pre-school children." *T. C. Contr. to Ed.* *323, 1928.

BURT, C. *Mental and Scholastic Tests.*

BURT, C. "The development of reasoning in school children." *Jo. Exp. Ped.*, v. 5, 1919.

DEWEY, J. *How We Think.*

HAZLITT, V. "Children's thinking." *Brit. Jo. Psych.*, v. 20, 1930.

HELSETH, I. O. *Children's Thinking.*

MOORE, T. V. "The reasoning ability of children in the first years of school life." *St. in Psych. and Psychiatry of Cath. Univ. of America,* v. 2 *2, 1929.

PIAGET, J. *Judgment and Reasoning of the Child and The Child's Conception of the World.* Selected chapters.

THORNDIKE, E. L. "Reading as reasoning." *Jo. Ed. Psych.*, v. 8, 1917.

CHAPTER XIV

PHYSICAL DEVELOPMENT

GOOD HEALTH AS A SCHOOL RESPONSIBILITY

It is a generally accepted educational principle that the school as well as the family has a definite duty with regard to the physical development of children. In discussion most teachers would admit this principle, but in actual practice not half enough is being done for the health of children, despite the tremendous changes of the last few years. There are several causes for this state of affairs. First, except in the case of infectious diseases, the parents have the final word with regard to the physical side of child nature. The school can act in things intellectual and things moral (to some extent), but it is the prerogative of the home to decide in most things physical. For instance, the school authorities may say that the child must stay in this or that class, although even this power is limited in some directions; they may suspend the child from school attendance for bad behavior, or perhaps send him to the truant school or the class for incorrigibles; but when it comes to a child's need for glasses, or to have adenoids removed, or for different food, or for more exercise, — the school can do little but recommend, — the parents decide. Second, although convinced in theory that it is part of their duty to conserve the health of the child, most teachers in practice allow the matter to be pushed into the background, or to be forgotten entirely by the pressure of the demands of lessons. Third, the lack of free clinics for treatment of all kinds handicaps the work seriously in all but the large cities. It is generally acknowledged that, in rural districts, the physical health of children is worse along some lines than in urban districts, despite the crowded conditions of the latter. These three difficulties will have to be met before the physical side of child nature will receive its fair share of attention.

Interdependence of mind and body. — The reasons for the responsibility of the school in this matter are, first, if the school is to train the minds of boys and girls, it must look after their bodies too, for the well-being of the one is dependent on the health of the other. We are slowly reinstating the aim of the ancient Greeks, "a sound mind in a sound body." Just how far the two are interdependent is a question not yet answered. How great a handicap is poor health, or the presence of various defects, or of unbalanced nervous condition, we do not know. That it is a handicap, that some defects are a very serious handicap, there can be no doubt. Physical superiority usually accompanies mental capacity. Therefore if the school would do its duty by the child intellectually it must not only prevent the spread of infectious diseases, but also must take measures in the line of both preventive hygiene and positive treatment.

Happiness depends on it. — Second, one of the definite aims of education today is health, not merely because health gives greater possibilities for intellectual development but because it makes for happiness. Emotions, temperament, morals, are all bound up very closely with health. Every child has a right to happiness, therefore give him health. Also every child has the right to be well-born. Much of the disease, deformity, and weakness in the world is a matter of inherited tendencies. In order that the next generation may be physically better than the present one, the children of today must be guarded, guided, and treated along all possible health lines.

Economic conditions make it imperative. — Third, the public schools are provided at state expense in order that the children of the state may be self-supporting citizens, contributing in their adulthood to its development and prosperity. A school that because of a one-sided point of view, or because of an unfair division of time, or because of lack of apprecia-

tion of its responsibilities, fails to achieve this end, pitiably
fails in its function. Of the thousands of incompetents who
fall back on the state for support each year, the thousands
always a drag and a menace, those found in the insane asylums, the jails, on the streets, how many of these are physically unfit, and have been so since childhood? Might not the
teachers of these children have done more for them and for
the community by discovering the physical trouble and maybe
setting that right, than by any teaching which merely drills
and informs the mind?

**The organization and demands of the school make it re-
sponsible.** — Fourth, a teacher must take cognizance of
the physical side of child nature because in the school she is
requiring certain tasks, forming certain habits, allowing certain opportunities, imposing certain deprivations, each of which
procedures has its own dangers so far as the physical well-being
of the child is concerned. The teacher must take measures
to minimize the dangers, and if definite harm should result
see to it that needed remedies are applied. Schools require
that children learn to read: have they any right to ignore the
resulting eyestrain no matter what the cause? Examinations
are necessary in most schools, but teachers should know the
attendant ills. Children must learn to write, but habits of
posture which result in curvature of the spine are not necessary as a concomitant. Is it wise to require much home study
of certain classes or children if it is done under conditions which
are definitely injurious to health? The very tasks which it
imposes, because they react upon or involve the physical child,
force responsibility upon the school and its teachers for the
health and growth of the children. Regard for health is not a
matter of choice or of philanthropy, it is a logical outgrowth
of the school's own requirements in other lines. All those who
deal with children, teachers especially, must realize the importance of this problem of the physical development. So long
as they are not alive to its significance, so long as they do not
know the facts of child development, so long as they are ig-

norant of the danger points of the causes of increased susceptibility, — just so long will the children, both of this generation
and the next, suffer.

DIFFERENCES BETWEEN CHILDREN AND ADULTS

In kind, not degree. — As children differ from adults in all
the intellectual and feeling processes, even so they differ in
things physical. It is just as true that "the child is not the
man writ small" in health and physical development as in
intellectual fields. Just as general adult psychology will not
answer the problems concerning the mental and moral processes
of children, so the hygiene of the adult will not meet the needs
of the child. Just as we need a child psychology, just so do
we need a child hygiene. The differences between the child
and the adult on the physical side are tremendous. Terman
says, "The child is different from the adult in every fiber, every
blood corpuscle, every bone cell, and in the relative proportions of all his parts. His resistance to disease, his powers of
recuperation, his food and sleep requirements are all unlike
those of the adult. He is differently affected by every element
of environment and regimen." [1] Not only is the child totally
unlike the adult physically, but a child of one age will differ
to a great degree from one of another age. What may be healthful exercise at one time may be a serious strain at another.
Work that is pleasurable to a little child may be the greatest
bore to an older one. Diet that is eminently suitable for a four-
year-old is quite insufficient for a ten-year-old.

Muscles, bones. — In childhood the muscles have less weight
per volume, are more watery in consistency than in adult life.
Strength, speed of action, co-ordination of groups of muscles
are attained only gradually. The fundamental muscles, those
concerned with coarse movements, develop co-ordination for
continuous work before the accessory muscles do, those involved
in fine, precise movements. Boys surpass girls in strength tests
at all ages; they are also superior in speed and accuracy of fine

[1] Terman and Almack, *The Hygiene of the School Child*, p. 54.

muscle control. Clearly, then, the type and duration of muscular exercise must be different at different ages. Exercise is necessary for development, but it must not induce strain, particularly in the early stages of growth.

The bones are soft and gelatinous in early childhood. X-rays of the bones in the wrist show clearly and conveniently the very slow ossification taking place in the first ten years. Girls are anatomically older than boys at all ages. At six they are about one year, at twelve about two years nearer their full development than are boys. In the skull, the various bones are not all joined at birth. The lower jaw, as also sometimes the nose, develops considerably in shape about puberty. The eustachian tubes connecting middle ears and throat are relatively shorter and wider in childhood. These facts make it possible to induce deformities by bad posture. They also show that, if we are to correct deformities, it is imperative to begin treatment early. Infections in the throat may affect the ears more readily in children than in adults.

Digestive system. — Dentition is changing for practically twenty years. The first set of teeth begins to erupt about the sixth month and is not complete till about the thirtieth. The permanent set begins with the sixth-year molars — so often supposed to be the last of the deciduous set — and is complete by seventeen years old all except the four "wisdom" teeth which may or may not appear before twenty-five. Metabolism is more rapid with children than with adults. The relative size and weight, even shape, of liver and stomach are constantly changing. These facts are evidence that children's diet must differ in kind, quantity, and frequency of meals.

Circulation. — The pulse rate of an infant is over 120 a minute and the circulation is completed in about 12 seconds. In the adult 72 is the average pulse and the circulation is nearly twice as slow. Blood pressure rises till the ninth year pretty steadily, then less rapidly till just before puberty, when the rise is more rapid again till about fifteen. The proportion of red and white blood corpuscles is different in childhood from what it is in adult life. These facts mean that children fatigue readily after brief spurts of hard physical exercise. Also, they have less resistance to disease.

Laws of growth. — (1) Growth and development are not synonymous. Development connotes an increase in complexity of structure, and in the interrelated functions of different organs. Growth means mere increase in size. If the newborn infant merely grew to adult size he would look all out of proportion. We should be shocked at the large headed, short legged, narrow shouldered monstrosity we should see.

(2) We need not expect every child to follow the "norm" revealed from massing statistics and finding averages. Every child follows his own rate of development, determined as it is by his own complex heredity, his own chance experiences in the way of disease, nutrition, a competent mother, and so on. For example, though on the average boys may grow three inches in the year of their most rapid increase in height, a given boy may add seven or even more inches to his stature in his pre-pubertal spurt. Individual differences must always be considered. We can, however, in the case of height, group children into tall and fast growing, medium, or short and slow growing, showing characteristic growth curves for all three groups. Thus, tall children are apt to mature earlier, and thus show the pre-pubertal spurt of height increase younger than do the medium or the short children.

(3) Individuals maintain their own rate of development. Thus, instead of children who are retarded early compensating by a rapid change and eventual superiority in physical measurements, they hold their own position relative to others, constantly. Similarly for those accelerated in development. Indeed, so far as height goes, so well are these relative rates of increase known that an expert can predict very closely from measuring children at six years old, and even more accurately from measuring at ten years old, how tall they will eventually be.

(4) Each part, each organ has its own rate of development both in size, volume, weight, and functional relationship with

other organs. A simple measure of the height and weight of a child by no means tells us all that is significant about him.

(5) Gradual, continuous development is the rule; sudden spurts, though striking enough, are the exception, and due to extrinsic causes such as illness rather than to intrinsic.

FACTS OF PHYSICAL DEVELOPMENT

Factors determining; heredity and environment. — There is great difficulty in assigning to each its share of responsibility because of the complexity of the problem. The internal factors, such as sex, family, and racial heredity, and the external factors, such as food, freedom from disease, exercise, sleep, ventilation, relaxation, climate, season of the year, etc., are all operative all the time and are inextricably mingled. The general opinion of both medical men and anthropologists seems at present to be that heredity is the more influential factor in determining stature, time of puberty, general development in height, weight, and other dimensions, and resistance to disease.

On the other hand this does not at all mean that environment has no effect. For instance, though in the Philippine Islands the Japanese children are lighter and shorter than the Filipinos, the Japanese in California are heavier and taller than the Japanese in Japan. College freshmen today are shown to be taller and heavier than they were thirty years ago, and presumably that is in part due to the greater freedom physically, the emphasis on activity and health.

Climate and season affect growth also, climate in that taller races are found in the temperate zones, and season in that boys have been found to increase in height more in the spring and summer than in the fall, and to put on weight relatively more from August to December. We need further investigations dealing with races emigrating from one zone to another, also on the annual variation, and on weekly and monthly fluctuations said to exist.

The various factors in the environment may be easy to catalogue, but they are difficult to control separately so that the influence of each can be analytically determined. If certain elements in the environment make the exposure of children to contagion much more common than under other conditions, there can be no doubt that environment is detrimental to normal physical development. However, we have but little scientific work upon which to base conclusions concerning the effect on an individual of insufficient food, light, air, exercise, play, etc. Probably the most dangerous of the environmental elements is improper feeding. Most of the work which has been done along even this line has not eliminated the factor of family heredity from the problem, nor have the many concomitant environmental influences been given recognition. For instance, children of the wealthy and the poor have been compared; factory children and others; those of the "more favored class and the artisan class; children of the professional class and the slums;" city and country children. Obviously this does not isolate the factor of nutrition. Either in the city or the country a child may be crowded with many others during sleeping hours in an ill-ventilated room, may be poorly housed, overworked or semi-idle, with a personal history of many or few diseases. The wealthy mother may feed and exercise her child just as improperly as the poor mother.

Two factors in connection with feeding seem fairly certain: first, that underfeeding, to have any permanent stunting effect, must be of long duration; second, that the feeding of the infant up to a year or a year and a half old is of the utmost importance.

Glands and growth. — Other than the sex glands influence growth, particularly the *thyroid*. Any defect or disease in the thyroid, or its absence, is accompanied by a lack of growth and by a special kind of mental defect, both of which can, however, be remedied if treatment is begun sufficiently early by supplying the constituents in the diet that the gland should normally have secreted. The thyroid controls the speed of metabolism, acts as a general energizer and helps the system fight against invading infections. The anterior portion of the *pituitary* gland affects the skeletal growth particularly. Lack of secretion means lack of growth of the long bones, resulting in dwarfism: conversely, oversecretion, occurring before puberty produces very tall people. If the overaction happens after the long bones have set, the extra growth shows in the extremities; the individual's face, hands, and feet appear coarse and too large for the body, a condition known as acromegaly. The outer part of the *adrenal* glands secretes a substance highly important in controlling the general maturation of the sex system. It also acts upon the development of the brain cells. The *thymus* gland is the direct regulator of growth and nutrition in childhood. It, too, affects the general maturity of the individual, and itself declines with puberty. The *parathyroid* glands regulate the utilization of lime in the blood and body cells, and the *pancreas* controls the sugar metabolism.

Growth in height and weight. — As has been indicated, racial and family heredity determine for the individual his ultimate height and weight, while the sex largely determines the rate of growth; so that statistics derived from a study of French boys would not be applicable, say, to Japanese girls. The figures here quoted are drawn from studies of American children.

The tables (pp. 300–303) show the relationship between age and height and weight. They may be read thus — taking the figure 56 in the left-hand column and reading across. A tall boy of eight years measuring 56 inches would be expected to weigh 75 lbs.: whereas a short boy of fifteen measuring only 56 inches would probably weigh 80 lbs. On the girls' table — a seven-year-old girl only 40 inches tall would weigh 36 lbs., whereas a seven-year-old who was 53 inches tall would weigh 66 lbs.

These tables [1] are printed by courtesy of the American Child Health Association, from the Baldwin-Wood revised figures,

[1] "These Tables were constructed from measurements made on a group of presumably healthy children, most of whom are native born. They show the *average* weight for height and age and sex. *Individual* children of the same age and height *normally* show wide variation in weight due principally to the width and depth of the skeletal framework. Body width and depth are as important as height in determining body weight. This fact should be kept in mind in interpreting the *significance* of deviation from average weight for height. Weight for height alone is not a dependable index of nutritional status." February, 1932.

with additional columns for the younger years from the Wood-bury data.

Taking the average length of a child at birth as 19 inches, and average adult height as 69 inches (M.) and 65 inches (F.) respectively, it will be seen that a total gain of 50 or 45 inches is made. Of this, the most rapid gain is in the first months of life, since at fourteen months old roughly one quarter the total increase, *i.e.*, 12 inches (M.), 11 inches (F.) will have been made. A male has gained his second quartile of growth, making him 44 inches tall, by the time he is slightly under six years old, taking therefore about 56 months to gain as many inches as he did at first in 14 months. His third quartile, making him 56 inches tall, is added by about eleven and a half years of age. He may reach his ultimate height anywhere from eighteen to twenty-three years of age. Very similar facts may be stated for the female, except that her third quartile's gain has been made by ten and a half. In weight, the total gain to the age twenty-two is approximately 138 and 117 lbs. respectively, of which the first quartile is gained before five years old for either sex, the second by eleven and a half (M.) and ten and a half (F.), the third by fifteen and a half (M.) and thirteen and a quarter (F.). Other rough statements that may be made are that a child is half his ultimate height at two and a half years old or slightly less. Between the ages of five and ten a child grows about two inches a year, adding 2 to $2\frac{1}{2}$ lbs. for every inch gained.

The *rate* of increase then, in both height and weight, gradually diminishes from birth, though by no means evenly. There is a slight retardation in growth at about six years old, an acceleration at eight (M.) or seven (F.), reaching a minimum rate at eleven (M.) and nine (F.). Following this period of slow growth is one of rapid growth, reaching its maximum at fifteen (M.) and twelve and a half to thirteen (F.). The increase in height up to the time of maximum growth is principally due to growth in length of legs; after that time the trunk grows rapidly. Rapid increase in height is followed by gain in weight. Development, *i.e.*, qualitative rather than quantitative change in the cells,

WEIGHT — HEIGHT — AGE TABLE FOR BOYS

Height Inches	6 Mo.	1 Yr.	2 Yrs.	3 Yrs.	4 Yrs.	5 Yrs.	6 Yrs.	7 Yrs.	8 Yrs.	9 Yrs.	10 Yrs.	11 Yrs.	12 Yrs.	13 Yrs.	14 Yrs.	15 Yrs.	16 Yrs.	17 Yrs.	18 Yrs.	19 Yrs.
23	13																			
24	14																			
25	15	18																		
26	17	19																		
27	18	20																		
28	19	21																		
29	20																			
30	22	22	22																	
31		23	23																	
32		24	25																	
33		26	26	26		34	34													
34			27	27		35	35													
35			29	29	29	36	36													
36			30	31	31	38	38	38												
37			32	32	32	39	39	39	39											
38				33	33	41	41	41	41											
39				35	35	44	44	44	44											
40				36	36	46	46	46	46	46										
41					38	47	48	48	48	48										
42					39	49	50	50	50	50	50									
43					41		52	53	53	53	53									
44							55	55	55	55	55	55								
45																				
46																				
47																				
48																				
49																				

										9 Yrs.	10 Yrs.	11 Yrs.	12 Yrs.	13 Yrs.	14 Yrs.	15 Yrs.	16 Yrs.	17 Yrs.	18 Yrs.	19 Yrs.
50							57	58	58	58	58	58	58							
51								61	61	61	61	61	61							
52								63	64	64	64	64	64	64						
53								66	67	67	67	67	68	68						
54									70	70	70	70	71	71	72					
55									72	72	73	73	74	74	74					
56									75	76	77	77	77	78	78	80				
57										79	80	81	81	82	83	83				
58										83	84	84	85	85	86	87				
59											87	88	89	89	90	90	90			
60											91	92	92	93	94	95	96			
61												95	96	97	99	100	103	106		
62												100	101	102	103	104	107	111	116	
63												105	106	107	108	110	113	118	123	127
64													109	111	113	115	117	121	126	130
65													114	117	118	120	122	127	131	134
66														119	122	125	128	132	136	139
67														124	128	130	134	136	139	142
68															134	134	137	141	143	147
69															137	139	143	146	149	152
70															143	144	145	148	151	155
71															148	150	151	152	154	159
72																153	155	156	158	163
73																157	160	162	164	167
74																160	164	168	170	171

PREPARED BY BIRD T. BALDWIN, PH.D., AND THOMAS D. WOOD, M.D.

WEIGHT — HEIGHT — AGE TABLE FOR GIRLS

Height Inches	6 Mos.	1 Yr.	2 Yrs.	3 Yrs.	4 Yrs.	5 Yrs.	6 Yrs.	7 Yrs.	8 Yrs.	9 Yrs.	10 Yrs.	11 Yrs.	12 Yrs.	13 Yrs.	14 Yrs.	15 Yrs.	16 Yrs.	17 Yrs.	18 Yrs.
23	13																		
24	14																		
25	15	17																	
26	16	18																	
27	17	19																	
28	19	20																	
29	19																		
30	21	21	21																
31		22	23																
32		23	24	25															
33			25	26															
34			26	27															
35			29	29	29														
36			30	30	30														
37			31	31	31														
38				33	33	33	33												
39				34	34	34	34												
40					36	36	36	36											
41					37	37	37	37											
42					39	39	39	39											
43					40	41	41	41	41										
44						42	42	42	42										
45						45	45	45	45	45									
46						47	47	47	48	48									
47						49	50	50	50	50	50								
48							52	52	52	52	53	53							
49							54	54	55	55	56	56							

Height				9 Yrs.	10 Yrs.	11 Yrs.	12 Yrs.	13 Yrs.	14 Yrs.	15 Yrs.	16 Yrs.	17 Yrs.	18 Yrs.
50	56	56	57	58	59	61	62						
51		59	60	61	61	63	65						
52		63	64	64	64	65	67						
53		66	67	67	68	68	69	71					
54			69	70	70	71	71	73					
55			72	74	74	74	75	77	78				
56				76	78	78	79	81	83				
57				80	82	82	82	84	88	92			
58					84	86	86	88	93	96	101		
59					87	90	90	92	96	100	103	104	
60					91	95	95	97	101	105	108	109	111
61						99	100	101	105	108	112	113	116
62						104	105	106	109	113	115	117	118
63							110	110	112	116	117	119	120
64							114	115	117	119	120	122	123
65							118	120	121	122	123	125	126
66								124	124	125	128	129	130
67								128	130	131	133	133	135
68								131	133	135	136	138	138
69									135	137	138	140	142
70									136	138	140	142	144
71									138	140	142	144	145

Weight is stated to the nearest pound; height to the nearest inch; age to the nearest month.

Weights of children under 35 inches were taken without clothing; those of children above 35 inches with clothing (shoes, coat, and sweater removed).

should always follow growth. Times of rapid growth are times of increase in vigor and energy, hence these periods are of great educational value. Though periods likewise of high fatigability they are dangerous only in the way that a rapidly moving machine is in more danger than a slow moving one.

Growth and development of various parts. — The growth of the body does not proceed as a whole, but by parts and successively. The various organs seem to follow a rate and rhythm of their own, and to develop quite independently of other organs. Thus the time of maximum growth of one part may be the time of minimum growth of another. For example, the brain increases in size two or threefold during the first year, but only 10 per cent more during the second year. There is a continued slow growth till puberty though by the sixth year it has almost reached adult size. By the twelfth or fourteenth year its growth has practically ceased. The muscles and intestines are largest relatively, in the fifth, the heart and lungs in the eighth decade. At birth the size of a cross section of the heart compared to a cross section of the large arteries is as 25 to 20; at puberty it is as 140 to 50; for the adult it is as 290 to 61. At fifteen years old a boy's limbs are relatively longer than they are either at eleven years old or in adult life. Detailed facts are too numerous to be given here; but that does not lessen the danger of lack of acquaintance with them on the part of parent or teacher. For instance, they should know of the risk of too vigorous exercise of an eight- or nine-year-old child while his heart is still small in proportion to his arteries; and that a child of six needs twice as much oxygen for his weight as does the adult. They should realize that the greater plasticity of the child's bones makes deformity from bad posture a very real danger. They should remember that boys are at every age superior to girls in lung capacity and in strength of hands. They should know that children of three require 40 per cent as much food as adults although they are only about one fifth as large. The danger is of underfeeding or improper feeding, not of overfeeding. The answers to many school problems and the principles of much of school discipline must be found through a careful study of the physical growth and development of the child.

Physiological and chronological age. — The differences in the rate of growth in every organ of the body, the skeleton, and nervous system are important; but even more important for the individual child is the fact that there are large variations from any "average" rate of development within any one year. The number of years a child has lived is no sure sign of his physical development. The distinction between chronological age and physiological age is an important one. The fact is that children who have lived the same number of years are not the same physically.

We have come to speak of the *physiological age,* as referring to the general state of maturity of the reproductive system, and the *anatomical age* as referring to the development of various other organs, and generally measured by noting the dentition and the degree of ossification. We cannot treat all nine-year-olds alike — putting them all in the same school grade, expecting them all to be the same height, demanding the same quantity and quality of mental work, assigning tasks requiring the same fine muscle co-ordination — just because all have passed their ninth birthday. Severson,[1] measuring one hundred ten-year-old children found an anatomical age range from eight to fourteen. Girls are anatomically older than boys even as young as before the second birthday, and by twelve and one half are as old, physiologically, as boys of fifteen. In a group of boys fourteen years old some may be still in the pre-pubescent period, some may be at that time in the stage of transition, and some may be post-pubescent. Crampton [2] in his work with the boys of New York City found that by the time they reached high school age, about thirteen and one half, the number of pubescents, pre- and post-pubescents was almost equal. Physical maturity brings with it certain ideas, ideals, attitudes despite

[1] Woodrow, H., *Brightness and Dullness in Children,* pp. 114–115.
[2] Crampton, C. W., "Influence of physiological age upon scholarship," *Psy. Cl.,* v. 1, 1911.

the lack of school training. Simply because a child has lived fourteen years is not enough to insure either the physical strength and maturity or the intellectual development that factory, mill, or any other form of work demands. The twelve-year-old, non-English-speaking child cannot well be taught with ordinary second-grade children. The eighteen-year-old moron with ten-year-old mentality is by no means ten years old in other ways. The question of co-education, junior high school, methods of instruction, especially in religion and morals, must take account of these facts. The religious school that classes all fourteen- to fifteen-year-olds, boys and girls alike, together to take its graded course marked for that age is probably making a mistake far-reaching in its effects, and much worse than a similar classification of all seven-year-olds would be. The treatment of the juvenile delinquent, both before and after conviction of crime, would be materially altered if these distinctions were kept in mind.

Relationships of physiological age. — On the whole, taller children mature earlier than do shorter ones, and their pubescent processes take place more gradually.

We know too that, contrary to popular opinion, in cases of delayed puberty, the individual is not so tall eventually as those who begin to mature earlier; though the adolescent acceleration is more marked, it is briefer in duration. At any one chronological age those older physiologically tend to rate higher mentally. At any one chronological age those with delayed dentition and younger anatomical age have, on the average, a lower mental age than those advanced anatomically. There is a slight but positive correlation between superiority in height and weight and mental ability.

Consider the following facts. (1) Porter [1] found in his examination of 34,500 St. Louis school children that pupils of any age who were above their normal grade were heavier and taller than those of the same age who were below their normal grade. For instance, the average weight of eleven-year-old boys in the sixth grade was 73.34 lbs.; in the fifth grade 71.29 lbs.; in the

[1] *Trans. Acad. Science*, St. Louis, v. 6, 1894.

fourth grade 69.24 lbs.; in the third grade 68.12 lbs.; in the second grade 65.45 lbs.; and in the first grade only 63.5 lbs. (2) Adult mental defectives are on the average more defective all around physically than normal men and women. (3) Warner [1] and Ayres [2] both found a larger percentage of physical defects, of poorly nourished and nervous children among the dull than among average children. (4) The removal of certain physical defects and the improvement of health conditions have been followed in numerous cases by definite, and in some cases by remarkable, changes in mental capacity and moral balance. (5) Mead [3] found mental defectives below the norms for their age in height and weight. (6) Goddard [4] found mental defectives in nineteen institutions shorter and lighter than children of normal mentality; and those lowest mentally, the idiots, were lowest in physical measures. (7) Terman [5] found his six hundred gifted children above the norm in physical measurements. (8) Buford Johnson [6] found the relationship of mental ability and complex muscular control higher than between mental ability and mere strength of muscles. We may conclude, then, that there is a positive, even if slight, correlation between physiological and mental development.

The pubertal changes are usually closely related in time to religious and æsthetic awakenings. At sixteen, the age when the majority have matured, we note a turning point in several ways. For instance, the point of view with regard to vocational possibilities and responsibilities is markedly different after sixteen from what it is in the two preceding years. Sixteen, also, has come to be taken, statistically, as the limit of development of mental age.

---

[1] Warner, *The Study of Children*, ch. 13.

[2] Ayres, *Laggards in Our Schools*, p. 125.

[3] Mead, C. D., "The relation of general intelligence to certain mental and physical traits," *T. C. Cont. Ed.*, *76, 1916.

[4] Goddard, H. H., "Height and weight of feeble-minded children in American institutions," *Jo. Ment. and Nerv. Dis.*, v. 39, 1912.

[5] Terman, L., *Genetic Studies of Genius*.

[6] Johnson, B. J., *Mental Growth of Children in Relation to Rate of Growth in Bodily Development*.

CONSTRUCTIVE MEASURES FOR HEALTH

Inspection, hygiene, special studies. — The establishment of the school nurse and of the medical inspection of school children has done much to prevent the spread of contagious diseases and to promote the early detection of some of the grosser defects. The hygiene of special subjects, such as reading and writing, and the equipment of the schools with books, blackboards, seats, etc., in accordance with the physical demands of the child, have done much to prevent eyestrain with its train of evils, curvature of the spine, etc. The studies in fatigue with their resulting influence on length of class periods, length, distribution, and character of recess periods have worked for the nervous betterment of children. School lunches, out-of-door classes, free clinics of all kinds have both improved the health of the school children and alleviated some of the suffering due to defects. But the health of the children will not be properly conserved until each individual teacher recognizes her responsibility in this direction. In some districts, such measures as have been indicated are not possible; then the teacher alone is responsible. In all cases the initial step must often be taken by the teacher. This problem is not one which can be adequately solved by providing specialists. They are necessary in the long run, but the greater responsibility for close observation and detection of trouble, for suggestions of remedies, and for persistent endeavor to have means taken to relieve must be on the teacher in the schools.

Oral hygiene. — Care of the teeth has been urged in times past for two reasons: first, because bad teeth are ugly and good teeth are an element of beauty, and second, because such care prevents suffering caused by toothache. These two reasons are still in force, but today much evidence is being produced to show that the care of teeth is necessary not only for bodily health, but for mental health as well. "Defective teeth may affect the health of the entire body. The influence is chiefly of four kinds: (1) decreased power of mastication, due either to decay or irregularities of the teeth; (2) the toxic effect of pus which is absorbed directly into the blood or taken into the stomach and intestines; (3) reflex nervous disturbance due to pain, impaction of teeth, etc.; and (4) the possibility of acting as a breeding-ground and distributing-point for bacteria which cause infectious diseases." [1] Indigestion, anemia, and even rheumatism have been traced directly to defective teeth. The extent to which defective teeth are found among school children all over the world is appalling. Reports of examinations of children's teeth in England, Germany, Austria, Australia, and several cities of the United States agree in the large percentage of children found with defective teeth, as high as 70 per cent for a conservative estimate. Decay, diseased gums, impacted teeth, jaws closing improperly are the most common defects. The younger children showed more defects than the older ones, as the milk teeth are more susceptible to attack than the permanent teeth. The age most free from troubles of this kind is about ten years for girls, for boys a little older.

The teacher has three duties with reference to this defect: (1) she should teach something of the hygiene of the mouth and teeth; (2) she should co-operate with the home in promoting habits of sanitary care; (3) she should find out whether there are defects if there is no one else to do it, and then do all in her power to get the defects remedied before the child's health suffers.

Adenoids and enlarged tonsils. — Adenoids[2] and enlarged tonsils are defects of the throat. They have somewhat the same effect on the health of children, although the former is the more serious mentally of the two. Conditions of high-arched, narrow palate, impacted teeth, and nasal obstruction are frequently found together. The signs of these obstructions should be well known to every teacher so that the treatment could begin while the child is young. Adenoids usually appear before the child is

[1] Terman and Almack, *op. cit.*, pp. 173–174.
[2] Adenoids consist of the overgrowth or infection of the lymphoid tissue forming the third tonsil. They occur above and behind the soft palate.

nine and the commonest age seems to be six. Removal of the adenoids and tonsils if they are large enough seriously to obstruct the nasal passages, should occur preferably when the child is six or seven. The effect of these obstructions is to cause: (1) irregular and shallow breathing; (2) mouth breathing with its attendant evils; (3) lowered general vitality; (4) defective hearing and speech; (5) a greater frequency of certain diseases by providing fertile ground for infection. Besides all these effects on the health of the child, there is very great reason to believe that the mental development of the child is delayed, so that sometimes he may be permanently retarded. Lack of physical vitality means lack of mental vitality. Deafness, wandering, fickle attention affect mental development. Just what is the relation between these defects and mental capacity has yet to be worked out; but we are pretty sure that the adenoidal child does not develop normally, and there have been some startling changes in mental power and moral character upon the removal of adenoids. But the teacher's duty is not ended when the adenoids are out. There are all the bad habits of the child's life to undo. Many parents and teachers seem to think that all will be well when once the operation is over, — that the child will breathe through his nose, hear the first time he is spoken to, be interested in his school work, — whereas these particular habits of response have to be formed gradually, and the old ones inhibited. It must be made a definite educational problem.

Tuberculosis. — Childhood, particularly the earliest years, is the time when nearly all people contract this disease. Many recover from the primary infection without any one's being any the wiser, but a large number retain it to develop later in some form or other. The lymphatic glands or the bones are the most common seat of secondary infection, showing in the familiar swollen neck, hip disease, "white swelling" of the knee, or hunchback. Early diagnosis and treatment is of extreme importance in such cases; by six years old it may be too late to effect a cure or prevent a deformity.

The form we know best, pulmonary tuberculosis, is, then, the tertiary form: it is most likely to develop in later adolescence in those previously infected whose general resistance has been weakened by malnutrition, colds, "grippe," pneumonia, and other respiratory diseases. Proper hygienic habits and thorough instruction on the topic of tuberculosis are the main safeguards here, with special attention to vocational guidance, general nutrition, and care during periods of convalescence from attacks of scarlet fever, measles, whooping cough, and the like.

Contagious diseases. — Of these and other infections and contagious diseases little detail need be given here. Any book on hygiene can give the symptoms, the periods of incubation and necessary quarantine, and the teacher should acquaint herself with these. Her better work for the community would be to combat the prevalent idea that these diseases are inevitable and therefore the sooner over with the better. The resultant evils possible from scarlet fever alone are too serious to permit the careless exposure of children to it. One great help in preventing the spread of many of these is, as we are coming to realize, rigid insistence in public and in private on proper care of the secretions from the mouth and nose. Carelessness in sneezing and coughing will soon be recognized as criminal negligence; a sex difference in the need for expectoration will no longer be supposed to exist, so that printed regulations on the subject may disappear as surely as the common drinking cup. Teachers must remember that this is distinctly a matter of educating the public.

Nutrition. — Perhaps the most fundamental handicap from which a child can suffer is malnutrition. This, besides its effects on height and weight, is apt to interfere with development in general, particularly to delay puberty. By lowering the general vitality of the body it increases its susceptibility to any infections, lessens the chance of recovery once a disease is contracted, and increases the danger of a relapse. Especially is it likely to precede tuberculosis, and, in the very young child, to produce rickets, a soft condition of the bones shown in severe cases by enlarged joints, overgrown head, bow legs, or knock knees.

From 6 per cent to 30 per cent of our children may be said to be poorly nourished. In any classroom of from thirty to forty pupils, the teacher may expect from three to ten cases, we might say.

The causes of malnutrition are various. Physical conditions such as unsound teeth, a weak digestive system, reflex nervous disturbances including eyestrain, disorders of the lymphatic system, will aggravate the evil of malnutrition; so will also lack of sleep, or of exercise in the open air, and any overexcitement, anxiety, or worry.

An obvious cause is an insufficient amount of food, but more frequently a lack of the right sorts of food. Investigations too often reveal a poor home control of food due to the incompetent mother, or to ignorance rather than chiefly to poverty. We find a considerable number of pupils coming to school with no breakfast at all, more with an inadequate meal such as coffee and bread. If this is followed by a poor lunch of the doughnut and ice cream variety, with "piecing" and candy at impulse, headaches and irritability will soon be symptomatic of the damage being done. Food that is badly prepared and eaten at irregular intervals or too hurriedly will not serve the child's need, nor will an oversupply of certain articles such as candy, stimulants, and highly seasoned foods.

A good diet means, first of all, sufficient intake of calories. A calorie is a measure of the heat or fuel value in food. Metabolism is the process by which this fuel value is utilized in the body; it includes the building up of the living cells, and the separation, for excretion, of their waste products. Children's organic processes are more rapid than those of adults; and, since they have to build not only for present needs but for growth as well, it is evident that their caloric intake must be large relative to their size. Proportionately, they require more food than adults. Thus, a boy of twelve needs as many calories a day, 2200 to 2400, as does a grown woman at a rather sedentary occupation. Children entering school at six years old need about 1400, the ten-year-olds 1800 to 2000. Boys of fifteen need around 3000, girls of the same age about 2300. Boys of eighteen need from 3000 to 4000 according to the amount of muscular exercise they are taking, girls, similarly, from 2300 to 3300.

All foods, obviously, do not contain equal numbers of calories per unit of volume or weight. A 100 calorie portion is represented roughly by such different things as one egg, two average sized apples, one (large) chocolate cream, four tablespoons of beefsteak, six tablespoons of green peas, one pound of lettuce.

All foods are not equal in value in other ways. We could not recommend thirty chocolate creams as the sole and entire daily diet for a high-school boy even though they would contain enough calories. The body needs a balanced diet of (1) protein foods for repair, such as eggs, meat, (2) carbohydrate foods for energy, such as sugar, starches, fats, (3) mineral salts, iron, lime, and so on, and (4) the substances known as vitamins about which so much has been discovered by patient research.

The typical diet of fruit, cereals, milk, potatoes, green vegetables, eggs, meat, bread and butter contains all the vitamins normal children, who can be out in the sunshine, need. *Vitamin A*, contained in whole milk, the yolk of egg, spinach, carrots, promotes growth and also prevents eye disease. *Vitamin B* is found in tomatoes, unpolished rice, whole wheat, fresh fruits and green leaf vegetables. It is known as the anti-neuritic vitamin. *Vitamin C* occurring in carrots, cabbage, potatoes, apples and the citrus fruits, prevents scurvy. *Vitamin D* is perhaps the most famous and well known, as it prevents — or cures — rickets. It is produced in the body by the direct action of the sun on the skin. Cod liver oil and the newer viosterol are rich sources of this vitamin. *Vitamin E*, less well known, but preventing sterility in laboratory animals, is found in lettuce and in the germ of wheat. *Vitamin G*, the pellagra preventive, is found in yeast, milk, eggs, and lean meat.

Without fruit and vegetables, then, the body is not well provided for. The teeth, bones, and blood need their mineral constituents; and their alkaline ash residue must counterbalance the high acid-forming properties of cereals, eggs, and meat.

Pure water, to the extent of at least three pints a day is needed to keep the body working well.

Teachers have several duties relative to nutrition.

(1) They may interest children of all ages in the study of foods as related to the body's needs. Little children's hunger and fondness for sweet things will be an obvious source of motivation. Even young children can be habituated to choose a lunch wisely. Gradually the relationship of different food values, the scientific principles behind the choice can be appreciated. About the sixth-grade level boys and girls alike are easily interested in the right preparation of food. The economic aspects can be studied in more detail in high school, as may also the varied group's needs, rather than that of the individual.

(2) Co-operation with the homes is especially necessary. Parents may need assistance in promoting good habits in regard to food. Some may be helped to greater competency in budgeting and planning diets. The school lunch must be related to the total diet, not considered as a thing by itself.

(3) As indicated by the community's needs, the clinic, the nutrition class, the lunchroom may make demands upon individual teachers, who should in turn be on the alert for cases which need expert attention.

The undernourished child is more subject to neuroses. He is high strung, easily fatiguable, having little endurance.

In appearance, a child who is ill nourished is usually pale and thin. Slenderness, due to heredity, should not be confused with the thinness due to a slight, flabby covering for the bones. Underweight for height may be accounted for by small bones, and cannot, alone, be taken as an index of malnutrition. The face may be puffy, giving a plump appearance, but with dark circles under dull eyes. He may be either listless or overexcitable, with other signs of nervousness, particularly twitchings. Decayed teeth, foul breath, and other symptoms of indigestion may be evident at a closer inspection. A teacher on observing a child with manifestations such as these should refer him to a physician for proper examination.

PRACTICAL EXERCISES

1. On square ruled graph paper chart the tables given below. Make one graph for height, using different colored inks for boys and girls. Make a second graph for weight, differentiating the sexes as before. Arrange your chart thus:

```
Inches
  69
  68
  67
  66
   :
   :
   :
   :
   :
   :
   :
   :
  19
   :
   :
   :
   :
Age 0  1  2  3 .........................................18
```

How does your chart show that girls in their teens are taller than boys of the same age?

How does it show the periods of acceleration and retardation?

2. Spend 30 to 60 minutes in a classroom, noting as follows:
   (a) how many, and which children have a poor posture habit;
   (b) which appear poorly nourished;
   (c) how many have poor eye movements, or hold their work nearer than 10 inches to the eyes;
   (d) the profiles of any who are unusual in forehead or jaw, sketching them for reference and comparison;
   (e) any cases of speech defects, any evidence of bad hygienic habits, any asymmetry of ears or eyes.

3. Find out what clinics for children exist within a mile radius of your school.
4. A formula offered by Oppenheimer for identifying malnutrition is as follows:

Arm girth × 100   (halfway between elbow and shoulder)

    chest girth   (average between inspiration and expiration).

If the result is less than 30 the child is considered undernourished.

Try this on one or two children whose appearance suggests malnutrition and see what is the result.
5. For the child selected for individual study: — look up all available physical records. Supplement by any measures you can make, and by consultation with his parents.

HEIGHT IN INCHES		AGE IN YEARS	WEIGHT IN POUNDS	
BOYS	GIRLS		BOYS	GIRLS
19.5	19.3	At birth	7 or more	7 or less
29.5	29.0	One	21	20
33.5	33.0	Two	26	25
36.5	36.0	Three	31	29
39.0	39.0	Four	34	33
41.5	41.5	Five	39	38
44.5	44.0	Six	44	42
46.5	46.0	Seven	49	47
49.0	48.5	Eight	55	54
51.0	50.5	Nine	61	60
53.0	52.5	Ten	67 +	67
55.0	54.5	Eleven	74	74
57.0	58.0	Twelve	80	84
59.0	60.0	Thirteen	86	92
62.0	62.0	Fourteen	96	102
65.0	62.5	Fifteen	109	110
67.0	63.5	Sixteen	118	118
68.0	64.0	Seventeen	127	120
69.0	64.5	Eighteen	135	121

FOR DISCUSSION

1. Can you suggest any physical facts that might explain the poor penmanship often found about eleven or twelve years old?
2. By what signs would you suspect the presence of adenoids? What would you, as a teacher, do after thus suspecting?
3. What is one result to the child's own feelings of the fact that bones may grow faster than the muscles and skin covering them?

4. What facts given explain that the rate of growth of height taken sitting differs from the rate of growth of height taken standing?
5. How could you co-operate to educate the parents in the matter of nutrition?
6. What facts about the home would you want to know to understand a child's physical condition?
7. What practical work can be done to interest children ten to twelve years old in public hygiene?
8. What facts about children's endurance, fatiguability, etc., should camp counselors know, (a) for a junior camp, children seven to twelve, (b) for a camp for fifteen years and older?
9. What health problems are particularly pressing in the junior high school?
10. The incidence of smallpox is higher in the United States than in any European country. Is this a problem of public education?

SELECTED REFERENCES

BALDWIN, B. "Physical growth of children from birth to maturity." *Univ. of Iowa St. in Ch. Welf.*, v. 1, 1920.

BRACE, D. K. *Measuring Motor Ability.*

INNSKEEP, A. D. *Child Adjustment in Relation to Growth and Development.* Chs. 1–11.

ROBERTS, L. J. *Nutrition Work with Children.*

SEHAM and SEHAM. *The Tired Child.*

TERMAN and ALMACK. *The Hygiene of the School Child.*

VITELES, M. S. "The influence of age of pubescence upon the physical and mental status of normal school students." *Jo. Ed. Psych.*, v. 20, 1929.

CHAPTER XV

MORAL DEVELOPMENT

Of the many current definitions of morality perhaps one of the most significant is that which calls it the *intelligent choice by the individual of habits of action for the good of the group.*

Intelligence a factor. — It should be noticed that at least five things are involved in this conception. *Intelligence* implies that an individual, to be moral, must know the accepted standards of right and wrong. On this account the very young child or a feeble-minded person is obviously not moral. The first needs instruction, the second may not be able to profit by it. So, too, from the stranger in a community, be he newly arrived immigrant, freshman at college, pupil in a new school, or rural visitor in a city home, breaches of social customs are tacitly ignored while the newcomer is allowed a period in which to shed his greenness. No plea of ignorance of the law is sufficient, however, to enable the adult citizen to escape the penalties of breaking it. Training in morality will include then (1) instruction in desired standards, (2) the formation of ideas of right and wrong by empirical means.

Personal choice. — A second constituent of morality is *personal choice.* This involves a motive and a decision rather than a blind keeping of the law. A hypnotized subject or a sick patient are extreme cases of people whose actions may be conformable to law but who entirely lack individual motivation and impulse. Their outward conformity is therefore not moral. In this matter we should not make the mistake of supposing that a routine compliance with orders on the part of any one, together with an absence of thoughtful decision or

318

purposeful control of emotions, is moral. Our complaisant adult conduct is, however, largely of this type. Most of us have not *chosen* to refrain from murder, theft, arson, and the like; we have simply not had the occasion for such conduct arise opportunely. In fact, were such occasion now to present itself, especially without a strong emotional setting or appeal to an instinct, we should probably refrain, not from any moral choice, but from sheer inertia with regard to a non-habitual line of action. Our law-abidingness, then, has never risen to the moral level with respect to these and many similar things; it is merely non-moral. Not that this neutral, non-moral conduct is valueless: quite the contrary, it has its main social utility in that it constitutes a stabilizing force helping to conserve standards, restrain or support the weaker ones among us, and provide the stepping stone to higher levels. As individual preparation for dealing with new situations, however, especially in moments of strong emotional urge, it is dangerous in its narrowness. Training, then (3), must provide opportunities to reason and to choose in matters of right and wrong conduct, or else children cannot learn independence of will nor acquire clear vision of ethical values.

Individual responsibility. — The third requisite in morality is to have *responsibility* thrown upon the *individual*. Each must stand accountable for his own deeds, learn his standards, do his own choosing. In this matter no moral person may shelter behind the community as a whole, nor behind any other person in the guise of counselor or friend, nor behind any institution. Each, as he comes to years of discretion and elects to whatsoever small unit of society such as club, political party, church, profession he will give his adherence, by thus pledging his loyalty, takes a definitely moral stand, and shares the responsibility for the good of that unit and for its value to the larger social group of which it is a part. Should his greater intelligence show him ways in which his unit is running counter to the general social good or is failing to further it, it devolves upon him to point out that fact and to help make such changes in policy and function as will carry his vision into reality. Should a person have charge of others, the morals of leadership imply that he look out for the well-being and the well-doing of his followers; in that case he must expect blame or praise for others' acts as well as for his own. Moral education will have to include (4) the refraining, on the part of adults, from giving directions or advice too freely, (5) the intrusting of special commissions to children, (6) positions of command and care of others.

Habituated action. — The fourth fundamental in morality is *action*. In fact morality is in its very essence, action, and, moreover, *habits* of action rather than isolated acts. Too often a person prides himself, not only on the things he doesn't do, but on the beautiful sentiments or the fine ideas he has either in the abstract or those which criticize other people's conduct. But ideas and sentiments without expression other than in words whether oral or in print do not begin to give us morality any more than steam from the spout of the kettle will accomplish anything; both have to be directed, transformed into working power. A quite limited intelligence backed by earnest effort may produce a constructively moral character provided the individual lives out the best that he knows. But to have the knowledge, the vision, and to fail in living up to it — to have the power and the insight and to neglect to use them for the social good, is more than the negative act of a shirker. It is as positively immoral deliberately to refrain from a recognized good as it is to go and poison one's neighbor, a truth we have frequently heard proclaimed and at last are beginning to realize.

Further, an occasional moral act does not make a man moral or the reverse. Character is composed of fixed tendencies or habits rather than of spasmodic deeds. A woman who has once refrained from slandering her neighbor is not thereby virtuous any more than the youth who has taken one drink of whisky is an alcoholic. Perhaps our thinking is not yet sufficiently clear on this point, for we unfortunately are apt to condemn a girl permanently for one lapse from chastity, and to condone all a wastrel's offenses for one act of bravery. Particularly should we be cautious in passing judgment as final on characters still in the making, of penalizing an adolescent for a few misdeeds, or of affixing derogatory adjectives as labels on to the persons of immature human beings in consequence of single immoral acts. Likewise, we should not rest content with instilling moral precepts, nor with hearing professions of idealism, nor with supervising a few performances of moral acts. We must (7) enlist the children's co-operation in the long process of habit forming with all that that means in the way of perseverance, provision of extra chances to practice the virtue, and eternal vigilance against exceptions.

Social relationships. — The fifth constituent of morality, already touched on, is that action shall be *for the social good.* Not all conduct, then, has a moral bearing; but no conduct which has a social effect either immediately or more remotely can escape being either moral or immoral. To overeat, to sit up constantly till 1 A.M., to invite injury through negligence while engaging in sports may be, at first blush, a purely individual matter and non-moral; but in so far as they impair the efficiency of one's services to society such acts are immoral. Clearly too, habitual indulgence in actions having a deleterious effect upon one's work is more immoral than is any single act; likewise a deliberate repetition of conduct realized as having a harmful consequence is worse than a chance repetition. Training children in morality will include (8) observation of the effect of others' actions on themselves, and, (9) consideration of their own actions as affecting other people.

Historic changes. — The term "social good" must be taken in a relative sense, however. Standards of good differ first of all with the age in which one lives and the degree of civilization reached. To eat one's enemy, to kill one's aged grandparent, to burn a heretic alive are no longer considered moral acts though they all were permissible at one time or another. At present we are convinced that dueling and slave-holding are not for the social good, and are in the early stages of realizing that sweat-shop conditions, the cutthroat business competition, and the advertising of quack medicines are likewise immoral.

Racial differences. — Racial and national differences in moral standards also exist. Hatred of lying, ideas of honor, reverence for the old or weak, for instance, are not the same among Chinese, Scotch, and Italians; marriage and divorce laws are different in England, Turkey, Japan, and various parts of America.

Size of group. — The relativity of moral standards depends not only on the age and nation in which one lives but upon the size of the community one considers. An act non-moral for an individual in a small family becomes immoral for any one living with two hundred others in an institution. A single family living isolated on a mountain may dispose of its garbage, sewage, and waste in any way it chooses; not so the family living in a small town. The town may use a near-by stream for sewage disposal, but not the city situated upstream from another city. Only recently, however, have we begun to suspect that if it is immoral for an individual to lie, steal, and murder, it is also immoral for a corporation, a society, a nation, to do these things. Our social horizons and our estimates of what is moral widen and stretch together. Moral training will necessitate, therefore, (10), introducing children into wider and wider social environments, as well as instructing them, presenting opportunities for choice, throwing increasing responsibility on them, and insisting on actions being coordinated into habits.

Distinction from immorality. — If morality consists in these things, then to be an ignorant follower, or to live in isolation may leave one non-moral; but to know right and wrong and choose the wrong, or to choose in thought merely and refrain from doing the right, to habituate conduct by a narrow gauge only makes one immoral. What can be said of those who can think, but carelessly don't consider the maximum social good?

Or who think but stop short of decision? Or who have ability but shirk responsibility? In these matters perhaps most of us have not "done growing."

MORALITY AS ACQUIRED

" **Conscience.** " — Innate tendencies that are primarily social soon become modified by contact with other human beings, emotions are gradually controlled and utilized in one way or another, but all this is a process of learning. Little children find that certain impulses that tend to further individual satisfaction come into conflict with other impulses which tend to further the good of the group, — the family, the playmates, the working unit; thus occasions are provided for choice and inhibition of one set of impulses rather than the other. Whether children become moral or immoral depends upon the way in which their original tendencies are modified. Their "conscience" is the outcome of education in a community and will, of necessity, reflect its standards; but the concepts and ideals are only gradually formed as their knowledge and experience is extended.

Habits. — One of the strongest factors in fixing habits of all kinds is pleasurable results; to have punishment follow violation of a desirable habit or an exhibition of its opposite is not nearly so efficacious. Punishment is a negative procedure, and results in a cessation of the desired response as soon as the punitive measure is removed. Positive satisfaction connected with the sought-for response is the method far to be preferred. This means that the environment must furnish satisfaction of some kind when the child is truthful, obedient, generous, self-controlled, helpful. The social habits formed in the early years must be put on the same level as all other habits and treated in the same way. Responses that bring satisfaction are the ones which are stamped in, whether moral or immoral. The child having no power of discrimination, no distinct moral sense, welcomes with equal readiness responses leading to criminal habits and responses resulting in upright living. The element he instinctively responds to is satisfaction. If that is present, then the response will, to his mind, be worth while. Of course what brings satisfaction must vary with the age of the child and his previous experience. The motives appealed to might vary from obtaining the physical pleasure of eating candy to satisfaction from the belief in divine approval. The essential part to be borne in mind is that the desired result brings a real satisfaction to the particular child. Because the motive appealed to influences children in general, or because the response required is right, means nothing in getting a particular child to form a particular habit so that it will be permanent.

Transfer of training. — We have no right to expect in the realm of morals any direct transfer of a habit from one line to another dissimilar one with no focalization of an ideal, no learning how to stand the strain of attention. Because a child is courteous to one person it does not follow that he is polite to all others; that he tells the truth in some situations does not mean that he is veracious in reality; that he is careless, disorderly, or forgetful in some matters does not involve negligence of others. It was a wise mother who warned her six-year-old boy on the eve of a visit to relatives to mind and obey his aunt just the same as though it were mother; but it was poor policy on the aunt's part to go off for the day omitting a similar precaution with regard to another adult left in charge. Here as elsewhere there must be training in holding the attention to difficult ideas, in formulating judgments in moral situations, in making many specific bonds between situation and response.

PUNISHMENTS AND REWARDS

Principles. — Mankind's ideas about punishment have evolved from mere retaliation to its use as a deterrent and as a remedial, constructive measure. The bad effect of the wrong kind of treatment is chiefly in the emotional life. Antagonism, fear, hardness are only too easily engendered. Dishonest and cruel acts may be actually habituated by improper punishment; and, in any case, a wrong idea of discipline is built up in a child's mind. The *negative* principles that should guide the teacher are, then, that no humiliation of the child should be brought about. No excessive severity should be used, nor should punishment be given according to the adult's impulses, especially the angry, irritated ones. One child should not be made a scapegoat for others, nor treated differently from the rest of a group all of whom have been at fault. Unusual, ingenious punishments should not be devised.

The *positive* principles are that the child should know, quite definitely, the charge against him. The association between deed and unpleasant result should be clear in his mind. This necessitates prompt treatment the younger the child, in view of the limited time sense and interest span. Punishment should be adapted in severity progressively with age or with repetition of the offense. Threats are useless by themselves; a consequence that has been mentioned as warning must ensue. The adult must speak of the offense as bad rather than the offender, keeping an objective, impersonal attitude throughout. Secure the child's own co-operation in the deterrent and remedial measures proposed. For persistent bad conduct a superficial treatment is useless or dangerous. The anti-social habits may be symptomatic of some maladjustment very different in its real nature from its face value. Only after a careful diagnosis of the underlying trouble can remedial treatment be wisely given.

Forms. — Spencer,[1] writing at a time when *impositions* of set tasks and *corporal punishments* were the most frequent types administered contrasted such artificial means with the *natural punishment*, in which a child is made to feel the logical consequences of the misdeed. He advocated natural punishments because they are impersonal and build up an idea of cause and effect, of law and order in a child's mind, thus helping him to control himself and avoiding feelings of antagonism and in-

[1] Spencer, H., *Education*.

justice. For instance, the boy who has broken his sister's doll
should, instead of being whipped by father who buys a new
doll, be required to make restitution even at the cost of deprivation to himself. Heartily as we could agree with this, the
difficulty in keeping only to logical, natural consequences arises
from the fact that (1) such are sometimes wholly disproportionate. Carelessness and ignorance may bring horrible disaster,
involving others who are innocent. (2) Individual differences
are not allowed for. What one child can dare with impunity
another attempts only to suffer at once. (3) The consequences
are often so long delayed that the child either sees no connection
with his deed, or is tempted to take a chance.

Therefore, one function of punishment is to foreshorten the
effect, and bring home to the offender here and now even in
exaggerated form, but certainly in terms adjusted to his maturity, what would be the natural consequence if he persisted for
years in his poorly chosen conduct. For example, distrust is
the eventual social consequence of lying, or rather of being
found out in a lie. We scarcely want to wait to let a child discover that — meanwhile forming a habit of lying; so we give
him at once an intensive experience of lack of confidence, with a
challenge to him to demonstrate unmistakable trustworthiness.

Though *deprivations* of pleasures and imposition of unpleasant
tasks all figure as customary modes of punishment, yet *social
disapproval* is the most widespread, and most widely applicable
form of all. It is most potent in bringing an emotional condition
of unhappiness which, in general, stimulates the individual to
effort to regain approval. Unless suitable channels are available
for this effort we are as likely to find undesirable actions as
desirable ones. With the more introvert type of child the
unhappiness brings self-pity and sulky brooding rather than
definite, objective attempt for reinstatement in others' esteem.
With such children it is particularly necessary to treat the
offense in matter-of-fact manner as a mistake to be greatly
deprecated, understood in its causation, and corrected in future,
just as any arithmetical or manual skill mistake would be

treated. At any age it is important to realize the source of social approval or disapproval for which the individual cares most. While the little child is oriented by his parents we must realize the social pull of the gang for the boy over nine years of age, of "the others" of similar age and social status for the young adolescent. The esteem of friends and of idealized personalities is increasingly important in adolescence, as is also public opinion of large groups.

Rewards. — The arguments for natural punishments apply equally well to rewards. Rewards may function as incentives to action and as potent factors in hastening the learning of desirable conduct. Poor results may come if self-display, selfishness, jealousy, are aroused, or if children are incited to dishonest means to gain the reward. To avoid this the objective rather than the subjective attitude needs to be emphasized. Where little children may be freely praised for good behavior children of school age must be directed away from self-glorification to the realization of the social value, and worthwhile achievement of their course of action. Competition, though a strong motive, can be dangerous unless transferred in middle childhood from individuals to groups, and supplemented by interest in good work for its own sake, real sportsmanship in games, and so on. Again, artificial rewards are far less desirable than those belonging naturally to the activity. Long continued use of artificial rewards may fail to develop any permanent, intrinsic interests since the individual has come to rely on outside stimulation and misses it when it is no longer supplied. Too many of our graduates fail to develop further activity along lines encouraged in school by artificial means only.

Social approval is the most permanent of rewards. To win it, any kind of behavior may be shown. Much of our moral training consists in seeing that approval follows only the conduct deemed desirable. Much of our treatment of maladjusted children consists in substituting opportunities for worthwhile action in place of the peculiar methods they have hit on by themselves hoping for attention and approval. More of our training for all should make clear to children at the opportune moment exactly what element in their conduct it is that is socially pleasing; thus we could shorten the process of moral learning.

Children's ideas and attitudes. — Barnes,[1] Schallenberger,[2] and others long ago investigated children's own attitudes towards punishment. Recent, unpublished work by Whitley confirms most of their findings. The technique in general has been to tell a story describing a piece of "naughtiness," giving the age, sex, motives of the offender and the social results, then asking the children what should be done in the matter. The findings may be stated as follows: —

Younger children, up to about eight or nine vote for punishment which they regard as personal, arbitrary, a retaliation for the wrong done. They disregard the possible motives of the offender and judge only by the result. After nine or ten an increasing number suggests ways of preventing a repetition of the offense, and still older they would appeal to reasoning, and try to understand the individual's motives. Boys are less merciful in their recommendations than are girls. In suggesting penalties children are inventive and merciless, ignoring any prescribed legal punishment that may have been mentioned in favor of severe measures of their own. By twelve years old approximately half of them show regard for the authorized legal penalty; by sixteen three quarters of them do.

As to a punishment they themselves have received, children consider it just if it balanced the misdemeanor in some way, if they were really in fault, and if the regularly constituted authority administered it. Conversely they consider it unjust if it was too severe, unusual, administered by any one not in direct relation to them, or, naturally, if they claimed innocence or no deliberate intention of wrongdoing. Their feeling of justice either for themselves or others is less a matter of reasoned judgment than it is of emotion.

[1] Barnes, Earl, *Studies in Education.*
[2] Schallenberger, M., "Children's rights as seen by themselves," *Ped. Sem.*, v. 3, 1894–96.

In the question of punishing a whole class for the offense of one unknown member Frear [1] found that as children grew older they developed an increasing sense of the injustice of it, because "the good are punished along with the bad." There is, however, an increasing feel of group responsibility both to compel the guilty member to confess and to prevent the possibility of recurrence.

SEQUENCES OF MORAL LEARNING

Conduct and age level. — Though we have no " moral age " defined for us by extensive testing in the way mental age and physiological age norms have been established, yet we have a few sorts of statistical observations on moral difficulties, and plenty of opinion as to standards of good behavior we might reasonably expect at various age levels. For instance, teachers' ratings of behavior of children from six to fifteen years old reported by Haggerty [2] indicated that boys at seven and eleven years old, girls at thirteen were more likely to be reported for bad conduct. Blatz and Bott, [3] in a longer continued study, found most misdemeanors at eight and nine years old for boys, and a slight increase again at thirteen. Boys were reported for bad conduct more frequently than girls. Marro, [4] in an older study of boys from eleven to eighteen noted that teachers graded their conduct as good 70 per cent of the time at eleven, only 58 per cent of the time at fourteen, while the age of fifteen led in positively bad conduct. From the teachers' standpoint, then, boys and girls are having a more difficult time at some ages than at others. We should remember, however, that bad conduct in the teachers' minds is likely to mean aggressive behavior, rather than docility, whereas from the mental hygienist's point of view docility might be a warning symptom.

[1] Frear, Caroline, in Barnes' *Studies in Education.*
[2] Haggerty, M. E., "The incidence of undesirable behavior in public school children," *Jo. Ed. Res.*, v. 12, 1925.
[3] Blatz and Bott, "Studies in mental hygiene of children," *Ped. Sem.*, v. 34, 1927.
[4] Marro, *La puberté*, quoted in Hall, *Youth.*

Teachers also rank inattention as a first-class offense; parents speak most frequently of disobedience — illustrating anew that we tend to judge as bad that in other people's behavior which inconveniences ourselves. The ages fourteen, fifteen, and sixteen are most frequently given by cases appearing in the children's courts, though delinquency may have existed one or two years before its discovery.

Typical difficulties of different ages. — Observation of specific problems which beset the youngest children reveal clearly their emotional origin. Nervous habits, negativism, temper tantrums, fears, much crying are manifestly emotional difficulties; but thumb sucking, enuresis, masturbation, feeding problems, are generally traceable to some emotional maladjustment also, and are not cured till the root difficulty is discovered.

From a study of six- to eight-year-old children's undesirable responses made by Carmichael [1] the following frequencies were found. Talking harmfully about or to others, 19 per cent. Non-co-operation, 17 per cent. Acts involving property rights 15 per cent. Various socially ineffective reactions, 13.5 per cent. Various forms of fighting, 10 per cent. The remainder included insubordination, lying, disturbing others, and so on. Bühler [2] found the age peak for frequency of lying to come between seven and eight years old, though the greatest number of selfish, malicious lies occurred between ten and twelve. A study of the charges for which children between the third and ninth grades inclusive in the schools of Philadelphia were referred to the clinic gave approximately 37 per cent for stealing, 33 per cent lying, 25 per cent truancy, 20 per cent each for uncontrollable temper and disobedience, 17 per cent running away, 16 per cent each for bullying, sex experiences, masturbation, 11 per cent enuresis, 3 per cent other bad habits.

Adolescents' problems are fivefold according to Holling-

---

[1] Carmichael, A. M., "Moral situations of 6-year-old children as a basis for curriculum construction," *Univ. Iowa St. Ed.*, v. 4, *6, 1927.

[2] Bühler, C., "Are lies necessary?" *Ped. Sem.*, v. 33, 1926.

worth.[1] (1) They must achieve emotional and volitional independence from the home group, a process called family weaning and which should, of course, have started in young childhood days, but culminate now. Their attempts to run away, the bitterness in their criticisms of their parents exemplify the difficulty which this problem presents to them, as do also extreme homesickness and lack of initiative. (2) The emotional life connected with sex has to be understood in its biological and its social relations. The sex knowledge acquired in pre-adolescent years must integrate with the new experiences consequent upon maturation. Habits of self-control learned in regard to satisfying other physical desires must be transferred to this new realm. A balanced heterosexual relationship must be the goal. (3) An appraisal of self must be objectively undertaken to decide upon vocational aptitude. Intelligent choice of occupation and its prerequisite training can then be made. There is, further, the stress and strain of finding the job and learning to function in it. (4) An appraisal of beliefs and points of view presents a mixture of intellectual and emotional problems sometimes precipitating mental conflict which disrupts conduct. This may begin as early as fifteen, and may not be a pressing necessity till nearer twenty. Many inconsistencies in conduct, now as well as later, are explained by the lack of having arrived at an integrated point of view. (5) They are faced with the desirability of forming a life plan. These other appraisals help here; but many are content to drift along, their course deflected by chance, rather than to pick out some goal for which to steer. Many dissatisfactions of adults are explainable by the general aimlessness which has characterized them.

Standards. — We might state then, roughly, that there is a maturation sequence discernible in the degree of difficulty found with various modes of social adjustment. Certain problems are more likely to occur at certain ages than at others, and probably the successful adjustment in later periods depends upon the degree of mastery of moral lessons at the appropriate

[1] Hollingworth, L. S., *The Psychology of the Adolescent.*

earlier age. Our moral and religious curricula could be much more intelligently devised if we were clearer in our understanding of the sorts of moral problems peculiarly acute at different stages.

We may reasonably expect achievement of bladder control by two years old. The nursery school age child wrestles with negativism and temper tantrums which for the five-year-old should have been conquered. Learning to take turns, to share toys, is a lesson for the kindergarten age. The seven-year-old should have overcome earlier timidity and be engaged in learning to speak and act fairly. How to act when laughed at is best learned before nine. If by ten a child does not follow the rules of the game and show substantial progress in veracity and square dealing he stands a poor chance of self-control, honesty, and generosity. To share work on a team, to be loyal to a larger group, to be fair to opponents as well as friends, are tasks that challenge the pubescents. Clean thinking about sex matters presents itself as a problem before twelve years old; if not well handled the chances are slight for healthful attitudes in adolescence. To get enjoyment without injuring others is a problem of prime importance between ten and fourteen; if not successfully met then it is difficult to form good social habits later. Property rights of groups other than one's own, of large public groups of which one is vaguely a member, are not within the conceptual grasp of pre-adolescents, though specific habits of care of such property, of keeping public places clean and whole may well have been built in. If by fifteen these concepts are not developing healthily we are likely to have an adult markedly retarded in sensing social property rights. We seem lax in training these ideas, permitting willful damage from college students that from a gangster of like age would involve a jail sentence. The incredible pilfering with which hotels have to contend, the bad reputation of sightseeing tourists, illustrate behavior development arrested on, say, an eleven-year-old level. The disorder left by picnickers, the vandalism in parks and museums, the litter tolerated in our streets are no credit to our methods of training however they demonstrate the psychological fact that habits are specific, and will not transfer even to similar situations unless people purpose consciously to have them carry over.

By the middle teens we expect standards of personal cleanliness and hygiene, care of personal and group belongings to have been habituated. Girls should show an intelligent interest in the needs of little children. Adequate conduct as guests and when exercising hospitality should be exhibited. Courteous behavior in public gatherings, control of speech when angry, responsibility in completing delegated tasks for the group are evidently looked for, since those who have not achieved them are looked upon as undeveloped. By the later teens, and here we are more vague, ideals of thrift, of chivalry and fair play with regard to sex relationships, of heroism as applied to daily trivial tasks should so motivate the behavior that the individual is consistent, integrated, well oriented to his fellows.

MEASUREMENT OF CHARACTER TRAITS

Honesty. — The most extensive, well-planned and reliable tests that we yet have for certain character traits were devised and given by Hartshorne and May, later with the assistance of Shuttleworth and Maller.[1] They would emphasize the psychological fact that the terms we use for traits are, after all, abstractions; and that character is formed in a concrete way by habituated responses to specific situations. To think of a child as generous, or deceitful or well-controlled means only that in certain observed situations he has acted in such a way as to make us think of the categorical expression. In other situations he might respond by actions we should interpret in the opposite fashion. Very gradually do children grow towards a consistent, integrated, organized sort of personality.

The whole series of tendencies to action which we think of as a unitary trait is not claimed to have been measured. Numerous controlled situations of very varied kinds were set up, and

[1] *Studies in Deceit. Studies in Service and Self Control. Studies in the Organization of Character.*

the honesty, or the service or the self-control exhibited in the responses to these was scored. In the tests for deceit, for instance, opportunities were offered to cheat in games, in school work, in making change, to tell the truth or lie under varying types and degrees of motivation. Similarly there was a great diversity of situation for the studies in self-control and willingness to be of service. Their subjects were mostly children in grades five through eight.

Some of their findings may be summarized as follows. Older pupils were slightly more deceptive than younger ones. There was practically no difference between boys and girls. Children from homes of bad discipline and examples of discord cheated more than others. Children from homes of better cultural background and homes of higher socio-economic level cheated less. The more intelligent children, and those emotionally stable cheated less than the average. There was a general resemblance in amount of cheating between friends, and between members of the same family. There was a positive though low correlation between scores for honesty on the one hand and such things as school marks for deportment, school placement, the general morale of the school, and enrollment in Sunday School. There was no correlation found between honesty scores and religious affiliation, attendance at Sunday School, or membership in clubs.

Other findings on the subject of cheating in school situations have been that 25 per cent or more of students of high-school and college level will cheat if possible.

Service. — The investigation into " service " — that is, willingness to work for the good of the group rather than just for one's own benefit, brought out no special relationship with age or grade. The older and further advanced children were not measurably different from the younger ones. Girls were slightly superior to boys, and the more intelligent children slightly better than others of the same age. There were positive correlations between scores for service and membership in a team. Friends and members of the same family tended to resemble each other in score. Children from homes of moderate cultural background were better than those from homes scoring either high or low in the culture scale.

Self-control. — Self-control does not mean, as so many children suppose, doing nothing rather than doing what one wishes to do. A car is in control when its movements are guided in accordance with a definite purpose. Self-control involves a clear aim for conduct, inhibitions of impulses contrary to the furtherance of the aim, persistence in face of distractions or discouragement. The little child's impulses to action soon meet checks of one sort and another. Counter-impulses of his own, such as fear and curiosity, may lead to inhibitions or encourage perseverance. Restrictions imposed by others, directions, requests, commands, all help to train in habits of obedience. Both in physical and social adjustments there is ample opportunity to learn control of action, though there may be a lack of clear purposing for one's self and in conjunction with the group, and lack of regard for others in forming the purpose.

Hartshorne and others devised some measures of self-control in the two aspects of persistence and inhibition, the purpose being formulated by the experimenters. They found a slight increase in the upper grades in power to inhibit, also a slight but variable correlation between age and inhibition, though none between inhibition and the more intelligent children of any one age level. Girls were rather better inhibited than boys. Children who were neurotic or emotionally unstable made poor scores in persistence. Foreign born children made better scores than American. Again a family resemblance was noticeable in the scores. Children who reported least frequent attendance on moving pictures scored better both on persistent effort and on amount of restraint.

Hartshorne concludes from all the investigations so far made that there is little evidence of efficiency in the type of moral education offered by our religious and other organizations supposedly engaged in character training. Possibly they are too theoretical, too verbal, too general and abstract and not sufficiently practical when it comes to the forming of all sorts of specific habits. Children learn honesty, self-control, and things like that by meeting situations which call for actual responses. Ideals are not objects of æsthetic devotion so much as tools by which to shape conduct. The mere possession of a fine set of tools does not confer the ability to use them well. Practice in applying ideals is all important in the fashioning of character traits. A child will be motivated by the ideals and codes of that group, chiefly, to which, because of its small size he feels he belongs. Such codes are never mere verbal formulæ but are emotionally tinged.

TRAINING SUITED TO THE AGE

Growth is gradual. — There is obviously plenty of growth involved from the condition of the infant to that of the moral adult: and naturally, morality is not achieved in any other than a gradual way. Without a distinct feeling of self there can be little development, and this ego sense grows but slowly, dependent as it is on memory, imagination, and the companionship of other people of all ages. Ideals, too, are generalizations; and these take time to be formulated independently of the particular situations and the immediate groups of experiences from which they arise. Ability to discriminate, judge, and reason is refined little by little. Habits are formed by degrees, especially the higher hierarchies concerned with wide social adjustment. Here as elsewhere there is a gradual unfolding, ripening, becoming. With increased knowledge and larger scope of judging, more opportunity is given for conduct to be rationalized, rather than merely habituated. With increased age and a less sheltered, controlled home life, children are forced to individual thinking, testing, deciding, choosing. With a widening environment, earlier standards may be recognized as temporary or inadequate, and a process, more or less explicit, of reconstruction may be set up. With frequent contact with all sorts of people inducing friction, emulation, dislike, admonition, affection, and the like, motives change both in kind and in amount of impulsive power. But these changes come about unevenly, so that children may be, at one and the same time of their physical life, in different stages with regard to different phases of their moral life. However, there are predominant characteristics of each stage more or less typical of different ages of childhood.

Early stage. — The first stage may be called the non-moral since at the beginning children are too young for rational choice, and their conformity to law is secured mainly by the law of effect modifying original tendencies. In this stage such control is attained first by incidental pains and pleasures sequent to actions, second by the systematic administration of pains and pleasures by members of the society in which children find themselves. As imagination and memory develop the controlling factor is supplemented by the anticipation of blame or praise, and still later by some sort of ideal. The emotions of young children which training may utilize are largely fear, love, and wonder. As young children depend on adults for the needs of the body and for the need of love, so towards them the earliest trust, love, and reverence are directed. Not only do adults relieve pain, they occasionally inflict it to bring about obedience; thus personality becomes the strongest factor in developing the sense of self, and a greater mystery than the forces of physical nature. Other persons, too, stimulate imitation and imaginative play. From the experience with these surroundings is born the "conscience," which inevitably reflects the customs, standards, and characters of those nearest. What is right, is what results in satisfaction to the children themselves and brings approval from other people. Little children need an atmosphere of love, trust, and social harmony, full and healthful provision for physical needs including rigid training in habits of regularity and cleanliness. They should find that it pays to do right, or to wait for the greater good, or to endure pains and disappointments bravely.

Middle and later childhood. — The age from six or seven to about ten forms part of what Kirkpatrick [1] calls the period of

---

[1] Kirkpatrick, E. A., *The Individual in the Making.*

competitive socialization. During these years children are influenced by a greater diversity of factors in their moral education than in the preceding years. They begin to go to school and to live more independently of their own family; they meet and deal with many others near their own age. In their games and companionship with other children they form a rough ideal of give and take, of justice, fair play, and physical bravery. Being keen and zealous for their own rights and pleasures they soon come to guard against any actions of others that curtail these; but they find that their own deeds are in turn submitted to the same jealous scrutiny by their playmates. Thus cheating in a game, or greediness, early rank, from the child's point of view, as wrongs, undeniably if they themselves are the sufferers thereby, vaguely so if their fellows resent such conduct in them. From the pure individualism of the earliest years they progress to membership in a clique or gang the units of which may indeed quarrel and nag among themselves, but are at least united against outsiders. Thus, empirically, they adopt into their moral code as wrong, cruel teasing, the lie, excuse, tale-bearing, or cowardice that betrays a friend. Meanwhile their standards of courtesy, truth-telling in the abstract, obedience, and those other virtues to which the adults about them may or may not be training them, are most likely quite undeveloped, chaotic, or formulated in talking-machine fashion. The moral sense is derived from custom; shame arises not from the consciousness of having performed an unlawful deed, but from having been found out. Virtues are acquired by imitation, not by conviction. Approbation of one's social equals becomes gradually more important than that of those in authority, as many a teacher knows to her cost. There is a rising desire for independence.

There should be consistency in the matter of rewards and punishments, so that the earlier desire to please others may be clearly directed to pass over into a conscious determination to do what is known as the right. The habit of implicit obedience begins now to be transformed into rational obedience. Self-control must be developed in newer and newer fields. They must learn that though there are many matters in which their preferences may be consulted, there are also very many occasions when "I don't like to," or "I don't want to" makes not a particle of difference to the necessity for action. Not to learn this lesson early is a tremendous handicap in the later, adolescent period. Adults should help children to distinguish clearly between times when they may choose what is to be done, and times when it is not a question of choice, only of loyal and prompt carrying out of orders. There must be an inexorable holding to account for deeds good or bad that children may feel the force of social law and individual responsibility. Impulses to mischief or teasing which result in unhappiness to others or harm must be inhibited in favor of impulses leading to generous, kindly, courteous behavior. Habits that are the foundations of later sexual purity must be formed and their opposites carefully guarded against. The natural childish curiosity in sex matters should be satisfied simply and with absolute veracity rather than met with refusal to answer or equivocation. Repression will lead only to their seeking, and usually getting, misinformation from impure sources, working harm that is difficult to undo; evasion or falsehood will engender a distrust of the adult when later enlightenment comes, and raise a barrier of silence perhaps never to be torn down in adolescent years when boys and girls need a wise confidante. Sex information should be given incidentally, but simply and as a matter of course, changing the probable atmosphere of mystery into reverence, perhaps scientific interest and poetic appreciation.

Adolescence. — Rapid physiological changes take place, and these, together with the probable changes in home life and the sharing of wider community activities, make the period peculiarly difficult to live through with poise. Though there is already a large system of organized personal habits, yet strong, intense new impulses from within, fresh customs and standards without, the new feeling of individuality and the immaturity of the will combine to provide ordeals that test the adolescent in all sorts of ways. New possibilities open up in the way of emotions, interests, feelings of self, capacities for reasoning, reorganization of the personal life in its relationship to the larger social wholes. There is a heightened sensitiveness to the phenomena of nature, greater appreciation of the beautiful, the good, and the true, with the beginning of abstract questionings. The whole being is likely to be in a ferment from twelve to sixteen, though temperamental differences are an important factor in determining the length and intensity of the emotional activities of the period. The social nature is being born, as it were, at a psychic crisis, so that at no time is there apt to be greater disparity between insight and power to act, between judgment and moral control; at no time is the moral equilibrium more easily upset.

Authority should gradually relax and greater responsibility be thrown upon the individual. "Obey me" should become "Obey yourself." Boys and girls must learn to meet crises for themselves, to readjust their actions to the demands of the larger social unit of which they are coming to realize themselves members. They must face and decide questions for themselves, and relate the value of their individual acts and immediate activities to the broader system of morality which they can now appreciate. Problems should seldom be solved for them, but many interests should be provided, especially those leading to wholesome activities. A healthy body, plenty of mental occupation, and abundant outlet for physical, æsthetic, social, and ethical needs will help form habits of untold value. Physical disturbances may be the sole cause of a morbid conscience which has, indeed, been described as a case of "nerves." Action rather than theory should be emphasized.

PROGRESSIVE SOCIALIZATION

Enlarging groups. — The art of living together involves practice in meeting groups of one's fellows which differ in size, differ in their immediate interests, differ in age, differ in the kind of people composing them; if this practice is not afforded, stereotyped, inflexible habit bonds are formed not only in action but in attitude. The provincialism, race prejudices, violent partisanship of many adults evidence an outlook on life narrow and egotistical for lack of socially widening groups in younger days, in contact with which more flexible habits could have been formed.

The connotation of the word "we" is a fair index of an individual's stage of social growth, the kind of extension of the personality that has taken place, the various sorts and sizes of groups with which he will identify himself. The bragging of the four- to seven-year-old of the what-is-done-at-our-house, "my daddy can beat yours" type, shows the *we* to mean the family. For the eleven-year-old *we* is a group of six or eight like-sexed, like-aged individuals, while the rival gang is *they*. In the junior high-school age *we* may mean the club; to the college sophomore it means those of a given graduation year.

"We don't do that — as you people do." What does the adult most frequently mean by *we?* Often, one very narrow group felt as different from, antagonistic towards others. At the club level so many seem to suffer arrested development. Snobbishness prevails, cliques persist, barriers are set up. The better developed personality seeks contacts with ever-widening circles of human beings of diverse interests, of various levels culturally, economically, racially, religiously. The ideally social-ized individual is at home wherever he goes, for he is brother to all mankind.

Means of socialization. — The psychology of the means by which this progressive socialization takes place is worth analysis if our character training is to be effective. Since the younger the child the more concrete minded he is, the group idea is first dependent on *being with* others physically. Already in the family contacts a group meaning has been given to "we." In the nursery school and kindergarten age the "we" comes to be used for "me and another child," occasionally for three. *Doing* things together is the next means of development. Routines established by adults as well as spontaneous activities precipitate social adjustments of all sorts. As playing in the presence of other children changes to playing with them, and egocentric talking changes to conversation we have the next step of *purposing* together. The so frequent "Let's play — " of children over seven evidences the enlarged *we* and the formation of group purposes. Purpose now directs the group activity, and together the members discover their capacity for enjoyment. Hard work, endurance, self-sacrifice may be called for, and experiences thus shared weld the group emotionally. By ten or eleven, the gang, club, set, likes to have a name for itself — sometimes a visible badge of membership, to have a local habitation as well as a name, and, soon thereafter, to *own property*. As children get older their purposes carry over a longer period. As the purposes become more complex a metamorphosis takes place. Mere synchronous activity becomes co-operation. The couple becomes a pair. The group becomes an organized team.

Though illustrations have been given from different age levels yet the same process is necessary at any age before group consciousness develops when new people meet. First is a period of being together, then activity ensues during which purposes become classified to direct complementary action.

Other means in the socialization should be noted. *Comparison* with similar groups defines the concept of the group self, just as other concepts are evolved by comparison of similar, but not identical particulars. Differentiation helps in distinguishing one group from another. Here, probably, is the cause of the oft heard emphasis on differences which sounds like bragging, and which may be misdirected into contempt for the others. Friendly comparison is what is needed, objective, scientific interest in likenesses and differences with no self-glorification at the expense of others, if we would avoid a lifetime of prejudices. *Opposition* from others consolidates the members of a group, just as the resistance of the physical environment gave the baby his first idea of his self-limitations. Many a group has awakened to keen self-consciousness under the necessity of presenting a united front of defense to the "enemy." Hence the swift development of gang life in the warfare of our city streets. *Collective ownership* involves important aspects of group consciousness. Purposes formulated by the group may involve labor and financial responsibility with respect to property. Its care soon favors diversified duties in the group and promotes team work. Simultaneously an understanding of property's value to other groups is gained.

Levels of purposing. — Three sequent stages can be observed in social relationships equivalent to the function, fiction, factum development in play with objects. At first a group mills around, getting acquainted, testing each other's possibilities. There is no concerted action. This *exploratory stage* is a function interest. When a purpose becomes defined, limited by the group's immediate enjoyment we have the similarity to the fiction use of play material. The purpose may be to have, to do, to know, but solely for *the group's self-satisfaction*. There is considerable use of symbolism, too, at this level, with enthusiasm over artificial values. The secret society is a fair illustration of this. Within the group there may be either similar parallel action of its members, or the integrated design of action characteristic of the true team. That will depend partly on how long the group has been together, partly on the general maturity of its members. When a group is unified to the point of conceiving a *purpose beyond itself*, for which it serves as a tool, we have a level of purposing parallel to the factum stage of use of play material, when the work idea dominates.

Here is a critical point in social development. To fail to pass to the third level indicates, for the group, an arrest on a selfish, individualistic plateau. If a club's only reason for existence is to give itself a good time it is as selfish, corporately, as a single person with a similar aim in life. When the group envisages service to another group, when it articulates with other groups in diversified service to large sections of humanity which it could scarcely reach physically, for which, indeed, it may have an abstract name, that group is mature socially.

Group interrelations. — This is a matter of the utmost significance. A group unit must sense its relationship to other groups, learn to co-operate rather than to fight precisely as, at an earlier stage, the individual child had to find his place in a group and learn exactly the same lesson — by quarrels at first — that small units must pass beyond the stage of aloofness, antagonism to other groups to find harmony of action in allied groups. Hence the Boy Scout troop is interrelated with other small units and integrated in a national, international organization. We try to develop not only squad and class feeling in a school, but bring the classes together in a common school undertaking. School and school are brought together in a town enterprise.

These affiliations, interrelations, integrations are of special importance in the adolescent period. Failure to arrive then at group consciousness wider than one's immediate, small unit may mean arrested development, or, at best, a belated lesson learned with greater difficulty in later life. The noisy home town booster, the tourist who compares all foreign places unfavorably with "way back home" is as immature in his group's relations with other groups as is the boasting five-year-old child in his individual relationship to his first group outside the family.

That large group units find still larger interrelations a difficult social problem is seen in our economic, political, religious, national misunderstandings today. Apparently, what with cut-throat competition, graft, intolerance, jealous watchfulness we are, as such groups, still in the self-contained, suspicious, ready-to-fight stage of the small gang numbering eight or ten members. In the fields of science and art such large group integrations seem easier, possibly because the ideals there are already impersonal, a search for truth and beauty rather than gain, an evaluation which fosters purposing on the third level.

Use of imagination. — One other point is important. We transcend the limits of mere physical nearness to produce group consciousness by the agency of language communication. Words can bring people together in thought though distance and time separate them; pictures can stir the imagination to wander where the body cannot go. Books and stories have long served this purpose. As our means of language and picture usage improves it opens possibilities of understanding people far off, and identifying ourselves with them emotionally as the little child does at first in his actual groups. Our use of sound pictures, radio, and similar devices serves not only to inform but to awaken interest in others' feelings and thoughts. Our various schemes of world friendship projects among children illustrate an attempt to harness this potential sympathy for efficient work. Through the imagination, too, comes a feeling of affinity that dispenses with barriers of time as well as space. The ideals handed down from our heritage of the past become factors in our own lives. The youth whose historic or time sense permits can arrive at pride of religious tradition, pride of racial origin, pride of economic, political, professional affiliation not simply because his present-day friend groups belong to this or that, but because of all that these unities have meant in the past. He feels the obligation to "pass on the torch."

Some principles of training. — From these psychological facts some principles for the cultivation of group consciousness may be formulated.

A mere aggregation of children is not a social group. It takes time to get acquainted. Activity in common, whether self-chosen or suggested from without, will promote the discovery of mutual interests and of identical, or complementary abilities. The younger the children the less this process can be hurried.

Children must practice belonging to small groups before they can sense membership in large ones.

Growth is from within. A superposed organization, even of the simple adult pattern of president, secretary, treasurer is quite artificial for third graders, just as no yearning for a constitution and by-laws is felt by sixth graders. Forced growth may bring unhealthy results. The fourteen-year-old boy-mayor-for-a-day probably learns more of how to secure individual notoriety than he does of civic responsibility. Faculty domination of high-school clubs will fail to develop a biologically sound organization with its natural polarization toward leadership.

Such group attitudes as civic consciousness, patriotism, are only vague terms to pre-pubescents, attached to a few specific habits such as keeping the school yard free from litter, saluting the flag, and the like. The city, the state, the country are too abstract to be apprehended. The city is embodied perhaps in the park policeman or the town librarian. The state is a colored patch on the map, a signpost on the road. "Our country" is something sung about, with an annual connection with firecrackers. The group feeling can grow only as multifarious, differentiated activities are undertaken in company with various sorts of people.

A period of aggressiveness, self-sufficiency within the group is as natural for a time as it is for an individual child under seven. Unless this stage is passed, however, the gangster may develop, loyal to his own small group but antagonistic to every other, and ruthless in the means taken to establish the supremacy of his own unit.

Since stealing in order to own is a gang delinquency frequent from fourteen to sixteen, there is need for concomitant training in fellowship and in property rights. A group should own something in common and take responsibility for it financially and by labor. Such ownership should inhere in a small group to begin with.

Visits to other groups, information about them, will help to better understanding of their purposes, their struggles against handicaps. Understanding leads to more intelligent co-operation than a mere sentimental interest does. Constructive planning with one group for the benefit of another group may be undertaken at any age.

Every boy and girl should have opportunity to feel the inspiration of team work in more than one line. However clearly the needs of team unity are sensed during middle and later adolescence in sports and games, yet athletics is only one field. Chorus singing in parts rather than in unison may be a lesson in social organization as well as in harmony. Musical children should have experience in a school orchestra with all the diversified effort for the total unity that that involves. Projects such as plays and pageants provide splendid opportunity for, and development of, team work. For those of introvert tendencies such experiences are invaluable.

Groups must not be composed invariably of the same age level. We are in grave danger of perpetuating antagonisms between the generations by our too ready acceptance of segregation by ages. Life is not like that, stratified in horizontal layers; there are vertical combinations of vital importance to the organic whole. Adjustments to old people, middle aged ones, young ones, little children must be easy for every one and can be learned only by practice, as are other reactions. If adolescents are left to return to family life solely through the promptings of the sex instinct they are ill prepared to function socially in a home of their own. In vocational life they most decidedly must integrate with people of all ages.

If our hope of making this world a better place to live in is to be realized we must lose no chance of helping young people integrate their small group units with still larger units. If barriers of distrust are to be broken down, the job that is preeminently the teacher's, that of helping pupils gain information through social studies, can do much to facilitate this. Purposes and ideals that reach beyond the immediate group's need must be formulated.

PRACTICAL EXERCISES

1. If possible, visit a session of the Children's Court. Report on the procedure.
2. Refer to the ratings and rankings done in connection with Chapter I. Can you analyze the reasons for your judgments any further?
3. When you hear the term "we" used by a five-year-old, a nine-year-old, a thirteen-year-old, ask at once what he means by "we."
4. For your selected child, find out what rewards, bribes, punishments and

threats are commonly used in his home. Does his father ever talk over with him his moral difficulties?

5. Read the following story to groups of various aged children asking them to write the end of it. Study the results for ideas of retaliation, reform, restitution, parental responsibility as correlated with the age of the children. Are any sex differences manifest?

"Bobby had just had a birthday. He was six. His father had given him a set of tools for a present, a hammer, a saw, a screwdriver, some nails and screws. Next day while mother was out he found a little box. He sawed off a piece of it and nailed the box with lots of nails on to the window sill. "There," he said, "now mother will have a place to put her flower pot." When mother came home she found her box broken and the woodwork by the window all spoiled with nails and with hammer marks. What do you think Bobby's mother should do?"

FOR DISCUSSION

1. What moral responsibility is involved after you have realized such things as the following: (a) that a large class passes more easily from a room if the movable seats and book-rests are turned back and the doors opened wide? (b) that to spit is unsanitary? (c) that a station platform is dangerously narrow for the crowds that use it? (d) that obscene picture postals are being sold near your school? (e) that you are overworking?

2. Under what circumstances is it non-moral or immoral to (a) drop candy-wrappings, fruit skins, nut-shells, etc., wherever one is eating? (b) to conceal the fact that one has tuberculosis? (c) to delay decision in a plan of action? (d) to read novels or do nothing every afternoon for a month?

3. Are these things moral or otherwise? (a) loyalty in a partisan way to such things as "the gang," a secret society in high school, (b) ignorance of the civic health regulations.

4. What do your answers to the preceding questions suggest as to requisites in the moral training of children?

5. In what way is a child brought up alone likely to be deficient morally? Why?

6. Of what moral value is the "gang" tendency in the years ten to fifteen?

7. What accounts for the constant disputes and bickerings of children from nine to thirteen? Would you check it? Why, or why not?

8. What is probably lacking in the moral education of children brought up in an institution run on the congregate plan?

9. How would you deal with obstinacy in a little child?

10. What can you do for the very selfish fifteen-year-old?
11. How would you help cure exaggeration in a ten-year-old?
12. Give some suggestions for dealing with cruelty in a six-year-old; impudence in a twelve-year-old girl; obscenity in the years eight to twelve; bullying on the playground.
13. Outline procedure in conformity with the principles of habit-formation to train in "honesty."
14. Do the same, to train a child to like being with others, to try to understand them and to please them.
15. Why might a child get the idea that to spill water on the floor is a worse offense than to tell a lie?
16. What has the money sense to do with morality?
17. With whom can you co-operate in the matter of character building?
18. Why is it significant that friendship ranked so high as a factor in scores for cheating, and for service?
19. What is suggested by the fact that in the grades six to eight to be a member of a small team was more of an incentive to "service" than to work for the good of the whole class?
20. Would you expect older children to cheat less than the ten-year-olds? Why or why not?
21. In what ways does training in making plans help in learning self-control? Training in foreseeing consequences?
22. Is there anything to indicate that maturity rather than intellectual superiority correlates with power to inhibit?
23. Discuss the results of the exercises above.

SELECTED REFERENCES

BLANTON and BLANTON. *Child Guidance.* Chs. 12, 13, 19.

CARMICHAEL, A. M. "Moral situations of six year old children as a basis for curriculum construction." *Univ. of Iowa St. in Ed.,* v. 4 *6, 1927.

HARTSHORNE and MAY, etc. *Studies in Deceit. Studies in Service and Self Control. Studies in the Organization of Character.* Selected chapters from above, or the summaries given.

HAVILAND, M. S. *Character Training in Childhood.*

MACAULAY and WATKINS. "An investigation into the moral conception of children." *Forum of Ed.,* v. 4, 1926.

McGRATH, M. D. "A study of the moral development of children." *Psych. Mon.,* v. 32 *2, 1923.

MORGAN, J. J. B. *Child Psychology.* Ch. 13.

ROBACK, A. A. *Psychology of Character.*

CHAPTER XVI

RELIGIOUS DEVELOPMENT

The beliefs, customs, motives that spring to mind at the mention of the word religion illustrate the great variety of individual experience that may exist, and the diversity of forms under which religion may operate. The prejudices, bigotry, intolerance, and persecutions we know of indicate the divisive force it may become. Religion can sanction the most fantastic beliefs, the worst depth of vile behavior; it can inspire the purest devotion, the noblest heights of heroic achievement.

MEANING OF THE TERM

A way of living. — Religion is not easily definable. From the psychological point of view we should describe the behavior we observe, seek to analyze the controlling ideas and impulses behind it. We find, characteristically, a tendency to organize life round values other than material. There is a positing of belief in powers other than human with which or with whom man has definite relationship. This power controls the universe, life and death, and may, in consequence, control man's conduct in the rough or in minute detail. We notice the familiar mechanisms of idea forming, of wish fulfillment, of projection, identification and the like, the ubiquitous impulses of love, mastery, fear determining behavior in religion as elsewhere, both towards this posited Power, and towards fellow beings.

James,[1] in his *Varieties of Religious Experience* says: "We and God have business with each other, and in opening ourselves to His influence our deepest destiny is fulfilled. . . . In the sober moments of life every man instinctively appeals to or leans upon the larger and stronger spirit whom he, perhaps

[1] Page 516.

vaguely, regards as the original and final authority over the affairs of men." Religion is not to be identified with the performance of many acts of public and private worship, nor with the possession of information about religious literature, history, and theology, nor with susceptibility to emotional transports, though in the popular mind the term "a religious person" may easily call up a mental image of an adept in any one of these three lines. It is true that religion does involve acts, knowledge, and feelings, since religion is a way of living. Its peculiarity as a way of living is in its point of reference to some power or powers other than human with which man has some kind of relationship. It will be seen that roughly this description fits the Moslem, the witch doctor, the Parsee, the Presbyterian, the modern Japanese, the Jew, the Hindu, the Quaker, the Catholic, and many other types equally well. Coe says, "Religion exists at all because men find themselves and their world standing over against each other in an antithesis, even opposition, that needs to be resolved. . . . The religious impulse is thus toward the progressive unification of the man with himself, his fellows, nature and all that is. It is man's effort to be at home in his world and with himself." [1] Religion, then, is the unification of life in terms of principles which prove themselves true. It is the regulation of life by ideals of universal and everlasting truth. It is the attempt of the human being to live the best that is in him, to be the best that he can; and that attempt comes only through communion with the Infinite.

" **Religious** " **acts, emotions, thinking.** — The expressive formal *acts* universally recognized as religious include seclusion for purposes of meditation and introspection, fasting, the need of objective symbolic objects, self-torture, burial customs, collecting of sacred literature, pubic initiations, pilgrimage, prayer of all types from mere incantations up to friendly communion, sacrifice, concerted worship, including the use of music, fasting, dancing, various rites and ceremonies.

Wherever we went in the world, if we saw these things going

[1] Coe, G. A., *Education in Religion and Morals*, pp. 200–201.

on we should recognize their connection with the religious beliefs of the people.

On the *emotional* side the feelings of wonder and fear in the presence of the forces of nature which we do not understand or control, inspire the sentiment we call awe. Gratitude, which includes the attitude of submission as well as a tender feeling, a relief from strain, may be compounded with this awe and give the typical religious sentiment of reverence. The sense of mystery, then, a certain filial relationship enters into man's feeling for his god. With community of ideas and aspirations he may feel sympathy with his fellow men, and come to connect his moral ideas with religious concepts.

On the *intellectual* side the instinct shows itself in a consciousness of increasing uneasiness, a realization of a gap between what is and the ideal. This duality, disturbance, opposition, is resolved as salvation from wrong by the deliberate connection with the higher: the Ideal beyond limitations is postulated as the only Real. The self is identified with this higher Ideal, which in turn is probably identified with the force operating in the universe at large. All feel that this force exists and functions, though the various religions and theologies may differ in their belief of the nature of this force and the way in which it acts. The first idea of God may arise from observation of the forces of nature, in other words animism. Belief in the immortality of spirits is the next stage, with its accompaniments of ancestor worship, superstitions, fetichism, incantations, and magic. Local and tribal deities are adopted, then national deities with assigned seasons and places of worship. As the tribal god inspires to loyalty, so the national god inspires to righteousness. From a zoömorphic conception man passes through polytheism, an anthropomorphic conception, symbolic presentation to a philosophic concept as Final Cause or as Power making for righteousness.

Essentials. — To be religious requires, first, that the individual, through *experience*, realize the inadequacy of various endeavors; the lack of adjustment between man and man; the warfare within himself between a better and a worse self; the need to explain and account for nature. Religious instruction, which is mere telling, giving information, will not meet this need. Religion, the progressive and the final adjustment, is Life, and Life means action. The feeling of maladjustment must arise from actual living, not from mere head-knowledge, otherwise the individual may be non-religious but he could never be truly religious. The value of law, the need of human sympathy, the meaning of divine love, the function of punishment, the dependence of the individual upon others and upon unseen, often unknown, forces, — all these facts and many others must come to the child growing up in human communities. Too much protection and care often prevents wholesome experience. Dogma and creeds are accepted when not understood, and the normal questioning and investigation that would have led to a true realization of some of life's problems, are snuffed out.

Realization of opposing forces. — With the realization of the inadequacy of responses along the lines indicated, there must be present a desire to make things "better," to have things what they are not. In other words, there must be ideals — ideals real, vital, ideals that can influence conduct. Of course they will vary with the maturity and surroundings of the individual. From childish ideals and principles such as of being "Papa's brave boy," and of "God who is just like a big Santa Claus who wants me to be good"; or of explaining thunderstorms by saying "God is rolling barrels"; or of sharing with sister because she shared with me yesterday, we progress to the highest ideals the human race has yet evolved.

Habits, knowledge, and thinking. — As in morality, knowledge, thinking, and habits are all necessary and for the same reasons as there discussed. Since religion is a matter of constant, steady living towards an end, controlled habits of conduct must be formed. Real control involves thinking, and without knowledge thinking goes astray and some habits cannot be formed. Further, unless religion is the outgrowth of judgment, of choice, it is blind, — not rational, — it does not take in the whole man, and therefore is not true religion.

Religion includes morality. — From this it will be seen that religion, in its true and biggest sense, includes morals. A man cannot seek to unify life in accord with ideal ends without working with that phase of it which requires the adjustment of man to man, which we mean by the term "morality." It is hard to see how a man could be really religious, and yet be immoral. On the other hand, it is possible for a man to be truly moral without being fully religious. He may unify his experiences in regard to his fellow creatures under moral laws; but he has taken into consideration only one phase of life, he has not reconciled the opposing forces along other lines, and therefore is not religious. Morality, included in religion, is a stepping stone to it, but morality is not religion. Religion is Life at its broadest and best. It is man finding himself in God. This ideal requires every power of the human being to think, to feel, and to do; all are required in this greatest problem of the human race.

Original nature. — Somehow or other, in our original nature are formed the roots from which religion develops. Six of the most important native tendencies are curiosity, sex, æsthetic interests, fear, gregariousness, kindliness. *Curiosity* has led us to questionings about nature, and so, ultimately, has had a large share in formulating the god beliefs. *Sex* love gives personal meaning to emotions. Sex life has suggested innumerable analogies of the relationship between gods and humanity. Phallic worship, symbols, similes of all sorts permeate our religious ceremonies of today. Religion always seeks to control sex practices in some way and therefore to shape the ideals concerning them. *Æsthetic* interests have been entwined with our ideas of God and of behavior. The most beautiful we can conceive in architecture, literature, music, color, pageantry, etc., has always been at the service of religion. We find expression of devotion most fittingly through beauty. *Fear* has not only entered into the god belief, it is a most powerful motive for the control of conduct. The terror of punishment after death, for instance, has been a familiar weapon of religious leaders. *Gregariousness* brings us together for worship rites. Emotions peculiar to the suggestibility of crowds have been deftly stimulated for all sorts of purposes by preachers. Gregariousness also provides the frequent social contacts from which moral and ethical problems arise. The impulse to *kindliness* promotes philanthropy through sympathy and benevolence, attitudes which manifestly work for greater human happiness, and which are interpreted in religious thinking as pleasing to deity.

Nature and nurture. — The responses made because of these original tendencies, modified as they are by all the experiences which life brings, come to be controlled by conscious ideals, and thus the religious personality develops. Coe would go even further. He says, "Man has a religious nature. The definite establishment of this proposition is perhaps the greatest service that the history and psychology of religion have performed." "To speak positively, the possession of a positive religious nature implies three things: (*a*) that a child has more than a passive capacity for spiritual things. . . . A positive spiritual nature goes forth spontaneously in search of God. (*b*) That nothing short of union with God can really bring a human being to himself. . . . Failing to find Him we lose even our self. (*c*) That the successive phases in the growth of the child personality may be, and normally are, so many phases of the growing consciousness of the divine meaning of life." [1]

Need of training. — Whether we agree with the foregoing statement or not there can be no doubt that the main thing for us as students of child psychology to bear in mind is that children have a religious nature. To ignore it is to deprive them of some of their inheritance, — after all, the most important part. But the fact that children have by original nature a religious impulse, is no reason to suppose that they will grow up religious, or that they will necessarily have any conscious religious experience or realization of God. This

[1] Coe, *op. cit.*, pp. 37, 62.

tendency needs developing, pruning, directing, feeding, just as any other does. All children have the kindly instinct, yet how many brutes there are, and how many more who are never rationally moral. We all have the instinct of curiosity, yet how few of us become scientists. Much and careful training is necessary before a child grows up into a truly religious adult.

LAWS OF LEARNING, AND RELIGIOUS EDUCATION

Principles involved. — A way of living to include relationships with a higher being and with one's fellows implies the development of the intellectual, volitional, and emotional aspects of children's natures. They must be informed, they must think, they must choose, they must gain independence of thought and choice, they must be inspired and motivated, they must act, and act consistently. The self must be oriented with regard to other human beings and the higher powers. Since there is no one thing recognizable as *the* moral or *the* religious impulse, but simply the whole self employed about moral and spiritual matters, and as education is a unitary and continuous process, it follows that there is no special education to be termed religious; it is merely one aspect of the whole. Its material may vary slightly but scarcely its methods, since it deals with the same highly complex organism of feelings, affection, impulses, aspirations, habits, and intellectual capacities as do other aspects of education. No new psychological laws are needed, therefore. However, since we are conscious that many adults remain on low moral levels in all sorts of ways due to defective training or inadequate environment, it may not be amiss to emphasize a few of the most important factors in the development of children during the non-moral and transition periods.

Laws are not different. — It must be continually and forcibly emphasized that the same laws do apply in the development of religious responses that apply in the development of any other type. Most people even today, if one can judge from observing the training of children in these fields, believe that some mysterious force reigns here, and that although every law of child psychology and every law of teaching be broken, yet faith and prayer will make children both moral and religious. Witness the subject matter, the methods, the material used in the majority of our religious schools, Jewish, Catholic, and Protestant, save the few progressive ones. Where are the motivation, the interest, the life situations, the provision for initiative and motor expression which are considered so important in the secular schools? How many of the teachers who serve Sunday after Sunday would be tolerated in a day school? How many parents who declare their inability to teach their children arithmetic or history yet do not question for a moment their ability to teach them to be moral, God-fearing men and women? The fact is that instead of being easy, this problem is one of the most difficult of child education, because of its complexity. It is surely one of the most important, because the effect of training and environment is more influential here than in the field of intellect. Parents are, to a large extent, responsible for a child's character in so far as it is the result of his environment, whereas his intellect is a result of heredity over which they have less control. In the field of morals and religion perhaps more than in others we need to apply our scientific knowledge of the development of the child. We need further to apply all our methods and principles of good teaching. We need continually to bear in mind that this field is in no way innately different from others, for it involves all others and is involved in every other.

Law of maturation. — This is often overlooked entirely in planning for a child's education in religion and morals. When this law is ignored, teaching is futile, no matter what the field. Here, just as in every other phase of child development, progress is gradual, and is limited by the content of the child's experience. It must be from known to unknown — the unknown interpreted in terms of the known, here as elsewhere. A child's maturity, his experience, his interests and ideals, his habits, his knowledge determine his growth and interpretation in re-

ligion and ethics just as surely as they do in arithmetic or literature. Why, because adults enjoy thinking of children as little
lambs, should the self-respect of a twelve-year-old be injured
by having him join in singing a request to be made a lamb?
Or, for the same reason, why should six-year-olds be compelled
to memorize the twenty-third psalm with its unfamiliar metaphors and mature experience? Again, to appeal to motives
of abstract right in Sunday School is no more effective than to
appeal to those same motives in day school. To expect a child
to be governed by moral abstractions, or to appreciate them,
when his advancement in science is still in the nature study
stage, and in arithmetic he is still using apples and pencils
and boards, is silly. And yet in our choice of subject matter
that is just what has happened over and over again in these
departments. The teachings of the fourth gospel, the Beati-
tudes, in fact, much of Pauline theology has been made the
subject matter of Sunday School lessons for children under
twelve years of age. This material embodies the highest moral
and religious ideals of the adults of a highly intellectual people.
It contains much more than many mature minds can grasp;
how then is it possible for children to get anything from it
save misconceptions? Such abstractions and ideals must grow
gradually from knowledge and experience. To be shocked
when a little child tries to bargain with God, — "if God will
give me a pony, I will be a good boy," is simply to show complete misunderstanding of child nature. God, religion, other
people, — are simply for the child's own use and pleasure, at
first. His attitude is the same towards all his world. To put
adult prayers and purposes into a child's life before he can
possibly appreciate or understand them — when his general
life is quite contrary to them — is useless, even dangerous.

On the other hand, why confine a ten-year-old to nothing
but stories when in his fifth grade day-school work he has been
introduced to so much more? And why omit the character
studies, debates, literary criticisms, historical outlines for the
sixteen-year-old when they are so familiar a feature of high-

school study? To fail to go on to the unknown, to stay with the known to the point of nauseating boredom, is no way to teach. In religious and moral matters, as elsewhere, dependence on growth and experience must be the guiding principle in planning a child's education.

Law of suggestion. — Third, the important place occupied by *suggestion* in this field of religious training should not be forgotten. The human personalities surrounding a child are the chief source of the suggestions which to such a large extent influence his habits and mold his ideals. The baby by reflex imitation shares the moods and emotional attitudes of those about him; later, conscious imitation finds its material in the actions and words of his companions. Chums, characters in books, on the stage, in history, in public life offer suggestions of tremendous importance. People do tend to grow like those with whom they constantly associate. The more immature the character, the more this is true. Hence the vital importance of having little children surrounded by people whose moral and religious lives are worthy to be copied, for copied they surely will be, both consciously and unconsciously. Hence the need of having the friends of childhood and adolescence, and the characters, whatever their source, that are held up to admiration those whose habits and ideals are good. So important is this matter of the power of suggestions furnished by characters in the child's environment that some psychologists will go so far as to claim that a child's moral character is set before he enters the schoolroom.

Law of exercise, or frequency. — Part of the law of habit-formation most conspicuously neglected by the organizations that exist for imparting religious instruction to children, is that of frequency. Really to know the formulæ of mathematics, or the facts in history and literature, requires plenty of drilling, the expenditure of many hours a week for many weeks in the year with continual review and use in new ways as the years succeed each other. All this is well understood and provided for in the day school. But apparently in a total of fifty-two,

perhaps of only thirty, hours in a whole year, each such hour
given over to many and varied performances, much of it wasted
by poor administration, our Protestant churches expect children
to get hold of facts historical, literary, and doctrinal, formulæ
of public worship, to say nothing of inspiration towards right
living. And, upon examination of the elaborate courses published
by some of our leading houses or denominations, it is evident
that next to no provision is made for any drill, repetition, or new
use of material once presented. A cycle of four to six years may
go by before a child ever hears a given story a second time. This
is an economic waste of machinery as well as a pedagogic error.

Law of exercise as expressive use. — The danger that theory
becomes divorced from practice is a very real one. As has
already been shown, religion must be defined in terms of conduct. Ethics is not morality, nor is theology religion. A man
may recite a creed or pass examinations in theology, and yet
be irreligious. Too much of our time and energy has been
used in developing the knowing side in religion and ethics,
while the conduct and the emotions have received but secondary attention. It should be clearly understood that in no
sense is it being suggested that conduct should be blind; in
fact, the reverse point of view has been urged. On the other
hand, knowledge which does not function in conduct is futile.
Because instruction in ethics and in religion is so often given
as mere classroom exercises, as a matter of books and memory,
it often happens that such instruction does not influence conduct. Vital instruction in these fields can only be given in
connection with some living situation that calls for a response.
Knowledge of facts is surely necessary in order that judgment
may be exercised, but here as elsewhere, such knowledge means
most when it is the natural answer to a question aroused by life
situations. In this field we may need to seek out, or to create
opportunities for social experiences so as to provide a stimulating environment for the developing child.

Law of effect. — Here, as elsewhere, tendencies to act which
bring pleasant results are likely to recur; conversely, reactions

which bring discomfort are unlikely to be repeated. Whatever conduct, then, is sanctioned as worth while in itself must be made immediately worth while to the children. Their kindly impulses must find reward when expressed; their strivings for the beautiful, especially the beautiful in character, must be given appreciation. Worship must be made a thing of delight to them. If church going, Sunday observance, and the like are associated in their minds only with restrictions and inhibitions they are sure to conceive a dislike for the whole situation. If the teacher in the school of religion has an unpleasing personality the entire set-up he or she represents may be avoided by the pupils.

Law of variability. — Individual differences count quite as much here as in other fields. Children will not all respond alike to instruction and training in religion any more than they will to instruction in history or science, in fact greater differences are likely to show in the former field than in the latter. Moral and religious conduct are both so tremendously complex, involving as they do intellect, emotion, and action, that the chance for variation in response is very great. The difference in the power of suggestion over children of different natures offers another problem. Discussions of big moral problems, sex questions, questions of individual responsibility may for one child be the very thing necessary to set him upon his feet and steady his judgment; for another child in the same class, such discussion offers all sorts of suggestions which may be directly harmful. Hence the need of much individual instruction in religion and morals, and the danger of relying exclusively on classroom instruction.

Among us adults there seem to be four different dominant interests in religion; and, partly according to the general maturity of children, partly due to their different temperaments we see these varied interests in them too. One is in the *intellectual* side. To such people religion is synonymous with the faith, the creed, the precise shade of theological opinion held. Some children will respond always in terms of thought. These are they who ask the questions so difficult to answer. In the main this aspect of religion becomes interesting in the teen age, when abstractions are better understood and when the personal belief and point of view become acute problems. Other people's chief interest is on the *emotional* side. To be religious means, for them, a personal experience of union with the divine. The more ecstatic, the more transcendant the experience the more meaningful, also the more inexpressible it becomes. They are the mystics, found in all religions, in all ages. These people are more suggestible by nature, and rather less intellectual, as far as we can measure these characteristics. They are likely to be introverts. Many young people go through a phase of this, particularly in early or middle adolescence when the emotional life becomes a dynamic center of behavior control.

A third interest, sometimes but not necessarily associated with either of the other two, is represented in the *rites*, the *symbolic ceremonies* of worship. To be religious, for such persons, connotes frequent and painstaking carrying out of ceremonial observances. Quite little children are often sticklers for form and easily adopt standards of ritual. Adolescents often show a phase of ultra-conservatism in adherence to prescribed forms, taking a deep satisfaction in the pageantry of worship. Or their private devotional life assumes an unusual importance. A fourth interest, sometimes a mere emphasis as expression of some of the other three but also capable of complete separation from all of them, is that shown in the *ethical conduct* side. The relationship with fellow men polarizes behavior rather than the believed or felt relationship with deity. This is more likely to be the interest between seven and eleven years old than any of the other three; it is also characteristic of the older adolescent whose emotional life has been polarized around human love, who is of an executive turn of mind, who feels irritated by symbolism, repelled by theological hair splitting.

RESEARCH WORK

Amount of religious teaching. — Taking this country as a whole, figures show that about one child in four is enrolled in some religious school. Of those enrolled not all attend, and few attend 100 per cent of the time. We might estimate that, under Protestant influence one child in five has about twenty hours per year of direct instruction, as many more in worship and other church contact. Those who attend the longer sessions of Jewish religious schools clearly get more than this short time, likewise children attending Catholic parochial schools. In many communities the percentages and hours would be higher, but in the United States at large approximately 25 per cent of the children under twelve are definitely indoctrinated, given specific ideas as to what they should believe, how they should worship, what religious attitudes are desirable, what social conduct has religious sanction.

What of the 75 per cent remaining? Religious ideas they must surely encounter in casual contact with others and in their reading. Attitudes, points of view are being impressed with all degrees of clear formulation. Prejudices are formed just as surely, though the emphasis may be different. Moral standards have been set. In other words, indoctrination has occurred just the same but in hit or miss fashion. A few children there are whose parents, either in revolt against the form their own early teaching took, or bewildered and uncertain what to teach, have endeavored to guard them against any ideas with theological coloring. Too few controlled studies of children's development under those conditions have been undertaken to give any dependable results.

Reliability of investigations. — Statistics, results of investigations dealing with religious knowledge, attitudes, training, and the like are not so meaningful as we could wish for the following reasons: (1) The subjects used are usually a selected group. Thus, questionnaires are given to college students, people obviously selected for intelligence. Diaries and literary compositions of adolescents are analyzed, probably a sampling of temperament to start with. Children and young people within one special religious group are observed and measured in various ways. (2) If a more random selection of subjects in the ordinary school system is made the scope of the inquiry is greatly restricted, even if the law sanctions any inquiry whatever. The state, in endeavoring to safeguard parents' rights to individual liberty in thinking limits the topics and methods of any investigation connected with religion even in countries such as England and Germany where the curriculum provides for religious instruction. We are thus unable at present to disentangle the influences of the particular environment in which children grow up till unbiased, wider inquiries are made including children of different races in fifty or so varieties of religious atmosphere.

Representative findings. — With full recognition of the limitations above, and in spite of them, the following findings are interesting to the student of child psychology.

After analytic study of the ideas presented in the textbooks used, MacLean [1] tested 575 Protestant children of elementary school age on their ideas of God. He found a great similarity between the children's reactions and the textbook teachings, conservative on the whole. Ethical ideas were relatively unimportant. Lack of discrimination and of consistency was the most striking characteristic of their thinking.

Bose [2] tested 2500 subjects between eight and eighteen in church schools on sixty selected concepts commonly met in religious teaching. He found few definitely erroneous ideas but a large number of very vague ones. The teachers made scarcely any better score than the children did. Little growth was evident after fifteen. There was no correlation between score made and either regularity in church school attendance or family worship, a slight correlation with intelligence, somewhat higher correlation with church membership.

Case [3] and others found, even in middle childhood, strong prejudices being formed against children of other "faiths,"

---

[1] MacLean, H., "Idea of God in Protestant religious education," *T. C. Cont. to Ed.*, *410, 1930.

[2] Bose, R. G., "Nature and development of religious concepts in children," *Rel. Ed.*, v. 24, 1928.

[3] Case, *et al.*, Unpublished studies, Teachers College.

coupled with the most grotesque pieces of misinformation of others' beliefs and practices.

Matthew [1] found, among 400 junior high-school pupils accustomed to frequent ritual use of a brief prayer form, only 22½ per cent could write it out correctly.

Kupky,[2] Dehn and others note the prevalence of doubt in the adolescent period. The incidence of these doubts was reported as discrepancies between earlier traditional beliefs and the new vistas opened by science, or their own unanswered prayers, or inconsistent, unethical conduct of people professing to be religious, or their own moral problems, especially those connected with sex, or a worry over social injustice, evil in general, over the mystery of life as a whole. A minority of adolescents questioned recounted nothing that had awakened a feeling of reverence in them; most report situations such as a death in the family, sickness of their own, gazing at the stars, sunsets, mountains, forest scenes, hearing beautiful music, the occasion of their first communion.

Hartshorne and May [3] found no observable difference in the forms of behavior called self-control among children of Catholic, Jewish, or Protestant background. In the tests of willingness to co-operate and be of service those with Catholic background scored less well than the others. The tendency to cheat and deceive bore little or no relationship to enrollment in or attendance at a church school. The same was true for membership in organizations stressing ethical teaching about honesty.

The same investigators found the moral ideas of children to resemble that of their parents roughly two hundred times as much as that of their church school teachers.

Hightower [4] found no correlation between biblical knowledge and conduct.

[1] Matthew, M. T., "A written reproduction test for the Lord's Prayer," *Sch. and Soc.*, *240, 1927.

[2] Kupky, O., *The Religious Development of Adolescents*.

[3] Hartshorne, *et al.*, *Studies in Service and Self Control*.

[4] Hightower, P. R., "Biblical information in relation to character and conduct," *Univ. Iowa St. in Character*, *186, 1930.

Though we hear judges in some children's courts stating that seldom, if ever, do boys and girls come before them who have had any religious training, yet Mursell [1] found, in Ohio reformatories, delinquents scoring higher than non-delinquents on a religious training questionnaire, and about the same in biblical knowledge and religious attitudes tests. Allowing for the influence of intelligence and socio-economic status, he concluded there was no significant relationship between religious training and delinquent or non-delinquent behavior.

Among college students in widely different communities a high correlation was found between the beliefs retained in deity, immortality, the value of prayer, and having been brought up in a religious home. Between present activity in church organizations and home training it was fairly high; between moral judgment, cheating, and home training it was zero. On tests for ethical and liberal points of view the "non-religious" groups scored about the same as the "religious."

From the above, our conclusions are reinforced that younger children express ideas which they have been taught, and are non-critical. The need to organize thinking may precipitate conflict in the adolescent period. The home is more potent than the designated agent of religious education. What religious teaching is given does not affect conduct very greatly; mere knowledge affects it not at all. Antagonistic attitudes are early formed.

CHILD DEVELOPMENT AND RELIGIOUS EDUCATION

Children under six. — This first stage is often called non-religious. True, from three to six years old a child may ask more questions about the causes of things and the nature of God than the most erudite theologian can answer; but this curiosity does not mark, necessarily, the beginning of either a scientist or a devotee. These questions, as also the early fears, personal attachments, and sociability, show us the line of least resistance for the development of a religious consciousness.

[1] Mursell, G. R., Unpublished study.

How amazing to the modern psychologist is the regret of Cotton Mather and others like him that a child under seven did not show much sense of sin nor concern for her soul's salvation! Scarcely less arresting, however, is the spectacle of the pious ten-year-old who anxiously scans a line of conduct before embarking on it to see if it is right and acceptable to God, and who begs to be told of her faults that she may eradicate them. The normal mental activity of the first, the healthy, animalistic unconcern of the second, the morbid introspection of the third case are none of them religious or irreligious, though from each may come a contributing factor to the later religious consciousness. Little children are extremely credulous, accepting undoubtingly much of what is told them. They have a strong sense of the mysterious, too. The wind is felt but not seen, the light is seen but not felt, voices are neither felt nor seen, only heard; so by analogy, it is not a far step to a postulating of a mysterious Being neither felt, heard, nor seen. Stories of nature, myths, and wonder tales should intensify the emotions of awe and mystery, while God may be represented as something rather vague and distant rather than as an indulgent parent. Almost invariably children form an anthropomorphic concept of deity at this stage based on analogies of father and mother; beyond that, they may posit either a watchful presence judicially or beneficently inclined according to the teaching received, or a magic worker, or a confidante to whom they may chatter of the day's doings.

As discussed in the chapter on thinking, qualities are spontaneously attributed to the parents which mankind has posited about deity such as omnipresence, omniscience. Authority and love come from the parents, submissive and accepting love is shown to them. This reciprocal attitude is transferable to that assumed between God and man. We must realize that if a child fears or dislikes his father that attitude may be associated with the term father as applied to God. It should be remembered that the main appeal in instruction should be to the emotional, imaginative, intuitive side rather than to the higher intellectual, presenting dogma which cannot be assimilated and may later have to be rejected. Children in this early stage may have simple habits of private and family worship inculcated, and begin before six to share in social worship with a large group also.

The daily problems of keeping the temper, obeying parents, sharing toys form the obvious approach from the conduct side.

Middle childhood. — The age from six or seven to about ten, covers a period during which we see several important changes taking place in children's thinking and feeling. It is also for most a time of broader social contacts. Their acquirement of reading ability has opened up a world of books, and, in consequence, a new channel through which ideas may come, a new means of satisfying curiosity. Their earlier credulity is modified by the widening range of knowledge and by their far more realistic imagination. By nine they usually develop a keen interest in "real" children in other lands, and so are ready for a more intelligent sympathy and world fellowship. In their construction play the work idea and task idea should have developed. In their play in general they act far more in groups than before, and play games with rules. Competition and rivalry become increasingly dominant after eight, so that questions of cheating and quarreling constantly arise. Fighting, teasing, showing off, truth-telling are frequent social relationship problems. They are more independent of their parents' control, and are shifting their loyalty to some outside source of approval, possibly the teacher and the school group. Their training and instruction must allow for these characteristics.

On the instruction side, the more realistic imagination, curiosity instigating eyes and hands to explore are signals all too frequently ignored in the direction of religious teaching of children from six years old on. During this period they should be approached mainly through action and feeling rather than through ideas and abstractions. It is easy to talk to children in symbolic or abstract terms, but their daily experience is far behind in its degree of abstraction; we should remember that symbols are appreciated only after the things for which they stand have been felt as realities. Meanwhile, children understand conduct in terms of personality; morality for them is concrete and immediate, to be lived rather than discussed. We should work with them on the active and practical rather than on the passively intellectual and theoretical side. Action and feeling can be right before concepts are formulated; in fact, all concepts need this very broad basis of particular instances, even though they are religious ideas.

In imparting religious facts, catechisms and homilies should be replaced by a giving of information through dramatic stories of the duties and virtues expected at this age; any code given must be true for all time, especially in its disciplinary values. It is cruel to teach religious doctrines that cannot be understood, and that may have to be unlearned or rejected later. As the character may be formed largely by suggestion and imitation, the surrounding personalities must still provide the fitting material for the spontaneous expression of the child's highest self. Consistency, as well as correctness of example, is of the highest importance. Children soon see the discrepancy between the teaching and actions of other people, and as this is a gap which needs closing in their own lives, it is well to present the example of "applied ethics" before creeds.

Later childhood. — Since the years ten to twelve are dealt with more fully in another chapter only a few salient characteristics will be mentioned. Emotionally, the feeling of loyalty is becoming more intense, especially in the boys, than any other social feeling. To be part of the gang, share its fortunes good or ill, is the most significant thing in boys' lives. They may have a special chum, as, indeed, girls are more likely to have. Friendship and love, then, are learned in practical ways, with members of the same sex. The reading craze culminates towards the end of this period, and may introduce children to appreciation of historical settings for heroic adventures, so valuable for religious instruction. Advantage should be taken of the power of memorization to present the best of the sacred literature such as can be approximately grasped, and the poetic beauty of which can be partly appreciated. To fail to do this in the years before twelve is to deprive children of what they would otherwise come to look back upon as one of the most valuable means of arousing and sustaining their interest in spiritual things. There is scarcely any limit that need be set to the degree of familiarity with the biography, history, and poetry of sacred writings. In them children have a birthright such as they have not in the stories of the *Odyssey* or *Iliad*. Emotionally and inspirationally the effect of this early, everyday acquaintance with the literature and history of their religion is as noticeable as any other single thing in their environmental influence. The dramatic and imaginative interests may be appealed to in religious ceremonies, the love of competition and rivalry by emphasis on progress. The interest in language so often shown in the use of a secret tongue, in enjoyment of puns, conundrums, epigrams, and the like has not been so widely utilized as it might have been. It may be the foundation of acquaintance with, and appreciation of, the wisdom literature; but the teacher should ascertain that it meets a felt need in individual cases, and is not merely a matter of rote memory. The idea of God is more that of a big Father than that of a big Man as in the preceding stage. Girls are more prone to superstitious beliefs than are boys, apparently.

Their most acute moral problems center around property rights, honesty in word and deed, clean thinking about life processes, and need interpretation and assistance from the religious angle. At the age of twelve, just before the pubertal changes, comes for some a spiritual awakening, a longing to be definitely devoted to a cause deemed ideal, symbolized perhaps by joining some special group. Religious teaching may have fostered this, and prepared the way for its own pubic ceremonies. The form in which this longing will be expressed may vary considerably, then; but the interesting psychological fact is that it is so clearly there in some cases. This readiness for consecration, the simplicity and earnestness of purpose is so lovely a climax to the period of childhood that the student of human nature should be on the watch not to let it pass unrecognized.

Adolescence. — Stanley Hall early directed our attention to the characteristics of this period. Others who have studied the religious side of our nature at this time are Lancaster, James, Leuba, Coe, Starbuck, Kupky, Ames. The psychiatrists report many anomalies of growth, curious fanaticisms, perversions of religious interests that may result if satisfactory adjustments are not made, especially with regard to mastery of others, and to sex love. Psychologists like Bühler, Furfey, Hollingworth, Slattery, Moxcey, Mudge, Richmond depict sympathetically the adolescents' difficulties in the stage of transition from childhood to adulthood.

From the study of their letters and diaries as well as by questionnaire and observation we realize that adolescents are likely to come to personal grips with such questions as these: — What is life all about anyhow? What is my life worth? What am I going to do with my life? Is there a life after this one or does death end it all? What makes things really right and wrong? What is the power that rules this universe? Is it friendly or indifferent? These are religious questions. No matter what stereotyped answers may be given by the doctrinal teaching encountered, many adolescents feel bound to evaluate them personally. Opinions, philosophy, a point of view of their own, these are a felt necessity; and often the feeling side is much stronger than the thinking. Around fifteen or sixteen the emotional side is likely to be more prominent, and about nineteen the intellectual. Expressions of religious doubt become more frequent as adolescents learn to think for themselves. If the early teaching has been narrow, or differs greatly from what they meet in a larger environment the conflict may be severe. Those less well able to analyze, weigh, and judge are impelled either to fling away all the old and turn rebel, or to denounce the new vehemently. Some, less aggressive, crave guidance, and, by a sort of trial and error process, become violent partisans of one form after another of religious faith. Those who are not so bothered by doubts beseech help for character and conduct difficulties, the boys mostly in connection with sexual problems. What is known as the "storm and stress" period is characteristic of many. It may last from months to years and present one or more acute phases. Essentially it is that realization of duality needing unification referred to earlier. Other individuals experience a very gradual, quiet religious awakening, an orderly maturing of the ethical, intellectual, and æsthetic nature while the progress in morals comes about imperceptibly, keeping pace with the felt deeper meanings of the intellectual life till intelligence controls and directs the feelings. A third type are conscious of some definite surrender of personality to the Divine. This phenomenon, known as conversion, lasts in its various stages about one fifth the time that the storm and stress period lasts, so that, psychologically, it is much like a foreshortening or epitome of that experience. Conversions, awakenings spontaneous or special, storm and stress acute stage, or period of carelessness, come at about the same age, fifteen to seventeen for boys, fourteen or so for girls.

Girls mature earlier not only physically but in allied emotional and social modes of adjustment. The looked for "awakening" to a deeper sense of values need not concern itself mainly with philosophical issues. Æsthetic appreciation, scientific curiosity, altruistic impulses may also be centers around which life revolves, so that those not primarily interested in religion may experience an awakening in these other spheres.

Early adolescence — up to the completion of the pubertal changes — is ushered in by a negative phase, when girls feel especially unhappy, lost, misunderstood. Inarticulate from the force of the new complex emotions, they long for help and "some one who really understands." Boys' negative phase is rather later, and causes less unhappiness apparently. Both are moody, broody, apt to daydream extensively. While the romantic theme may be uppermost in these dreams yet life plans enter too, and ideals are formulated. Boys' social life is still centered in the gang.

In *middle adolescence* — approximately fifteen to seventeen — they have a greater realization of the real character values in others, their own parents included, if the family weaning process is progressing satisfactorily. They are more ready to express ideas and share emotional experiences than in early adolescence, and are ready to debate and criticize. Mental growth ceases in this period, if it has not already done so at fourteen. There is ability to grasp and define abstractions, to deal logically with complex judgments, though the heat of enthusiasm may obscure the light of reason on religious issues. Social life is apt to become absorbingly bisexual. Vocational problems take on an ethical significance for many.

In *later adolescence* comes a greater willingness to accept responsibility, a mature view of the individual life work in relation to its social background which is not characteristic of the more self-centered, day-dream-like plan for the future of the fourteen-year-old. It is a time of stabilizing the character, fixing special trends, organizing interests toward a conscious goal. The vocational goal, when clearly conceived, may be shaped by economic needs chiefly, or by the love impulses, or by ideals of social service. With these last religion has much to do. The motivation of action is an ethical problem frequently discussed. There is an increased control by principle rather than by the emotion of the seventeen-year-old. Appeals to altruism and self-sacrifice are far more effective now than they have been earlier. The quiet example of devoted personalities is more permanently inspirational than the most eloquent exhortations, however.

Treatment. — From all this consideration of the adolescent period there come some clear suggestions for the religious education. In a general way it may be said that the needs should be met fully at every point. The process of gradual, even, symmetrical growth should be aimed at rather than violent experiences of any kind. It is better not to bring great pressure to bear from the environment towards definite religious experiences. With some natures these things are possible, with some they are not, whereas development is possible for all; and it is the part of wisdom to provide all things necessary for a normal growth rather than to attempt any surgical reconstruction of an individual. Much emotional excitement will only aggravate the less desirable features.

A sane, healthy home atmosphere will be of the greatest possible help to the adolescent, with wise, sympathetic toleration of any extremes and vagaries. The secretiveness so common to both sexes makes it difficult to be certain, in individual cases, of the best channel through which to offer help. However, the attitude of "common sense" on the part of the adult, of taking the boy's or girl's experiences as only natural, to be expected, as a matter of course — when they occur, not inducing them — will do much to encourage openness with some natures and help counteract the agony of doubt or the morbid introspection. Some others are best helped by a treatment of their case as especially interesting though not dangerous, and not to be classed and massed with other typical cases. Either way, difficulties should be treated seriously rather than minimized, and confidence inspired by wise counsel.

Foolish questioning may be replaced by wiser study, by careful direction of the reading, and by making opportunity for larger social service. At no time is the doctrine of "learning by doing" more important, nor the need of living up to the faith of which one is possessed. Introspection and spiritual vivisection should yield to the impetus from within outward. "Something to love, something to know and something to do" is necessary for the unfolding nature. Personal friendships should be watched over, though discreetly at a distance, and guided and controlled as far as may be courteous and possible. Hero-worship in literature, history, or in current life may be partially directed at least by presenting and dwelling on characters worthy of such devotion. Abstract ideas may also be presented and ideals formulated; though, paradoxically, personality has a new meaning and influence. Broader studies should be gradually introduced in history, literature, and ethics.

Religious history will give greater content to the individual experience. Sacred literature should be taught for its beauty and inspirational value rather than for its dogma; but in later adolescence doctrinal studies and the study of church history or of comparative religions will prove fruitful. Instruction in dogma and doctrine will be in place earlier with girls than with boys, and with some natures than with others. When doubts come, adolescents should be taught to be very patient and tolerant with them, and on no account to let them interfere with their morality. They must regard doubt not as extinction of belief, but as reconstruction with exclusions, a phenomenon of change of concepts. Historical and critical study of sacred writings will be a help here, followed by philosophy and ethics.

The organizing impulse must be met successfully, and social companionship provided with some physical activity as its immediate end. For both girls and boys, sex instruction is absolutely imperative; purity and consistency of life should be linked forever with their religious experience. Religion should pick up all tendencies which are organizing in a new way and give to them its own specific, deeper meaning.

Religious experience cannot be standardized. Differences in temperament must be recognized and met by a wide diversity in the program of education. Intellectual, emotional, and social service activities must all be available, with increasing opportunities for the third of these as the later years bring the ideal of losing self to find the worthiest, integrated self-expression.

PRACTICAL EXERCISES

1. Examine three or four different hymn books in use in your community. How do they provide for the interests, the reverent feelings of groups of children and young people?
2. If possible, use the Chassell questionnaire (*Religious Education*, Feb., 1922) with a group of children eleven to thirteen years old. Prepare a set of answers first you would consider "right." Tabulate and score the children's answers as agreed. What religious concepts do you find?

3. Similarly, with groups thirteen to sixteen or older, use the Whitley Biblical Knowledge tests [1] or the Laycock Test of Biblical Information.[2] Check the scores against teachers' character ratings, and against attendance at church school. What does it show?

4. Find out what opportunities the various churches in your community offer for adolescents in (a) social and service activities, (b) instruction likely to lead to better understanding of others' points of view.

5. For your selected child — what, if any, religious instruction does he receive? What is the family influence on religious thinking?

FOR DISCUSSION

1. Do we tend to love more those who serve us or those for whom we render service? What does this suggest for awakening love in children for each other?

2. How are typical church schools handicapped in the field of character building?

3. What national religious values are emphasized in the celebration of special seasons such as Mother's Day, Decoration Day, Thanksgiving, etc.?

4. Did you ever invent a god, an idol, or a ritual of your own? If so, at what age? Have you known of this in other children?

5. Comparing several religions, what instances can you give of the sex instinct being controlled or sublimated by religious emotion, or of religious rites and practices degenerating into sexual orgies? What possibilities does this suggest for the training of adolescents?

6. At what ages, if any, have you felt in yourself or seen in others impulses to improvise sacrifices, to institute some form of blood covenant, to use self-torture, to indulge in a dreamy mysticism, to start out to reform the world, to overestimate the use of symbols, to organize a philanthropic cult or society?

7. What was wrong with training that led children to consider Sunday as a day when they could not do anything they liked?

8. Recall your own adolescent religious experiences. How did they differ from those of later childhood? From your interests today?

9. For what ages would you consider the following suitable, from the psychological point of view: Why?

Lives of heroes, adventure standpoint.

Fables, parables.

Inspirational biographies.

[1] Old Testament Series A. New Testament, Forms A and B. Teachers Coll. Bu. of Publ., N. Y.

[2] Univ. of Alberta Bookstore, Edmonton, Alberta.

Myths and wonder tales.

Literary study of single books of the Bible.

History in story form.

History from Exodus to 4 A.D. in ten lesson periods.

Memorizing proverbs, liturgical forms.

Doctrinal teaching of the parents' religion.

10. Should week-day sessions of religious schools include time for play? Why or why not?

11. Are the young people — fifteen to eighteen — of your acquaintance more interested in religious doctrines or in the application of religion to problems of living?

12. Of what ages, roughly, are these statements [1] true?

    (a) "There is a keen intellectual appetite for facts. The child wants to know of every story 'Is it true?' . . . At this age the choicest literature can be memorized even though the meaning be only partially understood, . . . there is reasoning but not abstract, . . . concrete examples alone appeal. . . . Habits of conduct are rapidly formed, the proper motive for which may not be deeply felt. . . . The capacity for unselfishness is . . . as yet only budding."

    (b) "This age is characterized by a feeling of personal honor, by a keen sense of justice manifesting itself rather more in insistence upon one's own rights than in regard for duties to others, by a strong love for the heroic and desire to emulate it, by a longing for larger activities . . . especially by the growth of a sense of relationship to other persons. . . . Through other lives . . . the child may . . . be led to find God in his or her own life."

    (c) "Surplus energy is the most prominent feature . . . there is only a small amount of knowledge . . . undeveloped thought power and little power of attention. . . . This is the age in which the child is gathering knowledge not by study or thought but through the senses. . . . Its training in ethical and religious knowledge must be quite largely by concrete illustrations. . . . His desires are largely selfish, the teacher should therefore . . . appeal primarily to the feelings . . . so that the child is led to want to do right.

13. Suggest activities in which young people could engage that might remedy narrow attitudes.

14. An eight-year-old girl, who had been taught that God was everywhere, within us as well, suggested writing a letter to God and eating it so that the part of God who was in her could read it.

    "He is some kind of spirit, not a man like my dad."

[1] Taken from the Bible Study Union Series of teachers' manuals.

"We have a picture of God at home."

"Sometimes when God is in a box they carry him through the streets."

"God is like a bush on fire."

What do the above illustrate as to the mechanisms of children's thinking?

15. Comment on the following: (1) Children's religious nature will develop only if the environment does not prevent it. (2) Unless a child is disposed to it from the beginning, religious influences alone will not make a child religious. (3) Pubertal changes usually precede religious and æsthetic awakenings. (4) Religious growth is, in general, promoted by a rich development of human love. (5) Indirect suggestions are usually more potent in shaping adolescents' conduct than direct commands. (6) Early adolescence resembles childhood in being relatively uninterested in the intellectual doctrines of religion. (7) In cases where religious feeling is not aroused in early or middle adolescence some other strong interest usually takes its place.

16. A fourteen-year-old girl came hysterically to her biology teacher. "Those aren't cells you see under the microscope. My (religious teacher) told me God made us out of dust. You're all wrong anyhow, I shan't believe it." What would you say if you were the biology teacher?

SELECTED REFERENCES

BAIN, R. "Religious attitudes of college students." *Am. Jo. Soc.*, v. 32, 1927.

FAHS, S. L. "The beginnings of religion in baby behavior." *Rel. Ed.*, v. 25, 1930.

FOREST, ILSE. *Child Life and Religion.*

FOX, H. W. *The Child's Approach to Religion.*

GRIGG SMITH. *The Child's Knowledge of God.*

KUPKY, D. *The Religious Development of Adolescents.*

PRATT, J. B. *The Religious Consciousness.*

SHUTTLEWORTH, F. K. "The influence of early religious training on college sophomore men." *Rel. Ed.*, v. 22, 1927.

STREIBERT, M. A. *Youth and the Bible.*

STURGES, H. A. "What college students think of Sunday school." *Rel. Ed.*, v. 22, 1927.

WATSON, G. B. *Experimentation and Measurement in Religious Education.*

WILSON, D. F. *Child Psychology and Religious Education.*

CHAPTER XVII

EXCEPTIONAL CHILDREN

BOUNDARIES OF ORDINARY AND EXCEPTIONAL

We cannot classify children, any more than we can adults, into discrete groups consisting of ordinary and exceptional. Whatever quality we consider, whatever group of abilities we measure, we find that pupils are distributed along a continuous scale the whole range of which we are perhaps unable to discover. Distribution does not occur evenly along this scale, however, but most ratings of ability cluster around a mediocre point, while the further we look in either direction the fewer ratings are found. Thus, in measurements of the height of a group of adult women of the same race we should find most of them around 5 ft. 3 to 4 inches, fewer between 5 ft. and 5 ft. 3, or 5 ft. 4 and 5 ft. 7, fewer still between these points and 4 ft. 8 on the one hand and 5 ft. 9 on the other, fewest of all beyond these last points. Yet where is the line to be drawn between ordinary and exceptional? And just as we find all degrees of stature rather than distinct groups differing from each other by an inch, so we find all degrees of variability in any trait we examine, blindness, nervousness, morality, or general intelligence, and we must keep in mind that to be "exceptional" is a matter of fine shadings of differences. Just, however, as the dwarf or the giant or the idiot or the genius claim our attention because they are so obviously towards the vanishing point of the possible range of abilities, so it becomes a relatively easy task to describe such extreme variations from mediocrity.

There cannot be a hard and fast line between intellectual and physical scales of measuring. Such are artificial divisions of a unitary being. Relief of physical disorder may facilitate intellectual development. Training along volitional and emotional lines may relieve nervous disorders just as undue pressure may induce them. However, for convenience sake we may think of deviations from the normal on the minus and on the plus side in different planes. We have the diseased, anæmic, blind, deaf, and what not, shading up to the healthy, thoroughly sound, superenergetic among us. We have the idiots, dull and so on, shading up through normal to the bright and the geniuses that exist. It is noteworthy that as so many more causes are likely to bring people down in the scale than to send them up, so our attention has been centered more on those that deviate in a minus direction from the norm, and even our nomenclature is fuller here than in the upper end of the range.

EXCEPTIONAL PHYSICAL CONDITIONS

Cases of physical divergence from the norm on the minus side will include abnormalities in growth, nervous disorders of various kinds, sense defects, conditions due to disease or injury. Some are discussed in another chapter; one, such as cretinism is described in connection with feeble-mindedness.

The deaf. — Children who are totally deaf are fortunately rare, comprising about .05 per cent of the population. Deafness may be *caused* by defective structure of the ear, defects in the nervous system, by injuries, hemorrhages, accidents, infections which affect the hearing mechanisms. Approximately 40 per cent of the cases are congenitally deaf; over 30 per cent become so following scarlet fever, cerebral meningitis, and other diseases. The earlier children become deaf the harder it is for them to learn. The task of acquiring speech, of understanding language is prodigious. Congenitally deaf children never develop a normal speaking voice however intensive and painstaking their training. The simple vocabulary habits picked up before four years old by ordinary children must be tediously built in through the few daily hours of school experience, beginning perhaps at five years old. This four-year retardation in language is never made up; in eventual understanding and usage of language they remain greatly deficient.

Physically, they exhibit a muscular tension in strong contrast to the limpness of the blind child. The alert, strained attention necessary during their school hours seems to fatigue them readily. A shuffling gait is characteristic of some. Emotionally they tend to be introvert. Mentally they compare unfavorably with children of normal hearing whatever sort of mental tests are employed, though in motor ability they differ very slightly from hearing children.

Educationally, socially, and vocationally the difficulties of deaf pupils are colossal. Residential schools have been greatly favored in the past. Recent opinion stresses the value of training deaf children in day schools rather than keep their total social environment so different, most of the time, from that to which they must learn to adjust. Special schools or classes are necessary in any case for the unique methods of instruction needed, and for the long, hard task of learning language. Oral methods, both of lip reading and talking, are insisted on for all by some authorities; manual methods are permitted by others, chiefly for those pupils who do not succeed by the oral method. Probably a mixture of the two would be advisable for the wider possibilities of social adjustment. Each word has to be learned as a thing-in-itself. It is not apprehended rich with relationships and connotations from varied usage hundreds of times a week as it is for the rest of us. Consequently, progress in academic subjects, information from books, anything usually mediated through speech, is exceedingly slow. Except for those proved superior mentally it would seem well not to attempt much in formal subject matter such as history and mathematics, but to concentrate their energies on acquiring such knowledge as is immediately helpful in social adjustment. Adequate industrial training must be given, and such education as will make for safe and happy leisure.

The blind. — Though the actual number of blind people in our total population is small, far less than 1 per cent, their evidently needy condition has always excited sympathy. Analysis of the 1920 census report of the United States shows that about one eighth of all who are blind are under twenty years old, and 8 per cent are under fourteen; therefore they present a school problem.

Over 16 per cent of all blindness is *caused* by accidents, and almost as much following various diseases such as measles. But over 54 per cent of all cases is due to diseases of the eyes themselves. Of these, glaucoma is conspicuously frequent, and, among certain classes, especially the foreign born, trachoma. Over one third of all blind people lose their vision in childhood or youth; and of all blindness occurring under twenty years old two thirds is congenital. Blindness from birth may be hereditary; but it is more than likely to be due to infection during birth. The preventive measure of treating newborn infants' eyes with silver nitrate has noticeably reduced the numbers of the congenitally blind.

Physically, blind children tend to be undervitalized, anæmic. This is easily the consequence of the sedentary habits which are so characteristic. Vision is so necessary for orientation and for guiding movements that without it muscular actions are halting, much restricted, badly co-ordinated. Blind babies do not walk till long after the normal age and then only with every evidence of timidity. Later it is rare to find an erect carriage. They slouch, remain limp and relaxed muscularly except during the prolonged strain of reading with the finger tips in the Braille system. Lacking the many pleasant stimuli that fill the sighted child's hours they resort to other means of satisfaction; nervous, wandering movements of the hands are common, rhythmic swaying of the whole body, or twisting and rocking the head. Masturbation is a very easily formed habit.

Emotionally they reflect the treatment they receive. The family tend to do things for them which, with care, they might learn to do for themselves, and, in so doing, fasten dependent attitudes on them socially as well as physically. They come to expect help and attention instantly, have difficulty in adjusting to the needs of others, develop a complacency that may hinder a balanced social attitude.

Mentally they do not, as has been erroneously supposed, compensate by any greater keenness of other sense organs. Their acuity of hearing, smell, and so on, proves no greater than that of sighted people. They do, however, learn to attend to fine differences in other sense stimuli which we ignore, and interpret these in meaningful ways. Their training develops much skill in touch discrimination. For information subjects, for computation, auditory memory is relied on intensively. From such few comparisons as are available on the basis of intelligence tests it would seem that dullness to feeble-mindedness is from two to three times as frequent among the blind and partially blind as among normal children, and superiority about half as frequent. At every age, no matter what tests are used, children handicapped thus are inferior in intelligence to normal children.

Treatment. — Blind children need to be stimulated and encouraged to move about. For their general health, physical activity other than with the arms must be motivated. Such things as rhythmic drill, dancing, guided running, even basket ball can be modes of enjoyment as well as means to promote physical well-being. Self-reliance must be fostered, ambitions wakened, and the ideal held up not only of independence but of contribution to the welfare and happiness of others. The tendency of the older ones to be introspective, satisfied with words rather than realities, must be prevented by as varied and rich a contact with reality as possible. Some stereotyped devices, such as relief maps, give ideas, after all, of symbols for reality rather than reality itself. Their vocational training offers a difficult problem. Only too many drift, even yet, as they do in such large numbers in the Orient, into prostitution and begging for their means of subsistence. The manipulative skills they can develop fare poorly in this machine age. Only the musically gifted — and they are no more frequent among the blind than among the rest of us — can do such work as piano tuning. Few would be engaged as organists or teachers of music in preference to sighted applicants for the position. Yet handicrafts must be the main reliance of most of them. Methods of education for normal sex adjustment are difficult to work out, too. Provision must also be wisely made for their recreation and hours of leisure.

Fatigue. — Chronic fatigue means a reduction in ability to do mental or physical work. Pallor, dark circles under the eyes, complaints of dizziness, insomnia, and loss of appetite are warning symptoms that, taken together, may indicate fatigue. Poor posture, badly co-ordinated muscular action especially of the face, are other suspicious signs. Fatigue may be congenital. Chronically tired parents, women worn out with factory labor and much childbearing tend to produce children handicapped from birth by lack of stamina. Subefficiency, with no discoverable disease, has been found in related members in different generations. Defective hearing and eyesight causing constant strain upon the attention bring on nervous irritability conducive to fatigue. Malnutrition may coexist; but fatigue is possible without any trace of malnutrition. Pubescent strain, convalescence, overwork may all be factors, but the outstanding cause is an unhygienic way of living. Investigation into home life and the daily routine reveals hurried eating, scanty sleep, lack of exercise, little relaxation, too long home study, continual over-stimulation, poor emotional atmosphere. Until these conditions are corrected the symptoms do not disappear. Crowded living quarters affect poor and moderately well-to-do families alike. Noise, hurry, pressure to keep up are very general accompaniments of city life. Remedial measures must reconstruct the fundamental habits if fatigue is to be overcome.

Epilepsy. — *Kinds and cause.* — Epilepsy is known in four forms — grand mal, petit mal, Jacksonian, and psychic epilepsy. The first is marked by fits of unconsciousness lasting from five to twenty minutes, preceded in some cases by premonitory signals; the second by unconsciousness lasting only a few moments, so that its existence may pass unnoticed. Jacksonian epilepsy is distinguished by localized rather than general convulsions and by no unconsciousness; the psychic form involves abnormal behavior, emotional outbursts rather than rigidity of muscles, and violent spasms, but is like the first form in that the child does not remember afterwards what he did.

The immediate *cause* of epilepsy is not well understood. A morbid condition of the brain tissues is generally present, sometimes grave lesions. Toxic substances produce the Jacksonian form, which may be relieved by their removal. By far the greater number of cases occur in poor heredity in which alcoholism, syphilis, or insanity is present. It may be coincident with genius or with feeble-mindedness, with health otherwise good, or with insanity. Frequent and severe attacks bring about mental deterioration. Over one quarter of cases appear before ten years of age, over three quarters before twenty years old.

Diagnosis and treatment. — The detection of epilepsy in the first and third forms described is easy even for the layman, not always so with the fourth, scarcely ever with the second. In consequence of the difficulty in these forms, much injustice may have been done to sufferers from this disease. True epilepsy is practically incurable. Children subject to it should be taught in special classes, both for their own sakes and to avoid upsetting other children.

The *emotional* life of epileptics is unstable. Most are melancholic, lazy, markedly egocentric, also irritable, unreliable, and insincere, often sentimentally interested in religion. Their sexual feelings are too easily aroused. Before a seizure there is frequently an increased emotionality, occasionally hallucinations. A quiet, regular life, free from excitement, with plenty of occupation, is what is chiefly needed. Any habits that might increase the general instability, such as the use of alcohol, should be avoided. Sometimes a treatment with bromides is ordered, or, in special cases of the Jacksonian form, surgical measures will afford relief. Epileptics should not marry.

Chorea. — Chorea, or St. Vitus's dance, as it is popularly called, is a disease commonest between the ages of eight and fifteen, especially prevalent in the spring months, and from two to three times as frequent in girls as in boys. About 1 per cent of children suffer from it. It is characterized by intensive, uncontrollable jerks and twitches of the face, head, limbs, or sometimes all of them, in severe cases by interference with speech and swallowing. The mental characteristics are capriciousness, instability, poor sleep, perhaps with nightmare. It may come on so gradually as not to be noticed in the early stages; it lasts from six to twelve weeks and may then entirely cease. In most cases there is a history of rheumatism as well as nervous instability, and a majority have heart symptoms also. As the onset is so gradual, it is often not properly diagnosed nor treated early enough. The children are considered clumsy, peevish, awkward, and are perhaps scolded. At a later stage there is little difficulty in recognizing what is the trouble. Choreic children should be immediately removed from school — partly to prevent psychic contagion — and put to bed for absolute rest away from relatives and friends till all symptoms have subsided and there is no danger of a recurrent attack.

Tics. — Habit spasms, or tics, are sometimes mistaken for chorea, but consist of violent contractions of an isolated muscle, or group of muscles, rather than the irregularly distributed, non-predictable jerks of chorea. They represent a functional disorder and are often associated with reflex irritation, anæmia, obsessions, and other emotional complexes. Great effort to control them may result in a temporary cessation, but the spasm may reappear in some other location. Sympathetic help in self-control is needed rather than severe attempts at repression.

Speech disturbances. — From 2 to 3 per cent of the school population exhibits some speech disorder, chiefly lisping and stammering. *Lisping* is generally explainable as failure to outgrow the infantile emotional stage of social behavior. In other cases, slovenly enunciation may be due to hearing bad examples of speech, or to carelessness and sheer lazy habits themselves motivated by young adolescents' desires to be like the crowd. Sometimes a defect of teeth, palate, harelip or tongue-tie is responsible. A few lisp from a general neurotic condition. The particular cause must be ascertained before effective remedial procedure can be undertaken.

Stuttering is less common, but more disadvantageous. About twice as many boys as girls have some form of this defect. "Nervousness" is generally associated with stuttering and may be both its cause and the result of emotional conflict produced by social maladjustment. The well-known characteristics of stuttering are muscular inhibitions of breath control, of the larynx, lips, tongue, often a widely diffused bodily tension. A large number of theories have been propounded as to the cause of stuttering ranging from the purely physical through mental, such as the absence of verbal images, to purely psychic such as an anxiety hysteria. The treatment advocated varies, in consequence, from surgical operations, retraining the attention, to psychoanalysis. The best results come from treating the nervous instability as primary cause. If this condition can be remedied then the "nervousness" and the stuttering both improve.

Neurasthenia. — About 5 per cent of children of school age are neurotic, meaning by that that they are sufficiently far down the scale of nervous stability to make them susceptible to emotional complexes which will interfere with good adjustment to the outside world. We may notice eccentricity, oversensitivity or sometimes its opposite extreme listlessness and indifference to the opinion of others, timidity amounting to fear, oppressive terrors, ready fatigability from any exertion, absorption in imaginary situations, rare joining in with other children's occupations, difficulty in reaching decisions. This inner sense of uncertainty, this lack of self-assurance shows outwardly not only in timidity, refusal to face facts, especially disagreeable ones, squarely, but in an apparently opposite characteristic — that of extravagant, aggressive, egotistic self-assertion. Adler explains this predominant characteristic as a compensation for the concealed inner state.

Diagnosis. — The tendency to neurasthenia is markedly hereditary, aggravated by unhygienic ways of living such as short sleeping hours, the use of stimulants, much social dissipation, and by unwise training such as narrow repressions, over-development of religious scruples, lack of sound sex education. The teacher may well watch for symptoms such as those noted above, and for others including inability to sit still or to keep the hands still when outstretched, extremes of emotionalism, sex perversions, morbidity, excessive daydreaming, attacks of dizziness, malnutrition.

Treatment. — The treatment must be along the following lines: (1) removal of any irritant causes, such as adenoids, bad teeth; (2) replacing unhygienic living habits by much quiet rest, overfeeding, and outdoor life; (3) habituation to courageous acts, prevention of imaginary fears by quiet reassurance, and a reasoned, sympathetic investigation; (4) habituation to brave moral acts, particularly in facing painful consequences of conduct, accepting failure or blame at face value, deciding about problems rather than evading the issue, and facing difficulties promptly. This may save them from the disturbing influence of repressed emotional complexes; (5) provision of opportunities for social interchange with other children, especially in free play and in all sorts of games. This engenders self-confidence, teaches many moral lessons of cause and effect, gives an outlet for the overwrought imagination, and lessens the chance for an unwholesome withdrawal into self; (6) establishment of impartial adult control, neither vacillating nor strict, which shall train to self-control and steadfastness, which redirects sympathetically rather than endeavors to repress, which encourages a frank relation between the child and the adult so that grief, sex trouble, humiliations, disappointments, and so forth may be confided instead of dwelt upon morbidly, ventilated, so to speak, rather than being left to generate an unhealthy atmosphere; (7) the supply of useful activity, work that shall be interesting and adapted to the child's ability, which will occupy his attention and favor further normal development.

SUBNORMAL MENTALITY

General description. — Cases of divergence from the norm in intelligence will include the dull, the backward, the aments on the one hand, and bright, precocious children on the other. On the minus side the degrees of intelligence grade down through the backward, the moron, the imbecile, to the idiot. Backward children are those whose mental growth is retarded from some environmental condition, such as a disease. Improvement up to normal may be expected if the adverse condition can be removed and special measures taken. Morons are the highest division of the class known as feeble-minded, or, more properly aments, and are defined as those capable of earning a living under favorable circumstances, but incapable, from mental defect existing from birth, or from an early age (a) of competing on equal terms with normal people, or (b) of managing themselves and their affairs with ordinary prudence. Imbeciles are defined as those who by reason of mental defect existing from birth, or from an early age, are incapable of earning their own living, but are capable of guarding themselves against common physical dangers. Idiots are the lowest in the scale and are defined as those so deeply defective in mind from birth, or from an early age, that they are unable to guard themselves against common physical dangers. Each step of the scale may be further divided into high, middle, and low grade, so that we may speak of a high-grade moron, middle-grade, or low-grade moron, similarly for the imbecile and the idiot.

The above definitions have been in use since 1908, when they were used by the Royal Commission on the Care and Control of the Feeble-minded on the recommendation of the Royal College of Physicians, London. Some confusion has existed, nevertheless, in regard to the use of these terms. In America the designation "feeble-minded" has been popularly applied to cover all three steps of the scale rather than to only the highest step, as in England. There "mental defective" signifies any of the three steps. Norsworthy in 1906, following

Ireland, has used "idiot" in the same generic sense. The student will do well to standardize his nomenclature, using amentia as a preferred generic term for the condition found in the various stages of idiot, imbecile, or moron. Amentia means "a state of mental defect from birth, or from an early age, due to incomplete cerebral development, in consequence of which the person affected is unable to perform his duties as a member of society in the position of life to which he is born." [1] The condition must be distinguished from dementia and from insanity. While in amentia the brain tissues have not developed properly, uniformly, to the normal degree, in dementia they are degenerating, and in insanity they function in perverted manner. (Compare a piece of machinery with some parts missing, some parts worn out, some parts geared wrong.)

Besides these grades of mental deficiency certain clinical types exist, amounting perhaps, taken all together, to about 15 per cent of all cases of amentia. Such are the microcephalic, the mongolian, the hydrocephalic, and the cretin.

Physical characteristics. — The characteristics of aments in general may be considered from the physical and mental standpoints. Physically there is among them a greater prevalence of "stigmata of degeneration" than among children higher in the scale of intelligence; that is, they show more anomalies per individual than do their more favored companions. This does not mean that any are necessarily present, nor that their possession indicates amentia. These stigmata include defects of the palate, delayed and bad dentition, badly shaped ears, nose, lips, a peculiar tongue with considerable slavering; a malformed skull, anomalies of the genital organs, certain skin secretions, poor circulation, stunted growth. Of the special types, the microcephalic has a specially small, "sugar-loaf" head and generally small stature. The hydrocephalic has usually a much enlarged skull. The mongolian is small, has a small skull, flattened face with slanting eyes — hence the name — a large, fissured tongue, broad, clumsy feet and hands

[1] Tredgold, *Mental Deficiency*, p. 2.

with generally a small, incurved little finger. The cretin is greatly dwarfed, with short, bow legs, badly formed extremities, a protuberant belly, a short, thick neck, large head, eyes wide apart, a flat nose, large, coarse tongue, swollen eyelids, coarse hair, dry, rough skin. The peculiar appearance of these special types should not make us forget that from 80 per cent to 90 per cent of all cases of amentia belong to no special type, and may have no distinguishing physical signs. Paralysis may complicate the condition, affecting the growth of the limbs on one side; epilepsy is another frequent concomitant.

Mental characteristics. — The mental ability of aments may be affected by special sense defects; even if not, their sense discrimination is usually weak. On the expressive side, we may notice poor motor co-ordination, poor control of bladder and bowels, delayed walking, instability of emotions contrasting with almost no excitability, possibly some degenerate habits arising from perverted instincts such as masturbation, eating filth. Talking is frequently delayed, and a speech defect is common, known as "lalling"; this involves difficulty in enunciating certain consonants, particularly th, r, y, s, g, ng, sh, k, v, l. Considering the higher mental processes they are sluggish in their thinking, are unduly suggestible, have a poor memory span, have little creative imagination. They form habits, or learn, very slowly. Their reasoning is almost non-existent, since they are scarcely able to analyze or to generalize. They have scant power of attention. Of these characteristics, the last few named are the most significant for the teacher to remember. Naturally these abilities are present, or rather absent, in varying degrees, as we descend the steps of the scale.

Causes. — Amentia results, in about 90 per cent of all cases, from hereditary influences. Of these, by far the largest factor is some disease of the nervous system; other less important factors are alcoholism and syphilis. The other 10 per cent of cases result from environmental influences, such as some disease, or alcoholism of the mother during pregnancy, injuries received to the head before, during or after birth, certain toxic poisons resulting from infectious diseases, defective gland action affecting nutrition. More specifically, the great majority of cases of simple amentia of whatever degree are due to neuro-pathic taint, as is also microcephaly, while the mongolian type is due possibly to syphilis, possibly to malfunctioning of the pituitary gland. These may be called primary amentia. Of secondary amentia, due to extrinsic conditions, paralysis may be produced by lesions due to hemorrhage, cysts, and tumors pressing on the brain. General amentia, hydrocephaly, or paralysis may result from poisons following diseases such as diphtheria, syphilis, or encephalitis. Cretinism is due to a lack of the secretions of the thyroid gland. Other conditions, such as rickets, tuberculosis, deprivation of the senses, may complicate amentia, but it is doubtful if they can cause it. Among other doubtful causes are tuberculosis of the parents, great discrepancy in the age of the parents or advanced age, con-sanguinity, though these are often mentioned as possible causes.

Diagnosis. — The diagnosis of backwardness or feeble-mindedness is a matter for the joint action of the teacher, the social worker, the physician, and the psychologist. With the discovery of the lowest degrees of amentia, and with the special types, the teacher has commonly nothing to do. They are the concern chiefly of the doctor and of the institution to which they are sent. It is with the retarded and dull pupils, the "borderline cases," the high- and middle-grade morons that the teacher will come in contact. General intelligence tests, given to whole classes simultaneously, serve as a preliminary sieve to separate the exceptional children from the rest. Such group tests are now available for every age level from the kinder-garten up to college. Some require knowledge of reading and writing; others, the non-verbal, use pictures which children mark in various ways, or even ask for drawings. All kinder-garten and first-grade level tests are non-verbal. A few tests, known as non-language, are given by pantomime and demon-stration, and are therefore particularly suited to foreign-speaking children.

From this preliminary sorting, the children who make low scores, and any doubtful cases, should be further examined individually. Where there is no one to administer group tests it is the teacher's business to watch for and report children two years or more older than the normal age for the grade in which they are working, and to send them to the proper expert for examination. The social worker might likewise discover cases of children several years behind their fellows in ability, but her chief work is to investigate for environmental conditions which may help the physician in his diagnosis or the psychologist in his prescription of treatment. It is the physician's business to make a thorough physical examination of the selected cases, and to get the family — heredity — history and the personal history of injuries, diseases, dates of development, and so forth, to date. The psychologist's business is to examine the school record of the selected cases to date, and to make a mental examination. Upon the combined results of all these investigations the diagnosis depends, but the final word should be left to the clinical psychologist, the problem lying mainly in the field of psychology.

The best known scale of intelligence tests is that devised by Binet, published in 1905, revised by Goddard in 1908, by Binet in 1911, by Terman in 1916. In this the various tests are arranged by age groups, each group representing what 75 per cent of normal children can do at that age. Thus, the VIII group consists of six tests which three fourths of normal eight-year-old children can pass. The groups range in difficulty from what a three-year-old can do through a fourteen-year-old level to "average adult" and "superior adult." Each test in each age group is credited with so many points in months. In applying this series, a child of eight who was so scored that his points added up to the equivalent of VIII, would be rated "at age." His mental age (M.A.), a concept we owe to Binet, would be eight.

The relationship of M.A. to chronological age, C.A., is found, as suggested by Stern. Terman, in standardizing the Binet scale for American children adopted this ratio for common use. Dividing the M.A. by the C.A. gives the intelligence quotient, or I.Q. as it is commonly called. The eight-year-old child testing at age has an I.Q. of 100. A child of eight so scored that his points added to VI is below age. He is M.A. 6 and his I.Q. $(6 \div 8)$ is 75. About one third of our population have I.Q.'s from 95 to 105. Children whose I.Q. ranges from 90 to 110 are considered normal. In the I.Q. range from 80 to 90 children are diagnosed as backward, or dull normal: in the range from 70 to 80 they are called dull, or borderline cases. Nine per cent, roughly, lie between 70 and 85 I.Q. and these constitute the problems of our special classes. About 1 per cent of the population have I.Q.'s of less than 70. The I.Q. of morons lies from 50 to 70, of imbeciles from 20 or 25 to 50, of idiots below 20. We may also speak of morons having a mental age of from about six to eight and one half or nine. Imbeciles have M.A. from three to nearly six, and idiots below three years.

The Herring revision of the Binet-Simon tests, published in 1922, provides a convenient form similar to the Terman revision, specially useful for retesting children after a brief interval provided they are not much below 90 I.Q.[1] Both, however, necessitate reading and lay great emphasis on the knowledge of the meanings of words, which penalizes illiterates and foreign-speaking children unduly. For them, and for deaf children, tests of the non-verbal, better still non-language, variety should be used. In them, children are required to do things rather than to talk. The Pintner-Paterson Performance Scale, published in 1917, and the Drever-Collins series published in 1928, as well as others, have been prepared with the needs of handicapped, especially deaf, children, in mind. They may be used with very young children, as well as with those of low mental age.

Treatment. — The treatment of subnormal children depends partly on whether they belong to any special type, partly on the degree of amentia found or the lowness of the I.Q. Good hygienic conditions may check tendencies to disease due to

[1] The Herring revision is less valid for extreme deviates.

poor circulation and weak digestion. Cretins, if taken very young, can be considerably improved by doses of extract of the thyroid gland systematically and permanently administered. A complication of epilepsy or paralysis obviously indicates specific treatment. For some, tumors may be removed, or other surgical measures employed. Of these, a social safeguard rather than a personal remedy is that of asexualization. This is advisable from the eugenics point of view, since aments have less control of their instincts than normal people, are prolific, and are almost certain to produce offspring with their own deficiency. Considering aments especially, idiots require constant physical care; they are scarcely improvable in any way but may sometimes be trained to cleanly habits. Imbeciles can acquire habits of care of the body, and can learn to do simple industrial work under permanent, close supervision. Morons can benefit by manual training and by intellectual as well; but we must remember that they can never be raised by training to the level of normal mentality which has been denied them by heredity. It is useless to try to teach them along with normal children; the pace at which they learn, the methods necessary, and the selected subject matter advisable make it imperative that they should be separated from the regular school classes and taught by themselves. The dull will never catch up to the brighter children, and whether taught in special or in regular classes may be expected to be permanently "retarded" and to drop out of school at about the grade designed for the mental age of twelve. For those of I.Q. 70 to 90, a pedagogical and psychological examination usually reveals special inaptitudes which will indicate methods of training. In general their small ability to think abstractly or to use creative imagination necessitates a somewhat different curriculum from that of the ordinary school, as well as a slower rate of progress. Omission of abstract arithmetic and grammar, emphasis on concrete facts, sense-training, and industrial work seem to be indicated. Wholesome amusements should be provided as well as opportunity to learn a trade. Suggestion and imitation should be the chief methods employed, with simple, prompt rewards for efforts and for work carefully done. After leaving school such children need sympathetic social supervision.

Retarded development. — From 30 to 35 per cent of school children are retarded one or more years, more boys than girls. The fact of being retarded, that is, being over age for the grade where found, might be due to extraneous causes such as foreign parentage, to having entered school late, to truancy, to much moving about from one school district to another, to periods of illness, or it might be due to real dullness. Opportunity to make up for lost time is what the temporarily retarded chiefly need, and this can best be gained by individual attention in extra, supervised study periods or in the small, special class.

Special disabilities. — Sometimes retardation is due to a disability in one school subject which is made the basis for promotion, such as arithmetic, or reading, which is so fundamental to later study habits of all kinds. *Arithmetic* ability is of at least two kinds, which are not necessarily present in the same person. They are ability in computation and in problem solving. The latter demands a certain degree of intelligence, so that generally dull children will lack in this respect. However, there may exist good reasoning ability but slowness and inaccuracy in computation very slightly amenable to ordinary drill. Little diagnostic work has been done on this. There are theories of persistent number forms in imaging which slow up mental manipulation, also of faulty early training. An emotional difficulty, combined with a negative auto-suggestion may be the cause for the arithmetic disability. This needs psychiatric treatment.

Case studies of *reading disabilities* reveal various and complicated causes. Poor mechanics such as bad eye movement habits are frequently involved, which sometimes may be fairly easily corrected. Diagnostic reading tests help to locate the field in which the child's difficulty lies. If there is no nervous instability, no general lack of comprehension, there may be a peculiar condition of word blindness. Theories of lack of imagery of one sort or another, of lack of co-ordination between the two hemispheres of the brain have all been advanced to explain this, and correspondingly varied remedial measures have been advocated. Individual instruction is almost always needed, and may have to continue for a long time.

Special disabilities in *spelling* are claimed to exist; that is, we may note a discrepancy between spelling achievement and I.Q. Not enough experimental work has been done in this field to make us sure if it is mainly an educational problem for the psychologist or the psychiatrist.

SUPERNORMAL MENTALITY

General description. — Turning now to exceptional children who diverge from the norm on the plus side we find degrees of ability ranging from the bright up to the genius. Any I.Q. above 100 indicates a superior child, and about one fifth of our school population may be so considered. Our nomenclature at this end of the rating scale is less precise than that at the lower end. We hear the terms precocious, bright, gifted, superior used rather loosely. The connotation of premature, unseasonably developed, has inhibited the continued use of precocious; the other three describe more pleasantly even if vaguely, the upper 10 per cent of the population. The term "gifted" is used more frequently to balance the term "feeble-minded" at the other end of the scale. Children with I.Q. over 120 are denoted very bright or very superior. About 5 per cent have an I.Q. over 122, and 1 per cent only, reach or exceed 130. Over 140 I.Q. would be considered near-genius.

Physical characteristics. — Rapid mental growth does not, contrary to popular opinion, argue unstable mental health, nor physical delicacy, nor early degeneration. By itself, it is rather a sign of ultimate superior attainment. Of course, where a neuropathic taint is present there may come a breakdown, accelerated by the pressure of longer hours of school work, and harder tasks; but the nervous instability is not a concomitant of mental superiority any more than it is of mental inferiority; it is a separate factor to which the credit should be given in explaining cases of degeneration. As a matter of record, children who are advanced in school work are more often than not taller and heavier than the average for their age. Terman's [1] intensively studied 600 cases of children of high I.Q. revealed general physical superiority. More of this group had been breast-fed than of his control group. Their average weight at birth was slightly greater. They exhibited weaknesses 30 per cent less frequently, and showed fewer symptoms of nervous instability. Both sexes reached puberty earlier than children in the control group.

Mental and social characteristics. — In school, gifted children show greater interest in subject matter that requires thinking than in drill subjects; and they accomplish more in them than do ordinary children. They are less different in school accomplishment in history and civics according to Terman's study, and are not distinguishable from the others in manipulative subjects. In judgments requiring mechanical ingenuity his control group exceeded his gifted group. They are marked by an intellectual curiosity, a better power of attention and concentration, better ability to understand relationships — shown too in their ready sense of humor — better ability to deal with abstractions and to generalize. They frequently excel in writing and dramatizing stories. Though they tend to grade higher than average in all subjects, nevertheless there is marked specialization of interest, and abundance of hobbies. They make a larger number of collections than other children, and more than twice as many that have scientific value. They are fond of reading. Many of them learn to read at an early age — four or five years old — and by eight they read about three times as many books in a given period as do children of average I.Q. Their reading interests, then and later, are of wider range. The gifted boys studied spent longer time in reading than did the girls. Other sex differences found were that the boys exceeded the girls in arithmetic and in general

[1] Terman, L., *Genetic Studies of Genius.*

information, while the girls over ten years old exceeded the boys in language usage.

In their *play* life they are less interested in purely competitive games than other children, preferring the quieter, mildly social, more intellectual forms. They choose playmates older than themselves. In *character* ratings both by teachers and parents and by such testing procedures as have been applied, gifted children as a whole far exceed the average. Terman's gifted nine-year-olds were about equivalent to the average fourteen-year-old in character development. With such children in school the discipline problem, as such, almost disappears. Their moral learning is rapid, as they are far more amenable to the reasonableness of the control required in social situations. Girls rate higher than boys except in the trait of honesty. The more highly gifted are less egotistic than the less gifted.

In *leadership*, children of I.Q. up to 125 or so do better than those still more superior. They are more like the normal group and so are accepted by them willingly. The very superior, the genius type of 140 or more, are less likely to be leaders. They are as far removed from the 100 to 110 I.Q. group as the latter are from high-grade morons, after all; so it is not surprising that they should fail to get on well. The gifted ones suggest occupations too much in advance of the interest level of those of like C.A. and are probably bored by what the others find absorbing. Yet they cannot compete physically, say at nine or ten years old, with those adolescents whose M.A. they equal. They are particularly likely to withdraw to a more solitary type of play. That they do not necessarily lack qualities of leadership is shown, however, in the fact that when segregated with children all of I.Q. of 135 or over, these of highest intelligence develop leadership within that group. The range of difference is less, and they can understand and appreciate each other better in consequence.

Cause. — The cause of exceptional mental ability is, in 90 per cent of the cases, superior hereditary endowment. Environment may develop wisely what is there, or, more tragically, may work in conjunction with moral traits of laziness and the like so as to discourage full development, but it cannot create what is not originally present. Some few advanced children may owe their position in school to environmental factors such as having begun school at an early age, having used spare time and vacations for tutoring so that added to intensive study they have had a continuous and rapid school progress. The advancement in these cases does not argue unusual intelligence, only unusual opportunity, and is not prophetic of exceptional ability in adult life.

Taking the family histories of gifted children always reveals a preponderance of superior parentage and eminent relatives in the first degree. Those people who have ability enough to succeed in professions and occupations requiring superior intelligence produce superior children. In Terman's study, 2 per cent of the population were parents of over half the total number of children testing above 130 I.Q. There was a negligible amount of parentage from the semi-skilled and unskilled classes of occupations. In that California group he found an excess of Jewish, and a deficiency of Latin, negro, and Indian ancestry, facts in harmony with other studies of race heredity and intelligence in the country at large.

Diagnosis. — The discovery of gifted children is still too often left to chance, or, what is almost as inadequate, teachers' reports. Unfortunately, teachers seem to compare the young child in their room with others in the grade rather than with others of like age, and so fail to estimate aright the superiority that is there. Time and again they do not report children as markedly superior who are instantly revealed as such by a testing procedure. Another cause of poor judgment is a regrettable prejudice found sometimes against the young bright child. A further reason may be that the better behaved, quiet children have not attracted their teachers' attention nor worried them as have those in danger of failing to win promotion. Still another reason is that teachers probably judge by achievement, and this does not always parallel aptitude. Sooner than trust to judgment then, it is advisable to do actual measuring. The group tests mentioned above will discover the exceptionally superior children with slight expenditure of time. When such are found, the individual test scales already described can be used for more intimate knowledge of their mental make-up.

Treatment. — It is highly advisable that children of superior ability be early discovered and given every opportunity possible for their best development. We need to prevent them from forming habits of idleness, of slack effort, of listless attention by performing tasks too easy for them. It is fatally easy to develop indolence by missing the challenge to put out one's best effort. If superior children are allowed to dawdle along as far as the fifth grade at the pace average children set, they are very hard to cure. For their own good as well as for society, gifted children need to be motivated to attempt the best possible for them, to persist, to win strength of character by striving against real difficulties. It is a debated question whether the ordinary school work should be more intensive than usual, or more extensive, whether gifted children should be taught with others older than they are but of the same mental age, or segregated and given special attention. Other than intellectual superiority matters here. We do not want to interfere with normal social adjustment by separating gifted children from others, but it is not always well to mix immature near-geniuses with adolescent boys and girls of average ability.

Baldwin [1] favors rapid promotion through the ordinary school provided there is also a superior physiological age. If there is much discrepancy between mental age and physiological age there is risk of maladjustment socially. Terman [2] found, following up two years after his first study, that those who had skipped grades reported a decreased fondness for school, while the most accelerated of all were below average in social adaptability. Classes specially formed for superior children seem,

[1] Baldwin and Stecher, "Mental growth curves of normal superior children," *Iowa Ch. Welf. Res. Studies*, v. 3, *1.
[2] *Op. cit.*

from experimental evidence, to be a better solution of the problem their training presents. Here they may go at a faster pace than usual, and cover a wider range of subject matter. Less emphasis need be placed on drill, and more attention given to intricate, abstract thinking, to stimulating the creative imagination. Here they may be under the guidance of specially gifted teachers, with insight and creative ability of a superior type. Here, though newcomers at first may be indolent, all may learn the value of hard work, and, by meeting competitors of like caliber, develop a democratic spirit rather than snobbishness.

Special abilities. — Just as certain disabilities are found, so superior abilities may exist. To put it differently, some abilities are relatively independent and may coexist with inferiority, mediocrity, or superiority in general intelligence. Such are mechanical aptitudes, drawing, carving and modeling, arithmetical computation, music. The independence of these traits is attested by the facts such as the following. We have "lightning calculators" of very limited mentality as well as of general superiority. Skilled jewelers, dentists, bone setters, surgeons are found over a wide range of intelligence. There is no correlation between achievement in other school subjects and in representative drawing, and none between linguistic ability and ability to draw. A selected group of superior children did about the same as ordinary children on tests for musical capacity. Students in music and in art departments at the college level test rather lower in intelligence tests than do their fellows in the general courses, however that may be interpreted. It may be that they represent a group of ordinary intelligence who would not normally have come to college at all were it not for their special gift, whereas the others are selected on the basis of higher intelligence. It should be noted, too, that imitative work in art and in music demands less intelligence than original, creative work. It is probable that those who will achieve eminence in these lines are also superior in intelligence.

These special gifts may be discovered early, and the greater the ability, apparently the earlier it shows. Thus, musical talent can ordinarily be detected before ten years old, whereas the musical prodigy is demonstrable before five years old. Artistic talent is evident before fifteen, and many times in the first decade. Rapid and accurate calculating, and fine manual skill likewise manifest themselves in early or middle childhood.

These special abilities seem to be hereditary.

RESPONSIBILITY TOWARD EXCEPTIONAL CHILDREN

Early diagnosis. — In all fairness to children, in adjusting their training to their needs, a comprehensive view of their abilities should be obtained early in life. Blindness can scarcely escape detection in infancy. Deafness, surprisingly, can, as witness the case of the boy who reached kindergarten before his handicap was discovered. His supposedly fairly well-educated parents thought, when he did not talk like other children, that he would begin suddenly and make up for lost time. As an example of what might be done, but is not done, it is interesting to note that Kerschensteiner happened to give drawing tests to the school children of Munich, by which it was apparent that a certain few possessed unusual artistic ability. As a result of this finding, arrangements were made by which those children might receive special training in art from experts in the same line. But had it not been for Kerschensteiner and his research work, those special aptitudes would have gone unprovided for. Similarly for other gifts. Unless the parents are aware of them and are able to allow time for their development, it is likely that little opportunity will be afforded these exceptional children to make the best use of their powers. Yet for their own sakes and for society's best good, we ought to have the means for discovering these special talents, and to apply such tests regularly, at least annually.

There is little reason why parents, would-be adopters, and others interested should not be able to find out very early the relative native capacity of any child now that testing methods have been developed for even the infant level. Charlotte

Bühler [1] has a battery of baby tests for the first two years of life. Kuhlmann [2] has extended the Terman series from the three-year level down to the first few months. Gesell [3] publishes norms for language, motor, adaptive, and personal-social development by monthly increments during the first year, and by wider spacings up to six years old. Stutsman [4] and others have elaborated pre-school age performance tests. Once at the C.A. of admission to public school there are numerous group tests which will speedily classify children of different grades of intelligence. Even without a regular test procedure dullness in children is soon recognized by the average teacher on account of their slowness in learning. Brightness in children should be suspected if they see a joke readily, if they show interest in number or learn to tell time early, particularly if they learn to read much younger than usual. Spontaneous interest in encylopedias, dictionaries, and atlases is another symptom of superiority which manifests itself rather later than school entrance age.

Constancy of I.Q. — Follow-up work on individual children by Gesell, Kuhlmann and others shows that those who test relatively low in general intelligence do not compensate later on. Their mental growth is slower than the average, they therefore remain relatively low whenever tested. They reach the limit of their development earlier than superior children do, and, in extreme cases of deficiency, they even tend to deteriorate. To illustrate, an infant of twelve months testing at ten months would probably show four months' retardation at two years old, a year's retardation at six years old. By nine years old he might still be in the second grade. He may cease his mental growth by the time he is fourteen years old at a mental level of eleven and one half. Conversely, the infant of twelve months testing at fourteen months would show four months' acceleration at two years old, a year's acceleration at six years old,

[1] Bühler, C., *The First Year of Life.*
[2] Kuhlmann, F., *A Handbook of Mental Tests.*
[3] Gesell, A., *Infancy and Human Growth.*
[4] Stutsman, R., *Mental Measurement of Pre-School Children.*

when he would be capable of doing second-grade work. His mental growth will continue till sixteen or past. He could do good work in high school and fair work at college. In general, superior children maintain their lead, finish the school course at an earlier age than usual, and are by no means found occupying low stations in life. We ought to be able to add that they are always found to achieve eminence in adult life; however, statistics are lacking here. Moreover, it needs effort, directed purpose, and a certain strength of character to achieve eminence, not high I.Q. alone. We can reverse the statement above and note that eminent adults have usually been noted as exceptional in childhood, though not always recognized for the superior beings they were by tradition-bound teachers.

Provision for exceptional children. — Though our percentages of children with special defects look small, yet the actual numbers in the United States needing special provision constitute an enormous problem. It has been estimated that we have about ten million handicapped children to care for, tubercular, crippled, cardiac cases, blind, deaf, of low mentality, disordered mentally. Caring for their bodies is not sufficient, or it might be a medical problem alone. Children such as these are in need of education and vocational training which will look for their assets and develop them to a life of happy social adjustment.

Special classes, special schools, have been provided for the benefit of exceptional children. Such include schools for the blind, the deaf, the crippled, the epileptic, the nervous, mental defectives, truant schools, schools for incorrigibles, open-air schools for the tuberculous or anæmic, schools of music, art schools, technical schools, classes for backward and for gifted children. Of these, the first two types were among the earliest to be established, from the manifest need for special methods. In 1817 the first public residential school for deaf children was opened, and in 1832 the first school for the blind, following similar provision in several of the European countries. In 1931, the sight-saving classes numbered 350, less than one tenth as many as we need, according to expert estimate. Provision for open-air work, for cardiac cases, and for the supernormal mentally are among our later developments.

So far as amentia is concerned, institutions for the care of idiots were long ago provided, sometimes, however, in connection with insane asylums. Famous examples are the Salzburg school for cretins, the school at Bicêtre, the Earlswood asylum, the Massachusetts School for Idiots and Feeble-minded Youth. In many such, not only idiots but imbeciles, low- middle- and high-grade morons are received. The presence of these has led to the inclusion of formal instruction in some school subjects, by which, of course, mere idiots could not profit. The emphasis is generally on training in industrial arts, agricultural work, speech training, with a minimum attention to the three R's, history, and geography. The majority of borderline, dull, mentally sluggish children are almost never sent to special institutions. Such are the charge of teachers in the ordinary school system, and merit special attention both for their own sakes and for the social good. Classes for such children have been formed in connection with the public schools since compulsory elementary education laws have directed the attention of administrators to the need for them. Beginning in 1867 in Germany, the decade from 1890 to 1900 saw many such classes and schools formed in France, England, and later in the United States.

Supernormal children have received less careful attention. A very common custom, and perhaps the least sensible in a closely articulated graded system such as prevails in the United States, is to allow them to skip a grade. Besides this, there are formed special classes in which a faster pace is possible than in the ordinary schoolroom, so that three years' work may be completed in two, or even two in one. Segregating the brighter pupils, as described above, seems to bring excellent results. Whether this should be for the entire school course, or, if only for certain years which years, is a matter of debate. Experiment will settle it; but, obviously, since the full results cannot be well estimated till the erstwhile pupils are twenty-five to thirty years of age, patient waiting is in order while the experiments are made. Final judgments cannot be passed on the basis of four or five years' trial.

PRACTICAL EXERCISES

1. Make an age-grade distribution of six different grade rooms. Study the cases two years or more either retarded or accelerated for the grade-age norm.
2. For your selected child — has an individual intelligence test been given? With what result? Is he "exceptional" in any way?
3. Visit any school or class for physically handicapped children that is provided near you. Study the children rather than the methods by which they are taught. What emotional strains do you see? Are they under any strain of attention-giving? How is self-control fostered? Are they interested in each other and learning to be sociable? What sort of play do they have?
4. Find out what types of special schools exist in the town where you live.
5. Find out what your State provides in the way of special institutions for exceptional children of any kind.
6. If convenient, observe the expert administration of a set of mental tests to a child of exceptional mentality. Compare the physical condition of such child with the normal.

FOR DISCUSSION

1. Review the facts presented in chapters VIII and XIV. What is their bearing on the education of exceptional children?
2. Review from chapter XIV what was stressed about neurasthenia. What does that suggest about watchful care in the schoolroom?
3. Just what should you do if you suspect that a child in your care is exceptional? Discuss this from as many points of view as possible.
4. Recall recommendations from the study of eugenics which have a bearing on the topic of exceptional children.
5. Should more time, energy, care, money be spent on children of sub-normal, or of supernormal intelligence? Why?
6. What else beside intelligence tests would you want to help diagnose or understand an exceptional child?
7. From the standpoint of vocational guidance what should the adviser know about an exceptional child?
8. How would you deal with a ten-year-old of 130 I.Q. who says, "I'm smart, I don't have to work"?

9. What sort of treatment in school is likely to develop anti-social tendencies in well-grown boys of about 80 I.Q.?
10. Are there "opportunity" or other special classes in the school nearest you? What sort of children are in them?
11. What difficulties in social adjustment do exceptionally bright children have in the ordinary high school, particularly if they are of normal physical size for their age?
12. What might help explain the fact that truants and delinquents are in the majority of cases rather below the normal I.Q.?
13. Should the public schools provide for specially gifted children, *e.g.,* in music?

SELECTED REFERENCES

BAKER, H. J. *Characteristic Differences in Bright and Dull Pupils.*

COY, G. L. "The interests, abilities and achievements of a special class for gifted children." *T. C. Cont. to Ed.* *131.

GODDARD, H. H. *School Training of Gifted Children.*

GROSZMANN, M. *The Exceptional Child.*

HOLLINGWORTH, L. S. *The Psychology of Subnormal Children.*

HOLLINGWORTH, L. S. *Gifted Children, their Nature and Nurture.*

JONES, A. M. "An analytical study of 120 superior children." *Psy. Cl.,* v. 16.

LAMSON, E. E. "A study of young gifted children in senior high school." *T. C. Cont. to Ed.* *424.

PINTNER, R. *Intelligence Testing.*

SCHEIDEMANN, N. V. *The Psychology of Exceptional Children.*

TERMAN, L. M. *Genetic Studies of Genius.*

WOODROW, H. *Brightness and Dullness in Children.*

Yearbooks of the National Society for the Study of Education for 1922 and 1924.

CHAPTER XVIII

MISDIRECTED TENDENCIES

MOTIVES, WISHES, DESIRES

The unit of experience. — The psychoanalysts emphasize to us that we should think not so much of the observed actions of an individual as try to discover what motive lies behind them. This motive is spoken of variously as a desire, a drive, an urge, a libido, a wish. A different total of these dominant urges is recognized by the different psychoanalytic schools, and they are classified in diverse ways. For Freud, indeed, they all reduce to one, the sexual. This term, however, is used in a far more inclusive sense than is customary for the layman. If, instead of being a blind devotee of one theory or another, we trace through history and sociology, and observe in ourselves and in growing children the motives that inspire most of mankind's conduct we shall probably agree on the following as of chief importance.

To eat. — The securing of food is the prime necessity of living. Our struggle for existence, our migrations, wars, our economic life in all its diversity, all are expressions of this basal need. The control of the appetite, the learning of social manners, the understanding and correct treatment of the whole digestive tract are personal problems with which each child has to deal. Failure may bring not only physical, but moral troubles.

To reproduce. — Beyond the necessity of self-preservation is that of race preservation. The urge to mate, the desire to have and care for children, is of equal importance with the urge to eat. Our development of family life, many of our social institutions, our educational systems are complex expressions of this fundamental drive. The two somewhat separate factors in it are referred to commonly as the sex instinct and the parental instinct. The control of the sex appetite, the balanced direction of the emotions, the varied relationships of male and female, of old and young within the home are, taken in their entirety, life-long problems. Opportunities for failure are correspondingly numerous, bringing poor hygienic results to the individual both physically and mentally, besides the moral consequences and social disasters that keep our legal institutions busy.

To achieve, succeed. — Whether in conquering the physical world about him, in beating competitors to a socially desired goal, or in the more abstract realms of thought, and of art, man feels the lust for power. Joy in construction, in creation, in executive ability, is easily recognizable. To fail, can be the cause of most acute misery.

To attract attention. — This, together with the last is some-times called the *ego* tendency, but may well be considered separately. It is more self-centered than the desire to achieve. Much "bad" conduct can be readily explained as due to this par-ticular drive, with no additional desire to achieve or dominate.

To be safe. — This, like the first, is directly conducive to self-preservation, and takes precedence of all others in emer-gency. It is allied also with the parental urge, and may conflict, at times, with the desire to achieve. It modifies our economic systems, enters into our philanthropies, inspires many of our inventions, and thus our scientific research.

To have new experiences. — Curiosity, the quest for thrills and adventures are due to this drive. Linked with the desire to achieve we have the activities of the explorer or the scientist on the one hand, those of the vagabond and the criminal gang-ster on the other, the wild conduct of the adolescent who wants to "get a kick out of life" somewhere in the middle.

MECHANISMS OF ADJUSTMENT

Maturation. — The developmental sequences of some of these desires have been carefully studied. For instance, the love impulse is at first directed by the infant to his own body, by the little child to the mother, father, and those who care for him. In middle and later childhood it goes to friends of about the same age and either sex; in later childhood and early pubertal years to persons of the same sex. In adolescence it goes to persons of the opposite sex and of varying ages, eventually to one of the opposite sex of suitable mating age. Maladjustments may occur because the individual does not continue his progress from one stage to the next, but suffers *arrested development*. Thumbsucking by a five-year-old demonstrates a prolonged infantile method of getting satisfaction from one's own body. Extreme vanity at any age may be looked upon as the expression of infant self-love. The seventeen-year-old who cares for none but those of the same sex has not developed beyond the naturally homosexual stage of later childhood.

The feeling for the parents changes from the early, unquestioning faith, dependence, and assured acceptance of all they give through parent hero-worship, parent criticism, even parent antagonism, to the parent appreciation of the fully matured individual. The mother-bound child so often encountered in the clinic has not passed successfully from the first and second stages. Many adolescents show themselves still bitterly critical of their parents' conduct, (not that which is related to them) feeling ashamed, chagrined, resentful. They are in danger of being arrested at this immature stage instead of passing on to that of seeing parents as human beings just as others are, individuals in their own right, fallible but lovable.

The urge to be safe is likewise bound up at first with habits of dependence on the parents for food, shelter particularly at night, security, money, and so on. A child's homesickness shows not only unreadiness to form new habits but a possible arrest on a level of dependence natural to a young child. Many parents cause permanent arrest rather than retardation of their children's development by their own desire to dominate. Poor economic training keeps innumerable older children and adolescents dependent on parents unthinkingly for all the items men-

tioned. Our lengthened requirements for some forms of vocational and professional training tend to keep our abler young
people financially dependent well after the legal age of twenty-
one. The disproportionate amounts adolescents spend of their
parents' money on unnecessary eating, drinking, amusements,
and the like evidence the fact of arrest on the young child level
of economic security.

Regression is another fault of development. Whereas in
arrest we have failure to develop beyond the point normal for
a younger age, in regression we have an individual who has progressed beyond but, because of meeting dissatisfaction, now
retreats to the earlier levels where he did, once before, experience pleasure from his adjustments. The young girl who assumes
a lisp or indulges in baby talk satisfies her desire for attention,
or her love impulses by the little child's methods. The excessive
masturbation of the degenerating dementia præcox patient is a
return to the self-love of the infant. Our psychopathic cases
show abundant evidences of regression to a child, even an infantile level of satisfaction.

Adjustment to conflict. — Thwartings and conflicts inevitably occur in the course of satisfying these various desires.
One impulse may obstruct another; or something outside proves
an obstacle to the original action. Energy thus interfered with
will find some outlet. Much of our training of children might
be described as directing their attention to the approved outlets
and rewarding them when they choose such. If we neglect
this and leave them to find some outlet of their own by a blind
trial and error method there is more than an even chance that
they will hit upon an undesirable reaction. The well-known
methods by which outlets are found vary according to the
individual's general temperament as well as according to the
particular circumstances of the environment. These methods
function in the field of imagination largely, but also in language,
and in action. They may be briefly described as follows:

Introversion. — Rather than face unpleasant realities with
action the individual realizes his wish in imagination only.

The imaginary companion of the little child, the daydream of the adolescent provide a pretense world where no conflicts need disturb. The desire to achieve and the desire to attract attention are satisfied by the *conquering hero* type of dream, or by the *suffering hero*, princess in disguise sort. The mechanism of *identification* finds frequent use as the adventures and love affairs of others are followed in books and on the stage.

Rationalization. — Instead of taking refuge in imagination the individual may put into words what is intended to convince others, and which sounds plausible but is really an excuse or a lie. The failure is explained away rather than admitted, and in the process the self loses the balance that comes only from absolute sincerity, as well as the ability to see things as they are. One form of this self-deception is called *projection*, in which all blame is placed on circumstances or on other people instead of on one's self. We all know children ready to complain of everybody and everything as at fault except themselves. The *sour grape* mechanism explains that the goal we have failed to reach was not worth striving for; and the *sweet lemon* method insists that the third rate present achievement is the best, most to be desired after all. By these three respectively, whole systems of ideas of persecution are built up, states of jealous resentment develop with slander and blackmail as possible consequences, or a false philosophy of sanctimonious resignment is formulated.

Repression. — People are likely to deal with fear, sex, and curiosity, or any of these in combination by trying to shut them away from attention, neither thinking nor acting in response to any impulse. This is an impossibility, and the attempt is a potent cause of trouble in the emotional life. What we term an *emotional complex* is analogous to a festering sore stupidly plastered over; it poisons a local area, and eventually the whole system, unless explored with a probe and allowed to drain off.

Surrender. — The desire to be safe balancing badly with the desire to achieve, the individual gives up effort and is tormented with anxieties and dread. The young adolescent's general restlessness, unhappiness, some morbid fancies, are largely an expression of obstructed love impulses, of aroused and frustrated sexual desire. Special fears, called phobias, may be projected substitutes for the general fear of failure. A disproportionate, cringing sort of humility, meek acceptance of blame, is another form of surrender. Great readiness to confess to all sorts of wrongdoing may prove a means to gain attention.

Attack. — An opposite appearing form of adjustment is a resistance carried to the point of fighting others. Rather than admit error the individual points to others who are worse than he is, and magnifies their shortcomings. Much malicious gossip is rooted in this effort to compare one's self favorably with one's fellows by running them down.

Defense reactions. — A barrier is erected against unwelcome ideas by actions which eliminate the necessity of doing what is disliked. A frequent case of this is the convenient headache which incapacitates the individual when a distasteful task is at hand. Opportune illnesses are termed *conversions*. A boastful habit may act as an auto-suggestion for the one who fears he is not succeeding. A superdignified mien is assumed by those of short stature. Such defenses we call *compensations*.

Substitute activities. — A conflict in any field may manifest itself in any conceivable form of conduct. The stream of energy, dammed at one point, simply overflows elsewhere. Many teachers and nurses express through their vocation the obstructed parental urge. Hunting with a camera is suggested instead of slaughtering wild life for fun. The small child forbidden to strike her brother finds relief in making faces at him. The eleven-year-old, failing to win the admiration of teacher and pupils takes to stealing. The feeble-minded fourteen-year-old girl finds herself of value as a prostitute where before she could not succeed in others' estimation. Unable to own a gun for the hunting and fighting adventures he craves, the young boy practices with pea shooters and sling shots on cats and unsuspecting passers by. A human target, more understanding than some, provided substitution in the form of an archery club in the play yard.

Little children's difficulties. — A *feeding* problem, so common in the early years, is often explainable as a refusal to eat because then the mother shows alarmed concern. In other words, the child has been conditioned into satisfying his attention-getting desire that way. *Temper tantrums*, though originating as an obvious reaction when any wish has been suddenly frustrated, soon become a means of getting attention. Wholesome neglect of these manifestations with much friendly notice of the child when he acts in a desirable way can work a cure in a surprisingly short time. Poor toilet habits, especially prolonged *enuresis*, if not due to a physical condition, is explainable as arrested development in adjustment. The child's own volition must be challenged to learn the self-control which should normally have been his by at least two years old. A greater number of cases are brought to the clinic for counsel for this problem than for any other, in the years before six. Negativism, temper tantrums come next in order of frequency, excessive fears rather low down on the list. *Negativism* may be caused by active dislike of the adult, but is often a sign of timidity. Again, a child may be so bewildered with hurried, conflicting demands on his attention that his own volition is apparently paralyzed.

Obstinacy. — Time was when this trait was looked upon as a symptom of a "strong will," and a child who exhibited it was admired so long as he did not obstruct adults' wishes, in which case they talked of "breaking" his will. The psychologist sees in it, however, misdirected persistence, or a sulky, negativistic sort of inhibition. The bodily symptoms are sometimes startling. A child may become rigid, as tense muscularly as though he were in a cataleptic fit. Or, with slowed pulse and shallow breathing he may be so limp that he cannot retain a sitting posture. Or a flare of temper may be followed by a prolonged period of refusal to eat or speak. The emotional and mental conditions with the aggressive sort of obstinacy are akin to the obsessions and impulsions of the more abnormal case which result in persistent, senseless following of the forbidden course of action. The opposite, the passive, inhibited children, are emotionally unable to fix their attention on anything except their repugnance and dislike for the action desired by others. This they fixate till they are practically self-hypnotized. Absence of body being impossible for them they retreat behind barriers of silence and are difficult to arouse. We have, then, a paralysis of volition rather than evidence of strength. The angry temper and sulky fit is a natural response to being frustrated, but easily becomes a means to satisfy the desire to get attention if the adults show themselves worried and solicitous.

The *causes* for these conditions may be (1) some physical difficulty, especially in the endocrine glands. Till we know more of the bio-chemistry involved in our schizo-phrenic and manic-depressive cases we cannot say for certainty that unusual inhibitions or impulsions which we now call obstinacy may not be due to glandular imbalance. (2) Bad training in the younger years is a potent factor. Parents who threaten or promise but fail to keep their word only confuse little children as to what authority really is, or how adjustment should be made. Parents who are inconsistent, alternately indulging their children and being severe with them according to their own passing whims, give no firm foundation for an objective idea of law and order. Some children, too, are encouraged and laughed at when little for actions which later bring reprimand and scolding. All such treatments predispose to obstinacy. (3) Immediate causes may be a sense of injustice, or a special dislike for the person or the task. After eleven or twelve years old the growing feeling of independence is strong enough to incite to open rebellion against outside compulsion.

Just as for a balky horse, distraction of the attention is effective *treatment* for many cases. The motive that causes persistence must be directed to a substitute outlet, and reward attached to the new action. The shock of cold water or violent active exercise may arrest and divert the flare of temper. It may also force a beneficial reaction from the limp, passive fit. The timely laugh with — not at — a child may happily avert or release the tensions. Whatever the form, the child must discover that he gains nothing whatever from his behavior, not even concerned attention, in fact that he is losing in social esteem as well as in the physical satisfaction of his hunger in refusing to eat. He must also find that self-control brings definitely pleasurable returns socially. A conflict of wills should be avoided if possible. Since self-mastery is the aim, it is of little value if the adult conquers the child by sheer force; and of course if the child wins the battle over the adult there is a very bad precedent established.

Lying. — Not every departure from the truth can be called a lie. We should analyze the situation and penetrate the motive behind the falsehood. The imaginative tales of little children are discussed elsewhere, likewise the pathological lying of the young adolescent. Real lying, the intent to deceive, may be due to motives of antagonism, of self-display, of fear, of sheer selfishness.

Antagonism favors the lie to enemies where only the truth would be told to the inner circle of friends. The greater spread of good will, the enlargement of the social group to which a child feels he belongs, the opportunity to belong to several different groups, will help eliminate this type of lie. Girls, more than boys, are apt to betray confidences and to suggest untruths about others for whom their attachment is waning. The motive of self-display leads children to boast and exaggerate. Some more legitimate means of attracting favorable attention and proving their worth socially will usually cure this form of over-compensation.

Timid children who are harshly treated are particularly likely to lie to escape blame and punishment; and almost any child would agree with the boy who described a lie as "an ever present help in time of trouble." Indeed, the escape motive functions only too frequently in their elders for children to miss examples of lying of that sort. It is difficult to reward for truth-telling under these circumstances so that real justice will be done. Some children have actually learned that they can get away with any kind of bad behavior so long as they own up freely. Yet truth-telling must be made more advantageous than lying if we would help form the right habit. Strengthening the less courageous to stand up to the consequences of acts, to assume responsibility, to take blame where it is due is part of the constructive program.

The selfish lie, as the cowardly lie, is a grave fault. It is likely to be deliberate rather than a matter of hurried impulse, therefore it is the more serious of the two. Cheating in games is a frequent form that this motive takes. It is the falsification that plans for the advantage of self regardless of, sometimes intentionally at, the expense of others' welfare. Unless a child can be rescued from this basic selfishness and helped through his friendships and love to treat others as he would like to be treated, he risks growing up into the hopelessly mean, unreliable adult.

Most children would justify the heroic lie for noble ends. Many have queer little superstitious practices such as making certain gestures, whispering "no" when they have said "yes," and the like. They half believe that such measures can disinfect the lie, so to speak. A few children may be found honest to the point of being over-scrupulous, worried unduly over any slight deviation from the truth.

About four years old to five is often found the first intentional deception of the cowardly or selfish sort. If the occasion is dealt with promptly and thoroughly much future trouble may be spared. For many children the tendency to lie is particularly strong at eight years old just as the rules of the group games they play and the marking systems in school assume a new importance and offer chances to cheat. If the motives and acts of liars, hypocrites, sneaks, and crooks are held by the family standards to be abhorrent in the extreme, children will most likely grow up honest, fair, and just in their social dealings. If by ten years old they are not well on the way to habituate truth-telling they stand a poor chance in later development.

Truancy. — This problem is more common among boys than among girls, and is more typical of younger boys. Mere wandering away occurs oftenest in April, May, and June according to Burt's [1] London findings, when the lure of outdoor life is more potent than that of book study indoors in a schoolroom. Though easily explainable as a yielding to the desire for new experiences, curiosity, a vague unrest, and sheer love of wandering, the need for lying excuses both at home and at school soon fastens further undesirable habits on the boy. Since it is so often found as an earlier offense among adolescents later brought to the children's court, we may look upon it as an easy first step in a delinquent career. With other like-minded adventurers and rebels against school authority, mischief and pilfering soon become outlets for the high spirits within, and an anti-social attitude is all too easily developed. Since the criminal gangster of seventeen years or so is typically an individual arrested at the ten- or eleven-year-old stage of social development, the truant group merits special remedial work of a constructive sort. The dominant motives functioning in their activities must be carefully sought and legitimate outlets brought to their attention in a friendly spirit. Punishment merely aggravates the conflict of desires. One understanding teacher, put in charge of some notoriously difficult boys in the seventh grade, won their confidence to the extent of being allowed to go along on some of the gang's outings. After some weeks of picnics and games she discovered their plan of investigating for themselves in a near-by cemetery the truth as to the resistance of bones to decay. She was fortunately able to redirect this scientific curiosity into safer methods of work. A study undertaken by Hiatt [2] on 100 typical cases to determine the causes of truancy showed that there were many complex factors rather than one dominant

[1] Burt, C., *The Young Delinquent.*
[2] Hiatt, J. S., *U. S. Bureau of Education*, 1915.

one. It seemed to be the fault of the home in 29 per cent of
cases, and a dislike of school in 26 per cent. Analysis of this
dislike revealed poor school placement, curriculum or methods
unsuited to the particular boy, or antagonism towards one
teacher. Some who gave the reason of wanting to go to work
were probably actuated by these same feelings of dislike. The
general instability of early adolescence is undoubtedly a factor
many times. Bad companions was a contributing cause in 2 per
cent of the cases studied.

Cruelty. — Even quite little children act toward others and
to animals in such ways as to bring great suffering. Granted
that their own ignorance of pain and death partially explains
this, likewise habits transferred from manipulating dolls and
stuffed animal toys, there yet remain deliberate attacks on
others which indicate an emotional maladjustment somewhere.
Many such are due to the disappointment at the lessened
attention given three-year-old when the new baby comes.
One child was found jabbing the baby's face with pins. The
lust for power instigates some cruel acts. The eight-year-old
who beat her puppy nearly to death when it did not do as she
commanded, illustrates this. Sheer curiosity and desire to see
exciting things happen explains many thoughtless, unsympathetic actions. Habits of cruelty, when a real thrill accompanies the causation and witnessing of suffering, are a perversion
of the sex impulse. Unless this sadistic behavior is understood as such, and corrected, the child may develop into a
depraved character.

DELINQUENCY

Definition. — Technically a delinquent is a person whose
offense is punishable by law. Obviously, some conduct classed
as delinquency, for example "gaming on the Lord's Day" as
in Boston, might be far less serious than other actions not so
punishable. The problem of juvenile delinquency is of immense
social significance since most of our adult criminals show early
history of delinquency. Our task is, then, to discover the crim-

inal in the making and do the best preventive work possible. Between four and ten years old tendencies may be so perverted that very difficult work is involved in redirecting a child. The teacher will need, therefore, to be on the lookout for symptoms in behavior which may indicate such maladjustment as may lead to delinquency and adult criminality. A noted procuress describes the most frequent characteristics in childhood of girls who later readily become prostitutes as greediness, selfishness, idleness, mendacity, extreme vanity, and inordinate love of finery, with complete absence of feelings of responsibility towards others. Here, then, is an arrested development of the ego impulse rather than a strong sex urge. The very slight amount of constructive training given to the urge to eat, and to the practical development of the concept of property may account for much of the predatory habits of boys.

Types of offenses. — Outstanding investigations of delinquency in children have been made in London, England, by Cyril Burt; in Chicago and Boston by Healy and Bronner.[1] Other important contributions to our knowledge have been made by Slawson,[1] Breckenridge and Abbott,[1] Lindsey,[2] Fearing,[3] and Julia Mathews.[4] Though the statistical details differ considerably from the various cities and states in which both extensive and intensive types of studies have been carried on, yet in the main facts all are agreed. Boys, more than girls, get into trouble for stealing in its different forms. From 65 per cent to 79 per cent of all charges can be so classed, against 30 per cent to 40 per cent of girls. Offenses such as truancy, vagrancy, mischievous or malicious damage to property are also more frequent among boys than girls. Girls, more than boys, get into trouble for sex offenses with the opposite sex, from 35 per cent to 70 per cent of cases being so charged, against

---

[1] See titles in bibliography.

[2] Lindsey, B. B., *Revolt of Modern Youth.*

[3] Fearing, F. S., "Some extra-intellectual factors in delinquency," *Jo. Del.,* v. 8, 1923.

[4] Mathews, J., "A survey of 341 delinquent girls in California," *Jo. Del.,* v. 8, 1923.

less than 8 per cent of boys under sixteen years old. Excessive lying and general incorrigibility are more frequent among girls than boys. Both boys and girls are brought to court for running away from home, staying out at night, excessive bad temper, attacks on other people, cruelty, obscenity, sex perversions, alcoholism, begging, and so on.

Correlated factors. — When investigation is made, poor home conditions are found in over half the cases. This includes a broken home, with one or both parents dead, parents divorced or separated, desertion, mother out all day working. Poor discipline at home — with only a subjective rating of "poor" to be sure — is given as cause in from 40 per cent to 80 per cent of the cases. Here the combined influences of heredity and environment undoubtedly weigh against the child. Poverty is given as a large contributing factor in about one fifth of the cases. Bad companions are a major factor in delinquency from 10 per cent to 60 per cent of the time. If we reflect upon the thwartings that poverty entails, the crowded conditions indoors and on the streets of our big cities, the paucity of worthwhile things for children to do and think about in our poor neighborhoods, it is a wonder that they keep as straight as they do when each one is potentially a "bad" companion.

Feeble-mindedness and mental abnormality, both of which may be due to heredity, are estimated very variously. For instance, from four to six times as many feeble-minded are found among delinquent as among normal children. Healy and Bronner consider it a main factor in 13.5 per cent of the 4000 recidivists studied, Burt in 8 per cent. The double conditions of intellectual inferiority and low social status are closely connected with delinquency. Emotional instability, according to both Mathews and Burt, is definitely present in one third of the cases studied. Mateer [1] judges delinquent children as defective and psychopathic in most cases. Healy and Bronner state that 72.5 per cent are definitely not abnormal or pathological. They emphasize general adolescent instability and

[1] Mateer, F., *The Unstable Child.*

mental conflict, including school and vocational dissatisfactions, as operative in the rest.

Psychological view. — The mere naming of offenses or rating of home conditions is superficial at best. As we trace the impelling motives of the juvenile delinquent and study the social treatment he has received we find a maze of compensations for thwarted desires, defense reactions against unsympathetic authority, and the like. The desire for adventure, alone, instigates much of the girls' sex experience as well as the boys' vagrancy and stealing. Re-education of the offender must include, then, legitimate satisfactions for these natural tendencies rather than the repressions of many so-called correctional institutions. Parental education is almost always needed, is, in fact, imperative when children are put on parole.

With the mentally inferior, the unstable, and the pathological cases, we have to contend with the fact that the reprimand, probation, punishment which serve the more normal children have little or no effect. They either cannot foresee and weigh the consequences of actions, or they can achieve no self-control, or they develop no "moral sense," that is, a feeling of the rights of others, a sensing of the self in relation to others. Such cases are most likely to become repeated offenders, and, by failure to respond to our therapeutic measures, continue into an adult life of vice and crime. Failure was reported by Healy and Bronner in about 55 per cent of the hundreds of case histories of repeated offenders studied. The proportion was higher among males than among females, higher in the homosexual group, higher also in homes of poverty, criminalism, alcoholism, and vice, as one might expect. Success did occur, however, under any of the conditions mentioned.

No stereotyped program of treatment can fit all cases. Flexibility and concerted attack on all conditions is necessary. The causes are so complex, the reactions so individual that each case requires not only diagnosis but treatment advocated for himself, carried out by all agencies co-operating. Here is where the school may have a large and important share in redirection.

The age before ten is the most hopeful for prevention, also for success in redirection.

Description. — A psychoneurotic child suffers from morbid emotional conditions; a psychopathic personality makes poor social adjustments, though no definite disease, no physical condition can be found as cause. Hence the distinction between the two is extremely difficult in practice. The terms are often used indiscriminately.

What we call neurotic children react in an exaggerated way to everyday occurrences. Some are overexcitable, violently enthusiastic over trifles, aggressive, very loquacious; others show lassitude, indifference, a dislike of others' company. Neurotic children seldom get on well with their fellows, or play contentedly. They find difficulty in concentrating attention and in persevering at tasks. Nervous habits are frequent, such as nail biting, face twitching, masturbation, sleep-walking, stuttering; motor co-ordination is often poor. They are very prone to headaches, digestive troubles, sleeplessness, and opportune illnesses which defer hated tasks and bring sympathetic attention in place of reprimand.

Obsessive ideas are common. Few have a well-developed sense of humor, especially with regard to human relationships. They seldom, if ever, achieve a well-balanced social sense. Some harbor resentment for long periods of time, or are deeply suspicious of others.

Pathological lying. — By this is meant a falsification quite out of proportion to any observable purpose, engaged in by persons not demonstrably insane. Whole systems of false tales, of accusations against others, even against themselves, are built up and adhered to for long periods of time. Those who indulge in it are apparently sincere but impulsive, without realization of the social consequences to other people of their charges, or of the disregard in which known liars are held. The motives for this sort of lying are difficult to discover.

Generally there seems to be no grudge against the person accused, no material gain to the individual who thus fabricates long, coherent tales, no escape from unpleasantness, no escape from blame. There is, however, an immediate gain in attention from others since many times there is widespread publicity, even court action resulting from the extraordinary statements they make.

Hysteria. — Hysteria is a functional disease resulting from nervous instability, manifesting itself in lessened mental control. Though not developing till middle to late adolescence, the earlier years are important in predisposing to this trouble. The characteristics are chiefly instability of emotional control, abnormal suggestibility, inordinate love of daydreaming, a tendency so completely to banish unpleasant emotional experiences that they drop out of memory and tend to originate a sort of dissociated personality. Various kinds of motor and sensory disturbances may occur, from simulated epileptic fits to the development of areas of anæsthesia. Real epidemics of hysterical origin are reported to have taken place among school children due to psychic contagion. Since hysteria may assume the outward form of almost any disease, ranging from deafness, dyspepsia, and the like, to paralysis, it is a difficult matter for even the physician to diagnose it. As mental hygiene is more important for its cure than mere physical regulation, the wise treatment of it lies largely in the hands of the teacher. Sometimes it may be well to remove the sufferer entirely from the influence of people in the home, if they are unintelligent and likely to foster attitudes of dependence and egotism. Any remedy that is in itself pleasant, that obviates the necessity of facing the disagreeable, of course prolongs the illness. So, too, if the sufferer is made the center of fussy attentions at home. Thus, the nine-year-old girl, whose nausea so interfered with school work that she was ministered to by a somewhat alarmed principal, taken home, eventually excused from regular attendance while much waited on by mother, was not strengthened either to fight the nausea or to learn the arithmetic during which periods the nausea had so conveniently incapacitated her. Better for her had she been matter-of-factly told to withdraw and be sick if she must, but to return as soon as possible and make up the work she had missed. It is surprising how many hysterical illnesses clear up when the remedy is unpleasant, even painful. One physician wisely uses strong electric stimulation this way, and seldom do the symptoms complained of give any further trouble after one or two such treatments and the certainty of more.

Self-control must be encouraged. The ideal must be built in of courage to do one's share in the world's work no matter what the handicap. Praise must be given for demonstrated efficiency, with the assurance of quiet scorn of all for malingering.

Dementia præcox. — Dementia præcox is a very prevalent form of insanity which attacks adolescents particularly. Its chief symptom is an aversion to things practical, and an excess of fantastic dreaming which gradually weakens effective volition so that the individual is content to substitute imagined for real deeds. A poor nervous inheritance is a large factor in this disease, and there is a possibility that a curious condition of the colloids of the brain cells, found in advanced cases, is the direct cause. We look hopefully to our bio-chemists for further light on this problem from their experimental work. Hitherto we have striven to arrest the progress of certain cases; if discovered early enough, this may be done, but in general the prognosis is bad. As the term *dementia* implies, a grave deterioration sets in. The patient may develop paranoidal symptoms, delusions of persecution or of grandeur, but more often withdraws from active social intercourse into an inner world of fantasy, eventually refusing to speak, even to eat — requiring the care and supervision of a young child in ordinary personal matters. The term *schizo-phrenia*, meaning shattered personality, preferred now to dementia præcox, aptly describes these individuals who live in a world of their own apart from their fellows, quite able to hear and understand but refusing to react to ordinary outer stimuli. Cases of this are more frequent than any other type of disease in our mental hospitals.

This fact alone should give us concern and make us all the more alert to observe the telltale symptoms. Full diagnosis is, of course, not the teacher's business; but the presence of the conditions noted, an unusual amount of daydreaming, a wide gap between thought-life and the life of actual, concrete application should arouse the teacher to a realization of the grave danger possible so that expert advice may be sought.

READJUSTMENTS

Diagnosis. — Obviously, a snap judgment based on casual observations of a child's behavior would be little use as a guide in redirecting him. What with disguises of compensations, substitutions and so forth, the observed actions are only symptoms that something is wrong.

Detailed, objective observation is the first step. Find out when the behavior was first noticed, how frequent it is, at what time of day. With what people does it occur, after what immediately preceding occurrences? How has such behavior been previously treated? Has this conduct brought the child pleasure in any way? How? Thorough investigation is the next step. Even without the services of the visiting teacher a good deal can be discovered as to the child's friendships, his hobbies and recreation interests, his home relationships. With the aid of the visiting teacher a great deal more may be found out about the whole field of social adjustments the child is making. A physical examination — which should not be left to the last — may reveal conditions calling for instant relief since they contribute in no small measure to the child's difficulties. An intelligence test may disclose poor placement in school, of itself a potent cause of dissatisfaction. The child himself may be able to tell his own story and explain underlying motives directly, or indicate the sources of conflict by indirect means. A knowledge by all the adults concerned of the dominant tendencies is of course necessary, as a key to many a hidden connection.

In a consultation center the expert services of physician and nurse, psychologist, psychiatrist, and social case worker are available for any child. From the combined findings of all the diagnosis is made and remedial treatment suggested.

Roughly, the longer the exceptional behavior has been going on as an outlet for the fundamental drive the longer the re-educative process may be. All we know of habit forming has to be brought to bear to help build up the new lines suggested as substitutes for the old. The re-education may have to include the parents and others in the home. The older the child is the more important it is to secure his own co-operation with parents, teachers, and others whose help is enlisted.

A careful perusal of the many case studies given in several books suggested below will do much to give the teacher a broader understanding of the many-sided problems involved in dealing with these misdirected tendencies.

Suggestions for teachers. — Find legitimate avenues for children to display skill, to gain attention, to satisfy sex curiosity, to do exciting things.

To be good must be made more satisfying than being bad.

A sense of humor in yourself, and a vivid recollection of your own escapades as a child should make you more of a comrade than a judge. When you find adolescents' vagaries and inconsistencies particularly trying, it is a very good time to recall similar conduct of your own. If you ever wrote a diary, and have kept it, reread it for evidence of longings, whims, absurdities, thrills, and rapid changes of mood you have since forgotten.

Analyze your own feeling of antagonism for any particular child. If you can't readjust sufficiently to win his confidence and give him what help he needs, find some one else who can. Not all personalities can overcome mutual antipathies.

Sometimes a special disability in a school subject is a transfer from a hidden, emotional conflict. If that is the case ordinary academic drill will not relieve the situation.

Do not take bad conduct at its simple face value. It is frequently symptomatic of some deep-lying trouble. The action is a distortion of a desire, a poor substitute outlet for a strong, but thwarted drive.

Ridicule is a dangerous weapon causing wounds that may necessitate a psychiatrist's healing skill.

Remorse and shame, if applied to self, are negative in their action. Self-abasement is not the goal, but evaluation of the social consequences of the individual's action.

Humiliation, abuse, and scorn do not help any one to find his balance. The use of them demonstrates maladjustment on the teacher's part calling for diagnosis quite as much as do the child's actions.

Encourage a prompt, matter-of-fact acknowledgment of error. None of us is infallible. Emphasize the good sense of analyzing the cause of the error so as to prevent repeating it. Disparage the thing that has been done wrong, not the child who has done it. Be friends with him while disapproving the misdemeanor.

Help children, adolescents especially, to see that the moral tumble is less disgraceful than the refusal to get up and try again.

Arouse a sincere feeling of contrition in a child before asking him to say he is sorry for something he has done. Above all things a child must be honest with himself.

The hypersensitive child who agonizes over having to ask pardon may be shown that prompt apology averts many a reproach. The timid child may be led to see that immediate acknowledgment of blame due disarms many a vexed complainant. Thus, speedy action of their own may pay them in less unpleasant social relationships. Both need a constructive means of re-establishing good will with those they have offended.

The child who broods over fancied wrongs, who is sure he is a victim of continual injustice, has an inflamed ego. He is not unhappy, he is enjoying his picture of himself.

A mistaken effort to overcome timidity may show in rough boisterousness, domination over younger ones, angry defiance of older ones.

To reason with a child who shows intense dislike or acute

fear will seldom help. The object of the emotion is frequently a substitute symbol to which a suppressed emotional attitude has been transferred. The real cause of the disturbance must be uncovered.

The child who is so scrupulously honest that she worries others with demonstrations of her truthfulness is probably having a real struggle with impulses to be dishonest.

If a child protests indignantly and constantly of one special sort of bad behavior in others suspect that he is guilty of it himself, and by this attack is satisfying his ego. Or suspect that he longs to do the same thing himself but does not quite dare.

Do not appear excessively shocked at the revelation of immoral behavior. This may function as just the reward of attention-getting that the miscreant craved.

Do not tell a child to forget unpleasant occurrences. Help him instead to understand why they were unpleasant, and so be intelligently able to prevent their recurrence.

Help young people to make the best of what they have and are, rather than claim that whatever they have is intrinsically the best, or that what they cannot have is no good.

Be wary of the pupil who always has a glib excuse for unpunctuality in handing in assigned work. What other responsibilities does he shirk?

Do not ignore the quiet, biddable child who "gives no trouble." He may be in the early stages of the worst kind of trouble for himself.

The child who would rather read than play with the others is not necessarily super-intellectual. He may be giving up the attempt to adjust socially, and taking refuge in an inner world of "have it as I please."

Find out the habitual content of the daydream, and you may be able to substitute an objective satisfaction for that gained in fantasy.

Writing out a daydream may open the way to the legitimate use of the imagination in the service of entertaining others in a literary way.

An opportune illness is extremely suspicious. True sympathy does not lighten responsibilities for the sufferer but calls upon courage to meet them. Retreat should be made unpleasant and illness an impossible refuge.

Do not think you can diagnose every kind of mental conflict. It takes an expert.

Remedial measures may involve parent and teacher re-education, and wider community responsibility for conditions found. Remedial treatment will not transform a child over night, even if immediate relief from emotional strain is secured. New habits must be given time as well as a chance to develop.

There is no one formula that will fit every manifestation. Each child is a problem by himself and must be studied, and treated, in his total social setting.

PRACTICAL EXERCISES

1. Arrange, if possible, to visit a local institution for truants, or for incorrigibles, or for law-court cases, etc., and note the following points:
   (*a*) What sort of motivation is used for good conduct.
   (*b*) What type of discipline, government, organization exists.
   (*c*) Whether the pupils play normally.
   (*d*) What means are provided for normal social development, especially for the adolescents.
   (*e*) How the pupils compare with others physically.
   (*f*) How they compare in school progress.
   Inquire about these facts:
   (*a*) What follow-up work is done when the pupils leave the institution.
   (*b*) What the statistics show as to the percentage making good after they leave.
2. Is there a children's guidance or behavior clinic in your neighborhood? If so, arrange to visit it, get its literature. Of whom is the staff composed? What age cases do they serve? Do parents in general in the area know of the possibility of help?
3. List all the agencies in your town that have to do with child welfare. Upon which could you call, in an emergency? What different sorts of problems do they handle?
   If you were teaching in a rural section where could you get help with a problem child?

FOR DISCUSSION

1. If no behavior clinic is available in a community, and you, as a teacher felt the need of one, how would you set about having one established?
2. How could the following help: — the local library, the children's court judge; the parent-teachers association; the local hospital; the state authorities; the Federal authorities?
3. What magazines carry useful articles from reliable authorities on the mental hygiene of childhood?
4. Review the material in chapters II, III, XV, and XVII that have a bearing on the prevention or redirection of tendencies.
5. Discuss the findings from the exercises above.

SELECTED REFERENCES

BENEDICT, A. E. *Children at the Crossroads.*

BLANCHARD and PAYNTER. "The problem child." *Ment. Hyg.*, v. 8, 1924.

BURT, C. *The Young Delinquent.*

BUTCHER, HOEY, and MCGINNIS. *A Study of Problem Boys and Their Brothers.*

GROVES, E. *Personality and Social Adjustment.*

GROVES and BLANCHARD. *Mental Hygiene.*

HARTWELL, S. W. *Fifty-five "Bad" Boys.*

HEALY, W. *Mental Conflicts and Misconduct.*

HEALY and BRONNER. *Delinquents and Criminals, Their Making and Unmaking.*

HEALY ET AL. *Reconstructing Behavior in Youth.*

JUDGE BAKER FOUNDATION. "Case Studies." *Series I.*

MORGAN, J. J. *Psychology of the Unadjusted School Child.*

SANDS and BLANCHARD. *Abnormal Behavior.*

SAYLES and NUDD. *The Problem Child in School.*

SEAGRAVE, M. "Causes underlying sex delinquency in young girls." *Jo. Soc. Hyg.*, v. 12, 1926.

SLAWSON, J. *The Delinquent Boy.*

ZACHRY, C. *Personality Adjustments of School Children.*

CHAPTER XIX

TWO CROSS SECTIONS OF CHILD LIFE

So far, the different tendencies have been considered group by group. A study of that kind, analytical as it must be, does not present us with a view of the whole child as we meet him in daily life, complex, changeable, developing as he is, constantly meeting and responding to all sorts of stimuli, varying from mood to mood, from year to year, from home to school environment, in sickness and in health. But neither does constant association with one child give us necessarily any idea of what children of a given age may be like. That one child observed may be atypical, may be very specially endowed by heredity or favored by environment, and is probably considered with prejudiced eyes in all but very few cases. In what follows, an attempt is made to present a sort of cross section of child life at two points, for the ages five and eleven. The facts stated will, of course, be generalized, and may not fit the mental image one calls up of some particular child in many traits: however, it may serve as a guide or map in the exploration of the land of childhood.

CHILD LIFE AT FIVE

Physically. — Children at five years old are anywhere from 36 to 46 inches tall, on the average slightly over 40 inches, growing 2 to 2.2 inches during the year. The weight will be from 31 lbs. to 46 lbs. with an average of 39 plus, adding 4 lbs. or a little more in the course of the year. A boy is very slightly taller and heavier than a girl at this age, and grows a little faster than the girl. The sitting height is large, relative to the standing height; the legs are increasing in muscle power rather than much in relative length. The brain has attained about eight ninths of its adult weight, while its development is proceeding rapidly.

433

Neural control of finger muscles is less well advanced than is that of arm muscles. They can drive nails better than they use needles and thread, they can carry full glasses of water without spilling better than they can weave cords. They should be able to lace shoes, given time and practice enough, even though rarely able to tie the laces: and they should be able to button clothing if the buttons are not small and inaccessible. Balancing on a narrow plank or on roller skates should be possible too. They should show ability to walk or skip in time to a 2/4 4/4 6/8 rhythm. Boys are somewhat superior to girls in accurate throwing at a mark and in running; girls are better in hopping on one foot. Climbing a rope is beyond their powers now, as also, for most, riding a bicycle, turning a somersault, swinging while hanging by the hands. They need exercise without strain or fatigue, therefore, with frequent rest periods. Trying to sit still is a tiring task. Standing still means using the same muscles continuously unless change of position is possible. We should not require either, then, for more than a few minutes.

The eyes are normally farsighted, and so do not accommodate easily for small objects near at hand. Only brief periods of focusing on such for handwork, and especially in connection with books, should be allowed if eyestrain is to be avoided. The very bright child who learns to read young should not read for long at a time

nor in print smaller than this which is 24 point type, in lines 6.5 mm. apart and 70 mm. long.

Small beads, tiny screws, fine needles and thread have no place in kindergarten equipment.

At this age children have long had their full set of 20 milk teeth and rarely start to lose even the lower incisors before another year has passed. The first of the permanent set, the "sixth-year molar," makes its appearance about as its name would indicate. Relative to their age, children of five need a large amount of food and at more frequent intervals than does the adult. Their diet should contain 1400 to 1700 calories a day, roughly 36 calories per pound of weight, and include plenty of milk, cooked rather than raw fruit, little or no meat. They need about one half as much fat, and one third as much carbohydrate food as does an adult. They require eleven hours or more of sleep out of the twenty-four, and plenty of outdoor air and sunshine. It is a time of less susceptibility to disease than in the years before three, but still very great compared to the resistance of children ten and twelve years old. Constant care must be exercised to guard against infection. Chicken pox, mumps, and German measles are less serious than are scarlet fever, whooping cough, measles, meningitis, or diphtheria. There is increasing possibility of immunization from some of these as our scientific knowledge progresses; but school and home need close co-operation in intelligent safeguarding of children's health.

Emotions, desires, and interests. — In a survey of 2000 cases studied intensively and reported on at a conference in Washington it was found that about half of the four-year-old children have definite *fears*. We may assume that at five years old from 40 per cent to 50 per cent have developed some specific fears. Those we frequently find are occasioned by unfamiliar animals or by people felt as menacing, by thunderstorms, by loud, sudden noises, often by the dark, by the feeling of lack of support in unusual physical positions or in water which is over waist high, or in untried movements that look violent, perhaps by grotesque carvings or even pictures of grim-looking people. There are considerable individual differences here, perhaps innate but partly due to the effects of early training. About 4 or 5 per cent of children are naturally timid and require special care in training to prevent or overcome tendencies to shrink and retreat under circumstances that others can easily be taught to understand and deal with effectively.

Anger is aroused less by taunts and jibes — which may not be very well understood — than it is by physical frustration. It is frequent, easily stimulated, but usually short-lived. Extreme fits, as in the temper tantrum — which should normally have been outgrown by this age — leave a child exhausted in a depressed reaction from the nervous excitement involved.

Desire for mastery is very strong, but is directed more to the physical than the human elements in the environment. That is, there is practically no competition motivating conduct in the sense of wanting to surpass another in skill. Interest can be more easily aroused in the function pleasure of the skill itself. However, some teasing may be explained as desire to dominate others. Pet animals must often be rescued from little children's ruthless handling due to this motive.

Emulation, though in a mild form as compared with the ten-year-old, is shown in such things as the effort to seize what a playfellow is pulling towards himself, struggling to retain a toy, leaving an occupation to run after some other child with an attractive plaything and trying to drag it away. Jealousy may follow with sulking; or if others get the treatment and notice for which they were aiming there is apt to be sulks, howls, or grief.

Jealousy may be the explanation for teasing, and for apparently cruel behavior as well as for sulks and varied forms of "naughtiness." Investigation will often show a resentment at missing attention formerly given by parents rather exclusively. *Desire for attention* may be seen in all kinds of showing off, commonly in the form of restless behavior, doing stunts, calling out, alternating with submissive behavior shown in shyness and self-conscious action.

Other tendencies, such as kindliness, motherly behavior, the sex instinct, certain forms of fighting, are not so strong at this age as they are likely to be later. In the case of the sex instinct, this is either in part of the period called by Moll the neutral, or in the period called the undifferentiated, when on the physical side the organs are immature and sensations unlocalized; on the psychic side the children's special affections may be centered on almost any one, even an animal, but chiefly on a parent or some older person of either sex. The curiosity exhibited about their own bodies or the origin of babies is not specifically connected with sex; it is rather a part of general information-getting, and should be so met.

Interest in food is strong, as it is for most ages. There are still habits of reaching and putting things in the mouth, cramming the mouth very full with pleasant tasting food. Sweet things are generally craved, but acid, pungent, or salty flavors are seldom enjoyed.

Play interests. — The games and plays enjoyed at this age are largely individual and solitary. Children of five will be intent for considerable periods on their own toys, construction work, occupation of whatever sort without desiring the co-operation of others in the way that older children do. Participation by others may frequently be resented and precipitate a fight; whereas seeing others busy with an object excites curiosity and acts as a suggestion to grab and handle likewise. Spontaneous groups of two or three children form transiently, sometimes for assistance in construction or an imaginative game; but more often five-year-olds play in the presence of or near others rather than actually with them. Their contacts are brief.

In play which is more or less directed by older children or by adults they join in an undefined group, *i.e.*, any number can play, and there is an absence of competition. It is play rather than a game with organization and rules. Ring games involving dramatic imagination, with rhythmic movement leading to some climax, especially if accompanied by singing, are popular at this age. Rhythm and repetition in speech and song is a prominent characteristic of the many traditional games played about this time.

If really interested in a self-chosen activity containing possibilities of mental and physical variability a child can occupy himself for as long as an hour. Otherwise it is not unusual to find changes of occupation every five or six minutes. Objects that stimulate the senses and can be manipulated are very attractive. Simple toys that will stand hard wear, that are not too liliputian, that offer opportunity for dramatic use or original construction work are the best to provide, especially easily handled variants of blocks and bricks. In using these, girls tend to care for ornamentation more than boys do, while the latter already tend to be more interested in the mechanics side of building. A few simple tools will be appreciated. Other materials also providing scope for the imagination but involving smaller muscles, are such as paper to be cut or torn, clay, colored crayons, the various things found in Montessori or kindergarten rooms, including the sand table. Medium-sized dolls, teddy-bears, other animals and their appurtenances are enjoyed by both sexes. The girls may do a greater variety of things with them than boys, and the same thing for longer at a time; also they begin to develop an interest in the details of doll's housekeeping appliances which may bore the boys. Anything suggestive of a cave is adopted rather than constructed at this age; the knee hole of father's desk, a hollow in a bank, empty crates, overhanging ledges of rock, area-ways arched with steps provide cubby-holes all ready for playing house without much further trouble.

Construction plays are increasingly interesting, taking precedence for many children over fiction plays. The majority of five-year-olds have arrived at the pre-plan stage of activity with such materials as blocks, sand, drawing implements.

Another marked feature of their play is the constant activity indulged in from sheer enjoyment of it rather than from any idea of acquiring skill in a movement. Five-year-olds love to jump, roll, slide, dig, climb, run, pound, throw, lift, and use their whole bodies in large movements; but there is little desire to run fast, to throw hard, to jump high, nor to excel the next child in these abilities. Playing in shallow water is a great delight whether in tubs on the veranda, or the small stream, or mere road puddles. Playing in the snow is sometimes a fearsome pleasure and is not so violent as it becomes four or five years later. Imitation and dramatization play a large part in the activities connected with their toys as also in their other play. They love to dress up and assume the characters they see daily, such as policeman, car conductor, etc., or those they hear about in stories, though this less often. In this way their imagination is greatly developed. They are interested in fairy tales, but especially in narratives of the culminative type with repetitions such as that of the old woman with the pig that wouldn't go over the stile.

Mental characteristics. — Children of five live in a world fascinatingly "full of a number of things," and they are constantly exploring their environment not only by getting sensations and making movements but by asking questions. Though the previous year may more truly be termed *the* age of questions, the tendency has lost but little of its strength, and, as every parent desirous of living up to his responsibilities knows, even the latest encyclopedia and the *Child's Book of Knowledge* combined sometimes fail to provide the necessary, satisfying answers. Children's attention is quickly caught by moving objects either seen or heard, but on the whole, things are noticed and considered important only as they contribute to present enjoyment. Voluntary attention is not easy to give, and any kind of attention is quickly distracted. As has been elsewhere indicated, imagination of both the creative and constructive type is very vivid at this age, being a strong factor in determining the type of story or play enjoyed. They begin to imitate not only people and things present at the time, but also those absent and simply remembered. Mere retentiveness is good, relatively, also rote memory; but the memory image is weak and inaccurate, neither is there much ability to recall voluntarily. Logical memory is scarcely developed at all.

Five-year-olds' methods of memorizing are obviously unlike

those of older children who have learned to read. Yet many can rattle off long tales of the Struwel Peter type. Careful observation by Stern [1] of a little child's learning processes convinces him that sense and meaning are less important now than later, while joy in sheer sound, in the rhythm, rhymes, refrains, duplications, alliterations, and so on, is relatively greater. He estimates that a repertoire of 200 lines of verse would not be unusual for a child of five. Space concepts are fairly well developed for empirical reaction to daily environment, but their time concepts are weak. This condition may be appreciated when we realize how much more frequent are perceptual experiences that involve allowing for space adjustment than are those requiring time measurement; and that beyond small portions of time which can be felt as rhythms, our very terms are abstract. What wonder then that "tomorrow," "last week," "next month" should be difficult to grasp, and that even darkness and light, which can be seen to be understood, do not always satisfactorily explain "today," "this evening," still less morning and afternoon. The type of meal soon becomes a fixed point of reference for time of day as do also habitual activities. Number concepts are few and weak. Though the series idea of number may be known as high as 10 — *i.e.*, there is ability to count up to 10 by pointing to each object in turn — yet it is the rare child of five who knows 10 as a group number, who could tell how many are in a group even after having counted them. Prepositions and adverbs expressing space relationship are correctly used at this age, but few expressing time relationships, still fewer dealing with causes, conditions, concessions, and the like. This indicates their vague, confused notions of logical, scientific relationships.

Stern,[2] tracing the development of inductive inference, concludes that real induction, in the sense of generalizing from all that is a common element in a series of examples, occurs normally not until five years old. Before then there have been vague

[1] Stern, W., *The Psychology of Early Childhood*, ch. 16.
[2] *Op. cit.*, part viii.

attempts at generalization, and suppositions put largely in question form. Very few purely deductive inferences are drawn. Specific statements and the use of crude analogies are common. The words "because" and "therefore" are not used in any logical relationship, if indeed the latter is used at all. "Because" means "and then," or else refers to human motives rather than real cause and effect relationships between events.

Interpreting from the facts of human agency which they experience daily in regard to themselves, their ideas of the world around are largely animistic. Things that move are alive, though they cannot go so far as to explain that things that move *by themselves* are alive however clearly that idea governs their interpretation, as may be brought out by skillful questioning. Their thinking, as their talking, is almost wholly egocentric. They are not socialized enough to be able to take the point of view of another even with regard to space, far less to objectify their ideas. Thus, they know their own left and right hands, but do not correctly give the right and left of some one opposite, and especially of the relationship of three objects in a row. Only one child in five can succeed with the brother and sister problem.[1]

They talk to describe their own actions, to express wishes, requests, commands, objections to others' actions, but not to convince another's thinking.

In language development, children of five may have a vocabulary of from 2000 to as many as 4000 or more words, depending almost entirely on the sort of home environment there is, and also upon definite training including possible ability to read. Many more words are understood than are commonly used in the child's own speech, of course, as with all of us. Substantives and verbs form perhaps three quarters of the entire stock of works used, while some pronouns and any

---

[1] Having ascertained how many brothers and sisters he himself has, suppose a brother X and a sister Y, the questioner asks, How many brothers has X? How many sisters?

irregular inflections give considerable trouble even when the environment supplies the correct forms constantly. Infantile pronunciation should no longer exist.

Intelligence ratings. — Whatever the heredity of a child, daily contact with minds sparsely equipped, functioning on a low conversational level of idle gossip hampers his mental development. We find that the degree of education and culture of the mother is very clearly related to the intelligence rating of little children, more so than is the fact of poverty or medium to high scoring of the home on the socio-economic scale. A poorly educated, superstitious nurse-maid can, then, hinder if not harm young children mentally.

The Gesell norms, the Detroit kindergarten tests, as well as the Stanford revision of the Binet-Simon tests give us an idea of the norm of general intelligence of five-year-old children. They can generally state their own age correctly. Their ability to understand simple instructions and to hold them in mind sufficiently to direct a process of comparison is brought out by the "comparison of weights" test, in which two weights looking exactly alike, but one weighing 3 the other 15 grams, are presented for a sense discrimination test. The same abilities contribute to success in other tests also, as for instance the "three commissions." In this the directions are to take a key and put it on a chair, then to open the door, then to bring a designated box to the experimenter. Most children at this age, if they fail in this test at all, do so from omitting one of the orders. Comprehension and attention are needed again in the "game of patience" test, in which two triangular cards are required to be placed together "so they will look exactly like" a rectangular card which is shown. Control by an idea is involved too, and of course judgment and comparison through the eyes of shape and position. By five years old normal children show discrimination in matters æsthetic by being able to pick out the prettier of two faces in three pairs, and show their interest in the world of color by having picked up the names of the four primary colors without having had any direct teaching in connection with them. Boys are somewhat inferior to girls in this test.

Most five-year-olds will prefer to match objects by color rather than by form, given the choice. Things around them are thought of more largely in terms of use than in terms of general characteristics, so that they will reply to such questions as "What is a table" by saying "To eat on," or "Where to write" rather than giving the fact that it is made of wood, or that it has four legs and a top, or that it is of a certain color and shape. True, they may be led off into irrelevant remarks such as "We have a new table in our parlor," as is readily explainable by the association laws of vividness or recency. For that matter, adults' imagery or mental judgments might well be colored the same way, but the latter would inhibit expression of this type of fact, while five-year-olds do not. Girls may do somewhat, but very slightly better in general intelligence tests than boys do.

Socially. — Kirkpatrick [1] calls the age from three to six the period of individualization, when children intelligently try to modify other people, their physical environment, and their world of fancy to suit themselves, and, through this self-assertion, develop a personality more independent of others than heretofore, also possibly different from that which they exhibited say at three years old.

For the great majority of children the influence of the family and the home life in general has been the biggest factor in their education. The daily training in habits of whatever kind which they receive has laid down patterns of character which make marked differences between children even as young as this. Already, their ideas of good and bad, of beautiful, of true, their implicit interpretations of father and mother functions have been modeled in ways which may determine the line of their thinking for life. Their attitudes with regard to modesty, generosity, good nature, personal hygiene, property rights, and so on have been fairly well set, even though not made explicit

[1] Kirkpatrick, E., *The Individual in the Making.*

in language. They learn pretty well what is expected of them in the family life, and, with the help of their dramatic imagination, begin to idealize conduct to some degree, using terms such as good, nice, kind, brave, "what — likes." Such moral standards are in process of formation unreflectively, being crystallized from either incidental pains and pleasures or from those administered systematically by the older members of the group to which they belong. Thus their "conscience" is derived wholly from the authority of the surrounding adults, and their moral habits are formed by the law of effect. They learn to be whatever will secure them the greatest advantage, coy, whining, patient and good tempered or vociferous and teasing, shy, obedient, polite, bold according to the value in personal returns which such behavior brings. Right is that which wins the approval of the elders, or which provides the satisfaction of a desire.

Their memory and imagination are developed sufficiently so that hope of reward, dread of ridicule, or fear of punishment can become a controlling factor in conduct. Neither memory nor imagination is a reliable guide, however, when it comes to reporting occurrences. Creative imagination is the generator of many of the so-called lies at this age, faulty perception or memory is accountable for more; but a little training in distinguishing actual from wished-for experiences will be of immense help in straightening out this type of falsification. Conscious and purposeful lying may occur from fear of some loss or punishment, or from a state of open dislike or warfare with unsympathetic adults. A majority of children probably take to lying in some form or other; and to prevent the venture from becoming a habit they should find convincingly, in terms of personal and social results, not only that deception does not pay, but that truth-telling does, even if it is owning up to some piece of mischief or disobedience. Because of the weak time sense at this age, both rewards and punishments need to be immediate to be effective, and closely connected in the children's own minds with the action. They must be fitted to the children primarily, to the deeds in logical fashion only as a secondary consideration.

Standards to be given. — Moral and social habits reasonably to be expected at this age include regularity and control of bodily functions, co-operation in cleanliness of person, the use of "please," and "thank you" and other simple courtesy forms, use of handkerchief, some inhibition of impulses to cry when disappointed or hurt, of impulses to kick and shriek when angry, of impulses to handle any attractive object known to be either another's property or dangerous, some sustained effort to stop sulks, or crossness, or contrariness, and to be pleasant, polite, courageous.

Negativism is a phase that most children have outgrown by the age of five. Any child showing marked inhibitions, fits of obstinacy either of persistence or refusal, evidences bad training and perhaps a neurotic tendency as well. In any case he needs special attention to help him develop self-control.

Habits of independence and responsibility may include watching for traffic lights and obeying the signals, memory of and execution of simple routine tasks assigned such as using dustpan and brush, watering the plants. They can be intrusted with take-and-fetch errands of many sorts provided no complicated set of directions beyond their attention-span is given. Thus, a child can be sent two or three short blocks to the grocer's with a written list and a dollar bill to bring back a couple of parcels and the change given him. Standards of bedroom and table manners differ so much that it is difficult to be specific. Compare, for instance, children in a typical, two-child, servantless home with parental supervision but many makeshift ways; those in a crowded tenement family with no privacy and no room to sit together at meals; those in an English-style nursery with its careful training; those in single-child millionaire establishments, overloaded with personal service; those in an institution on the congregate plan with the lack of intelligent, refined interest to direct in these matters. On the ground of sheer ability to handle forks, spoons, cups, etc., there is no excuse for poor table manners. Five-year-olds have all the skill needed for washing and drying faces and hands thoroughly, brushing teeth, and attending to themselves at the toilet. An ideal of health should not be expected to function at this age, so that drill and supervision is necessary to mechanize good hygienic habits. Children of five years should be made conscious that there is a standard in these things, and their training should have produced an approximate conformity.

One moral habit needed at this age is obedience, brought about either by personal influence on the emotions or by tangible results in pleasure or the reverse, but in any case secured promptly. Much help can be given here by never offering mere suggestions, which may be disregarded, in the form of commands which must be heeded. This is a bad, thoughtless habit on the part of adults, and necessarily confuses children who thus have no ready means of distinguishing between occasions when a choice is permissible and when it is not. Their "I don't want to" being met with "Oh, all right then" in one case, how are they to know that such an objection will be a source of contention another time? Fits of obstinacy may be helped by a little letting alone for a while, or by deliberately distracting the attention, as one does for a balky horse, till the inhibitions are released. By auto-suggestion, a child's "I won't" becomes only too literally "I can't," with an accompanying state of high tension; relief by relaxation is needed, which may frequently be secured by something which induces a good laugh. Obedience may then follow more easily, and the child has an experience in control to look back upon, rather than a scarring of a conflict with the adult.

CHILD LIFE AT ELEVEN

Physically. — Turning now to the consideration of eleven-year-old children, we find that at this age they are anywhere from 49 to 61 inches tall, slightly over 54 inches on the average, with boys a very little in the lead. During the year from eleven to twelve girls will start on their period of rapid growth, gaining nearly 2½ inches before their twelfth birthday, while for boys the acceleration has not yet begun. In weight, children of this age tip the scales at from 60 to 90 lbs., girls on the average at 70 and boys at 74. During the year boys will gain about 6 lbs. and girls more, as they overtake boys in height. In lung capacity or strength of grip, however, girls do not measure up to boys. A tall child will begin the period of acceleration rather earlier than a small child; and it will become noticeable in height sooner than in weight. There is a stimulated increase in growth of the bones, especially the long ones, at this period, making a change in the relation of sitting to standing height. Poor posture is frequently found since the rapidly changing bodily proportions do not find correct adjustments of seats and working surfaces. The large muscles of the back, in particular, tire easily.

In motor ability, Brace [1] found that eleven-year-olds passed, on the average, between eleven and twelve of his twenty tests; these require good balancing ability, particularly of legs and back. Boys are stronger muscularly than girls, and have greater endurance, according to Smedley. They are also slightly superior in steadiness of precision of manual movements. The hips and pelvic bones start to undergo changes in the girl which frequently result in a greatly modified carriage and gait. At this time lack of symmetry may show in the shoulders, hips, sides of the face, use of the hands, and so on. For many girls this marks the beginning of an "awkward" age, when uneven growth not only necessitates new habits of muscle co-ordination but has its effect in a dawning self-consciousness of a different kind to that previously existing, an increased sensitivity to personal criticism, and an instability of mood which are the forerunners of the metamorphosis that will take place in early adolescence. About 6 per cent of girls begin their pubescent changes before their twelfth birthday, so that sex differences are particularly variable as the tall girls start their spurt of growth and develop in other ways, while boys are seldom so precocious in physiological age. In both sexes the brain has all but ceased to increase

[1] Brace, D. K., *Measuring Motor Ability.*

either in size or in weight. The heart is still small in relation to the size of the arteries compared to the relative size obtaining in adult life. The general resistance to disease is high. Mortality statistics show that this is a healthy, disease-resistant age compared with the period before five or with the adolescent years. Approximately 25 per cent of all deaths now are from some form of tuberculosis, or over 40 per cent from that and all respiratory diseases combined. The other single large factor is accidents, which is probably evidence of the personal daring and social heedlessness of the age.

By eleven years old the incisors, the first molars, and the front premolars of the permanent set of teeth have appeared, and during the year the canines and back premolars may be changed, though there is considerable age variation here, and again the girl shows more precocity than the boy. Several teeth may be already diseased, especially the sixth-year molars;[1] only one child in five may have perfect, sound teeth at this age, the others having suffered chiefly from lack of inspection and proper care. Children[2] now require about 1800 to 2000 calories in food value daily, or from 28 to 32 per pound of body weight; this would be approximately six tenths as much as a man at moderate work. Their diet should be varied but plain, avoiding rich, heavy, highly seasoned dishes, and being bulky rather than concentrated, so as to somewhat satisfy the almost inexhaustible capacity for eating commonly found. They need at least 9½ hours of sleep during the 24, preferably more; though investigations[1] show that the hours actually spent in sleep average less than this.

Emotions, interests, and desires. — *Fear* is manifested chiefly in a sublimated form such as remnants of superstitions, responses to situations such as ridicule of companions, anticipated blame. Girls are probably more timid than boys about such things as going into deep water, dealing with strange animals, getting on high places, being hurt in a fight, touching firearms, and the like,

---

[1] Terman and Almack, *Hygiene of the School Child.*
[2] Rose, *Feeding the Family.*

unless they have been brought up with a good deal of physical freedom and encouraged in rough and tumble sports.

Fighting, especially of the counter-attack, rivalry-in-combat types, is exceedingly prevalent among boys at this age. Since it seldom leads to permanent quarrels or alienation and does help to develop fundamental, if crude, ideas of fair play, adults may well refrain from interfering to suppress it. Since when allied with hunting it easily degenerates into bullying, a wise control with substitutions and sublimations is desirable. Girls, less than boys, tend to use feet and fists when this instinct is aroused. They respond more often with indirect attack of language, gesture, facial expression, resorting to pushing, slapping, or pinching when more violent measures are called for. The two sexes very seldom engage each other in actual physical fighting now, though there are occasions permitting hair-pulling and scratching. Males will more often content themselves with jeers, hoots, and cat-calls, females with derogatory remarks to each other about the offending males in their presence, or with quiet planning to outwit them, injure their property, or make them appear ridiculous.

So far as the *sex* instinct is concerned, this year falls in the undifferentiated period. On the physical side, since girls mature earlier than do boys, there will be, besides the general spurt of growth, some development of the secondary sex characteristics, and in about 4 to 7 per cent of cases the appearance of the menses before the twelfth birthday. Instruction should include knowledge of this approaching change that there may be no psychic shock when it comes. Boys are probably more widely informed and more misinformed than girls in general sex matters by this age, and are also more likely to have formed undesirable habits. Indeterminate, uncomprehended sexual excitement may be induced by such activities as horseback or bicycle-riding, pole-climbing, sliding or swinging. On the psychic side there is rarely any genuine falling in love at this period. Rather are attractions and adorations casual, part of transient attachments, and felt for members of the same sex as often as not. It is probable that there is never any connection consciously realized between such physical phenomena as may be experienced and the emotional, psychic facts. Love stories are not cared for now, indeed there is a marked impatience with them. Towards the end of the year some few girls may develop a romantic streak remarkably far removed from everyday affairs. Forced into daily companionship with young men not of the family there may be a perfectly childlike, frank chumming, or girls may become restive, shy, uncertain in behavior, perhaps protectively rude without developing the coquetry or self-consciousness that would be natural at fourteen years old. To be caressed or kissed by such men would be an affront to the more mature, or a perfectly simple matter to the less mature, wherein lies a danger, of course. For a boy to be kissed by a girl would be overwhelmingly shameful. For him to be caressed by a young woman would be felt as indecent and undignified; in some cases there is risk of arousing unexpected instinctive reactions, and the practice is distinctly inadvisable. A big brother in the true sense is what a boy chiefly needs to steer him straight at this time. Both boys and girls are better managed by older members of the same sex. Allied with this instinct may be mentioned the added clothes consciousness of girls, and the budding chivalry towards girls and women in boys.

Among the social impulses *tender affection* is more likely to be found in girls than in boys, and in such forms as delight in babies, desire to "mind" them, and in patient care of little children up to about four years old, pride in showing them off.

Gregariousness is more marked in boys, and is shown chiefly in the formation of the gang. Although beginning at eight or so, this tendency seems to be stronger in the years eleven to fourteen. Girls, being left out of so many of the boys' social activities, must perforce congregate with members of their own sex; but it is to be questioned whether they seek each other's company as actively as do boys. We have no conclusive evidence on this point. With both sexes it is an age for chums. The particular friend chosen seems to be the result of casual propinquity rather than conscious selection for reasons of character or temperamental affinity.

Attention-getting, display, mastering and submissive behavior are all noticeable, but are not specially different from what they have been. There is a growing desire to mask attempts to attract attention, to feign indifference during acts of display on the part of boys. Towards women, girls may be quite demonstrative where boys will be shy, attempting to conceal the shyness with assumed rough rudeness.

Rivalry is a very strong tendency at this age and enters into almost all play and work undertaken. As noted before, it is individual rather than team rivalry, though the emphasis shifts somewhat during the year. Envy and jealousy are not so strong now as they may be later, and have developed beyond the little child's phase of coveting other toys, clothes, and so on.

Kindliness comes so often into opposition with teasing, fighting, and rivalry that it does not get much unhindered growth; nevertheless it is there, and is manifested in occasional beautiful outbursts of sympathy, generosity, efforts to relieve, self-denial for causes appealingly presented, thus giving good ground for the development of genuine altruism. In general there is a willingness to share food with those who need or with those who are friends, to help the weak or injured, to do things for the defective, to be glad at others' happiness.

Collecting, though it is at its height in the year from ten to eleven, now engages the interest of over 90 per cent of children. They will collect anything convenient and attractive, such as marbles, cigar tags, paper dolls, nature objects, pictures, and vie with each other as to who will have the largest collection. The predatory activities of the gang are also a manifestation of this group of interests; food is the principal thing taken at this age.

Migration, though not so strong at this age as it is in the teens or even at a much earlier period, appears in the imaginary plans for going to sea or becoming a bandit, in the delight in stories of discovery in all parts of the world, less frequently in attempts to run away from home, in stealing rides on trains and boats. This may be contrasted with the intense pangs of homesickness experienced by many children when away from familiar places and people.

Interest in food is shown in a strong tendency to gorge with food at all times and seasons; in an interest in roughly preparing and cooking food; in hunting and chasing, stronger in boys than in girls.

We note also the *language interest*, leading to appreciation of puns, conundrums, ciphers, puzzles, aphorisms, parabolic utterances, to the practice already illustrated of inventing verbal symbols, languages, and the writing of poems and stories, also to the ease with which new languages may be acquired.

A *sense of humor* is manifested in the use of nicknames, in contriving practical jokes, perhaps in the rather frequent and continuous laughter.

Play interests. — The kind of play enjoyed at eleven years old is usually in the form of a game rather than free play, with definite rules, a purpose, a beginning, and an end. In type of organization it is generally an undefined group or double group, with a very slight beginning of co-operative teamwork towards the end of the period. Chiefly, however, the feeling of rivalry dominates, each player desiring to star in his own part even if the contest is between groups. Sports and games of skill both single and social are in great favor. Children want to see who can pitch a ball hardest, send it highest, jump the farthest, skip longest, run fastest, win most marbles, do the most fancy movements in roller skating, slide most swiftly, etc. A good deal of the playtime is devoted to practicing certain movements, acquiring skill, perfecting accomplishments. Tree-climbing, swinging on rings, skating, bicycle-riding, and swimming are favorite activities that may be instanced in addition to the plays mentioned earlier.

The aim in the stunt is usually speed or accuracy, less often ease, least often grace. Running is a prominent feature of a great many games, though girls begin to slacken in this respect.

Girls seem to enjoy rhythmic movements more than boys do, and to be more interested in folk dancing, prearranged pageantry, and dramatics.

Doll-play is rapidly disappearing, and is probably in the stage of doll-dressmaking, or paper dolls. While girls will be busy with constructive activities allied to home making, and may be interested in ornamentation, finished detail, and the like, boys are more likely to use carpenters' tools, do simple engineering, experiment with pulleys, levers, electricity, water power, and especially to build some kind of house with whatever the environment offers as suitable material. Housekeeping activities appear in several forms of girls' play. Among boys it is seen in the group enjoyment of the wigwam, cave shelter, tree hut or other gypsy play house which the gang will construct. Guessing games and games of chance are increasingly enjoyed, also the more passive forms of amusement, table games of various sorts, and reading, for which a veritable craze now sets in for many children. Stories of adventure are the chief joy, tales of heroes and their exploits, mystery tales, pioneer narratives, and other thrillers. Individual tastes, of course, come out here, some children becoming veritable storehouses of information on miscellaneous topics, others on historical subjects, others on science, some on poetry, more on merely impossible fiction. The stimulated imagination frequently finds expression in long stories given orally to the inner circle of friends, or in written form; besides detailing episodes of the blood-curdling variety the young authors, or rather authoresses, may try their hands at verse-making. Here, or in plays where a conclave is felt necessary, is the occasion for developing a secret language, from the employment of a shibboleth, password, incantation or what not, to the possession of quite a large-sized vocabulary useful as a barrier between the favored few and inquisitive outsiders. Games involving an intellectual feature are played with interest — such things as acting titles, proverbs, quotations, word-building from long words, checkers and other board games, card games of authors, geography, and so forth.

According to the returns on the Lehman and Witty Play Quiz,[1] 50 per cent of the eleven and one-half-year-old children reported from 16 to 35 different play occupations in the course of a week. Taking 748 children questioned in January, the mean number reported was 36.86, rather fewer than in the immediately younger years.

Mental characteristics. — Intellectually, children at this age have learned a great deal through their perceptual experiences, and are tremendously interested in the physical world about them. Keenly observant of all sorts of details, they are less subject than are adults to such illusions as depend on ignoring things grown familiar through long use. Their school training has emphasized their natural eyemindedness in the process of learning to read and use books, but even yet it does not appeal to the eye in other ways as well as it might do with objects rather than pictures and diagrams rather than oral descriptions.

At this age the creative imagination is realistic rather than idealistic; so also is the constructive imagery and the attempt to imitate. The reproductive imagery, in whichever form it is employed, is fairly good at this time in point of accuracy. It is likely to be vivid and concrete, predominantly visual. Some few children may be found who possess eidetic images.

Memory itself is concrete rather than abstract. The personal memory is good, but, like older persons, children may be very inaccurate in a report of what happened, of what they did, unless they were unusually attentive and observant at the time of the occurrence.

Already there are well-marked individual differences in the type of thing best remembered, some children excelling with sensed and perceived facts, others with numbers, symbols, verbal systems, desultory facts, others with associated information about objects. From these facts about memory, and since the ideas of time are clearer, it is a good time to teach history as connected, sequential narrative. The interest and memory will center round the deeds rather than about such abstract

[1] Lehman and Witty, *The Psychology of Play Activities*, pp. 190, 191, and 207.

things as political motives, terms of treaties, changes in constitutions. Again, since the rhythm sense is strong, reproductive imagery good, and muscle dexterity being co-ordinated, it is a good time to have children of special ability trained at some musical instrument; to start only in the teens is too late, so far as technique goes. Again, since there is a language interest it is an excellent age for acquiring a wide vocabulary in one's own and foreign tongues, for memorizing the more formal aspects of geography, grammar, and the like, as well as literary selections. Verbal learning comes particularly easy at this age, an advantageous fact so far as remembering paradigms, lists of facts, mere words is concerned, disadvantageous so far as the habit of appreciating the meaning of whole passages is desired. Somewhere about now comes the greatest relative increase of immediate memory, though this sort of learning is less good than it is in adult life. The power of prolonged retention is still on the increase, so that, taken together, these two facts explain this "golden age of memory."

The power of forming abstractions is not good, nor is the interest in abstract truth, nor the memory for abstract things. Concepts of time, of space, and of number are fairly well developed within the limits of daily experience and of vivid imagination. On the whole, concepts are chiefly in the form of generic imagery or generalized analogy to some specific instance. As a result, reasoning for reasoning's sake seldom interests children at this age, conduct is seldom generalized, money values need to be personalized, æsthetic and ethical values need to be made specific and concrete. Their reasoning is for practical purposes, not for the sake of discovering truth in the abstract, nor for the fun of measuring wits and developing mental skill. The problems of constructing things that will work are increasingly interesting. They are no longer satisfied, as at nine, to have things merely look right, or be approximately correct; they must actually work. Function pleasure with materials, that is, gives way to a zest for reality. In this, girls are not nearly so advanced as boys.

Piaget [1] finds the years eleven to twelve a turning point, in more ways than one, in logical thinking. Not until this year are the following types of tests passed.

Three objects, a pencil, a key, and a coin are placed in a row. Six questions are asked as to the position of each object relative to the others. Younger children are confused by the key being simultaneously "to the left of" one object and "to the right" of another, and take refuge in the statement that it is in the middle. Eleven-year-olds show a grasp of objective relationship.

The similar test of Burt's [2] — Edith is fairer than Suzanne; Edith is darker than Lily. Which is darkest? — is successfully dealt with for the first time at this age, showing a grasp of logical relationships.

In like manner, they can realize that they would be "foreigners" to the Chinese if they were in China, just as the Chinese are foreigners to us here — showing ability to take not only a viewpoint other than their own, but to generalize the relationship. Relational judgments in general are possible, which in turn gives rise to the ability to give complete definitions rather than by genus alone, or by illustration of a particular.

Before this age children will not assume as premise a judgment in which they do not believe. — For instance, if we say "Supposing we all had two noses and there were three of us in the room how many noses would there be?" they will interrupt by declining to suppose any such thing. Sometime during the years eleven to twelve they will assume pure hypotheses as starting points. They become willing to take other points of view than the egocentric, they gain power to handle the logic of relationships and the logic of classes, to analyze a common element out of given facts. They are therefore ready to discover general laws, and to think formally.

Mental tests. — In the last revision of the Binet general intelligence tests there is no set for this special age; but a

---

[1] See all Piaget references in the bibliography.
[2] Burt, C., *Mental and Scholastic Tests.*

mental age of eleven would be attained by any child passing all the ten-year tests and half those for twelve years, or, of course, nearly all the ten-year tests and scattered tests in the higher ages. Thus he should be able to give the meanings of from thirty-five to forty words from the selected list, indicating a working vocabulary of 6300 to 7200 words. He should be able to detect the absurdities in the test sentences, draw the standard simple designs from memory, give the substance of a simple paragraph read, name at least sixty words in three minutes, and pass the "comprehension tests" of the tenth-year series. At twelve he should be able: (1) to define satisfactorily three out of the five abstract words *pity, revenge, charity, justice, envy;* (2) to rearrange mentally the scattered words of three dissected sentences; (3) to repeat backwards five digits given orally; (4) to interpret two out of five fables read; (5) to interpret rather than merely enumerate the objects in three designated pictures out of four shown; (6) to pass the practical judgment "ball and field" test; and (7) to show power of analysis in naming similarities between certain things. Burt gives samples of reasoning tests which are standardized for this age as well as others. Our various group intelligence tests, with age and grade norms, should be consulted for further illustration of the standard difficulty an eleven-year-old child in grade VI can tackle.[1]

Socially. — Socially, children of eleven are moving in a world made up mostly of their own kind, vaguely peopled with adolescents and younger children, occasionally touched by the orbits of adults. True, grown-ups are borne with in such necessary spheres as industrial and school life, are tolerated as convenient providers of food, money, and other things; but on the whole they are regarded as amazingly far from the interests, occupations, plans, and motives of the boy or girl of eleven. Many adult actions and points of view are incomprehensible, at best foolish, at worst unjust, and generally most uncomfor-

[1] For instance, Detroit Alpha, Otis Self-Administering, the Terman Group test, Kuhlmann-Anderson, etc.

tably non-predictable. At no time may there be such complete
mutual impatience or even misunderstanding, such falling foul
of each other's inclinations and guiding principles.

One reason for this is probably found in the fact that though
in eleven-year-olds the sense of ownership is well developed
so far as their own versus their friends' belongings are concerned, the sense of honor is not yet sufficiently generalized
to make them keep from meddling with the property of older
members of the family, adults in general or the public at large.
Their impulsiveness, imperfect reasoning abilities, wide-awake
energy, eagerness to be experimenting, investigating, making
things happen, lead them into all sorts of situations which
to the unsympathetic adult smack of sheer perversity or willful
mischief. Since they are not yet advanced enough to generalize
principles of conduct, orders or directions have to be specific;
these cannot usually be sufficiently numerous to cover all the
possibilities that will suggest themselves to a healthy, active
child. Hence the wail from the injured adult, "Who could
suppose they would ever think of that?" and from the chidden
culprits, "We weren't ever told not to do that"; or "How was
I to know they'd object to that? Whatever a feller does seems
wrong."

Another reason is that wider reading acquaints children
with all sorts of wonder and adventure tales, delightfully suggestive to the imagination and demanding to be worked out
in play. The fields and woods are full, not only of birds and
animals, but of probable knights, Indians, pirates, and other
vivid beings to whom adjustment must be made; but adults
prosaically refuse to recognize the existence of such, except
in rare instances. When engaged in strife with burglars, savages, one must needs act violently and express one's self by
whoops; it is inconvenient that grown-ups have a different
sense of the fitness of time and place, but so it is. Likewise,
it is stupid, nay provoking, of older ones not to recognize the
absolute necessity for the utilization of all sorts of objects to
further the realism of the atmosphere created; it is unfortunate

too that they object to the transformation of such articles, but so they do. Inevitably, when behaving at such cross purposes, a certain reticence will be induced. This, with the forced reticence concerning escapades that will be interpreted and rewarded in most variable manner, heightens the difficulty of making explanations in language and widens the gulf of misunderstanding. The adult who can appreciate the real motives at work in children, who does enter into the sport, who is serious and respectful at the right time, who is inventive enough to "play up" may cross a bridge over the gulf into the charmed land of boy and girl trust, love, even adoration.

A third reason for the usual lack of understanding is probably that the common adult impulses expressed in love-making, in industrial and social prudence are not yet vital to eleven-year-olds. They view these activities with amusement verging on contempt, at best assuming an attitude of tolerance towards behavior in grown-ups which interferes with their own purposes. Adolescents are, to them, near-adults in many ways, while younger children, unless they arouse pity and fostering care, are so visibly inferior in prowess that their company is unwelcome in the thrilling exploits which occupy the days for eleven-year-olds. Companionship of their own kind is what is urgently needed and constantly sought. Here there is wordless understanding, common aim, mutual interest, co-operative league against uncomprehending elders and babies. Here there are rivals of one's own sort and size, worthy coadjutors; here there is a true democracy, adjustment to which is the main business in life at this time. Girls do not chum with boys at this age, except in rare instances, nor do boys go in "gangs" with girls, though they may be attracted by some special girl of their own age. In general, there is a distinct drawing apart of the sexes, a dislike for each other's ways, a lack of sympathy with each other's interests. Boys think girls "silly, sneaky," and use the word girl as a term of supreme contempt. Girls find boys "horrid, noisy, rough, messy" and other similar things. Clubs for boys and girls together are not likely to flourish; boys respond better to the leadership of one of their own sex than to that of a young girl or older woman.

It is an age when the emotions are strong, the volitional impulses are also strong, but self-control is still weak. Although freedom for initiative in moral, æsthetic, and intellectual fields is very necessary, the opportunity for this must be restricted and balanced with frequent direction; impartial control is equally important for the developing eleven-year-olds, and is, moreover, appreciated by them.

Moral development. — Kirkpatrick [1] calls this the close of the period of "competitive socialization," when "the sharp corners of individuality are to a considerable extent rubbed off or suppressed, and the individual is made to conform to the rule of social life. . . . Only through companionship with those like himself can the child learn the natural laws of sympathy, ridicule, rivalry, etc." Through this association, children by the age of eleven have developed a sense of honor and loyalty to the group that condemns tale-bearing or lying to one's friends, but upholds the lie to enemies or mere outsiders, especially on behalf of one's friends. They have acquired also a contempt for physical cowardice, an admiration for fearlessness, grit, and ability to endure hardship. They will condemn any abuse of the really little by the big, in spite of the frequent bullying of those not so little, and the thoughtless cruelty towards insects, frogs, and very small animals. Their sense of justice is strong, especially within the group. Abstract considerations have little weight except as they sum up, perhaps in proverb form, some concrete experience; but, since this is also the age for voracious reading, ideals embodied in the deeds of favorite hero characters in fiction or history may play quite a large part in determining conduct. Tales of action, power, and courage appeal most to a boy, while for a girl, tales of devotion, romanticism, and sacrifice will also have an appeal. The keen desire for adventure, together with lack of personal ratification of civic law, makes predatory excursions of very

---

[1] Kirkpatrick, E., *The Individual in the Making*, p. 166.

common occurrence among boys. Activities that may go unnoticed in the country are apt to cause friction in the more
densely populated town or city, so that instead of an indignant
farmer appearing to give chase, a policeman may arrive to arrest
for petty larceny. Nevertheless, this age is remarkably "good"
compared with fourteen to fifteen, whether one takes the witness of the police courts or the gradings of conduct by day-
school teachers. By them, 70 per cent of the eleven-year-olds
were rated as good, in spite of the fact that the sixth grade is
proverbially difficult to handle from the standpoint of discipline.

Moral standards. — Moral conduct that may reasonably be
expected *if* there has been suitable training is: self-control
in the way of willingness to take the lesser good first that
future greater good may come, in choosing work before play,
in giving up desired objects for the sake of much smaller or
weaker ones, in prompt obedience to orders issued in a drill,
in persevering in effort at a task in spite of some consequent
discomfort, in inhibiting displays of violent temper, in inhibiting — at stated times and places such as social gatherings
for worship or other ceremonial — impulses to personal satisfaction at the expense of the group. The sense of honor should
by now include keeping promises, finishing tasks assigned,
acknowledging responsibility for deeds, protecting the weak,
old, sick, or very young, treating members of the opposite sex
in some differentiated ways, punctuality, respect for the property of others in the same age group. Ideals of loyalty to one's
friends, to one's family, and to some larger unit, such as the
school, the gang, the village, are usually developed, with a
more shadowy, remote loyalty to the still larger units. Obedience should be a well-formed habit, yet needs to change somewhat during this year to a more rationalized conformity with
social necessities. A conscience is being developed with regard
to duty, politeness, kindness. Table manners will reflect the
home conditions, as will also the personal, modest habits. An
eleven-year-old may have been trained to a very high degree
in these matters; and there is no reason for permitting behavior

far below the family's standards. Although some supervision will still be necessary, children of this age can be held responsible for the entire daily care of their own persons and immediate belongings, whatever new habits may have to be acquired in the next few years.

Superstition is somewhat on the wane, since there is an increasing interest in practical science, such as physics; yet girls may retain much belief in love-lore, and boys in general good luck. There is a great interest in stories of heroes, and a lack of interest in very brief stories, particularly in those presenting abstract ideals of duty, or some obvious moral. Biographies of adventure, such as David, are favorites in Biblical themes; but here it is unsafe to generalize, since interests and the range of information differ so tremendously with the kind of environment. If the religious teaching has been of the mild type, God is now felt as a watchful Father rather than as censorious parent. In quoting beliefs about heaven, death, etc., there is a greater caution shown by prefacing statements by such phrases as "I have been told that . . ." "It is supposed that . . ." Children of eleven to twelve are usually heartily averse to having an adult discuss with them anything religious from a personal point of view; and they are profoundly reticent on the subject with their fellows. Exhortations are tolerated only as they are imagined to apply to some one else. Some few girls and still fewer boys have a definite religious awakening at this period. Girls more than boys are susceptible to the influences of color, beautiful music, symbolic pageantry, and the like, in acts of worship, and may even develop a ritual of their own deeply tinged with mysticism. Usually, however, this is reserved for a later age.

PRACTICAL EXERCISES

1. Review the facts presented in this volume about the eight-year-old child. Observe in the schoolroom, at play, and in the homes if possible. Supplement by wider reading. Prepare generalized statements similar to those in this chapter for the eight-year-old (7—9) level.

2. If preparing for high-school teaching, do the same for the fourteen- to fifteen-year period.

3. If the special interest is with little children, do the same for the two- to three-year period.

4. Extend the list of works of fiction about child life given on page 6. Include only such books as you judge show real insight into child or adolescent behavior.

5. Go through the list of authors given below. Check off those from whose writings you have read. Look up from any good catalogue facts about any you do not know.

Addams, Jane	Furfey, P. H.	Morgan, J. J. B.
Adler, Felix	Gesell, Arnold	O'Shea, M. V.
Baldwin, Bird	Goodenough, Flo. L.	Piaget, Jean
Bigelow, Maurice	Groves, Ernest	Slattery, Margaret
Blanchard, Phyllis	Gruenberg, Benjamin	Starbuck, Edwin D.
Bott, Helen	Gruenberg, Sidonie	Stern, William
Burt, Cyril	Hall, G. Stanley	Swift, Edgar J.
Coe, George A.	Hartshorne, Hugh	Terman, Lewis M.
Curti, Margaret	Healy, Wm.	Thorndike, E. L.
Dennett, Mary W.	Hollingworth, Leta	Watson, John
Dixon, C. M.	Mateer, Flo.	Witty, Paul
Forbush, Wm. B.	Mead, Margaret	Woolley, Helen T.

6. If within reach of a large library, look up a dozen of the books you did not know; add descriptive remarks.

7. (a) Select from your total, completed list, eight volumes you would recommend some one with limited means to get as a *general* child-study library.

   (b) Select a library for a missionary going to India.

   (c) Select the best four to give a young father.

   (d) Select thirty for the library of a women's college.

8. Use the bibliography at the end of this volume, extending it in the line of your special interest.

FOR DISCUSSION

1. Of what value are such studies as these in this chapter?

2. What statements made would be invalidated by:

   (a) great differences in mental age?

   (b) differences in physiological age?

   (c) racial differences?

3. How far do your observations made in connection with special sugges-

tions through this volume corroborate the facts stated for these two age levels? Where do they lead you to disagree?

4. In what way would a preparation of this sort assist any one who was going to Persia, or India, or China to teach?

SELECTED REFERENCES

(Note. The literature on the pre-school period, and on adolescence is so voluminous that no attempt is made here to do more than to indicate a very few general treatises. For specific problems, and source material, the student should turn to the general bibliography at the end of the volume for suggestions to assist in the exercises outlined above.)

ARLITT, A. H. *The Child from One to Twelve.*

BALDWIN and STECHER. *Psychology of the Pre-School Child.*

CABOT, E. L. *Seven Ages of Childhood.*

HOLLINGWORTH, L. *The Psychology of the Adolescent.*

JOHNSON, H. M. *Children in the Nursery School.*

KENWRICK and KENWRICK. *The Child from Five to Ten.*

PECHSTEIN and McGREGOR. *The Psychology of the Junior High School Pupil.*

RICHMOND, W. *The Adolescent Girl.*

STRANG, R. *An Introduction to Child Study.*

TILSON, M. A. *Problems of Pre-School Children as a Basis for Parental Instruction.*

WHITLEY, M. T. *A Study of the Little Child.*

WHITLEY, M. T. *A Study of the Primary Child.*

WHITLEY, M. T. *A Study of the Junior Child.*

CHAPTER XX

INTERPRETATIONS OF CHILD DEVELOPMENT

BRIEF HISTORICAL SKETCH

Adults' interest in children. — There has always, we might assume, been an interest in children. They were so important a part of woman's life that mothers, at least, from the necessities confronting them, learned to interpret and anticipate child behavior, to provide stimuli to social and mental growth as well as physical nourishment, protection and love. That this learning was individual, the attitude partial and possessive, the results unorganized, perhaps not even made explicit, is also true.

The men's interest in children depended on their social viewpoint rather than on individual contact. In primitive communities they took little part in the education of the children till puberty approached. The needs of the tribe, the differentiated functions of men and women, the particular religious beliefs of the group dominated the type of training the young received. In more civilized communities the same thing was true. Children were of concern from the point of view of the state, from the economic and industrial relationships of the group, the sex customs prevalent, the philosophy current. It was taken for granted that, physically and mentally, children were adults in miniature, with an inborn nature either wholly good or wholly bad morally according to the philosophy of the time. Being adults in preparation therefore, children were considered in terms of what they ought eventually to be, according to the Chinese, or Greek, or Christian concept of man's destiny and of desirable social functioning. As beliefs about human nature and destiny changed so a varied influence was felt in education. Thus, children *must* reverence the past and memorize endless rules for behavior, or they *must* be let alone to develop with no interference, or they *must* be restrained and disciplined. (Today, too, the economic and political theories dominant, Soviet, militaristic, democratic, etc., will affect the content of the curriculum and the methods of teaching whatever the psychological interpretation of child development.)

Growth of idea of fitting education to child nature. — A few scattered men whose vocation as schoolmasters gave them contact with childhood seem to have arrived at conclusions that sound ultra-modern. Thus, *Vitterino da Feltra* (1378–1446), emphasized the importance of the nursery age, and stated that education was largely a matter of the right environment. But it was not until *Bacon's* persuasive influence was felt (1561–1626), that the way was open for scientific method to be used in the study of childhood. He deplored the deductive method of taking so much for granted before arguing, and advocated the inductive method of patiently assembling facts before attempting to make sweeping assertions.

Comenius (1592–1671) applied Bacon's ideas and principles to educational methods, with the result that younger children were taught by means of objects and pictures rather than through abstract language. The philosopher *Locke* (1632–1704) centered attention on child nature rather than on teaching method, and later that supreme individualist *Rousseau* (1712–78) put some of Locke's ideas in popular form. *Pestalozzi* (1746–1827) applied the constructive elements in Rousseau's theories in a practical way. His belief was that education was a growth, an unfolding from within in a natural order, from simple to complex.

While Pestalozzi's own emotional nature gave him a sympathy with children, *Herbart* (1776–1841), in a more intellectual way, brought together the best of Rousseau's and Pestalozzi's ideas, expanded the doctrine of working with children's interests, and worked out a psychological method of approach to instruction. *Froebel* (1782–1852), like Pestalozzi, participated in child activities and studied closely the mother-child relationship in the early years. He elaborated the doctrine of the continuity of growth and the necessity of self-activity for development.

These eighteenth and early nineteenth century men were united in the realization that a knowledge of child nature was necessary before suitable education could be undertaken. Each had his own peculiar interpretation of that nature, his own peculiar advocacy of method influenced more by his philosophic outlook than by empirical studies of childhood. Thus, Froebel's mysticism, Rousseau's childish lack of self-control and strongly sexed nature, Herbart's over-analytical mind, biased their interpretations and their exposition of educational doctrine.

Beginnings of scientific study. — In all sciences the method of experimentation was far less common than that of casual observation plus much speculation and rhetorical disquisition. It was not surprising that psychology, originally a philosophical subject, should not have adopted systematic observation and controlled investigation any sooner than it did, or that education, the field of application of child psychology, should be so long conservatively bound by its traditions.

However, we do find that *Tiedemann* in 1787 published a series of observations on his son, almost a century before a similar diary record, scrupulously exact, was given us by *Darwin* in 1872. The classical analytical studies of infant development by *Preyer* appeared in 1882, and are a valuable source of illustrative material in spite of the fact that our present interpretations may differ radically. Similar books by *Perez* and by *Compayré* appeared in the last decade of the century. In this country, *Sully's* "Studies of Childhood" came out, and *Bohannon* made early use of the questionnaire method, helping to center the attention of students in normal schools on individual case histories.

Growth of the idea of studying children directly. — *G. Stanley Hall* has been deservedly called the Father of the Child Study Movement in America. It was due to his indefatigable industry and boundless enthusiasm that widespread interest in the observation of children was aroused, leading to the organization of many adult study circles. From an investigation made in Berlin in 1869 he drew the inspiration for his famous Boston study of 1880 into the "Contents of Children's Minds on Entering School." The results of this were illuminating, even if shocking, to the average teacher, and provoked much further study. Under his guidance further pioneer work was undertaken on all sorts of manifestations — on play, social relationships, fears, jealousy, etc. Such well-known workers as *Kuhlmann, Goddard, Gesell, Terman*, to mention but a few, took part of their training under Stanley Hall at Clark University.

TWENTIETH CENTURY INFLUENCES

Testing, measuring, and experimenting. — *Cattell*, himself in contact with Stanley Hall, with Galton, and a student of Wundt, became particularly interested in individual differences, and early made attempts to measure typical mental abilities. *Thorndike*, utilizing the facilities available in Cattell's laboratory, undertook extended experiments on animal learning. From these, and from his observation of children, he formulated the laws of learning, those of exercise and effect. He familiarized us with the terms S-R bonds, trial and error, and inspired much research with the pronouncement "whatever exists, exists in some quantity and can be measured." The field of educational psychology bears witness to his prolific, scholarly activity as it does to no other one man. Stimulated by his multifarious inquiries and many-sided interests scholastic tests began to appear in great numbers, as well as studies of learning. Other fields related to childhood have benefited from the contributions of such people as *Stenquist, Fowler Brooks, McCall, Bonser, Gates, Agnes Rogers, Augusta Bronner*, to mention but a few names of people trained under him.

Individual tests. — From *Binet*, in France, came the other great impetus towards devising tests of mental capacity. Elaborated by *de Sanctis* in Italy, welcomed by *Goddard* whose work at that time was with feeble-minded children in Vineland, N. J., the knowledge of mental testing spread. Under *Terman* the technique was greatly improved and standardized for children of school age. Others, as described elsewhere, extended the use of tests for younger children and devised others more suitable for handicapped children. Because of the war experience in testing adults, and moved by educators' need to economize time, group tests of intelligence were developed by a group of psychologists, and, since 1920, have come increasingly into use.

Interest in the pre-school age. — A line of influence can be traced from the philanthropic traditions of day nurseries in England and France, and from *Séguin's* methods of teaching feeble-minded children. Madame *Montessori*, in Rome, where kindergartens were not in vogue, gathered little children, largely of the underprivileged class, and modified to fit their needs the methods which, as a student of Séguin's she had observed. Soon she had quite a following of disciples of her own. Not since the multiplication of kindergartens of the Froebelian type had so much public interest in the teaching of little children been aroused. Because of the peculiar philosophical and educational assumptions involved, rival sorts of schools soon appeared, particularly in this country, partly for the social needs they met, partly as fields of research and demonstration for university workers. Professional interest in child health soon focused upon these pre-school age groups, and found expression in nutrition studies.

Baldwin and *Stecher, Gesell, Woolley,* more lately *Goodenough, Blatz,* and *Bott* and many workers under their direction, have refined and enlarged our knowledge of infancy and early childhood. In England, *Grace Owen* and *Susan Isaacs,* in Switzerland *Piaget,* in Vienna the *Bühlers,* all from rather different angles of approach, have stimulated interest in or directed research towards the problems of development of young children. To knowledge of this period also *Stern* contributed largely. His method has been more of the intensive, personalistic type, used by himself and his wife, or by selected parents under his guidance. In this country similar studies of special phases of development have been carried on by Whipple, by the Brandenburgs, Mateer, the Nices, etc.

Mental hygiene. — From the work of psychoanalysts with abnormal and maladjusted adults came another influence on our thinking about childhood. It was so evident that the sources of the abnormal emotional conditions found lay in the earlier years that attention was trained on them to discover what had gone wrong, and when, and why. "Because of repression," was the conclusion. With that, under *Freud*, there developed a whole series of postulates such as (1) the subconscious mind — a sort of dingy subcellar into which unwelcome ideas and unfulfilled wishes were thrust — (2) the censor — a force in charge of the heavy trapdoor to the cellar — concepts which of course are not subject to any objective proof whatever.

For Freud, the repression of the sex instinct is the explanation of every conceivable mental disorder, emotional complex or everyday forgetfulness. Failure of little boys to orient successfully to their mothers, and of little girls to their fathers, is interpreted as the Œdipus or Electra complex respectively, and is considered a large and important factor in children's attitude towards sex matters all through life. *Adler*, an early disciple of Freud, considers the desire for power the greatest force, repression of which is accountable for the peculiarities of behavior we see, and which gives rise to the inferiority complex. *Jung* also dissents from Freud's idea of sex as the sole driving force or "libido," and imagines rather different contents for the subconscious mind. For him, the chief interest centers in the group of instincts that have to do with self-preservation, meaning by that preserving one's individuality socially. Introverts are those motivated chiefly from within, inclined to thinking and dreaming; extroverts are those whose motives turn their attention to objects outside themselves.

Morton Prince did much to make available the values of these points of view. Psychoanalysis was early popularized,

and its tenets greatly distorted, its methods abused by all sorts
of people.

When psychiatrists themselves are in such prejudiced dis-
agreement and would give radically different interpretations of
the same data — dreams for instance — it behooves the psychologist to consider calmly what are their points in common,
and why their methods are efficient to produce cures. They
all assume the importance of motivation of conduct. They all
warn against the unwisdom of repressing instead of sublimating.
They all emphasize the importance of the early years of childhood for shaping the emotional life, points of significance for
the teacher. They have all utilized the fact that to a person in
trouble one of the greatest possible reliefs is the opportunity to
talk it out in private to a sympathetic adviser. Apparently
they all neglect the fact of the very great suggestibility of
any emotionally disturbed persons who willingly consult an
expert. Yet history is full of examples of just such credulity,
showing that any medical or religious belief whatever may
be foisted upon the receptive mind of one who consults the
oracle.

Leaving to one side the many quack and pseudo-psychological
and religious developments of the various theories which lead
astray gullible and morbid people, we find we have a valuable
service rendered by psychiatrists, counselors, guidance clinics,
and so on who can probe into a child's difficulties, help parents
and children readjust, and prevent maladjustments. Our
magazines for parents carry good suggestions for training children with which teachers could well keep in touch. Men like
Ernest Groves, Douglas Thom, John J. B. Morgan do valiant
work in the field of literature.

View of child development. — Of what general facts about
child development can we be reasonably sure? What laws
can be formulated, always remembering that a law in this
field is not a statement of an absolutely uniform happening, but a prediction of the greatest probability of a happening?

First, we may reject the idea that children are adults in all but size. They are in process of becoming, they are continuously changing where adults are relatively stable.

Second, their development is continuous. Even though, for convenience' sake we speak of periods and ages when, by our measurements, certain abilities are now demonstrable that were not in evidence before, that does not imply overnight change from one condition to the next. Just as a plant grows from the two-leaf seedling stage to the two-foot specimen, and as we can at intervals count the leaves, show traces of color in the bud, find ripened seeds in the ovary, so with our measurements on children. We can refer to definite, quantitatively expressed characteristics of the changes we see, but the growth is gradual.

Third, an orderly sequence in development can be traced. Even though the rate of this development varies from child to child yet the sequence itself is predictable, because constant. To illustrate from physical development, the eruption of teeth follows a definite order. Squirming and rolling comes before ability to turn somersaults. Reflex grasping when touched, looking at that which has been grasped, grasping that which is seen are separable stages occurring in that order and no other. Mentally, orientation in space precedes orientation in time. Naming, describing, interpreting is the order of language reaction to pictures. Defining by function precedes defining by classification and differentiation.

Some practical consequences are that (1) with well-selected, graded tests we can discover, in a brief period, a given child's present level of development. (2) We may avoid in our educational procedure calling for abilities not yet manifest, and so avoid wasting time training in a skill before a child is sufficiently mature to profit by such training. For example, we need not endeavor to "rationalize" the process of long division when it is being taught as a habit skill, nor need we expect ten-year-olds to derive benefit from abstract explanations about anything whatsoever.

INTERPRETATIONS OF DEVELOPMENT

Recapitulation theory. — There are three main attempts to explain the sequences of maturation observed, the recapitulation theory, the utility theory, and the theory of correspondence.

The recapitulation theory sets forth that the various instincts, powers, and capacities appear in the individual in the same order as they did in the race, their strength being determined by their age and their importance to the race. Each individual duplicates, from the moment of his conception, in a condensed, somewhat distorted fashion, the history of the race's development. The following quotations express the theory as it has been held. Agassiz said . . . [1] "the phases of development of all living animals correspond to the order of succession of their extinct representatives." . . . "ontogenetic development is recapitulatory. Each individual passes through the stages through which its phylum has passed," [2] . . . "the child's development is only a condensed index of what took place on the larger plan of race history." "In play every mood and movement is instinct with heredity. Thus we rehearse the activities of our ancestors, back we know not how far, and repeat their life work in summative and adumbrated ways. It is reminiscent, albeit unconsciously, of our line of descent, — and each is the key to the other. . . . Thus stage by stage we re-enact their (our ancestors') lives. Once in the phylon many of these activities were elaborated in the life and death struggle for existence. Now the elements and combinations oldest in the muscle history of the race are re-represented earliest in the individual, and those later follow in order." [3]

Stern points out the dull life of the first few months, similar to the mere mammalian, the abilities of the six- to twelve-month stage, comparable to those of the apes. With walking and talking the child "becomes a man" and resembles primitive man for

[1] Burk, F. L., "From fundamental to accessory in the development of nervous system and of movements," *Ped. Sem.*, v. 6, p. 36.

[2] Slaughter, J. W., "The moon in childhood and folk-lore," *A.J.P.*, v. 13, p. 294.

[3] Hall, G. S., *Adolescence*, v. 1, pp. 202, 203.

several years in his dream and play life. He does not become capable of the co-ordinated, differentiated mental activity of present-day civilization till puberty.

G. Stanley Hall is the most ardent advocate of the theory in this country and all his writings contain references to it. It is practically the controlling principle in his discussion of Adolescence in the two-volume book of that name.

The evidence offered for the belief that "ontogeny recapitulates phylogeny" may be grouped under three heads. First that relating to physical recapitulation and derived largely from embryology. A second line of evidence, less important, is adduced from vestigial structures in man, and from the so-called "survival movements." The gill slits, the vermiform appendix, the muscles by which the external ear is moved are those most often quoted. The survival movements may be illustrated by the peculiar paddling or swimming movements, and the grasping and clinging movements which very young babies make. The same answer may be made here to both arguments. Even if a general method of development does not account for their presence, still such bodily analogies have no bearing on recapitulation of behavior.

A third line of evidence offered from genetic, social, and pathological psychology instances many superstitions, fears, customs, and other psychoses which suggest ancestral minds in the same way that vestigial organs in the body suggest earlier physical forms.

Utility theory. — A second theory which is being offered to explain the order of development of original tendencies is the utility theory. Thorndike says, [1] "Other things being equal, the date at which a tendency appears is that one of the many varying dates at which it has appeared in our ancestry which has been most serviceable in keeping the stock alive." The two factors of variation and selection account for the order of the appearance of the tendencies just as they account for their existence. The evidence for this theory is very scanty. The embryo must

[1] *Original Nature of Man*, p. 252.

develop somehow, and it seems extremely likely that in nature there has been evolved a general method for the development, the easiest and most economical; and that because it is a general method, traces of it can be found all up the animal scale. This is borne out by the fact that in instances where recapitulation seems clearest, the way taken for the development is the most simple — most economical, apart from any tendency towards recapitulation. It does seem true, however, that in cases of delayed instincts when the order is in opposition to that of racial development, it is in the direction of the useful order; for instance, walking erect precedes climbing trees.

Theory of correspondence. — This interpretation contents itself with pointing out that since development of organisms is under consideration we are surely apt to find certain characteristics which are similar in both ontogeny and phylogeny. This similarity may apply not only to early levels, but to later and higher levels of development. The individual's typical reactions at various stages indicate in a general way the racial development. This is sufficiently vague and cautious in its statements to allow considerable freedom of judgment. Meanwhile, too little is known of the actual equipment of man in terms of original nature as well as the dates of the appearance of such tendencies to make it safe to consider any theory verified. Such verification must depend on added knowledge.

VARIOUS SCHOOLS OF THOUGHT

The first two decades of the century saw the clearer differentiation of schools of psychological thought as the defects of some of the older methods of study were made evident, and as newer concepts in philosophy were formulated. Proponents of various theories inevitably turned to child life for evidence and, in turn, affected educational procedure by their pronouncements.

Purposivism. — The purposivistic school of psychology, spoken of as the hormic, finds its chief exponent in *William Mc-Dougall.* For him, any description of behavior which omits the motivation, the drive, the seeking of a goal, is absurd. Physical causes alone are an inadequate explanation. Active striving towards some end, a purposeful activity, is a fundamental conception of all behavior. We perceive a situation, anticipate an effect, use effort to attain, and experience satisfaction when the goal is achieved. This is the sort of conduct we know most about, and we should study it first before pushing back into the study of instinctive behavior and the learning of animals. Whether knowingly or not, much ethical discussion assumes McDougall's premises in dealing with child-training.

Behaviorism. — The rise of the behaviorist interpretation of learning is associated chiefly with *John Watson's* repetition on infants of Pavlov's methods of conditioning reflexes. Denying the validity of introspection as a method of psychological study, Watson endeavored to center attention on the observable muscular responses. Their early modification by controlled variation of the situation suggested that everything children do is learned. He took the stand that unless a response was manifest at birth it was due to learning and that therefore heredity, original nature, instincts might be ignored. The behaviorists proceeded to eliminate the terms "mind" and "consciousness" as unnecessary assumptions. *Lashley* and *Weiss* have continued experimental work with both animals and infants.

Perhaps their most valuable contribution to the business of child rearing has been the warning that it is fatally easy to form wrong habits in the first few months and years of life, and that it is tremendously important to secure the right environment, and placid, poised personalities for the care of young children.

Gestalt. — Another school of thought, originating in Germany but little heard of till the estrangement of the war years had lessened, making better interchange of thought possible, is known as the Gestalt, or configurational psychology. It denies that studying isolated abilities of an individual and then summing them up assists us to comprehend him as a whole, since no whole is the same as an aggregation of its parts. Just as a man's physical being is more than so many cents worth of the chemical elements into which it could doubtless be analyzed, so the mind is not so many units of perceiving, imaging, deciding, and so on. The individual is an organism, and acts as a related whole. Instinct is active and continuous. Learning is not a matter of accretion, it depends upon moments of insight, such insight being a release from periods of tension. We perceive, think, and act by patterns, configurations, which emerge and take form from ill-defined backgrounds. Development involves the perfecting of increasingly complex configurations in which purposes as well as objective data have a part.

Wertheim, Köhler, and *Koffka* are the chief exponents of this psychology, citing numerous experiments on animal and child learning to prove their points. *Wheeler* and *Ogden* in this country have written of its applications to education and interpretation of child behavior.

ATTITUDE OF THE PUBLIC IN GENERAL

Teachers. — And what of the average teacher? Will she subscribe heartily to one school of thought exclusively? Will she trust all the learning process to conditioning, or delve into the subconscious, or look for insight? Will she listen to the advice of all in turn? "These are the laws of learning: see that the children adapt to environment," says the functionalist. "Find the motive behind their behavior," says the purposivist. "Watch what they do, that at least is objective," says the behaviorist. "Beware the Œdipus complex — don't repress — rescue the introvert," suggest the psychoanalysts. "Don't pick your children to pieces and think you've explained them, you've destroyed the whole by your analysis," warns the Gestaltist. Will she be eclectic, or, as Woodworth [1] so comfortably puts it, a middle-of-the-roader, along with a goodly host of other psychologists and educators?

Wider interest. — One important aspect of the modern interest in the study of childhood is that not only parents and

[1] *Contemporary Schools of Psychology*, pp. 215 f.

teachers, who must inevitably have contact with children are vitally interested in the results of research, but that those in industry, in criminology, in sociology, in medicine have followed the lead of those in education and have realized that children are not miniature adults but beings-in-themselves whose growth from infancy merits special attention. Child Labor laws, the Children's Court, the Conservation of the Family, the concern of specialists in pediatrics are symptoms of social appreciation of childhood. Our various local associations, our state and Federal departments and Bureaus evidence the public's concern as a whole with its children, such as was undreamed of at the beginning of the century.

Good perspective needed. — In all this we can detect a confused thinking, particularly on the part of parents assailed by contradictory advice from all sides. They are afraid to kiss their children good night, they fear to refuse them anything they ask for, they do not dare object in any way to their activities, and so on. There is a tendency to deify the Child and let the household revolve about His personality, to allow Him so much freedom that he misses guidance. He is made self-conscious, he is habituated to get, to have, to do, to talk, to keep, to extract excitement from any source with little reciprocal adjustment to the community's welfare.

A recovery from this extreme of absurdity is due, as children are envisioned as one part only of the social whole, parenthood as one function only of adults, and the social integration of the whole far more important than exploitation of one of its parts.

In this work of sane, organized functioning teachers are called on to exercise wisdom and judgment to promote adult as well as child learning. The whole of the old-time advice needs emphasis and exemplification,

Come, let us live with our children!

FOR DISCUSSION

1. Do you know homes where the parents seem confused because of the conflicting advice on child-training which they receive?
2. What are the main differences it would make in dealing with children if one were
   (a) a behaviorist of the extreme type;
   (b) a purposivist;
   (c) an adherent of the Adlerian school?
3. For what did or do the following stand? Locate them.
   The Child Study Association of America.
   The Magazine *Parents*.
   National Society for the Study of Education.

James Sully	E. Claparède	Earl Barnes
Karl Groos	O. Decroly	Louise Hogan
Pierre Bovet	Charlotte Bühler	G. D. Compayré

SELECTED REFERENCES

GOODENOUGH and ANDERSON. *Experimental Child Study.* Chs. 1, 2.

HEALY, BRONNER, and BOWES. *The Structure and Meaning of Psycho-Analysis.*

KOFFKA, KURT. *The Growth of the Mind.* Chs. 2, 4, 6.

McDOUGALL, W. *Social Psychology.*

MURCHISON, C. (editor). *Handbook of Child Psychology.*

THORNDIKE, E. L. *Educational Psychology, Briefer Course.* Chs. 1, 6, 8, 10, 11.

WATSON, J. *Psychological Care of Infant and Child.*

WHEELER, R. H. *The Science of Psychology.* Pages 470–500.

WOODWORTH, R. S. *Contemporary Schools of Psychology.*

GLOSSARY

Adenoids. Enlargement or disease of the third tonsil.

Adumbrated. Foreshadowed.

Æsthetic emotions. Emotions that have to do with æsthetic judgments, feelings of beautiful, humorous, etc.

Affective states. Feelings of pleasantness or unpleasantness accompanying sensations and other mental states.

Alternate inheritance. Resemblance to one parent exclusively in some trait.

Amentia. Mental deficiency.

Anæmia. Deficiency of blood.

Animism. Belief that inanimate objects have a soul.

Anthropomorphic. Attributing human form and characteristics to Deity.

Apperception. Taking in and interpreting new material on the basis of the old.

Asexualization. Rendering neuter, sterile.

Astigmatism. A vision defect due to uneven curvature of the cornea or lens, causing uneven focus of light rays and varied brightness of objects.

Asymmetry. Lack of symmetry.

Atavistic. Reverting to remote ancestral traits.

Atypical. Irregular, divergent from type.

Automatization. Making habitual, mechanical.

Behavior pattern. A series of acts making up an effective whole.

Blended inheritance. Resemblance to a mixture of the parents' traits.

Calories. A unit of food value. (The heat required to raise 1 gram of water 1 degree centigrade.)

Carbohydrates. Foods containing 6 atoms of carbon, or a multiple of 6, hydrogen and oxygen in the proportion to form water. Usually in the form of starches or sugars.

Cephalic index. Ratios of width to length of head.

Chorea. " St. Vitus's dance "; muscle twitchings and jerks.

Chronological age. The time elapsed since birth.

Coefficient of correlation. An index of resemblance.

Conditioning. Attaching a response to a new stimulus by presenting the new one simultaneously with the old, effective stimulus sufficiently often to shift it.

Congenital. Existent from birth.

Consanguinity. A close degree of blood relationship.

Constructive imagination. Productive imagination which constructs according to directions objects the accuracy of which can be checked up.

Cornea. The front part of the outer coat of the eyeball.

Cortex. The gray matter of the brain on the outsides of the convolutions.

Creative imagination. Productive imagination which is unhampered, unrestricted, " fancy-free."

Cretinism. A clinical type of idiocy or imbecility due to lack of thyroid gland secretion.

Dementia præcox. An adolescent form of insanity.

Desultory memory. Memory for unrelated, heterogeneous material.

Disuse. A method of modifying instincts and habits by withholding any stimulus which might bring about a response.

Duration of attention. The length of time the attention is centered on a single stimulus.

Empirically. By first-hand, direct experience; by experiment.

Eugenics. The science of improving offspring, of insuring good birth.

Explicit judgment. An interpretation of experience in which the grounds for the inference are clearly expressed.

Forced attention. Attention involving effort.

Free attention. Attention given with no feeling of effort.

Generic images. Imagery not of specific things but with only the generalized features of a class of things.

Gestalt. German word usually translated configuration.

Graph. A pictured or diagrammatic way of representing statistical facts.

Hydrocephaly. A clinical type of physical and mental defect, characterized by too much fluid either between the membranes lining the skull or in the cavities of the brain itself.

Hyperopia. A vision defect due to too short an eyeball to permit the light rays coming to focus on the retina. Long-sightedness.

Hysteria. A nervous disease of adolescence.

Idiot. The lowest range of aments, those needing complete physical care. See page 389.

Illusion. A misinterpretation of sense experience, a false perception.

Imbecile. The middle range of aments, those able to avoid physical danger, but unable to care for themselves economically, socially. See page 389.

Implicit judgment. An interpretation of experience in which the grounds for the inference are used unreflectively, are presupposed.

Inhibition. Interference with a nervous discharge by an opposing force.

Intelligence Quotient. "I.Q." The ratio of mental age, as determined by tests, to chronological age.

Lalling. Mispronunciation of consonants.

Larceny. Theft.

Law of effect. If a response to a situation results in satisfaction, the tendency to respond similarly in future is strengthened. Conversely, if a response results in discomfort, the tendency to respond similarly is thereby weakened.

Law of exercise. The likelihood that a given response will be made to a given situation is in proportion to the frequency of its connection with the situation.

Law of regression. The characteristics of offspring vary, not about the parental deviation, but about a point between that deviation and the mode for the whole population.

Masochistic. Sexually excitable by experiencing pain or ill-treatment.

Mendelian. According to Mendel's theory or law. See page 25.

Microcephaly. A rare clinical type of ament characterized by a very small, peaked head.

Molars. Double, grinding teeth.

Mongolian. A clinical type of ament characterized by a facial resemblance to the Mongolian race.

Moron. The highest range of aments, handicapped mentally, socially, and economically, but capable of working under supervision.

Motor centers. Areas in the brain from which nerve impulses are sent out to the muscles.

Motor images. Mental representations of being in motion passively, or of moving parts of the body.

Myopia. A vision defect due to too long an eyeball to permit the light rays coming to focus on the retina. Shortsightedness.

Negative correlation. Index of resemblance varying from 0 to -100, indicating inverse relationship.

Neurasthenia. Nervous debility.

Neurones. Nerves, consisting of fibrils called dendrites, a cell body, a fiber called the axone ending in fibrils called the end-brush.

Neurone circuit. A chain of three types of neurones, those that receive impressions, the sensory; those that connect with various parts of the brain, the associative; and those that move the muscles, the motor.

Obliviscence. Forgetting.

Ontogeny. The history of the development of an individual.

Organism. A structure acting by means of organs; roughly, any living plant or animal.

Orgasm. Excitement and swelling.

Percept. Interpreted sense experience; consciousness of things present to the senses.

Phobia. Excessive fear of anything.

Phylogenetic. Pertaining to the history of the development of the species.

Phylum. The big branches of the animal or vegetable kingdoms.

Plasticity. The condition of capability of change, neither too sudden nor too temporary.

Plateau. A place in the practice curve more or less on the dead level, representing lack of measurable progress.

Positive correlation. Index of resemblance varying from 0 to 100.

Practice curve. The graphic representation of progress in learning. It shows a sharp slant at the beginning, one or several pleateaus, gradual flattening out to a level of efficiency.

Predatory. Plundering, pillaging.

Productive imagery. Images combined in new ways.

Protozoa. One-celled animal organisms.

Puberty. The age of sexual maturity.

Pubescent. Relating to the beginning of puberty.

Range of attention. The number of things that may be attended to, grasped, simultaneously.

Recall. Reviving past experiences.

Remote sensations. Those felt in the part of the body not directly moving; *e.g.*, in the eyes when walking.

Resident sensations. Those felt in the part of the body that is acting; *e.g.*, in the hand when writing.

Retention. Holding impressions so that they may be recalled.

Rickets. A young children's disease involving crookedness of the long bones and swelling of their extremities.

Sadistic. Sexually excitable by inflicting pain on others or watching it inflicted.

Senescence. Growing old.

Siblings. Offspring of the same parents, *i.e.*, brother-brother relationship, or brother-sister, or sister-sister.

Situation. A complex group of stimuli all of which together may evoke some response — roughly, the immediate circumstances under which an act is performed.

Skatophilia. Undue interest in excretory processes, excitement therefrom.

Span of attention. The number of things that can be grasped, understood, remembered, if presented successively.

Stimulation. A method of developing instincts and habits by providing extra situations to arouse the responses.

Strabismus. Lack of balance in the muscles moving the eyes, causing squint, cross-eyes, etc.

Sublimation. Changing the emotion connected originally with an instinctive response so that it is felt in other situations.

Substitution. Changing the instinctive reaction to a situation.

Tertiary. Third.

Threshold. The point at which the intensity of a stimulus is sufficient to produce a sensation.

Tics. Nervous twitching habits.

Toxic. Poisonous.

Trial and error. A method of learning in which successive attempts are made with no clear idea of their value or probable result.

Vitamins. Elements in foods of bio-chemical importance.

Voluntary attention. Attention given with a feeling of effort.

BIBLIOGRAPHY

Abbreviations used

A. J. P. — American Journal of Psychology.
Am. Jo. Psych. — American Journal of Psychiatry.
Am. Jo. Soc. — American Journal of Sociology.
Am. Phys. Ed. Rev. — American Physical Education Review.
A. S. H. A. — American Social Hygiene Association.
Arch. of Psy. — Archives of Psychology.
Br. Jo. Med. Psych. — British Journal of Medicine and Psychiatry.
Br. Jo. Psy. — British Journal of Psychology.
Ch. Dev. — Child Development.
Ch. St. Mo. — Child Study Monthly.
Comp. Psy. Mon. — Comparative Psychology Monograph.
El. Sch. Jo. — Elementary School Journal.
Gen. Psy. Mon. — Genetic Psychology Monograph.
Jo. Abn. Psy. — Journal of Abnormal Psychology.
Jo. App. Psy. — Journal of Applied Psychology.
Jo. Comp. Psy. — Journal of Comparative Psychology.
Jo. Del. — Journal of Delinquency.
Jo. Ed. Psy. — Journal of Educational Psychology.
Jo. Ed. Res. — Journal of Educational Research.
Jo. Ed. Soc. — Journal of Educational Sociology.
Jo. Exp. Ped. — Journal of Experimental Pedagogy.
Jo. Exp. Psy. — Journal of Experimental Psychology.
Jo. Gen. Psy. — Journal of Genetic Psychology.
Jo. Her. — Journal of Heredity.
Jo. Juv. Res. — Journal of Juvenile Research.
Jo. Med. — Journal of Medicine.
Jo. Pers. Res. — Journal of Personnel Research.
Jo. Soc. Hy. — Journal of Social Hygiene.
Jo. Soc. Psy. — Journal of Social Psychology.
Ment. Hyg. — Mental Hygiene.
N. S. S. E. — National Society for the Study of Education.
Ped. Sem. — Pedagogical Seminary.
Pop. Sci. Mo. — Popular Science Monthly.
Psy. Bull. — Psychological Bulletin.
Psy. Cl. — Psychological Clinic.
Psy. Mon. — Psychological Monograph.
Psy. Rev. — Psychological Review.
Pub. Sch. Pub. Co. — Public School Publishing Company.
Rel. Ed. — Religious Education.
Sch. Rev. — School Review.

Sch. and Soc. — School and Society.
Sci. Mo. — Scientific Monthly.
Soc. Sci. Mo. — Social Science Monthly.
T. C. Cont. to Ed. — Teachers College Contributions to Education.
Univ. Iowa St. Ch. Welf. — University of Iowa Studies in Child Welfare.
Univ. Iowa St. Ed. — University of Iowa Studies in Education.
Zeit. f. Psy. — Zeitschrift für Psychologie.

ADDAMS, JACOBY, etc. "The child, the clinic and the court." *New Republic*, 1925.

ALLEN, CHAUNCEY N. "Individual differences in delayed reactions of infants." *Arch. of Psy. 127*, 1931.

ALPERT, AUGUSTA. "The solving of problem situations by pre-school children." *T. C. Cont. to Ed. *323*, 1928.

ANDREWS, E. G. "The development of imagination in the pre-school child." *Univ. of Iowa St. 3 *4*, 1930.

ARLITT, ADA H. *Psychology of Infancy and Early Childhood.* McGraw-Hill, 1928.

    The Child from One to Twelve. McGraw-Hill, 1931.

ATKINSON, R. K. "A study of athletic ability of high school girls." *Am. Phys. Ed. Rev.* v. 20, 1925.

BAIN, R. "Religious attitudes of college students." *Am. Jo. Soc.* v. 32, 1927.

BAKER, HARRY J. *Characteristic Differences in Bright and Dull Pupils.* Pub. Sch. Pub. Co., 1927.

BALDWIN, BIRD T. "Physical growth of children from birth to maturity." *Univ. Iowa St. Ch. Welf. 1*, 1920.

    "The relation between mental and physical growth." *Jo. Ed. Psy.* v. 13, 1922.

BALDWIN and STECHER. *Psychology of the Pre-School Child.* Appleton, 1925.

BARKER, MARGARET. "A technique for studying social activities of young children." *Ch. Dev. Mon. *3*, 1903. T. C. Bureau of Publications.

BENEDICT, A. E. *Children at the Crossroads.* Commonwealth Fund, N. Y., 1930.

BERMAN, LOUIS. *The Glands Regulating Personality.* Macmillan, 1922.

BIGELOW, MAURICE. *Adolescence.* Funk and Wagnalls, 1924.
  Sex Education. Macmillan, 1920.
BLANCHARD, PHYLLIS. *The Adolescent Girl.* Moffat, Yard Co., 1924.
  The Child and Society. Longmans Green, 1928.
BLANCHARD and MANASSES. *New Girls for Old.* Macaulay, 1930.
BLANCHARD and PAYNTER. "The problem child." *Ment. Hyg.* v. 8, 1924.
BLANTON, SMILEY. "A mental hygiene program for colleges." *Ment. Hyg.* v. 9, 1925.
BLANTON and BLANTON. *Child Guidance.* Century Co., 1927.
BLATZ and BOTT. "Studies in mental hygiene of children." *Ped. Sem.* v. 34, 1927.
BOGARDUS, E. *City Boy and His Problems.* Los Angeles, 1926.
BOLTON, F. E. *Adolescent Education.* Macmillan, 1931.
BOOK, W. F. *The Intelligence of High School Seniors.* Macmillan, 1922.
BOSE, R. G. "Nature and development of religious concepts in children." *Rel. Ed.* v. 24, 1928.
BOTT, HELEN. "Observation of play activities in a nursery school." *Gen. Psy. Mon. 4 *1,* 1928.
BOTT, E. A., et al. "Observation and training of fundamental habits in young children." *Gen. Psy. Mon. 4 *1,* 1928.
BOWEN and MITCHELL. *The Theory of Organized Play.* A. S. Barnes, 1923.
BRACE, D. K. *Measuring Motor Ability.* A. S. Barnes, 1927.
BRECKENRIDGE and ABBOTT. *The Delinquent Child and the Home.* Charities Publ. Commission, 1912.
BRIDGES, K. M. B. "Occupational interests and attention of 3-year-old children." *Jo. Gen. Psy.* v. 34, 1927.
  "Occupational interests and attention of 4-year-old children." *Jo. Gen. Psy.* v. 36, 1929.
BRIDGES and BRIDGES. "A psychological study of juvenile delinquency by group methods." *Gen. Psy. Mon. 1 *5,* 1926.
BROOKS, F. D. "Rate of mental growth, ages 9 to 15." *Jo. Ed. Psy.* v. 12, 1921.
  The Psychology of Adolescence. Houghton Mifflin, 1929.
BROOKS and BASSETT. "The retention of American history in the junior high school." *Jo. Ed. Res.* v. 18, 1928.
BÜHLER, CHARLOTTE. *The First Year of Life.* John Day, 1930.
  Kindheit und Jugend. Hirzel, Leipzig, 1928.
  "Are lies necessary?" *Ped. Sem.* v. 33, 1926.

BÜHLER, KARL. *The Mental Development of the Child.* Harcourt, Brace, 1930.

BURKS, B. S. "The Relative Influence of Nature and Nurture upon Mental Development." *27th Yearbook of N.S.S.E.*, 1928.

BURNHAM, W. *The Normal Mind.* Appleton, 1925.

BURT, CYRIL. *Mental and Scholastic Tests.* London County Council, 1921.

   The Young Delinquent. Appleton, 1925.

BUSH and RIGBY. "The play hour." *Psy. Cl.* v. 18, 1929.

BUTCHER, HOEY, and McGINNIS. *A Study of Problem Boys and Their Brothers.* Crime Commission of N. Y. State, 1929.

CABOT, E. L. *Seven Ages of Childhood.* Houghton Mifflin, 1921.

CAMERON, H. C. *The Nervous Child.* Humphrey Milford, 1926.

CAMPBELL, C. M. et al. *Problems of Personality.* Harcourt, Brace, 1925.

CARMICHAEL, A. MAX. "Moral situations of 6-year-old children as a basis for curriculum construction." *Univ. Iowa St. Ed. 4 *6*, 1927.

   "To what objective stimuli do 6-year-old children respond with intentional misrepresentation?" *Ped. Sem. and Jo. Gen. Psy.* v. 35, 1928.

   "The behavior of 6-year old children when called upon to account for past irregularities." *Jo. Gen. Psy.* v. 37, 1930.

CHASE, J. H. "Street games of N. Y. City." *Ped. Sem.* v. 12, 1905.

CLAPARÈDE, E. *Experimental Pedagogy and the Psychology of the Child.* 1911.

CLARK, T. A. *The High School Boy and His Problems.* Macmillan, 1920.

CLEVELAND, ELIZABETH. "If parents only knew." *Children.* v. 2, 1927.

COE, GEORGE A. "A social theory of religious education." *Scribner*, 1917.

CONKLIN, EDWIN G. *Heredity and Environment in the Development of Men.* Princeton Univ. Press, 1923.

COOPER, M. L. *Seven Psychological Portraits, a handbook for parents and teachers.* Morehouse, 1928.

COY, G. L. "The interests, abilities and achievements of a special class for gifted children." *T. C. Cont. to Ed. *131*, 1923.

CRILE, G. W. *The Origin and Nature of the Emotions.* W. B. Saunders, 1915.

CURTI, MARGARET W. *Child Psychology.* Longmans Green, 1930.

DAVENPORT, F. I. "Adolescent interests." *Arch. of Psy.* v. 66, 1923.
   Salvaging of American Girlhood. Dutton, 1924.
DENNETT, MARY WARE. *The Sex Education of Children.* Vanguard
   Press, 1931.
DIXON, C. M. *Children are Like That.* John Day, 1930.
DOLCH, EDWARD W. "Grade vocabularies." *Jo. Ed. Res.* v. 16, 1927.
DOLL, E. A. "The growth of intelligence." *Psy. Mon. *2*, 1890.
DOUGLASS, A. A. "Vocational interests of high school seniors." *Sch.
   and Soc.* v. 16, 1922.
DRUCKER and HEXTER. *Children Astray.* Harvard Univ. Press, 1925.

EASBY GRAVE, CHARLOTTE. "Tests and Norms at the 6-year-old per-
   formance level." *Psy. Cl.* v. 15, 1924.
EAST, E. M. *Heredity and Human Affairs.* Scribner, 1927.
EAST and JONES. *Inbreeding and Outbreeding.* Lippincott, 1919.
EIKENBERRY, D. H. "Permanence of high school learning." *Jo. Ed.
   Psy.* v. 14, 1923.
ENG, HELGA. *Experimental Investigation into the Emotional Life of the
   Child.* Humphrey Milford, 1925.

FAHS, SOPHIE L. "The beginnings of religion in baby behavior." *Rel.
   Ed.* v. 25, 1930.
FARWELL, L. "Reaction of kindergarten, first and second grade chil-
   dren to constructive play materials." *Gen. Psy. Mon. *8*, 1930.
FENTON, NORMAN. "The only child." *Jo. Gen. Psy.* v. 35, 1928.
FISKE, GEORGE W. *Boy Life and Self Government.* N. Y., 1919.
FLETCHER, J. M. *The Problems of Stuttering.* Longmans Green, 1925.
FORBUSH, WILLIAM B. *The Boy Problem.* Pilgrim Press, 1913.
FOREST, ILSE. *Child Life and Religion.* R. R. Smith, 1930.
FOSTER, JOSEPHINE C. "Verbal memory in the pre-school child."
   Ped. Sem. and Jo. Gen. Psy. v. 35, 1928.
   "Play activities of children in the first 6 grades." *Ch. Dev.* v. 1,
   1930.
FOX, H. W. *The Child's Approach to Religion.* R. R. Smith, 1930.
FRANKLIN, E. E. *The Permanence of the Vocational Interests of Junior
   High School Pupils.* Johns Hopkins Press, 1924.
FREEMAN, F. N. *Mental Tests.* Houghton Mifflin, 1926.
FREEMAN, HOLZINGER, and MITCHELL. "The influence of environment
   on the intelligence, school achievement, and conduct of foster
   children." *27th Yearbook of N.S.S.E.*, 1928.

FRENCH, R. S. *The Education of the Blind.* California School for the Blind, 1924.

FURFEY, P. H. *The Gang Age.* Macmillan, 1926.

The Growing Boy. Macmillan, 1930.

"Case studies in developmental age." *Am. Jo. Orthopsychiatry,* 1931.

GARRISON, CHARLOTTE G. *Permanent Play Materials for Young Children.* Scribner, 1926.

GARTH, T. R. *Race Psychology.* McGraw-Hill, 1931.

GATES, ARTHUR. "The mnemonic span for visual and auditory digits." *Jo. Exp. Psy.* v. 1, 1916.

"Recitation as a factor in memorizing." *Arch. of Psy.* v. 40, 1917.

GESELL, ARNOLD. *The Mental Growth of the Pre-School Child.* Macmillan, 1925.

Infancy and Human Growth. Macmillan, 1928.

"Maturation and infant behavior." *Psy. Rev.* v. 36, 1929.

GILBRETH, LILLIAN. *Living with Our Children.* Norton, 1928.

GODDARD, HENRY H. *School Training of Gifted Children.* World Book Co., 1928.

GOODENOUGH, FLO. L. *Measurement of Intelligence by Drawings.* World Book Co., 1926.

"Racial differences in the intelligence of school children." *Jo. Exp. Psy.* v. 9, 1926.

GOODENOUGH and ANDERSON. *Experimental Child Study.* Century Co., 1931.

GROSZMANN, MAXIMILLIAN. *The Exceptional Child.* Scribner, 1917.

GROVES, ERNEST. *Personality and Social Adjustment.* Longmans Green, 1925.

GROVES and BLANCHARD. *Mental Hygiene.* Holt, 1930.

GROVES and GROVES. *Wholesome Childhood.* Houghton Mifflin, 1924.

GRUENBERG, BENJAMIN. *High Schools and Sex Education.* Washington Government Printing Office, 1922.

Parents and Sex Education. A.S.H.A., 1923.

GRUENBERG, SIDONIE. *Your Child, Today and Tomorrow.* Lippincott, 1920.

GUYER, MICHAEL F. *Being Well Born.* Bobbs-Merrill, 1927.

HAEFNER, RALPH. "The educational significance of left-handedness." *T. C. Cont. to Ed. *360*, 1929.

HAGGERTY, M. E. "The incidence of undesirable behavior in public school children." *Jo. Ed. Res.* v. 12, 1925.

HALL, G. STANLEY. *Adolescence.* Appleton, 1904. *Aspects of Child Life and Education.* Smith, 1907.

HALL, MRS. W. S. "First 500 days of a child's life." *Child Study Mag.* v. 2, 1897.

HARRINGTON, M. A. "Mental disorder in adolescence." *Ment. Hyg.* v. 4, 1920.

HART, H. N. "A test of social attitudes and interests." *Univ. of Iowa St. Ch. Welf. 2 *4*, 1923.

HARTSHORNE, HUGH. "Testing the knowledge of right and wrong." *Rel. Ed.* v. 26, 1926.

HARTSHORNE and MAY. *Studies in Deceit.* Macmillan, 1928. *Studies in Service and Self-Control.* Macmillan, 1929.

HARTSHORNE, MAY, et al. *Studies in the Organization of Character.* Macmillan, 1930.

HARTWELL, S. W. *Fifty-five "Bad" Boys.* Knopf, 1931.

HAVILAND, M. S. *Character Training in Childhood.* Dodd, Mead, 1921.

HAZLITT, V. "Children's thinking." *Br. Jo. Psy.* v. 20, 1930.

HEALY, WILLIAM. *Mental Conflicts and Misconduct.* Little, Brown, 1923.

HEALY and BRONNER. *Delinquents and Criminals, Their Making and Unmaking.* Macmillan, 1926.

HEALY et al. *Reconstructing Behavior in Youth.* Knopf, 1929.

HEALY, BRONNER, and BOWERS. *The Structure and Meaning of Psychoanalysis.* Knopf, 1930.

HELSETH, INGA OLLA. "Children's thinking." *T. C. Cont. to Ed. *209*, 1926.

HERRING and KOCH. "A study of some factors influencing the interest span of pre-school children." *Jo. Gen. Psy.* v. 38, 1930.

HETZER, H. "Kind und Schaffen; Experimente über Konstructive Betätigungen im Kleinkindalters." *Quellen und Studien zur Jugenkunde.* v. 7, 1931.

HICKS, J. A. "The acquisition of motor skill in young children." *Ch. Dev.* v. 1, 1930.

HIGH, STANLEY. *The Revolt of Youth.* Abingdon Press, 1923.

HILDRETH, GERTRUDE. "Resemblance of siblings in intellectual development." *T. C. Cont. to Ed. *186*, 1925.

HOLLINGWORTH, HARRY. *Mental Growth and Decline.* Appleton, 1927.

HOLLINGWORTH, LETA S. *Psychology of Subnormal Children.* Macmillan, 1923.

    Gifted Children, Their Nature and Nurture. Macmillan, 1926.

    Psychology of the Adolescent. Appleton, 1928.

    "The child of very superior intelligence as a special problem in social adjustment." *Ment. Hyg.* v. 15, 1931.

HOLZINGER, KARL J. "The relative effect of nature and nurture influences on twin differences." *Jo. Ed. Psy.* v. 20, 1929.

HUFF, R. L. "Percept content of school children's minds." *Ped. Sem.* v. 34, 1927.

HULSON, E. L. "Block construction of 4-year-old children." *Jo. Juv. Res.* v. 14 *3, 1930.

HUNT, N. M. "Factors influencing play of the pre-school child." *Soc. Sci. Mon.* *1, 1931.

HUNT, THELMA. "The measurement of social intelligence." *Jo. App. Psy.* v. 12, 1928.

HURLOCK and SENDER. "The negative phase in relation to the behavior of prepubescent girls." *Ch. Dev.* v. 1, 1930.

INNSKEEP, ANNIE DOLMAN. *Child Adjustment in Relation to Growth and Development.* Appleton, 1930.

IRWIN and MARKS. *Fitting the School to the Child.* Macmillan, 1924.

ISAACS, SUSAN. "The biological interests of young children." *Forum of Education.* v. 7, 1929.

    Intellectual Growth in Young Children. Harcourt, Brace, 1930.

JOHNSON, BUFORD. *Mental Growth of Children in Relation to the Rate of Growth in Bodily Development.* Dutton, 1925.

JOHNSON, HARRIET M. *Children in the Nursery School.* John Day, 1928.

JOHNSTON, G. A. "An experimental investigation of the psychology of moral judgment." *Br. Jo. Psy.* v. 15, 1925.

JONES, A. M. "An analytical study of 120 superior children." *Psy. Cl.* v. 16, 1927.

JONES, H. E. "Experimental studies of college teaching." *Arch. of Psy.* *68, 1923.

JONES, MARY COVER. "The elimination of children's fears." *Jo. Exp. Psy.* v. 7, 1924.

JONES, W. F. "A study of handedness." *Univ. of S. Dakota Bulletin,* Series 17 *14*, 1918.

JORDAN, ARTHUR M. *Children's Interest in Reading.* Univ. of N. Carolina Press, 1926.

JUDGE BAKER FOUNDATION. " Case Studies." *Series I.* Little, Brown, 1922-23.

KELLEY, T. L. *The Influence of Nurture upon Native Differences.* Macmillan, 1926.

KENWORTHY, MARION E. "The logic of delinquency." *Papers and Proceedings of the Am. Sociological Soc.* v. 16, 1921.

KENWRICK and KENWRICK. *The Child from Five to Ten.* Dutton, 1930.

KIDD, DUDLEY. *Savage Childhood.* London, 1906.

KING, IRVING. *The High School Age.* Bobbs-Merrill, 1915.

KIRKPATRICK, EDWIN A. *Fundamentals of Child Study.* 4th ed. Macmillan, 1929.

KLÜVER, H. "Studies on the eidetic type and on eidetic imagery." *Psy. Bull.* v. 25, 1928.

KNIGHT, H. R. *Play and Recreation in a Town of 6000.* Russell Sage Fdn., 1919.

KOFFKA, KURT. *The Growth of the Mind.* Harcourt, Brace, 1928.

KUHLMANN, F. "The results of repeated mental examination of 639 feebleminded over a period of 10 years." *Jo. App. Psy.* v. 5, 1921. *A Handbook of Mental Tests.* Warwick & York, 1922.

KUPKY, O. *The Religious Development of Adolescents.* Macmillan, 1928.

LAIRD, D. A. "Case studies in the mental problems of later adolescence." *Ment. Hyg.* v. 7, 1923.

LAMSON, E. E. "A study of young gifted children in senior high school." *T. C. Cont. to Ed.* *424*, 1930.

LANCASTER, T. J. "A study of the voluntary reading of pupils in grades 4 to 8." *El. Sch. Jo.* v. 28, 1928.

LANGFORD, F. W. "The religious nurture of a little child." *American Home Series *17*, 1920.

LA RUE, D. W. *Mental Hygiene.* Macmillan, 1927.

LASKER, B. *Race Attitudes in Children.* Holt, 1929.

LAYTON, E. T. "The persistence of learning in elementary algebra." *Jo. Ed. Psy.* v. 32, 1923.

496   *Bibliography*

LEAL, M. A. "Personality traits and maturing in children of normal I.Q." *Jo. Ed. Res.* v. 23, 1931.

LEE, A. L. "An experimental study of retention and its relation to intelligence." *Psy. Mon.* v. 34 *4, 1925.

LEE, JOSEPH. *Play in Education.* Macmillan, 1915.

LEHMAN and WITTY. *Psychology of Play Activities.* Barnes, 1927.
  "A study of doll play in relation to the onset of pubescence." *Ped. Sem.* and *Jo. Gen. Psy.* v. 34, 1927.
  "A study of play in relation to intelligence." *Jo. App. Psy.* v. 12, 1928.
  "A study of play in relation to pubescence." *Jo. Soc. Psy.* v. 1, 1930.
  "A study of vocational attitudes in relation to pubescence." *A.J.P.* v. 43, 1931.

LENROOT and LUNDBERG. "Juvenile courts at work." *U. S. Dept. of Labor Publ.* *141, 1925.

LEVY, J. "A quantitative study of the relationship between intelligence and economic status as factors in the etiology of children's behavior problems." *Am. Jo. Orthopsychiatry.* v. 1, 1931.

LINE, W. "Growth of visual perception in children." *Br. Jo. Psy. Mon. Supp.* *15, 1931.

LUCAS, W. P. *The Health of the Runabout Child.* Macmillan, 1924.

MACAULAY, E. "Some social, age, and sex differences shown in children's choice of ideals." *Forum of Education.* v. 3, 1925.
  "Some notes on the attitude of children to dress." *Br. Jo. Med. Psych.* v. 9, 1929.

MACAULAY and WATKINS. "An investigation into the development of the moral conceptions of children." *Forum of Education.* v. 4, 1926.

MAJOR, D. R. *First Steps in Mental Growth.* Macmillan, 1906.

MANGOLD, G. B. *Problems of Child Welfare.* Macmillan, 1924.

MARSTON, LESLIE R. "The emotions of young children." *Univ. of Iowa St. Ch. Welf.* v. 3 *3, 1925.

MARTIN and DE GRUCHY. *Mental Training for the Pre-School Age Child.* Harr Wagner Pub. Co., 1923.

MATEER, FLORENCE. *Child Behavior.* Badger, 1918.
  The Unstable Child. Appleton, 1924.
  Just Normal Children. Appleton, 1929.

MATTHEW, M. T. "A written reproduction test for the Lord's Prayer." *Sch. and Soc. *240*, 1927.

McCARTHY, DOROTHY A. "The language development of the pre-school child." *Univ. of Minn. Press*, 1930.

McCARTY, STELLA A. *Children's Drawings*. Williams & Watkins, 1924.

MEAD, C. D. "The relation of general intelligence to certain mental and physical traits." *T. C. Cont. to Ed. *76*, 1916.

MEAD, MARGARET. *Coming of Age in Samoa*. Morrow, 1928.
Growing up in New Guinea. Morrow, 1930.

MEARNS, HUGHES. *Creative Youth*. Doubleday, Doran, 1926.
Creative Power. Doubleday, Doran, 1929.

MEYER, ADOLPH E. "The lies that children tell." *Sci. Mo.* v. 23, 1926.

MILLER, ALICE M. *Children and the Movies*. Univ. of Chic. Press, 1930.

MOORE, D. T. V. "The reasoning ability of children in the first years of school life." *St. in Psy. and Psych.* v. 2 *2*, Catholic Univ. of America, 1929.

MOORE, K. C. "Mental development of a child." *Psy. Rev. Mon. Supp. *3*, 1896.

MOORE, R. C. "The evolution of admiration and its development in children." *Jo. Exp. Ped.* v. 5, 1920.

MORGAN, JOHN J. B. *Psychology of the Unadjusted School Child*. Macmillan, 1924.
Child Psychology. R. R. Smith, 1930.

MORTON, G. F. *Childhood's Fears*. Macmillan, 1925.

MOXCEY, MARY E. *Girlhood and Character*. Abingdon Press, 1916.

MURPHY, M. "The 10-year level of competency." *Psy. Cl.* v. 17, 1928.

MURPHY, GARDNER, and MURPHY. *Experimental Social Psychology*. Harper, 1931.

NATIONAL SOCIETY FOR THE STUDY OF EDUCATION'S YEARBOOKS.
Intelligence Tests and Their Use. 1922.
Gifted Children. 1924.
Vocational Guidance and Vocational Education. 1926.
Nature and Nurture. 1928.
Pre-School and Parental Education. 1929.

NEWMAN, H. H. "Mental and physical tests of identical twins reared apart." *Jo. Her.* v. 20, 1929.

NICE, M. M. "The speech development of a child from 18 months to 6 years." *Ped. Sem.* v. 24, 1917.

OAKLEY, C. A. "The interpretation of children's drawings." *Br. Jo. Psy.* v. 21, 1931.

OTIS, MARGARET. "A study of suggestibility of children." *Arch. of Psy.* v. 70, 1924.

OWEN, R. D. *Principles of Adolescent Education.* Ronald Press, 1929.

PALMER, LUELLA A. *Play Life in the First 8 Years.* Ginn, 1916.

PARKER, GEO. H. "Identical twins with dementia præcox." *Jo. Her.* v. 17, 1926.

PARSON, B. S. *Lefthandedness.* Macmillan, 1924.

PATRICK, G. T. W. *The Psychology of Relaxation.* Houghton Mifflin, 1916.

PECHSTEIN and JENKINS. *Psychology of the Kindergarten Primary Child.* Houghton Mifflin, 1927.

PECHSTEIN and McGREGOR. *Psychology of the Junior High School Pupil.* Houghton Mifflin, 1924.

PEPPARD, HELEN E. *The Correction of Speech Defects.* Macmillan, 1925.

PIAGET, JEAN. *The Language and Thought of the Child.* Harcourt, Brace, 1926.

Judgment and Reasoning in the Child. Harcourt, Brace, 1928.

The Child's Conception of the World. Harcourt, Brace, 1929.

The Child's Conception of Physical Causality. Harcourt, Brace, 1930.

PINTNER, RUDOLPH. *Intelligence Testing.* Henry Holt, 1931.

PLANT, J. S. "Some psychiatric aspects of crowded living conditions." *Am. Jo. Psych.* v. 9, 1930.

POPENOE, PAUL B. *Child's Heredity.* Williams and Wilkins, 1929.

PRATT, J. B. *The Religious Consciousness.* Macmillan, 1921.

PREYER, W. *The Mind of the Child.* Appleton, 1890.

Mental Development in the Child. Appleton, 1894.

PRUETTE, J. "What's happening in the daydreams of the adolescent girl?" *Jo. Soc. Hyg.* v. 10, 1924.

PUFFER, J. A. *The Boy and His Gang.* Houghton Mifflin, 1912.

RAUBICHECK, DAVIS, and CARLL. *Voice and Speech Problems.* Prentice Hall, 1931.

REAVIS, WM. C. *Pupil Adjustment in Junior and Senior High Schools.* D. C. Heath, 1926.

REEVES, W. R. "Report of commission on street play." *Jo. Ed. Soc.* v. 24, 1931.

REYNOLDS, MARTHA M. "Negativism of pre-school children." *T. C. Cont. to Ed.* *288, 1928.

RICHMOND and HALL. *Child Marriages.* Russell Sage Fdn., 1928.

RICHMOND, WINIFRED. *The Adolescent Girl.* Macmillan, 1925.

ROBACK, A. A. *Psychology of Character.* Harcourt, Brace, 1925.

ROBERTS, LYDIA J. *Nutrition Work with Children.* Univ. of Chic. Press, 1927.

ROBINSON, E. S. "A concept of compensation and its psychological setting." *Jo. Abn. Psy.* v. 17, 1923.

ROSANOFF, A. J. *Manual of Psychiatry.* John Wiley, 1927.

RUGG, KRUEGER, and SONDERGAARD. "Studies in child personality. I." *Jo. Ed. Psy.* v. 20, 1929.

SAER, D. J. "The effect of bilingualism on intelligence." *Br. Jo. Psy.* v. 14, 1923.

SANDS and BLANCHARD. *Abnormal Behavior.* Moffat, Yard Co., 1923.

SAYLES and NUDD. *The Problem Child in School.* Joint Comm. on Methods of Preventing Juvenile Delinquency, 1925.

SCHARLIEB, M. *The Psychology of Childhood, Normal and Abnormal.* R. R. Smith, 1930.

SCHEIDEMANN, N. V. *The Psychology of Exceptional Children.* Houghton Mifflin, 1931.

SCUPIN, E. and G. *Bubi's Erste Kindheit.* Grieben, Leipzig, 1907.
Bubi im 4 bis 7 Lebensjahre. Grieben, Leipzig, 1910.

SEAGRAVE, MABEL. "Causes underlying sex delinquency in young girls." *Jo. Soc. Hyg.* v. 12, 1926.

SEHAM and SEHAM. *The Tired Child.* Lippincott, 1926.

SHAFFER, L. F. "The measurement of children's concepts." *Jo. Ed. Psy.* v. 19, 1928.
"Children's interpretations of cartoons." *T. C. Cont. to Ed.* *429, 1930.

SHERMAN, M. and I. C. "Sensori-motor responses in infants." *Jo. Comp. Psy.* v. 5, 1925.

SHINN, MILLICENT W. *The Biography of a Baby.* Houghton Mifflin, 1900.

SHUTTLEWORTH, F. K. "The influence of early religious training on college sophomore men." *Rel. Ed.* v. 57, 1927.

SKALET, MAGDA. "The significance of delayed reactions in young children." *Comp. Psy. Mon.* v. 7 *4, 1931.
"The home play of young children." *Univ. of Minn. Inst. of Ch. Welf.*, 1932.

SLATTERY, MARGARET. *The Girl in Her Teens.* Pilgrim Press, 1910.

SLAWSON, JOHN. *The Delinquent Boy.* Badger, 1926.

SMITH, FRANK. "Bilingualism and mental development." *Br. Jo. Psy.* v. 13, 1923.

SMITH, MADORAH E. "An investigation of the development of the sentence and the extent of the vocabulary in young children." *Univ. Iowa St. Ch. Welf. 3 *5*, 1926.

SOARES, T. G. *Religious Education.* Chic. Univ. Press, 1928.

SPAULDING, E. R. "Important emotional trends in childhood." *N. Y. St. Jo. of Med.* v. 24, 1924.

SPECHT, L. F. "A Terman class in P. S. 64, Manhattan." *Sch. and Soc.* v. 9, 1919.

STANFORTH, A. T. "A study in social attitudes of a group of high school boys and girls." *Sch. and Soc.* v. 26, 1927.

STECKEL, M. L. "Intelligence and birth order in the family." *Jo. Soc. Psy.* v. 1, 1930.

STEDMAN, L. M. *The Education of Gifted Children.* World Book Co., 1924.

STERN, WILLIAM. *Psychology of Early Childhood.* Henry Holt, 1924.

STERN, WILLIAM, and CLARA. *Children's Speech.* Barth, Leipzig, 1907.

STILLMAN, B. W. *Training Children to Study.* Heath, 1928.

STOPES, MARIE C. *Sex and the Young.* Putnam's Sons, 1926.

STOWELL, W. L. *Sex for Parents and Teachers.* Macmillan, 1921.

STRANG, RUTH. *An Introduction to Child Study.* Macmillan, 1930.

STRAYER, L. C. "Language and growth." *Gen. Psy. Mon. 8 *3*, 1930.

STREIBERT, MURIEL A. *Youth and the Bible.* Macmillan, 1924.

STURGES, H. A. "What college students think of Sunday School." *Rel. Ed.* v. 22, 1927.

STUTSMAN, R. *Mental Measurement of Pre-School Children.* World Book Co., 1931.

SULLIVAN, H. S. "The onset of schizo-phrenia." *Am. Jo. Psych.* v. 7, 1927.

SULLY, J. *Studies in Childhood.* Longmans Green, 1896.

SUNNE, DAGNY. "Personality tests, white and negro adolescents." *Jo. App. Psy.* v. 9, 1925.

SWIFT, EDGAR J. *The Psychology of Youth.* Scribner, 1927.
The Psychology of Childhood. Appleton, 1930.

TERMAN, LEWIS M. *The Measurement of Intelligence.* Houghton Mifflin, 1916.
Genetic Studies of Genius. Stanford Univ. Press, 1926.

TERMAN and ALMACK. *Hygiene of the School Child.* Houghton Mifflin, 1929.

TERMAN and LIMA. *Children's Reading.* Appleton, 1931.

TERRY, P. W. "Social experience of high school pupils." *Sch. Rev.* v. 35, 1927.

THOM, DOUGLAS A. *Everyday Problems of the Everyday Child.* Appleton, 1927.

THOMAS and THOMAS. *The Child in America.* Knopf, 1928.

THORNDIKE, E. L. "Original nature of man." v. I of *Educational Psychology,* Teachers College, 1913.
"The permanence of school learning." *Sch. and Soc.* v. 15, 1922.
"Reading as Reasoning." *Jo. Ed. Psy.* v. 8, 1917.
Adult Learning. Macmillan, 1928.
The Psychology of Arithmetic. Macmillan, 1922.

THRASHER, FRED M. *The Gang.* Univ. of Chic. Press, 1927.

THURSTONE and JENKINS. "Birth order and intelligence." *Jo. Ed. Psy.* v. 20, 1929.

TIEDEMANN, D. *Record of Infant Life.* 1781, and Bardeen, 1890.

TILSON, M. A. "Problems of pre-school children as a basis for parental education." *T. C. Cont. to Ed.* *356, 1929.

TRAVIS, LEE EDWARD. *Speech Pathology.* Appleton, 1931.

VALENTINE, C. W. "The innate bases of fear." *Jo. Gen. Psy.* v. 37, 1930.

VAN ALSTYNE, DOROTHY. *Play Behavior and Choice of Play Materials of Pre-School Children.* Univ. of Chic. Press, 1932.

VAN WATERS, MIRIAM. *Youth in Conflict.* Republic Pub. Co., 1926.

VERTES, J. O. "Behalten und Vergessen des Kindes." *Zeit. f. Psy.* v. 22, 1931.

VITELES, MORRIS S. "The influence of age of pubescence upon the physical and mental status of normal school students." *Jo. Ed. Psy.* v. 20, 1929.

WADDLE, CH. W. *An Introduction to Child Psychology.* Houghton Mifflin, 1918.

WAGONER, LOUISA C. "The constructive ability of young children." *Univ. Iowa St. Ch. Welf. 3 *2,* 1925.

WALSH, WM. C. *The Mastery of Fear.* Dutton, 1924.

WARING, ETHEL B. "The relation between early language habits and early habits of conduct control." *T. C. Cont. to Ed. *260,* 1927.

WATSON, G. B. *Experimentation and Measurement in Religious Education.* Association Press, 1927.

WATSON, JOHN B. *Psychological Care of Infant and Child.* Norton, 1928.

WEILL, BLANCHE G. *The Behavior of Young Children of the Same Family.* Harvard Univ. Press, 1928.

WEISS, A. P. "The measurement of infant behavior." *Psy. Rev.* v. 26, 1929.

WHEELER and PERKINS. *Principles of Mental Development.* Thomas Y. Crowell, 1932.

WHIPPLE, GUY M. *Classes for Gifted Children.* Pub. Sch. Pub. Co., 1919.
Manual of Mental and Physical Tests. Warwick, York, 1910.
"The vocabulary of a three year old boy." *Ped. Sem.* v. 16, 1909.

WHITE, WM. A. *Mental Hygiene of Childhood.* Little, Brown, 1920.

WHITLEY, M. T. *A Study of the Little Child.* Westminster Press, 1932.
A Study of the Primary Child. Westminster Press, 1929.
A Study of the Junior Child. Westminster Press, 1923.
"Children's interest in collecting." *Jo. Ed. Psy.* v. 20, 1929.

WICKES, FRANCES G. *The Inner World of Childhood.* Appleton, 1927.

WICKMAN, E. R. *Children's Behavior and Teachers' Attitudes.* Commonwealth Fund. Publ., 1928

WILE, IRA S. *The Challenge of Childhood.* Seltzer, 1925.

WILLIAMS, T. A. *Dreads and Besetting Fears.* Little, Brown, 1923.

WILSON, D. F. *Child Psychology and Religious Education.* Doubleday, Doran, 1928.

WILSON, M. O. "Interests of college students." *A.J.P.* v. 38, 1927.

WINCH, W. H. *Children's Perceptions.* Warwick, York, 1914.

WISLITZKY, S. "Beobachtungen über das Gemeinschaftsleben im Kindergarten." *Zeit. f. Psy.* v. 107, 1928.

WOODROW, HERBERT. *Brightness and Dullness in Children.* Lippincott, 1923.

WOOLLEY, HELEN T. *An Experimental Study of Children.* Macmillan, 1926.

"Peter: the beginnings of the juvenile court problem." *Ped. Sem.* and *Jo. Gen. Psy.* v. 33, 1926.

WORCESTER, D. A. "The schoolroom attitudes and achievements of only children." *Jo. Gen. Psy.* v. 38, 1930.

YATES, D. H. "A study of some high school seniors of superior intelligence." *Jo. Ed. Res. Mon.* *2*, 1922.

ZACHRY, CAROLINE. *Personality Adjustments of School Children.* Scribner, 1929.

ZYVE, C. I. "Conversations among children." *T. C. Record.* v. 29, 1927.

INDEX

505